Race, Class, and Politics in Southern History

Race, Class, and Politics in Southern History

ESSAYS IN HONOR OF

Robert F. Durden

EDITED BY

Jeffrey J. Crow, Paul D. Escott, and

Charles L. Flynn, Jr.

LOUISIANA STATE UNIVERSITY PRESS *Baton Rouge and London*

98 97 96 95 94 93 92 91 90 89   5 4 3 2 1
First printing

Designer: *Patricia Douglas Crowder*
Typeface: *Linotron 202 Palatino*
Typesetter: *The Composing Room of Michigan, Inc.*
Printer: *Thomson-Shore, Inc.*
Binder: *John H. Dekker & Sons, Inc.*

LIBRARY OF CONGRESS CATALOGING-IN-PUBLICATION DATA

Race, class, and politics in southern history: essays in honor of
    Robert F. Durden / edited by Jeffrey J. Crow, Paul D. Escott, and
    Charles L. Flynn, Jr.
        p.   cm.
    Includes index.
    ISBN 0–8071–1512–6 (alk. paper)
        1. Southern States—Politics and government—1865–1950.
    2. Southern States—Race relations.   3. Racism—Southern States—
    History—19th century.   4. Reconstruction.   5. Populism—Southern
    States—History—19th century.   6. Durden, Robert Franklin.
    I. Durden, Robert Franklin.   II. Crow, Jeffrey J.   III. Escott, Paul
    D., 1947-   .   IV. Flynn, Charles L.
    F215.R13   1989
    975'.04—dc19   89–30172
                                                                      CIP

Contents

Race, Class, and Politics in Southern History

Preface

Since World War II, the study of southern history has become less and less a matter of insular regional self-examination and increasingly a matter of nationwide scholarly attention. As the South has become part of the Sun Belt, people from every region have perhaps broadened their perspective on this country's past. But perhaps, too, people across the nation, not just in its southern region, have recognized as their own the problems of racism and poverty amidst American plenty. The South, of course, offers especially rich soil for the study of the causes and consequences of these problems. In the South, the interplay of racial and class divisions has been starkly apparent in politics and in every other dimension of life despite its intricacy and, sometimes, subtlety.

The historical literature devoted to the study of race, class, and politics in the South is varied and rich, for though virtually all historians might agree that race and class are fundamental in southern history, they have differed substantially over the relative force with which each has helped to shape the life of the region. Many scholars have accepted U. B. Phillips' view that racism is "the central theme of Southern history"—the dominant influence on southern politics and society and a key source of unity among different classes of whites. Other scholars view class as primary, contending that it has shaped racial views and race relations. The issues in this debate are important, and they are a challenge to understanding a difficult past and, implicitly, to understanding a difficult present.

This volume of essays focuses upon the relationship between race and class in southern politics and culture in the period from the close of the Civil War through the Progressive Era. This period is receiving much attention from contemporary historians of the South because it embraces three climactic episodes or eras in which the South wrought its destiny. This volume of essays is organized accordingly.

During Reconstruction, white southerners fought not only with northern Republicans and freedmen but also with one another over different visions for their region's future. Of all periods in southern history before the civil rights movement of the 1960s, Reconstruction offered the greatest opportunity to create a racially egalitarian and just society. Historians have, therefore, debated the reasons for the failure to do so. Some have emphasized the power of racism among whites, both northern and southern. According to this view, the racism of northern whites ensured the failure of reform efforts by making the Republican commitment to racial equality weak, vacillating, and brief when confronted by the intransigent racism of white southerners united across class lines by appeals for white supremacy. Others historians have emphasized the class motivations of upper-class white southerners and their northern rivals. In this view, upper-class white southerners appear as counterrevolutionaries defeating less wealthy, reform-minded southern rivals and re-creating a system of subordinate labor to serve their own interests. Northern Republicans were all too willing to allow the victory of the upper-class southern whites as soon as their own industrial interests seemed secure.

The two essays in the first section of this book examine the relationship between racism and Republican reform during Reconstruction. In the first, Paul D. Escott describes the strength and endurance of the Republican biracial coalition for democratic reform in piedmont North Carolina despite the racism of its white members. And he studies the Ku Klux Klan terror to which antidemocratic Conservatives resorted when their appeals for white supremacy proved ineffective among white Republicans. In this essay, the class interests, not the racism, of both Republicans and their Democratic rivals seem to determine political conviction and behavior. In the second essay, Ruth Currie-McDaniel studies the wives and family lives of carpetbaggers as a means of understanding the motivations, preconceptions, and limitations of these important actors in southern politics. Exploring the connections between the personal and the political, she shows that the condescension and racism that so many northern reformers exhibited toward white and black southerners may go far toward explaining the failure of Republican reform during Reconstruction.

After "Redemption"—after the Conservative Democrats wrested control of southern state governments from the Republicans—there followed a period of uncertain, relatively quiet rivalry between commercial and agricultural interests within the South. This period also saw a relatively quiet but direful rivalry between many white and black southerners. Many whites hoped for the ever greater subordination of the already subordinate blacks, and many blacks struggled to maintain and expand the slim gains of Reconstruction in the face of white hostility. The uneasy equilibrium in this contest among competing groups was punctuated by the drama of the Populist revolt, a third-party insurgency that historians have interpreted in dramatically different ways. Some have described the Populists as reform capitalists whose views fell within the mainstream of the American political tradition. In recent decades, however, more numerous historians have described Populism as a challenge to the class interests and, to a lesser degree, racial orthodoxy of the Redeemer Democrats. These historians find in the Populist revolt, like Reconstruction, the opportunity to build an economically and racially more just South. But again like Reconstruction, it was a lost opportunity. The Populist challenge failed, and at the turn of the century, Democrats precluded the possibility of similar challenges in the future through their successful campaigns to disfranchise black voters and thus, with seeming permanence, to guarantee Democratic party victory.

The three essays in the second section examine the role of race and class in the Populist revolt and in the disfranchisement campaigns that made political rivalry outside the Democratic party a practical impossibility for the immediate future. In separate studies, Charles L. Flynn, Jr., and Eric Anderson challenge the notion that the Populists attacked the commercial values, the class interests, or the racist orthodoxy of the Democratic party and those it represented. Indeed, both authors find little difference between the positions of Democrats and their Populist challengers on the major issues of public policy during the 1890s. Both find that the Populists were frustrated and angry Democrats who sought to promote standard, local Democratic party positions through a new party organization. If both recognize conflicting class interests in the late nineteenth-century South, their portraits of the political battles in the tumultuous 1890s show that the bitter rivals nonetheless shared remarkably similar views. If the class configurations or racial injustice of southern society were to be dramatically challenged, it was not the Populists who were going to do it.

In the third essay, Richard L. Watson, Jr., explores the relative importance of racial and class motivations among proponents of disfranchisement in North Carolina. In conclusions consistent with those of Flynn and Anderson, he shows that though class interests may have been at stake in the campaigns, the evidence suggests that racism and partisanship figured most prominently in the motivations of those who pushed for disfranchisement. White supremacy was remarkably effective as a call for unity among white southerners despite class differences among them.

The failure of the Populist revolt and the success of the disfranchisement campaigns of the turn of the century allowed the final crystallization of a new southern orthodoxy that had been forming since the close of the Civil War. Like the exclusion of blacks from political participation, Progressivism for whites only was the logical conclusion of the late nineteenth-century Democratic party faith that equated economic development, white supremacy, and the public weal. Progressivism entailed a wide variety of intellectual, theoretical, and legislative initiatives that would define southern society for more than half a century.

The three essays in the third section explore the relationship between racial bonds and class divisions in the post-Reconstruction South. In doing so, they expose some of the awesome contradictions and ironies that underlay, and were often hidden by, the orthodoxy of the New South. In the first essay, Raymond Gavins analyzes the efforts of black North Carolinians to define their freedom and to develop autonomous institutions in the late nineteenth century. He describes an overarching racial unity, a shared sense of dignity and purpose with which middle-class black leaders and ordinary black folk met ever-increasing pressure from whites. But he also explores the often-ignored class tensions and divisions that existed within the black community as both leaders and ordinary folk struggled to find practical, principled, and effective means to win the substance of freedom.

In the second essay, Jeffrey J. Crow examines the views of Clarence Poe on race relations and segregation in the heyday of southern Progressivism, the period from disfranchisement to the First World War. Poe was an archetypal southern Progressive who rose from humble agrarian beginnings to edit and publish the most influential farm journal in the South. An advocate of scientific farming and numerous other reforms, he was also a firm believer in disfranchisement and segregation. In 1913 he launched a crusade to establish rural segregation in the South, and a constitutional amendment to effect such a program narrowly lost in the North Carolina Senate in 1915. Crow's essay analyzes Poe's political writings and activities to reveal the deep-seated contradictions in the Progressive movement. Crow shows how the fight over rural segregation is but one instance of a conflict between the New South orthodoxy of democracy, white supremacy, and segregation on one hand and the Progressive commitment to the existing class structure of the South on the other.

In the final essay, Bruce Clayton explores the views of W. J. Cash on race, class, and southern politics. Cash became one of the South's most influential writers and a powerful critic of the New South orthodoxy that united whites across class lines behind the banner of white supremacy, an alliance that he called "the Proto-Dorian Convention." Clayton describes the route by which this odd and talented man came to question the commitment to white supremacy that obscured important class issues and interests. But Clayton also explores the complexity, irony, and subtlety with which Cash attempted to explain the Proto-Dorian Convention and, in doing so, the role of race and class in "the mind of the South."

In this volume the South appears as a region of complexity, tension, and conflict, both overt and submerged. But it also appears as a region in which, in most instances, racism remained a powerful, even overriding commitment among whites. Class interests were apparent. Class conflict was perhaps common. But what seems striking is the frequency with which racism narrowly circumscribed the limits of dissent, the frequency with which racial bonds defined the limits in which

Part I

Reconstruction: Racism and Republican Reform

1 / PAUL D. ESCOTT

White Republicanism and Ku Klux Klan Terror: The North Carolina Piedmont During Reconstruction

The year 1868 brought a revolution to southern politics. The Republican party, aided by the support of the newly enfranchised freedmen, suddenly emerged and swept to victory in state after state. The victorious Republicans promptly rewrote southern constitutions and inaugurated new policies that furthered democracy, education, and opportunity. Yet, within a few years the Republicans had lost control of the government in most of these states, and by 1876 they had lost control in every southern state. Why did a revolution that seemed so promising turn out to be so short-lived?

The commonly accepted view emphasizes weaknesses inherent in the Republican party, weaknesses stemming from the corrosive effects of racism. Republican majorities rested upon a coalition of white and black voters; indeed, support from both races was necessary for victory, since blacks were a minority in all but two southern states. But historians of Reconstruction have pointed out that the Republican party had two very different centers of strength: the plantation districts, where blacks predominated, and the mountain areas, where there were hardly any blacks at all.[1] In the former, whites were reluc-

1. Allen W. Trelease, "Who Were the Scalawags?" in Edwin C. Rozwenc (ed.), *Reconstruction in the South* (2nd ed.; Lexington, Mass.: D. C. Heath and Co., 1972), 119–44.

tant to vote for a black Republican party, and in the latter the race issue was so irrelevant that it could not prevent divisions among whites.

These facts have led to the conclusion that southern Republicanism rested upon an uneasy combination of opposites rather than upon a true coalition. The Republican party, this interpretation suggests, was an unstable compound so lacking in real strength that it was fortunate to win even a few elections. Flawed from its inception, the party disintegrated in the face of racial pressures after a brief period.[2] The failure of the southern Republican party in Reconstruction thus becomes another example of the general proposition that racism has always prevented biracial politics from working in the South.[3]

There is much truth in this interpretation, but it does not accurately describe all of the South, and if taken too literally, it becomes misleading about the nature and role of racism in southern history. For it complements another common supposition about the South: that the most virulent racism has always resided within the lower class of whites. Proud but poor and disadvantaged, the lower-class whites, this argument goes, vented their frustrations on blacks and persecuted the subordinate race so that they could enjoy the feeling of being superior to someone. This view has long been popular with southern apologists.[4] It remains influential, despite a large body of scholarship pointing squarely in the opposite direction.

What happened in the North Carolina piedmont during Reconstruction challenges both of these propositions. Although racism did indeed hinder the South's Republican party, in at least one location a successful party came into being built upon a biracial coalition. In the North Carolina piedmont, Republicanism depended upon the votes of the freedmen, who made up an important minority in the region, plus

2. Trelease's essay suggests this point of view, to which he apparently still subscribes. In a letter to me dated January 8, 1986, Trelease described Radical Republicanism as "a precarious political coalition of blacks and middle-to-lower-class whites who lived to a large degree in different parts of the state," and he pointed to racial divisions among these diverse Republicans.

3. For a statement of this common view, see Joel Williamson, *The Crucible of Race: Black-White Relations in the American South Since Emancipation* (New York: Oxford University Press, 1984), 517. To Williamson, biracial politics was fragile, and Populism showed "that it would not work."

4. For a classic statement of this view, see William Alexander Percy, *Lanterns on the Levee: Recollections of a Planter's Son* (Baton Rouge: Louisiana State University Press, 1973), 20, a work originally published in 1941.

the votes of large minorities of whites. Although this coalition was always threatened, it was not inherently weak. It demonstrated its strength by winning stunning victories and overturning long-established local hierarchies. It proved its strength by building a strong core of Republican counties and by giving evidence of the ability to expand its base to include neighboring areas.

The white Republicans who were the larger part of this coalition did not behave as the stereotypical view of the lower class suggests. Rather than being the primary source of racism and repression, they acted as a progressive social force. Long resentful of undemocratic social and political arrangements in the state, they took the opportunity presented by Reconstruction to ally with black voters and work for a more open, more democratic society. It was the strength of white Republicanism and biracial cooperation that precipitated the Ku Klux Klan's campaign of terror, and the evidence of that campaign points toward an upper-class, not a lower-class, origin and inspiration for the Klan.

By whipping up racism and terrorizing white and black Republicans, the elite leaders of the piedmont Klan hoped to suppress a vigorous biracial alliance that had formed as a result of the effects of wartime suffering, class resentments, and emancipation. Eventually violence and the Democrats triumphed, but not before the Republicans had initiated significant change and not before many courageous and defiant people had suffered for their stands. White Republicanism and biracial coalition politics challenged upper-class hegemony in the North Carolina piedmont, and they created loyalties and habits that endured into the twentieth century. The evidence suggests that many lower-class whites in the Tar Heel State might be better described as insurgents rather than as racists.

The Biracial Coalition Comes to Power

Racism certainly existed within the North Carolina Republican party, as it did throughout America in the 1860s and 1870s. It is true also that North Carolina had one pillar of Republican strength in the western mountain counties and another in the east. But an examination of voting patterns reveals that the piedmont was vital ground for Republicanism and, correspondingly, a grave threat to Democratic chances.

A glance at several maps demonstrates the importance of the piedmont in North Carolina politics during Reconstruction. The piedmont encompassed a large and populous area in a state in which sectionalism had always had a profound impact on politics. Map 1 indicates the counties included within the piedmont.[5] For a number of reasons, this region included many counties that the Democrats, to be successful, would have to win. In the east, as Democrats knew, were the state's few real plantation districts, as well as other areas in which blacks constituted the majority of the population. The Republicans were certain to do well among those concentrations of freedmen, and the mountains likewise offered Democrats no comfort. North Carolinians in general had not wanted to secede, and unionism had been especially strong in the western districts. Some mountaineers had fought for the Union, and many more had opposed the Confederacy by means that included violent resistance.[6] Thus, the piedmont was crucial to Democratic success.

It also was an area with a predominantly white population. Map 2 shows that most counties in the piedmont had a black population that was less than 40 percent but more than 10 percent of the total population. Of the shaded counties, only four were more than 30 percent black, and only five were less than 15 percent black.[7] The typical county was roughly 25 percent black. Apart from Mecklenburg, whose population was 44.1 percent black, the only piedmont counties with large concentrations of black people were those bordering the coastal plain.

To win piedmont elections, the Republican party needed substantial numbers of white votes. Conversely, the Democrats could carry the piedmont only if they succeeded in dividing voters on racial lines and

5. Geographers and geologists have proposed two or three slightly different definitions of the boundaries of the state's three regions—mountains, piedmont, and coastal plain. My division is taken from James W. Clay, Douglas M. Orr, Jr., and Alfred W. Stuart (eds.), *North Carolina Atlas: Portrait of a Changing Southern State* (Chapel Hill: University of North Carolina Press, 1975), 6.

6. For an in-depth analysis of mountain Republicanism, see Gordon B. McKinney, *Southern Mountain Republicans, 1865–1900* (Chapel Hill: University of North Carolina Press, 1978).

7. To calculate percentages, statistics were taken from the *Ninth Census, 1870: Population,* 52–54, 633.

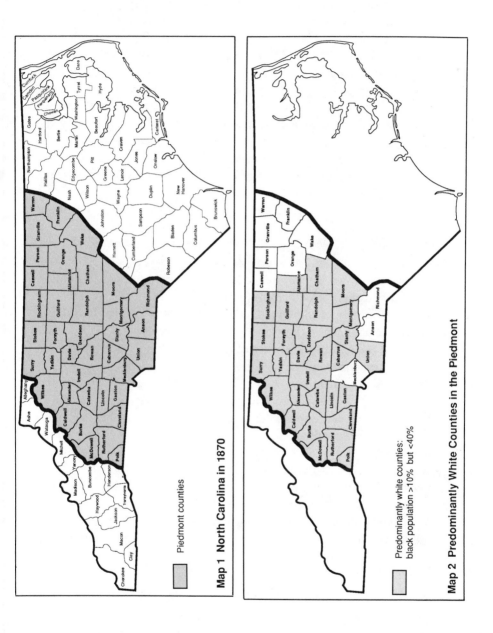

Map 1 North Carolina in 1870

Piedmont counties

Map 2 Predominantly White Counties in the Piedmont

Predominantly white counties:
black population >10% but <40%

holding a substantial majority of the whites. But Map 3 indicates that the Democrats were not able to do that. In his victorious gubernatorial election in 1868, William W. Holden, a former Democrat who had broken with his party and founded the state's Republican organization, captured twenty-six of the piedmont's thirty-nine counties. He nearly triumphed in Alamance and Caswell counties also, winning 48.8 percent and 49.9 percent of the vote, respectively, in those two counties. Several of the eastern counties in this upland section of the state were more than 40 percent black, it is true. But among the twenty-nine predominantly white counties of the piedmont, Holden triumphed in nineteen and came very close in a twentieth county, Alamance.[8]

Such Republican power in the piedmont gravely imperiled future Democratic efforts statewide, given the strongholds of Republicanism that existed in the coastal plain and in the mountains. Worse, Democrats discovered that the Republican party was competitive in some piedmont counties that Holden failed to win. In addition to Alamance, the Republican party had strength in the Democratic area just west of the four counties of the Quaker Belt—Forsyth, Guilford, Randolph, and Davidson—plus a chance to fill in the gap representing Cleveland County at the southwest corner of the region. Map 4 depicts the pattern that must have appeared in Democrats' nightmares. Every county covered by diagonal lines went Republican in at least one major election, defined as the gubernatorial and presidential races, in 1868 or 1872.[9] Soberly pondering their prospects, Republicans believed they had a chance to confine Democratic victories to a small portion of the piedmont.

Indisputably, these Republican victories were built upon the votes of large numbers of white men who allied themselves with the minority of black voters in the piedmont. The assumption that every black man went to the polls and voted Republican yields the largest possible *black* vote for the party. Subtracting that number from the total Republican vote cast thus yields a *minimum* estimate of the number of *white*

---

8. Election returns are from R. D. W. Connor (ed.), *A Manual of North Carolina* (Raleigh: E. M. Uzzell & Co., 1913), 1001–1002.

9. *Ibid.* Election returns for the 1868 and 1872 presidential races are from John L. Cheney, Jr. (ed.), *North Carolina Government, 1585–1974* (Raleigh: North Carolina Department of the Secretary of State, 1975).

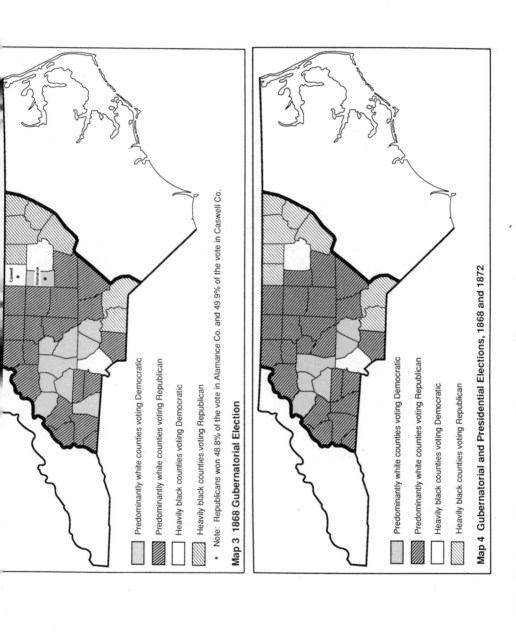

Predominantly white counties voting Democratic

Predominantly white counties voting Republican

Heavily black counties voting Democratic

Heavily black counties voting Republican

Note: Republicans won 48.8% of the vote in Alamance Co. and 49.9% of the vote in Caswell Co.

*

Map 3 1868 Gubernatorial Election

Predominantly white counties voting Democratic

Predominantly white counties voting Republican

Heavily black counties voting Democratic

Heavily black counties voting Republican

Map 4 Gubernatorial and Presidential Elections, 1868 and 1872

Republican voters. As Table 1 reveals, that minimum estimate includes a very substantial portion of the white population, even in 1872. Since 1872 was a year of Democratic victory after extensive Klan terror, the percentages in Table 1 may be taken as another kind of minimum calculation, an estimate of hard-core, unshakable white Republican strength. Table 2 provides higher minimum estimates of Republican support among whites in the piedmont, because it was calculated for 1868, a year that preceded Klan violence and intimidation.[10] It provides a more generous estimate of white Republican strength, though still not a maximum estimate. The Republican party was regularly attracting one-quarter, one-third, and even more of the eligible white voters to its banner. Among whites who actually voted, Republican strength was even greater, frequently exceeding 40 or 50 percent.

It is no wonder that this pattern of Republican victories and this extent of white Republican voting in the piedmont alarmed the Democrats. They had every reason to be concerned. But the question that demands more consideration is, What had caused the emergence of this kind of white Republicanism, with its readiness to form a winning coalition with blacks? What were its roots, and why had it come into being?

The Democratic Roots of Republicanism

Long before Reconstruction began, pressure for democratic change had been building in North Carolina. Since the Jacksonian period the Old North State had been out of step with the expansive thrust of American democracy. Economically and politically it had not participated in the liberalization and change that occurred almost everywhere else, and a rigid structure of power rooted in long-established county hierarchies lasted unchanged through the Civil War.

Americans generally enjoyed tremendous economic growth and change during the first half of the nineteenth century. In the North, a vigorous market economy developed and industrialization began; in the South, the cotton boom spurred settlement of new lands and cre-

10. *Ninth Census, 1870: Population,* 52–54, 633, provides the number of eligible black and white voters. Election returns are from Cheney (ed.), *North Carolina Government,* and Connor (ed.), *A Manual of North Carolina.*

Table 1 Extent of White Republicanism in 1872 Elections: Minimum Estimates

County	Minimum Number of White Republican Voters	Minimum Number of White Republican Voters Expressed as		
		Percentage of Total Republican Vote	Percentage of All Whites Who Voted	Percentage of All Adult White Males
Wilkes	1,502	84.1	70.2	63.0
Rutherford	532	52.5	42.3	27.9
Randolph	868	62.5	38.9	29.1
Davidson	810	53.4	36.9	29.3
Forsyth	657	58.9	38.9	31.2
Polk	158	46.2	41.4	25.2
Montgomery	266	40.7	35.9	27.3
Yadkin	599	69.2	44.1	35.0
Surry	574	64.7	45.7	29.5
Burke	363	46.6	36.4	27.1
Moore	294	33.4	22.1	16.8
Guilford	598	32.7	24.4	18.8
McDowell	136	26.2	16.2	10.8
Chatham	315	18.7	15.1	12.2
Stokes	325	39.2	26.4	19.5
Union	145	23.0	12.4	8.5
Alamance	257	25.3	16.8	11.6
Rockingham	167	12.2	10.5	9.1
Lincoln	189	26.8	17.3	14.8
Gaston	-30[1]	—	—	—

SOURCES: John L. Cheney, Jr., *North Carolina Government, 1585–1974* (Raleigh: North Carolina Department of the Secretary of State, 1975), 1324–25; R. D. W. Connor, *A Manual of North Carolina* (Raleigh: E. M. Uzzell & Company, 1913), 1001–1002; *Ninth Census, 1870: Population.*

[1] Eligible black voters could account for 30 more Republican votes than were cast.

Table 2 Extent of White Republicanism in 1868 Elections: Minimum Estimates

County	Minimum Number of White Republican Voters	Minimum Number of White Republican Voters Expressed as		
		Percentage of Total Republican Vote	Percentage of All Whites Who Voted	Percentage of All Adult White Males
Wilkes	1,144	80.1	68.1	48.0
Rutherford	851	63.9	64.6	44.7
Randolph	1,231	70.3	58.4	41.2
Davidson	1,137	61.7	57.7	41.1
Forsyth	803	63.7	50.5	38.2
Polk	221	54.6	53.3	35.2
Montgomery	340	46.8	49.9	34.8
Yadkin	573	68.2	47.9	33.5
Surry	517	62.3	46.5	26.6
Burke	511	55.1	40.8	38.1
Moore	480	45.0	39.5	27.4
Guilford	936	43.2	38.5	29.5
McDowell	357	48.2	37.0	28.3
Chatham	455	25.0	28.3	17.6
Stokes	278	35.5	27.2	16.7
Union	325	40.1	25.9	19.0
Alamance	344	31.2	24.6	20.1
Rockingham	260	17.8	14.7	14.2
Lincoln	124	19.3	17.3	9.7
Gaston	160	18.2	19.1	11.0

Sources: See Table 1.

ated many new planters and much new wealth. But North Carolina remained an exception to the general pattern, an economic backwater in a changing nation. Cotton planting in the state increased but then tailed off, as problems of comparatively poor soil and high transportation costs remained unsolved. The best opportunities lay elsewhere, a fact that led reformer Archibald Murphey to lament, "Thousands of our wealthy and respectable citizens," as well as "thousands of our poorer citizens . . . are annually moving to the west."[11] Although the state's elite would accept men whose wealth was new or derived from a variety of sources, there simply were fewer opportunities and less social mobility than elsewhere.

Perhaps for that reason, conservative leaders staunchly and quite successfully resisted the tide of democratic constitutional change. The 1835 state constitutional convention allowed citizens to elect the governor directly, but it retained high property qualifications for holding office and a system of legislative apportionment that favored slaveholding areas in the House of Delegates and wealthier districts in the state senate. Roughly half of the white men in the state did not own enough land to entitle them to vote for state senators. Most important, there was an appointive rather than elective system of county government. Justices of the peace, or squires, who were appointed for life by the legislature and governor, formed the county court to try cases, levy taxes, and adopt county policies. This "squirarchy" functioned as an oligarchy strong enough to control not only politics at the county level but often balloting for higher offices as well.[12]

But ordinary North Carolinians, black and white, were not immune from the democratic ferment that permeated America at that time. They heard the rhetoric of Jacksonian democracy and believed in it. Accordingly, they chafed at the undemocratic character of politics and society in their state. Signs of their discontent were especially clear in the late 1840s and 1850s. The surprise proposal by Democratic gubernatorial candidate David S. Reid for "free suffrage"—allowing all white men to vote for state senator whether they owned land or not—

---

11. Quoted in Harry L. Watson, "Squire Oldway and His Friends: Opposition to Internal Improvements in Antebellum North Carolina," *North Carolina Historical Review,* LIV (1977), 105–19.

12. Hugh Talmage Lefler and Albert Ray Newsome, *North Carolina: The History of a Southern State* (3rd ed.; Chapel Hill: University of North Carolina Press, 1973), 323.

aroused great enthusiasm in 1848 and helped to reestablish Democratic supremacy in 1850 after fifteen years of Whig ascendancy. Enthusiasm for "free suffrage" continued to grow until the proposed reform finally went before the voters and received overwhelming approval in 1857.[13]

No sooner was "free suffrage" enacted than a controversy arose over *ad valorem* taxation of slaves. Nonslaveholders and poorer citizens demanded that slaveholders carry a larger share of the tax burden by paying higher taxes on their valuable slave property. An organization of skilled white workers in the Raleigh area initiated the agitation for this reform, but its popularity spread rapidly and found favor among small farmers. The movement grew in strength until the Civil War began, at which point nervous slaveholders quickly engineered a compromise designed to mitigate nonslaveholders' complaints against the elite, whose property the yeomen would be defending on the battlefield.[14]

The appeal of these democratic reforms was so strong that it crossed traditional party lines. Whigs and Democrats vied with each other in support of them throughout the piedmont and the west. This continuing competition between Whigs and Democrats was itself another way in which North Carolina differed from regional and national patterns. After the national Whig organization broke up, North Carolina Whigs continued to be a viable party at the state level, calling themselves "the Opposition." This meant that in the Reconstruction period piedmont voters could remember an uninterrupted tradition of political dissent and competition, a tradition of opposition politics that encouraged some to join the new Republican organization.[15]

The Civil War itself was another major reason for the emergence of white Republicanism in the piedmont. For the war tested harmony as nothing had before and brought to the surface the clashing interests of different classes within the white population. The result was bitter

13. Paul D. Escott, *Many Excellent People: Power and Privilege in North Carolina, 1850–1900* (Chapel Hill: University of North Carolina Press, 1985), 27–30.

14. *Ibid.;* Donald C. Butts, "The 'Irrepressible Conflict': Slave Taxation and North Carolina's Gubernatorial Election of 1860," *North Carolina Historical Review,* LVIII (1981), 44–66.

15. See Marc W. Kruman, *Parties and Politics in North Carolina, 1836–1865* (Baton Rouge: Louisiana State University Press, 1983).

disagreement and conflict that often assumed violent forms. Deep and durable cleavages among whites developed during the war and strongly influenced postwar politics.

From the outset of the war, North Carolina's prosecessionists were notable for their unqualified support of Confederate policies. They called themselves the Confederate party, and by their support for the new southern government, they distanced themselves not only from their neighbors, who originally had not wanted to secede, but also from secessionists elsewhere, who often took issue with the Jefferson Davis administration in Richmond. As the sacrifices demanded by the war became extremely onerous, more and more North Carolinians felt resentment over the secessionists' attitudes. Ordinary citizens tended to sympathize with the rival Conservative party and agree with its characterization of the Confederates as "Destructives."[16]

The war was indeed destructive to the welfare of the citizens of North Carolina. In one of history's ironies, a state that had been reluctant to leave the Union became, in effect, the Hercules of the Confederacy. Judged by quantity of soldiers, taxes, the tax-in-kind, or any other category of resource or sacrifice, North Carolina contributed far more than its proportional share among the southern states. This occurred simply because most of the Tar Heel State remained within Confederate lines while the southern government progressively lost major parts of its territory. Circumstances compelled officials in Richmond to draw heavily upon the resources that they still commanded, and consequently North Carolinians had to shoulder unusually heavy burdens.[17]

The war brought profound suffering to the state. Not only were thousands of soldiers killed or maimed, but tens of thousands of soldiers' families lived in need and anxiety about where they would find their next meal. The combination of too many farmers away in the armies plus impressment, the tax-in-kind, and drought caused crop shortages in many areas. Surviving records from a variety of counties indicate that between 20 and 40 percent of the white families in the

16. Lefler and Newsome, *North Carolina*, 466, 468.
17. Paul D. Escott, "Unwilling Hercules: North Carolina in the Confederacy," in Lindley S. Butler and Alan D. Watson (eds.), *The North Carolina Experience: An Interpretive and Documentary History* (Chapel Hill: University of North Carolina Press, 1984), 265–84.

population became dependent upon government for enough cornmeal and pork to survive.[18] Residents of the piedmont frequently pointed out that their suffering was particularly acute because their region was preeminently an area of small farms and nonslaveholders. They had few slaves to furnish labor to grow what was needed, but they received much unwanted attention from Confederate impressment officers and tax officials.

Given the tight control of local elites over county governments and the interest of many officeholders in upholding Confederate authority, the cleavage between "Destructives" and Conservatives coincided with other divisions. The "Destructives," often wealthy officials with influence and with business interests in the towns and county seats, frequently enjoyed exemption from active service. Ordinary citizens who came to resent them were, by contrast, frequently poverty-stricken small farmers from the countryside who had little influence. When the *North Carolina Standard*, for example, began in 1863 to stress the poverty, suffering, and yearnings for peace of ordinary citizens, a correspondent from Randolph County reported: "I find the people throughout my travels almost a unit for peace. The opposition to propositions for peace I find mostly in the towns and villages."[19] Such patterns lent emotional power and a personal flavor to differing perspectives.

The Confederacy's exemption of the owner or overseer of twenty slaves from military service set off strong protests in North Carolina, and though the legislature was moved to make formal complaint, it could not remove the discontent. One foot soldier complained to the governor that "our soldiers cant understand why so many young magistrates are permitted to remain at home," and a woman in the piedmont likewise complained that militia officers and magistrates who had "remained at home ever since the war commenced" were rounding up "old grey headed fathers" and sending them to the front. From his vantage point in the army an unusually objective planter concluded: "The young men of wealth in our State have shown entirely too much reluctance to going into the field. Look around and see how few of those of your acquaintance are facing danger and enduring

18. Paul D. Escott, "Poverty and Governmental Aid for the Poor in Confederate North Carolina," *North Carolina Historical Review*, LXI (1984), 462–80.
19. *North Carolina Standard* (Raleigh, N.C.), July 21, 1863.

privations." Other citizens complained that Confederate units stripped "large numbers of people . . . of everything," and a growing number of men in the army concluded, in the words of one soldier: "A mans first duty is to provide for his own household[;] the soldiers wont be imposed upon much longer."[20]

Soon desertion became noticeably heavy from North Carolina units, as men returned to care for their families. When draft-exempt officials would not permit the deserters to work in their fields, and instead attempted to arrest them, these former soldiers often used their military experience to fight back and launch raids on the elite's storehouses and property. Conflict in many counties of the piedmont amounted almost to open war, with state treasurer Jonathan Worth admitting that "theft, robbery, and almost every other crime are common in almost all the rural districts." A member of the gentry in one county wrote fearfully, "We bolt & bar our doors every night, not knowing what hour they [bushwackers] may make their appearance." A postmaster summed up the state of public opinion in these words: "I have not known a man in the last two years [1863 and 1864] who would not willingly have given all he had and would have pledged all that his friends had to keep out of the army." This man also denied that conventional appeals and explanations would change people's feelings: "The time has gone by that the people can be maddened by such newspaper and pulpit slang as Yankee confiscation, appropriation of pretty women, &c." Nor, he said, would alarmist racial justifications be effective any longer: "We cannot afford to give up the white race for the negro."[21]

As internal war spread in the piedmont, William Holden began a risky political maneuver designed to capitalize upon the widespread dissatisfaction with the war and the Confederacy. Through his paper, the *North Carolina Standard,* and local allies, he launched a campaign for an armistice and peace. That Holden's organized, public peace movement existed at all was significant. The lack of a two-party system in the Confederacy powerfully inhibited organized dissent, since any rival movement appeared disloyal or illegitimate, a challenge to the author-

20. Escott, *Many Excellent People,* 72, 74, 39, 44.

21. *Ibid.,* 69, 64–70, 73–82; Emsley Beckerdite to Marmaduke Robins, January 21, 1865, in Marmaduke Robins Papers, Southern Historical Collection, University of North Carolina, Chapel Hill.

ity of the Confederate government. Criticism there was, often in ample quantity, but as David Potter has argued, the absence of an accepted opposition party hindered the process through which discontent leads to debate and then to renewed consensus around new policies. Fear of the taint of disloyalty kept opposition in other states at the level of criticism, but in North Carolina, Holden came out openly for peace and built a strong organization to press for that goal.[22]

During the summer of 1863, meetings took place in counties throughout the state, but especially in the piedmont. As many as a hundred of these public protests took place, with each one drafting resolutions to be sent to Raleigh and to Holden's newspaper. Just as Holden had declared in the *North Carolina Standard* that "the great mass of our people desire . . . a cessation of hostilities, and negotiations," the resolutions for peace typically argued for an end to the fighting and for a state convention to seek peace. The connection between Holden's paper and the meetings went further. Holden used the elected leaders of these peace meetings in his own gubernatorial campaign. The ties forged then would reappear in 1867 and 1868, when Holden organized the Republican party and ran successfully for governor.[23]

In 1864, however, Holden's gubernatorial campaign was unsuccessful. His ambition and frequent shifts of political position had alienated influential politicians. Moreover, Governor Zebulon B. Vance shrewdly met Holden's challenge by appealing to Holden's constituency. Vance emphasized his own efforts to bring about peace and repeatedly depicted Holden as the war candidate. The governor called attention to his own criticisms of the Richmond administration and to his advice to Jefferson Davis, at the end of 1863, to attempt "negotiations with the enemy." Charging that Holden's peace movement would cause conflict with North Carolina's sister southern states, Vance warned that Holden would provoke "a new war, a bloodier conflict than that you now deplore." Thus, Vance transformed the governor's race into a contest between two proponents of peace and made Holden appear the more dangerous choice. After a campaign that "tended to make all voters friends of peace," Vance won handily, despite the judgment of seasoned observers such as Jonathan Worth

22. Escott, *Many Excellent People*, 45–49; David M. Potter, *The South and the Sectional Conflict* (Baton Rouge: Louisiana State University Press, 1968), 285–86.
23. *North Carolina Standard* (Raleigh, N.C.), July 17, 1863.

that "*at least two-thirds* of the people" concurred with Holden's views or desired peace even more ardently than the editor did.[24]

Although Governor Vance won reelection, he soon reached the private conclusion that "the great *popular heart* is not now & never has been in this war."[25] The bloodshed and enormous sacrifices required by the war had produced a major change in the attitudes of many piedmont farmers. Their intense dissatisfaction during the war, and the violent resistance to Confederate authority that occurred in many parts of the piedmont, meant that many individuals had rejected traditional leaders and traditional policies. They were ready to demand a new, more democratic style of government.

Reconstruction Begins

A sign of the determination to have a more democratic political and social system came in the form of a meeting held in June, 1865. Nearly three thousand individuals from Surry, Yadkin, and Stokes counties, plus the adjoining mountain county of Allegheny, assembled in Mount Airy to express their views on postwar policies. Signaling their repudiation of the "Destructives," these citizens declared that the people of North Carolina never would have ratified secession at the polls. They asserted their loyalty to the Union, expressed sorrow over Lincoln's assassination, and pledged themselves to work with President Andrew Johnson. Although they offered to forgive the secessionists among them for past misdeeds, they put those leaders on notice that they would examine the character of future policies and leaders with great care.[26]

President Johnson appointed William Holden to be provisional governor. Holden, a man of humble birth (he was illegitimate), had many personal and political reasons to dislike the state's aristocrats, and he set about to make some changes. Holden did not try to overturn the whole system of government, but he did endeavor to infuse a new, more democratic element into the ranks of officeholders. Often relying on recommendations made to him by Union meetings, Holden ap-

24. Escott, *Many Excellent People*, 46–49.
25. *Ibid.*, 46.
26. *Ibid.*, 87.

pointed many individuals who had no previous experience on county courts to the post of justice of the peace. The provisional governor's broom was sweeping out the old squirarchy and replacing its members with officeholders who would be more responsive to the interests and discontents of the ordinary white farmer.[27]

Change came slowly, however. Although the Confederate experience had discredited the "Destructives," Conservatives were better able to defend their wartime record, and most Conservative leaders were unwilling to follow the lead of the provisional governor. Holden's followers, on the other hand, were in most counties poorly organized, if at all, and thus there was no party in existence to oppose the Conservatives or advocate new directions in the uncertain environment of Reconstruction. At this point Holden was shunning potential black voters and still hoping to gain the support of some of North Carolina's conservative elite; organization of a biracial Republican party remained two years in the future.

But poverty and suffering were very much present and pressing. Businessmen complained that commerce was at a standstill, and thousands of ordinary families continued to face the problem of hunger. Crops were short in several counties, prices often were high, and as a result many people were "very hard run for something to eat." It appears that the extent of suffering may have been less than during the painful last years of the war, but many families nevertheless faced a very troubled future. Undoubtedly a substantial number of yeoman farmers who later joined the Republican party were devoting their attention to desperate conditions at home when the conservative, old-line Whig Jonathan Worth defeated Holden for governor in the fall of 1865. There was a low turnout of voters (almost fifteen thousand fewer than the seventy-two thousand who had voted in 1864), and Worth scored heavily in eastern counties, including seven that refused to repudiate secession but gave Worth 82.3 percent of their ballots.[28]

Worth and the Conservatives steadily hardened their opposition to change, either within North Carolina or in the state's relations to the national government. Worth and many of his supporters in the government favored the full payment of all Confederate debts. They viewed with horror the North's determination to void the Confederate

27. *Ibid.*, 92–94.
28. *Ibid.*, 86–87, 98–100.

debt, and they opposed as immoral any moratorium or interference in the collection of debts owed by one North Carolinian to another. As the northern public became more critical of the course of Reconstruction under President Johnson, Worth adamantly denied that there was any disloyalty or violence in the state. He determined to resist the proposed Fourteenth Amendment, toward which he felt "detestation and abhorrence." By 1866 Conservatives had swung so far to the right that they decided to fight the proposed revisions in North Carolina's constitution.[29]

These revisions, drawn up by white delegates elected in 1865 under President Johnson's plan of Reconstruction, were hardly radical in spirit. They retained substantial residence and property-holding requirements for office holding, but they did make county magistrates subject to election, for terms of six years. Even more troubling to Conservative leaders was the basis of representation. Because slavery had been abolished, the "federal basis" of counting each slave as three-fifths of a person could no longer provide the measure of population for determining representation. In its revisions the constitutional convention turned to the "white basis," which would count only the number of white people. Led by Thomas Ruffin, who wanted former slaveholders and plantation districts to gain representation rather than lose it after emancipation, Conservatives assailed the proposed constitution. Its defeat, in another poorly attended election (the turnout was thirty thousand fewer than in 1864), showed that established leaders were unshaken in their rejection of democracy. With Worth they viewed "the universal suffrage principle . . . as undermining civilization." Government, they maintained, should be in the hands of "virtue and property and intelligence" and never given over to the power "of mere *numbers*."[30]

Thus, as Presidential Reconstruction failed and Congress began to seek a more democratic policy, white yeoman farmers in North Carolina had ample opportunity to see the undemocratic attitudes that worked against them at home. With anxiety they had watched repeated efforts to end debt moratoriums and feared a legislative repeal of the homestead exemption. They warned that debt collections would "ruin the country" and that "poore men will have to sell the Hat off of

29. *Ibid.*, 96, 104–105.
30. *Ibid.*, 105–11.

thare head to pay thare Debts."[31] The statements of men such as Thomas Ruffin clearly indicated that, if they could, Conservatives would roll the clock back and rescind "free suffrage" rather than allow the common citizens a larger voice in governmental affairs.

Not surprisingly, as Congress' policy evolved, piedmont yeomen also spoke of democratic change. One man expressed his hope to "beat the Oligarks in White voters by next election," and a voter from Alamance County wrote Holden that he would fight before he let "unhung rebels" take over the government again. He continued: "I do not want such men to dictate and domineer over me and my friend[s] as has [been the case] for the last 8 or 10 years. . . . Death is more preferable than such rule again. In my own County there has not been one instant as yet that the peoples wishes has been granted, both in the Convention and the legisla[ture]." By 1867 Holden and his supporters were organizing a biracial Republican party. "They are moving heaven and earth in this [Randolph] County," wrote one observer.[32] Two groups—the Union League and the Heroes of America—facilitated the Republican effort. The Union League concentrated its attention, as it did throughout the South, on mobilizing future black voters, while the Heroes of America, who had been secret supporters of the Union, joined with other supporters of the peace movement to fuse white dissidents' strength into a new party.

Congress' Military Reconstruction Act of 1867 gave these democratic forces their best opportunity to gain power. The act required that blacks be allowed to vote and participate in the drafting of a new state constitution, and prominent Confederates who would be barred from politics by the Fourteenth Amendment were likewise prohibited from political activity during the formation of the new state government. Thus, a new era in state politics commenced with the election of the Constitutional Convention of 1868. Republican delegates held an overwhelming majority in the convention, 107 to 13, and for the first time black North Carolinians—fifteen of them—took seats in the councils of government.[33]

31. *Ibid.*, 140, 96.
32. *Ibid.*, 139–40.
33. *Ibid.*, 142.

Republicanism Triumphant

From the first days of the convention, black and white Republicans signaled the kind of government that they intended to bring to the state. They stood for a new era of equal rights and opportunity for all. Under Republican auspices, there would be an end to privilege and aristocratic domination and an emphasis on education and economic growth, which were sources of opportunity for the common citizen, black or white.

The new state constitution clearly reflected these Republican values. It guaranteed universal manhood suffrage, for rich or poor alike and even for Confederate leaders who had fallen under Congress' prohibition. The constitution abolished property qualifications for the governorship and the General Assembly, and for the first time it gave the choice of judges to the people for terms of eight years. Most important, local government became democratic rather than aristocratic, as a new system of elected county commissioners replaced the squires, who had been appointed for life to sit as the county court.[34]

This new system of local democracy produced dramatic, immediately visible results. New faces appeared in office, replacing the familiar lineup of men who had sat on county courts for years or chaired them, in some cases, for decades. Between 1868 and 1877 in Randolph County, for example, twelve of sixteen county officeholders were new to politics. In Alamance County, where Democrats fared better, seven of sixteen were nonetheless new.[35]

Across the state, in counties whose policy makers had always been wealthy members of the gentry, county commissioners of both races and all stations in life now took office. The farmer, the mechanic, the wagonmaker, the brickmason, and the shoemaker came into positions that long had been the exclusive domain of planters or large landholders who combined planting with law, medicine, or commerce. The wealth of local officials also plummeted, both statewide and in the piedmont. In Alamance County, for example, the personal estate of county officials dropped from an average of $26,388 in 1866–1867 to

34. *Ibid.*, 142–44.
35. *Ibid.*, 167.

only $3,825 in 1868–1877. The value of officials' real-estate holdings also decreased from an average of $10,523 to $6,604.[36] County government under the Republican constitution truly included some men of the people.

Republican papers underlined this fact and promised that common men would have a voice under newly elected governor Holden. Recalling the dark days of the war, Republican editors identified their opponents as those "who wea[r] the cast-off clothes of the Secessionists and inheri[t] the animus and name of the old Democracy." In antebellum days, declared the Greensboro *Register*, "many of the white men of the State never knew what real freedom was." The Rutherford *Star* described the Conservatives, or Democrats, as "the same party [that] was the chief instrument in bringing upon the people the late unchristian war" and warned that if they regained power, "they will wield the reins . . . as during the existence of the so-called Confederacy, with *tyranny* and *despotism*." Although the Democrats claimed that they represented "the wealth and intelligence of the State," the *Star* asserted, "We glory in being called common people . . . we scorn the name of an Aristocrat, for in them we find nothing but selfishness, Toryism and Tyranny of the deepest dye."[37]

The state constitution also emphasized education as a new means of opportunity. Committing the state to a modern public school system, Republicans encountered the race issue. As Republicans did almost universally throughout the South, Tar Heel leaders compromised and agreed that classrooms would be segregated, but they fought successfully against any explicit reference in the constitution to separate schools. Black or white, North Carolina's children were to have expanded access to schooling, which ordinary citizens commonly viewed as the key to greater opportunity. Governor Holden, urging the legislature in 1869 to sustain the schools, declared: "Every hope for free government depends on the education of the masses. Taxes for such a purpose should be cheerfully paid." He made clear, too, that black citizens were entitled to their full share of funding proportional to population.[38]

---

36. *Ibid.*, 168.
37. Greensboro *Register*, July 7, September 1, 1869; Rutherford *Star*, May 30, 1866, June 9, 23, 1867.
38. Escott, *Many Excellent People*, 144; Greensboro *Register*, November 16, 1869.

Tar Heel Republicans joined other southern Republicans in efforts to couple this educational opportunity with economic prosperity that they hoped would come from inducements offered railroads and industry. To emphasize education and economic development, the masthead of the Greensboro *Register* defined the paper's creed as "THE ADVANCEMENT AND UPBUILDING OF THE MATERIAL PROSPERITY OF THE STATE AND THE VICINAGE." With warm approval it reported the organization in July, 1869, of a county Association of Friends of Education. The Rutherford *Star*, with an optimism that soon became standard in newspaper columns, predicted in 1867 that "capital will flow in, and our vast mineral resources will be speedily developed." In addition, the *Register* warned that violence would discourage immigration and damage hopes of economic improvement.[39]

The zeal with which Republicans promoted education reflected the depth of interest that ordinary citizens felt for this vital form of opportunity. In Randolph County, to take one example, the new Republican commissioners quickly set out to revive and improve the public schools. First they surveyed the existing system and its facilities, enlisting 114 citizens from every town and district to conduct a census of the school-age population and report on school buildings. They found 4,056 potential students and only fifty-four schools to serve them, with fourteen schoolhouses in "bad" or "not very good" condition. Working with eleven popularly chosen district school committees, Randolph's Republican commissioners resolved to increase the number of schoolhouses to eighty and to provide instruction for 2,400 students. This represented nearly 60 percent of the potential school population, a major expansion from prewar days. Moreover, the county allocated school funds strictly "in proportion to the number of children in each township" without regard to race.[40]

This was energetic, innovative, and democratic government that appealed to ordinary citizens, white and black, in the piedmont. It was a fresh approach to institutions that formerly had been ossified or rigidly under the control of a conservative elite. Rarely has change

39. Mark Summers, *Railroads, Reconstruction, and the Gospel of Prosperity: Aid Under the Radical Republicans, 1865–1877* (Princeton: Princeton University Press, 1984); Greensboro *Register*, July 7, 14, 1869; Rutherford *Star*, January 19, 1867.
40. Escott, *Many Excellent People*, 145–46.

been as clear or as dramatic as these innovations that came, at last, to local government.

The link between wartime discontent and resistance and postwar Republican strength was also evident in the piedmont. Opposition to Confederate policies had been strongest in the Quaker Belt—Forsyth, Guilford, Randolph, and Davidson counties—and in clusters of nearby piedmont counties, such as Montgomery, Chatham, and Moore, and Wilkes, Yadkin, and Surry. These counties proved to be sites of reliable Republican strength. Not only would that continuity worry Democrats, but it also could inspire doubt about their ability to hold other, similar piedmont counties. Caldwell, Catawba, and Iredell counties had also experienced large-scale desertion and resistance to authority during the war. Although each of these remained in the Democratic column, the possibility existed that Republicans could do well there. In the 1872 presidential election, for example, Ulysses S. Grant polled almost 46 percent of the vote in Iredell County.[41]

A careful study by James Lancaster confirmed these patterns and put into perspective the relationship of postwar Republicanism and prewar Whiggery. In North Carolina, as in some other southern states, the prominence of former Whigs in Reconstruction politics was quite noticeable. In addition, the Whig party had been strong in several of the piedmont counties that became Republican, notably Davidson, Guilford, Montgomery, Randolph, Wilkes, Yadkin, Rutherford, and Chatham. Consequently, old Whig loyalties have often been interpreted as the source of Republicanism. But Lancaster demonstrated that Whigs dominated both postwar parties. Although "Whiggery and relative poverty are strong in the scalawag profile," Lancaster concluded, "it is obvious that disaffection toward the Confederacy—especially support for the native peace movement of 1863–1864—was the principal catalyst in making Republicans of native whites." Overwhelmingly, the wartime supporters of the peace movement who became active in postwar politics went into the Republican party. Lancaster found that 87.9 percent of them labored for the cause of Republicanism.[42]

Through comparison of activists and leaders of both parties, Lan-

41. Calculated from Cheney (ed.), *North Carolina Government*.
42. James Lawrence Lancaster, "The Scalawags of North Carolina, 1850–1868" (Ph.D. dissertation, Princeton University, 1974), iii, 357.

caster found that 84 percent of the "mechanics," laborers, and tradesmen who became active in politics went into the Republican party.
Republicans also had a much larger number of leaders who had owned
no slaves prior to the war, whereas Conservative and Democratic activists and leaders were more likely to be wealthy, former slaveholders,
and college educated. Many yeoman farmers, laborers, or poorer
white voters remained attached to the Democratic party, a fact that
prevented Reconstruction politics from dividing cleanly and totally
along class lines. But, Lancaster argued, "the white North Carolinians
who adopted the name 'Republican' in 1867 saw theirs as the party of
unionism, economic opportunity, and social justice. For such men Republicanism represented a political phenomenon which both predated
and transcended the Reconstruction era."[43]

The Klan Counterattack

For piedmont Democrats, particularly local elite figures, triumphant
Republicanism represented a disturbing development that had broken
their customary control of county affairs. Moreover, it threatened to
destroy their power permanently. Important as Republican innovations were in state politics or county policies, the starkest reality for
local elites was the fact that they had been ousted from their accustomed seats of power and replaced by men of humble background.
To elite Democrats, long accustomed to dominance and control, the
new personnel of county governments seemed unqualified and un-
deserving. Ordinary citizens were not supposed to rule their betters,
and the proper order of society stood inverted.

In his diary piedmont lawyer and Democrat David Schenck lamented that "the old wealth and aristocracy . . . has been broken
down." He recoiled at the sight of "the 'dirty, unwashed scum of
society' like maggots revelling in the decaying remains of better days."
A Democratic newspaper from the east likewise condemned the "false
humanitarianism" that aimed at "breaking down every vistige [sic] of
honorable distinction and attempting to plant upon its ruin the unwise . . . doctrine of universal equality." In the once-proud South, the

43. *Ibid.*, 368, 376, 382, 381, 375, 393, 405.

paper bitterly observed, "the places once occupied by the best of our sons . . . are now . . . filled by men who can scarcely read plain english, or scrawl a mutilated cross for their signatures."[44]

Emblematic of the perversion of the social order was the elevation of former slaves to the status of citizens and voters. To Conservatives, this was the most egregious and unjustifiable of the whole series of outrageous changes in society that accompanied the Republican era. Accordingly, even before the Republicans were firmly established in power, influential Conservatives began a campaign to draw the color line. Former United States senator William A. Graham urged fellow Conservatives to define the issue in terms of "whether the negro or the white man is to be dominant," with "no middle ground," and Democratic newspapers adopted the technique of describing party meetings as a "Grand Rally of White Men." David Schenck observed, "The lines of society are being rigidly drawn . . . all the Intelligence and Virtue . . . are with the Conservative party and they treat with contempt and scorn the miserable wretches who have deserted their race." A Greensboro banker and Democrat condemned "the *native* radical called a 'scalawag'" and explained, "Scalawags are the ticky-scurry-scaly-mangy portion of a drove of cattle."[45]

Most appalling to Conservatives, however, was their realization that appeals to race consciousness were not working. In the piedmont, large portions of the white electorate stubbornly voted Republican despite the voluminous propaganda of the Conservative press. Wartime suffering and dissatisfaction had turned long-standing democratic aspirations and resentments into a potent political force. The black minority and a sizable portion of the white voters of the piedmont had made that section of the state a Republican stronghold. Local elites wanted their power back, and the Democratic party had to recapture the piedmont if it hoped to control a state that had durable centers of Republican strength in both east and west.

The Ku Klux Klan emerged to counter the political force of Republicanism.[46] Klansmen who later admitted to, and testified about,

---

44. Escott, *Many Excellent People,* 146–47.
45. *Ibid.,* 150.
46. The best treatment of the Klan in the South is Allen W. Trelease, *White Terror: The Ku Klux Klan Conspiracy and Southern Reconstruction* (New York: Harper & Row, 1971). It includes chapters on individual states.

their terrorist activities all agreed that the political purposes of the Klan were paramount. The Ku Klux Klan, stated one piedmont Klansman, "is a political organization of the Conservative party, in the interest of the Conservative party." Alamance County's John W. Long described whippings in which he had participated as "for the object of overthrowing the Republican party." Others explained that their purpose was "to strengthen the Conservative party" or "to keep down the style of the niggers and to increase the Conservative party." Klansman James E. Boyd of Alamance County added, "It was understood that on the night before election the Ku Kluks would turn out *enmasse,* and visit the houses of the colored people" with a message—"if [Negroes] went to election they would meet them on the way."[47]

That the Klan concentrated its activities in the piedmont was especially notable. There were incidents of intimidation and violence in the east but comparatively little sustained Klan terror there, where the black population was often greatly in the majority and Republican majorities were unassailable. The mountains also witnessed little Klan disorder. But the piedmont's Republican party rested on a coalition of black and white voters, and the Democrats had to regain the piedmont. Therefore their strategy focused on intimidating enough blacks, and frightening or using racism to recapture enough whites, to overcome the Republican coalition.

One of the counties in which the Klan was most active was Alamance, where Republican presidential nominee Ulysses S. Grant had obtained a forty-seven-vote majority in 1868. Obviously, that narrow margin could evaporate before a sustained campaign of terror. Alamance and Caswell counties, which suffered the most Klan violence in 1869 and 1870, were the only two counties that the Republicans had gained the year before, in the second (fall) set of elections in 1868. There was a strong correlation between counties recaptured by Democrats and counties in which night riders committed deeds of violence.[48] One observer described the changed situation in Cleveland

47. Escott, *Many Excellent People,* 155.
48. Otto H. Olsen, "The Ku Klux Klan: A Study in Reconstruction Politics and Propaganda," *North Carolina Historical Review,* XXXIX (1962), 340–62, especially 354, 360. Olsen's pioneering article notes that ten of fifteen counties that moved from the Republican to the Democratic column in 1870 had seen considerable Klan violence. (The first set of elections in 1868 was to establish the new state government required by the Military Reconstruction Act of 1867.)

County. Of "three or four hundred colored voters," he doubted that "twenty-five of them would dare to vote the Republican ticket."[49]

The old Democratic leaders, the traditional county elites, were the organizers and leaders of the Ku Klux Klan in the piedmont. James E. Boyd, who helped set up Alamance County's Klan, was the son of Archibald H. Boyd, who had often chaired the county court and also served as a legislator. Eleven other Klan leaders in the county had played prominent roles in the appointed county governments that preceded Reconstruction. Otto Olsen discovered the same pattern of dominance by the old local elite in Caswell County's Ku Klux Klan.[50] Thus, the Klan served as a kind of shadow government for the displaced former rulers of piedmont counties; they used its terror as their instrument to regain power and control by weakening the biracial Republican alliance.

Between 1868 and 1872, hundreds of terroristic attacks on Republicans took place across the Republican piedmont. In Rutherford County alone, there were one hundred to two hundred whippings, and far more in counties such as Alamance, Caswell, Lincoln, Gaston, Cleveland, Mecklenburg, Guilford, Orange, Randolph, Chatham, Montgomery, and Moore. Klansmen burned schoolhouses, the symbols of democratic opportunity for both blacks and many poorer whites, and maimed or murdered scores of Republican activists. There was so much danger that, during months of KKK night-riding, "quite a large number of respectable [Republican] farmers . . . [did] not sle[ep] in their houses any time."[51]

Piedmont Republicans did not surrender at the first sign of organized Conservative violence. Against charges that Republicans wanted to elevate the Negro above the white man, the Greensboro *Republican Gazette* replied: "It is a cardinal principle of the Republican party that the people as a whole should be protected in their rights. . . . Should the ballot be taken from them [Negroes], they would be reduced to absolute helplessness, for the elections would be controlled by men who would have no interest in their welfare, and who would make laws oppressive to their interests. This remark applies, not to the negroes only, but to all classes of the ignorant and

49. Escott, *Many Excellent People*, 156.
50. Olsen, "The Ku Klux Klan," 358.
51. Escott, *Many Excellent People*, 154.

poverty stricken." More simply, the Rutherford *Star* declared, "We desire North Carolinians whether they be white or black, to vote as interest might dictate, not as the would be aristocracy might wish."[52]

The Greensboro *Republican* accurately diagnosed much of the dynamics and personnel behind Ku Klux Klan terror when it asserted, "Under the countenance of . . . bitterly disappointed office seekers, the young scions of old Slave Aristocrats have been hurried into an organized system of rapine and murder." Evidence for the partisan purpose of the Klan lay in the Democratic party's "silence on ku klux violence, the extenuation offered for it, [and] the miserable subterfuges" used in its defense. "In 'sixty-one,'" observed the Greensboro *Register*, "Democracy rebelled because it could not rule. In 'sixty-nine' the same dog, grown too cowardly to rebel, stripes its face and hides its tail, and sneaks out by moonlight to beat an unarmed black man because he is a radical."[53]

The *Register* was not afraid to use, and excel in, invective against its opponents. To statements that Klansmen were only punishing immoral behavior between Negroes and whites, the paper taunted, "Why you know yourself there isn't a mulatto child in town scarcely whose 'daddy' isn't a Ku Klux." On another occasion, the *Register* turned racial assumptions on their head by commenting that a local black man who had offered to marry the colored mistress of "a brother of the white mask" had to be "awfully degraded" to tolerate such close association with the Klan. The paper also once mocked the Democrats' claim that they were "the party of refinement and culture. . . . Witness Joe Turner," the *Register* said, referring to the Democratic leader and editor of the Raleigh *Daily Sentinel*, "*scooping the flies out of his grog with nails as long and nasty as a buzzard's.*" In the fall of 1869 a letter to the paper signed "Retribution" urged formation of "an organization designed expressly to KuKlux the K.K.K. . . . Assassination must be met by Lynching, and midnight murder by midnight execution. A dozen hangings will save a hundred murders."[54]

But Republicans, black and white, lacked sufficient power to put down the Klan terror, and the whippings, beatings, and murders had

---

52. Greensboro *Republican Gazette*, August 26, 1869; Rutherford *Star*, July 25, 1868.
53. Greensboro *Republican*, March 24, April 28, 1870; Greensboro *Register*, July 7, 1869.
54. Greensboro *Register*, July 7, 14, October 20, 1869.

their inevitable effect on politics. As a piedmont black man named Essie Harris explained, "It is not worth while for a man to vote and run the risk of his life." Like many other individuals, Harris had stood for principle, resisted Democratic threats, and endured Klan violence. But eventually he felt compelled to put the safety and security of his family before his loyalty to the Republican party, so he stopped voting. That was precisely the result that the Klan sought to achieve through violence. In Rutherford County, Klan terror broke up an alliance of black and white Republicans that had previously produced a 590-vote majority from an electorate composed of 460 blacks and 1,800 whites. The Klan's violence intimidated many whites, and afterward an observer doubted that any "colored men would dare to vote at this time." In Cleveland County, Republicans lamented the effects of Klan terror, which had reduced black support for their ticket to almost nothing.[55]

The erosion of Republican strength involved more than the terrorism of hooded night riders. Republicans needed new taxes to pay for the schools they supported, and unfortunately for their party's cause, such taxes had to be raised from a tax base greatly diminished by war and emancipation. In addition, North Carolina's Republicans made serious mistakes, particularly in extending large amounts of financial aid to railroad promoters who failed to deliver or, in some cases, never intended to deliver on their promises of economic development. No incident of extravagance or corruption escaped the notice of the Conservative press. Coming on top of higher taxes, instances of waste or fraud angered the voters, and all these issues brought damage to the Republican electoral campaigns of the 1870s.[56]

But the Klan's reign of terror came at a crucial moment and delivered a blow from which the Republicans never completely recovered. Klan violence occurred at the height of Republican strength in the piedmont, turned Republican gains around, and established the downward trend that plagued the party during the remainder of Reconstruction. Map 5 shows the effects of terrorism in the piedmont. In the 1872 gubernatorial election Republicans carried only eight of the piedmont's predominantly white counties. Although the party still won six piedmont counties that had larger black populations, its strength in the crucial center of the state had been broken. With most of the piedmont

55. Escott, *Many Excellent People*, 156.
56. *Ibid.*, 160–70.

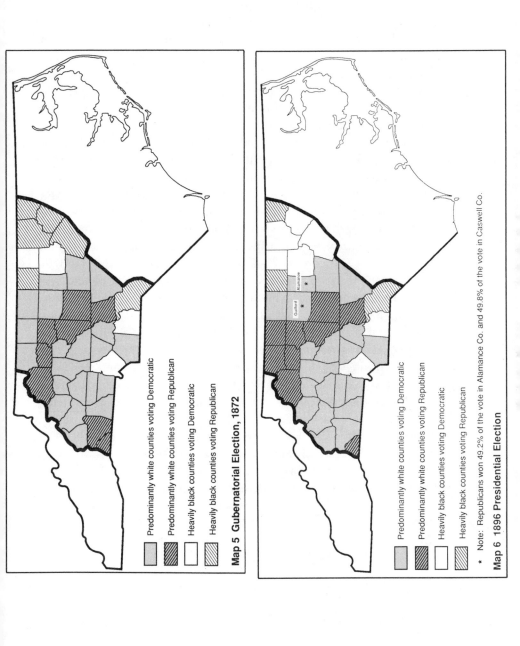

Predominantly white counties voting Democratic

Predominantly white counties voting Republican

Heavily black counties voting Democratic

Heavily black counties voting Republican

Map 5 Gubernatorial Election, 1872

Predominantly white counties voting Democratic

Predominantly white counties voting Republican

Heavily black counties voting Democratic

Heavily black counties voting Republican

* Note: Republicans won 49.2% of the vote in Alamance Co. and 49.8% of the vote in Caswell Co.

Map 6 1896 Presidential Election

Guilford

Alamance

in the Democratic column, the foes of the biracial Republican coalition were on their way to regaining complete control of the state.

Reconstruction failed in North Carolina, as it did throughout the South. The old-line conservatives regained control of politics and immediately tried to solidify their control by ending local democracy and restoring an appointive system of county government. The Klan's campaign overcame Republican strength, but it did not eradicate it. "Between 1880 and 1896," historian Jeffrey J. Crow has observed, "the Democrats never won more than 54 percent of the vote in gubernatorial elections."[57] The biracial coalition of white and black Republicans had been a meaningful and real alliance that sprang from long-established democratic aspirations and gained strength from the bitter experiences of wartime. Thus, it is not surprising that Republicanism in the piedmont did not die out. On the contrary, it remained a stubborn and persistent phenomenon through the rest of the nineteenth century and into the twentieth. As Map 6 shows, nine counties from the core area of piedmont Republicanism voted for McKinley in the 1896 presidential election, with Guilford and Alamance almost ending up in the Republican column as well. (The party polled 49.8 percent in Guilford and 49.2 percent in Alamance).

Even after disfranchisement the Republican party retained significant pockets of strength in the piedmont. During the twentieth century the counties of Wilkes, Yadkin, Surry, Davidson, and Randolph often voted Republican, with Forsyth, Guilford, and other counties also showing Republican loyalty. The contemporary Republican party has retained this base while trying to add support through a newer, more conservative strategy. Reconstruction Republicanism in the piedmont was neither an illusion nor a transient phenomenon. In North Carolina, at least, it was a significant movement, a biracial one, and a decidedly progressive and democratic cause contending against deeply rooted, undemocratic forces and traditions.[58]

57. Jeffrey J. Crow, "Cracking the Solid South: Populism and the Fusionist Interlude," in Butler and Watson (eds.), *The North Carolina Experience*, 335.
58. Clay, Orr, and Stuart (eds.), *North Carolina Atlas*, 76.

The Wives of the Carpetbaggers

Until recently, the relationship of gender to the forces of class and race has largely been overlooked in scholarship on nineteenth-century America and certainly in work on the carpetbaggers.[1] In tracing the political careers of these men, researchers have rarely noted the significance of whether they had wives and, if they did, what roles these women played. Historians have seldom asked, for example, whether the wives accompanied their husbands to the South, and what the implications of that choice may have been. What does a study of their wives reveal about the carpetbaggers? What do these wives show about women of their time? What does the relationship of the carpetbaggers to their wives and to the South reveal about class, race, gender, and politics in the nineteenth century? Before addressing these questions, however, one must first ask, Who were the carpetbaggers?

Of all the key players in the drama of Reconstruction, none have been more intriguing than the carpetbaggers. The name itself beclouds an understanding of this group. Writers have used it in various ways,

1. See Carroll Smith-Rosenberg, "Hearing Women's Words: A Feminist Reconstruction of History," in Smith-Rosenberg, *Disorderly Conduct: Visions of Gender in Victorian America* (New York: Oxford University Press, 1985), 11–52. Smith-Rosenberg's concise definition of gender is role divisions based on sex that are "man-made, the product of cultural definitions, not biological forces" (12). In this essay she gives an overview of the contemporary scholarship that inserts gender into a reexamination of social and political history, and the impact of that scholarship.

such as applying it to any northerner who settled in the South after the Civil War, to southerners who settled in the North, and to persons living in any region other than the one in which they were born.

Northerners had begun traveling to the South by the end of the first year of the Civil War, and by 1866 the stream had become a flood. They went for various reasons. Union army veterans frequently returned remembering a pleasant, warm climate and southern belles. Many migrants to the South from the North were idealistic teachers and members of the clergy—missionaries intent on assisting the former slaves in some way. Some of the newcomers had been assigned to various government agencies in the South. Others hoped to set up legitimate business ventures, having been lured by speculators who saw the need and opportunity for capitalists and entrepreneurs to rebuild the devastated region. According to one estimate, between twenty thousand and fifty thousand northerners moved to the South to try planting, and that took no account of those who migrated for other reasons.[2]

Whatever their original motives for going, it was the former Yankees' involvement in southern politics that led to the coining of a new epithet, "carpetbagger," that gained wide currency after Republican political activity increased in 1867. This essay uses Richard Current's definition, which is standard: "The men called carpetbaggers were white northerners who went south after the beginning of the Civil War and, sooner or later, became active in politics as Republicans."[3]

2. Lawrence N. Powell, *New Masters: Northern Planters in the Civil War and Reconstruction* (New Haven: Yale University Press, 1980), xii, 8–34; Willie Lee Rose, *Rehearsal for Reconstruction: The Port Royal Experiment* (New York: Vintage, 1964); Henry L. Swint, *The Northern Teacher in the South, 1862–1870* (Nashville: Vanderbilt University Press, 1941), 35; Jacqueline Jones, *Soldiers of Light and Love: Northern Teachers and Georgia Blacks, 1865–1873* (Chapel Hill: University of North Carolina Press, 1980), 14–48; A. T. Morgan, *Yazoo; or, On the Picket Line of Freedom in the South* (Washington, D.C.: n.p., 1884); David H. Overy, Jr., *Wisconsin Carpetbaggers in Dixie* (Madison: University of Wisconsin, 1961); Charles Stearns, *The Black Man of the South and the Rebels* (New York: American News, 1872); Jonathan Daniels, *Prince of Carpetbaggers* (Philadelphia: Lippincott, 1958); Richard N. Current, *Three Carpetbag Governors* (Baton Rouge: Louisiana State University Press, 1967); Current, *Those Terrible Carpetbaggers* (New York: Oxford University Press, 1988). Because it narrates the personal perspective, the latter book shows much about the wives, though it does not address the issue of gender.

3. Richard N. Current, "Carpetbaggers Reconsidered," in David H. Pinkney and Theodore Ropp (eds.), *A Festschrift for Frederick B. Artz* (Durham: Duke University Press, 1969), 144. Russell Duncan has recently challenged Current's definition by calling Tunis Campbell a carpetbagger. Campbell was black. Duncan, *Freedom's Shore: Tunis Campbell and the Georgia Freedmen* (Athens: University of Georgia Press, 1986).

The story of the northern involvement in southern politics of the time is well known. In the first year of Congressional Reconstruction, 1867–1868, the southern Republican parties made their bid for power with some optimism. The usual selection process had been altered by a combination of factors. Many white voters had been disqualified, and many others expressed their passive resistance to the new order by not voting. White unionist sentiment was also present, and the new black voters were participating for the first time. These factors led to the election of carpetbaggers (or allowed for their appointment) to constitutional conventions, local offices, governorships, state and national legislatures, and district and federal judgeships. The carpetbaggers' accomplishments came in the areas of public schools, penal and economic reform, and civil rights. But the changes they attempted were only partially successful, and Republican power eroded in each state in the face of its particular mix of recalcitrant southern opinion, violence or the threat of violence, other forms of resistance, the failure of the national government to enforce law and order, and Republican impropriety or mismanagement. The end of Reconstruction is generally denoted as 1877, when a new presidential administration shifted its strategy for dealing with the South. But by that time all of the former Confederate states had already marked the demise of Radical rule and the triumph of southern "Redemption."[4]

Not all the carpetbaggers were vindictive or corrupt, though the term once implied that they were. As business efforts failed or appointments ended, the transplanted northerners sometimes, out of perceived necessity or desire to remain in the South, turned to politics for their livelihood. Often coincidence or the desire to change some particular circumstance drew them into public life. Issues surrounding race relations in the South especially attracted Republicans from the party's

4. Of the numerous monographs on the politics of Reconstruction, a few of the more recent ones are Eric Foner, *Reconstruction: America's Unfinished Revolution, 1863–1877* (New York: Harper & Row, 1988); Michael Perman, *Reunion Without Compromise: The South and Reconstruction, 1865–1868* (Cambridge, England: Cambridge University Press, 1973); Perman, *The Road to Redemption: Southern Politics, 1869–1879* (Chapel Hill: University of North Carolina Press, 1984); William Gillette, *Retreat from Reconstruction, 1865–1879* (Baton Rouge: Louisiana State University Press, 1979); Dan T. Carter, *When the War Was Over: The Failure of Self-Reconstruction in the South, 1865–1867* (Baton Rouge: Louisiana State University Press, 1985); George C. Rable, *But There Was No Peace: The Role of Violence in the Politics of Reconstruction* (Athens: University of Georgia Press, 1984).

reform wing. Some of the carpetbaggers were former abolitionists and others were honestly desirous of seeing blacks attain civil rights, even if the former northerners' vision was blind to their own racism.[5]

Just as pertinent as their motives and integrity was the attitude of the carpetbaggers toward their new neighbors. Ambitious, usually young, and possessed of enormous egos and self-confidence, these men believed they could succeed not only in making a living in the South but also in changing it. The carpetbaggers, in many cases, evinced a certain contempt for soᴜthern culture and, largely unconscious of the flaws in northern society, seem to have been intent on "northernizing" the South.[6] They offer a perfect example of the interconnected forces of race, class, and politics. Politicians by definition, they displayed an arrogance toward southern whites that was grounded in class and regional pride. The chauvinism of their attitude was as natural and unquestioned as the racism that clouded their relations with southern blacks; both factors limited their effectiveness in many ways.

This essay adds the rubric of gender by examining the period from the perspective of some of its female participants and asking what gender roles reveal about the society that creates them. Like the carpetbaggers, the women who shared their lives were unofficial representatives of the victorious North, who brought with them northern mores and standards, which were sometimes quite different from the new ones they encountered. Engrained customs concerning such matters as choice of food, domestic accommodations, and preferences for entertainment or amusement were often contrary to those of southerners. Moreover, the strong anti-intellectualism in much of the South contrasted sharply with the academic vitality of the North. The wives of these politicians were an unusually well-educated group of women, whereas progress in women's education had barely touched the South. Women shared in the lyceums, temperance clubs, and debating societies of New York, New England, and the Western Reserve. The

5. Lawrence N. Powell, "The Politics of Livelihood: Carpetbaggers in the Deep South," in J. Morgan Kousser and James M. McPherson (eds.), *Region, Race, and Reconstruction: Essays in Honor of C. Vann Woodward* (New York: Oxford University Press, 1986), 315–47; C. Vann Woodward, *American Counterpoint: Slavery and Racism in the North-South Dialogue* (Boston: Little, Brown, 1971), 163–83.

6. Powell, *New Masters*, 123–24; Overy, *Wisconsin Carpetbaggers*, 11; Richard N. Current, *Northernizing the South* (Athens: University of Georgia Press, 1983), 50–82.

concerts and lectures of the cities, particularly within reformist circles, were a stimulating diversion for many women.[7]

The South's culture, on the other hand, was directly tied to family activities. Before the war, weddings and funerals served as social occasions, and dances and barbecues were a frequent and welcome chance for extended social events. Predominantly male activities of hunting, horse racing, and gambling left wives with few avenues for enjoyment outside the plantation or farm. Religious activities or domestic chores such as sewing, food preservation, and quilting became parties for females in an extended family or circle of friends. These patterns changed little immediately after the war except in ways mostly affecting men. A dearth of horses and money curtailed some male pursuits, leading to an increase in alcohol consumption. Although most of the South was rural, and therefore rural life was typical for most southern women, life in the cities, such as New Orleans and Charleston, before and after the war, was quite different from life in the country and more resembled northern culture (though it was perceived by northerners as inferior). Charleston boasted the first musical society in the United States and prided itself on its sophisticated cultural opportunities. After the war, even small cities, such as Natchez, boasted some public entertainment offered by traveling circuses, operas, and minstrels.[8]

7. Bertram Wyatt-Brown, *Southern Honor: Ethics and Behavior in the Old South* (New York: Oxford University Press, 1982), 96, 229–39. Wyatt-Brown underscores the paucity of activities for southern women, noting that plantation women had nothing to do at night. See also Catherine Clinton, *The Other Civil War: American Women in the Nineteenth Century* (New York: Hill and Wang, 1984), 44–46; Anne Firor Scott, *The Southern Lady from Pedestal to Politics, 1830–1930* (Chicago: University of Chicago Press, 1970), 42–43, 71; Powell, *New Masters*, 123–24; Edward Pessen, *Riches, Class, and Power Before the Civil War* (Lexington, Mass.: D.C. Heath, 1973), 111, 244; Ellen Carol DuBois (ed.), *Elizabeth Cady Stanton/Susan B. Anthony: Correspondence, Writings, Speeches* (New York: Schocken, 1981), 10–11; James C. Mohr (ed.), *The Cormany Diaries: A Northern Family in the Civil War* (Pittsburgh: University of Pittsburgh Press, 1982), 34, 53, 58, 162, 174.

8. Scott, *The Southern Lady*, 42–43; Wyatt-Brown, *Southern Honor*, 247–48; William C. Harris, *The Day of the Carpetbagger: Republican Reconstruction in Mississippi* (Baton Rouge: Louisiana State University Press, 1979), 579–80, 583–90; Pessen, *Riches, Class, and Power*, 230–34, 244; Stanley R. McDaniel, "Church Song and the Cultivated Tradition in New England and New York" (D.M.A. dissertation, University of Southern California, 1983). McDaniel discusses the "cultivated tradition" that thrived in Charleston as well as New England. See also Gilbert Chase, *America's Music From the Pilgrims to the Present* (Rev. 2nd ed.; New York: McGraw-Hill, 1966), 107–109. In a more recent book, Tess Hoffmann and Charles Hoffmann underline class similarities North and South by highlighting intermarriage and social interaction between the South Carolina and Georgia planter class and Rhode Island elites. See their *North by South: The Two Lives of Richard James Arnold* (Athens: University of Georgia Press, 1988).

These factors of culture and education divided northern and southern women and men. Recognition of similar gender roles might have drawn the women together. Popular literature consistently featured the role of the female in the entire nation as subservient to that of the male. The majority of people understood child care and domestic chores to be the woman's responsibility, regardless of what assistance she might have, whether from relatives and servants in the North or from slaves in the South. Although some scholars have questioned whether such a model person ever existed in reality, in her role as wife the nineteenth-century woman was expected to be the paragon of virtue and the transmitter of society's roles and traditions to the children. Opportunities for cultural outings and education depended on the region or city and on affluence. Nevertheless, despite her participation in community and church activities, the home was considered a woman's proper sphere; "ladylike" behavior was her approved demeanor, in the North and the South.[9]

Further, the primary form of sociability for women, in both regions, was visiting. In the South, according to one historian, it was "the essence of life." Equally important to northerners were the morning and afternoon "calls" of society ladies. Unfortunately, the mutual contempt between wives of carpetbaggers and southern women precluded the kind of friendships and bonding between them that tied southern females to members of their families and northern women to their "chums."[10]

Such barriers figure prominently in the lives of the women who are discussed in this essay. It cannot be claimed that they represent all the wives of the carpetbaggers, but they were chosen as a valid sample for several reasons. Their husbands came to the South with different motives and achieved different levels of success in southern politics. Each woman responded differently to her lot. Nevertheless, there is a

9. Scott, *The Southern Lady*, 28–32; Wyatt-Brown, *Southern Honor*, 226; Clinton, *The Other Civil War*, 40; Ann Douglas, *The Feminization of American Culture* (New York: Avon, 1977), 50–67; Nancy F. Cott, *The Bonds of Womanhood: "Woman's Sphere" in New England, 1780–1835* (New Haven: Yale University Press, 1977), 63–99; Carl N. Degler, *At Odds: Women and the Family in America from the Revolution to the Present* (New York: Oxford University Press, 1980), 52–74.

10. Scott, *The Southern Lady*, 43; Caroll Smith-Rosenberg, "The Female World of Love and Ritual," *Signs*, I (Autumn, 1975), 1–30. Ironically, no such barriers separated the wives of planters, who were at home in Newport society. Hoffmann and Hoffmann, *North by South*, 211–52.

thread of continuity in their experiences. The wives came with the unanimous view that the South was an inferior place. The heat, their accommodations, and southern hostility easily confirmed their pre-conceptions. Because of their reception, their attitudes, and their husbands' goals, the carpetbaggers' wives were unable to create a stable homelife with any sustaining community beyond that of other northerners.

The women highlighted are Emma Spaulding Bryant, wife of Georgia carpetbagger John Emory Bryant; Blanche Butler Ames, wife of Mississippi carpetbagger Adelbert Ames; and Emma Kilborn Tourgée, wife of North Carolina carpetbagger Albion Winegar Tourgée. Much is known about these women because of their extensive correspondence. Even though no letters of hers are extant, a short sketch of Etta Stearns is included because of her strong reaction to the South. Mrs. Stearns is highly visible in the memoir of her husband, carpetbagger Charles Stearns of Georgia.[11]

Emma Spaulding Bryant

Emma Spaulding married John Emory Bryant in June, 1864, while he was on leave near the end of his four years in the Union army. They had met in their home state of Maine, where he had boarded in her home while he also worked as her teacher in a subscription school. He was twenty-seven when they married, and presumably she was six to ten years his junior. Since John had been treated as an adopted member of the family, they had begun their relationship as "brother" and "sister," terms they continued to use in letters for some time. They corresponded throughout the years of the war, as he gradually revealed that

11. Ruth Currie-McDaniel, *Carpetbagger of Conscience: A Biography of John Emory Bryant* (Athens: University of Georgia Press, 1987); John Emory Bryant Papers, Manuscript Department, Duke University Library, Durham, N.C.; Ruth Currie-McDaniel, "Court-ship and Marriage in the Nineteenth Century: Albion and Emma Tourgée, a Case Study," *North Carolina Historical Review*, LXI (1984), 285–310; Albion Winegar Tourgée Papers, microfilm copy in Chautauqua County Historical Society, Westfield, New York (used by permission of the society); Otto H. Olsen, *Carpetbagger's Crusade: The Life of Albion Winegar Tourgée* (Baltimore: Johns Hopkins University Press, 1965); Blanche Butler Ames (comp.), *Chronicles from the Nineteenth Century: Family Letters of Blanche Butler and Adelbert Ames* (2 vols.; Clinton, Mass.: Colonial Press, 1957); Stearns, *The Black Man of the South*.

his brotherly advice concerning her behavior had a personal motivation. He also recognized her as his "little angel" and thought perhaps she could help him be a good person, though he admitted, "I am not remarkably bad now." He urged her to complete her college studies, even sending money from time to time to assist her. She graduated in May, 1864, from his alma mater, Maine Wesleyan, having led her class in at least one term.[12]

Emma Bryant remembered accounts of the sea breezes on the Georgia coast, where John had been stationed, and the abundance of flowers and vegetables. He had even mentioned the possibility of returning to the Sea Islands to live. Still, she had expected that he would follow his earlier plan of becoming a lawyer and residing in Maine after the war.

Bryant's work with black troops, however, had modified his perspective and given him a new sense of mission. In 1865, when General Rufus Saxton invited him to become an agent for the newly formed Freedmen's Bureau, John accepted and moved to Augusta, Georgia. He went without his new wife, for reasons that were unexplained but seem fairly obvious. The difficulties of that first summer after the war were overwhelming, with uncertainties and chaos the norm. Still, by the time Emma Spaulding Bryant joined her husband in early 1866, a pattern of living apart had been set for their marriage. The direction of his career had been established as well, since he had proved controversial and confrontational from the outset. Removed from the bureau in 1866 after he clashed with conservative Davis Tillson (who replaced Saxton as head of the Georgia bureau), John continued to work for the political participation of black males, organizing an equal-rights society and editing a radical newspaper with that goal.[13]

Emma Bryant, newly arrived but ostracized by white southerners because of her husband's political work with blacks, recalled that the ladies of Augusta "spoke insultingly" to her in the street. Then she was puzzled and hurt when her dog was cruelly poisoned. "I sometimes wonder whether the time will *ever* arrive when we shall be on friendly terms with the Southern people," she wrote in her diary. "If it can be,

12. Currie-McDaniel, *Carpetbagger of Conscience*, 17, 39.
13. *Ibid.*, 51, 56, 66–67.

without any concession of principle on our part, I would be glad but it seems scarce probable to me."[14]

Violence against her husband, as well as her poor health, caused her return to Maine by June, 1866. Pregnant by this time, and perhaps apprehensive about her condition, Emma retreated to a climate with cooler temperatures and a less stressful atmosphere. The stay was only temporary. After suffering a miscarriage, which she seemed to take in stride, Emma began what became a long-term, recurring effort to rejoin her husband on a permanent basis. But she was frequently dissuaded by his objections. Embroiled in Republican politics, he was totally taken up with the formation of the state's Republican party, the Georgia constitutional convention, and then the campaign to elect a Republican governor.

Even when in Georgia, Emma Bryant was alone much of the time. Like many other carpetbaggers, John often traveled to the North, conferring with Republican leaders in Washington, for example, seeking Union League support in New York, attending conventions in Philadelphia, and raising funds in Rhode Island. Also, the demands on the time of the state politician were seasonal. Just when Emma thought housekeeping might be possible in one town, the situation would change. When John was elected to the state legislature in Atlanta, housekeeping in Augusta became rather lonely. Little thought was given to Emma's accompanying John on political trips. Only once did her husband suggest that she assist him in campaigning in a congressional race; the idea was abandoned because she lacked an appropriate (and expensive) wardrobe. Although often separated, the Bryants remained close through an extensive correspondence. Emma was always eager for his letters, and John admitted that he was disappointed if a letter did not come daily from his wife.[15]

John Emory Bryant was never elected to national office. For a short time he attempted to maintain a law practice; he once held the post of deputy customs collector. But for the most part, he lobbied, campaigned, and wrote, always as a champion of black rights and usually arousing southern ire.

14. Emma Bryant Diary, June 20, 1866, Emma Bryant to John Bryant, December 30, 1866, in Bryant Papers.
15. John Bryant to Emma Bryant, August 7, 1874, May 14, 1872, in Bryant Papers.

In addition to being alone most of the time, Emma was always poor. She often lived in boardinghouses, which presented other problems, such as being forced to eat "starches and pork," which she detested. When she did maintain a rented residence in Georgia, Emma always had a freedman guard in the house when her husband was away, and she took a gun when she answered the door. Anxious about her husband's safety much of the time, she wrote in 1868 that he was in "constant danger." She remembered "the dark days" of her early southern experience with a certain amount of horror. But she learned to leave John's fate "in God's hands" and to think courageously about her own safety. Once, in 1872, when John expressed concern about her walking to town from their boardinghouse outside Atlanta, Emma answered, "I don't like much better than gentlemen do to feel cramped and prevented from going so short a distance as from here to town, if I have strength to carry me." She said that rather than give up the exercise, "I will arm myself."[16]

Emma endured family events such as childbirth alone, whatever her personal needs. After suffering the miscarriage in 1866, she was in Atlanta in 1868–1869 expecting another baby. She wrote her husband in plaintive letters of her fear of the impending birth. When the child came, she then had to inform John of their firstborn's brain damage and critical condition. He would have to hurry, she wrote, if he was to see the child alive. Involved in a campaign to be appointed postmaster of Augusta, he could not leave at once. The boy died before his father arrived. In 1871 Emma's only child who survived infancy, Alice, was born in an unfinished farmhouse in a room with a curtain instead of a door. John was absent on that occasion as well.[17]

Worried that they might drift apart because of separations that sometimes lasted weeks or months, Emma Bryant felt that "should our hearts ever stray from each other it would be a worse calamity than . . . death." On another occasion, weary of the long-distance marriage, she confessed her apprehension that the absences "will

16. Emma Bryant to John Bryant, October 2, 1866, October 10, 1867, December 12, 1880, June 27, 1872, in Bryant Papers.

17. Emma Bryant to John Bryant, March 12, 13, April 2, 18, 1869, in Bryant Papers; Alice Bryant Zeller Autobiographical Sketch (Typescript in Bryant Papers); Currie-McDaniel, *Carpetbagger of Conscience*, 103, 124; Smith-Rosenberg, "Hearing Women's Words," 22.

weaken the bonds that have always held our hearts and lives so closely together." "Does that fear ever trouble you, husband mine?" she asked.[18]

Her husband expressed his concern differently. In 1873 he grew absolutely irrational when Emma traveled to Cleveland without him. She had begun to paint as a diversion and planned to visit art shows and talk with fellow artists. She also took Alice for a medical examination and was treated by a physician herself as well. John questioned the propriety of his wife's being alone with the doctor and of the doctor's examination of her, though Emma reminded John that his own sister had been treated by this physician for three years. Emma enjoyed the doctor's company and accompanied him on some house calls. Afterward, he drove her to a hotel in his buggy, careful to be there before dark. But John, defensive and feeling helpless to alter the situation from long distance, sent insulting wires and letters commanding his wife to cease this behavior and return home.

Emma Bryant, reeling from the condemnation, completely rejected his interpretation of her actions. In all her life she had never been so "grossly insulted," she declared. "Do not dare to write me again, or expect ever to receive another line from me until you can assure me of your *unlimited confidence* in me and feel *sincerely repentant* for the terrible things you have said to me. I have never lived with you on other terms than those of the most perfect *love* and *trust* and *equality*. I never intend to live with you on other terms." John later explained that "freedom" of "the wife" led to "free love." Nevertheless, he apparently made the right apology. He wife's next letter began with the familiar "My darling husband."[19]

Emma probably would have preferred a more nearly normal existence for them in the North, but she manifested a keen interest in Georgia politics and kept up with the events and persons in John's life. Likewise, her genuine piety made her anxious about the corrupting influences in the political career that absorbed her husband. Throughout her correspondence she reminded him of his commitment to Christian principles. She wrote him that he must never "in political

18. Emma Bryant to John Bryant, December 21, 1880, in Bryant Papers. The Bryants' longest separation was two years, 1879–1881.
19. Currie-McDaniel, *Carpetbagger of Conscience*, 126.

scheming be induced to take yourself or encourage in others any step inconsistent with Christian dignity of character. I had rather that we would live poor all our days than you should do so." She prayed, she said, that he would "be kept from wrong in the midst of political intrigue."[20]

For Emma Bryant, the years after "Redemption" in Georgia (which came in 1871) did not change her poverty and loneliness. While her husband continued to work in Republican politics and to travel, perhaps even more than before, she assisted in the publication of the last of the party's ill-fated radical newspapers, the *Georgia Republican.* When it failed in 1879, she believed it was time for a reassessment. "You cannot continue," she wrote, "using up your energies at the lavish rate of the past four years with no material and pecuniary reward." The time was "fast approaching," she continued, "when there must be some element of certainty in our affairs."[21]

In 1883, rather than promising certainty, John offered his wife's services to help in his new school for poor white children in Atlanta, a project that he hoped would begin to reeducate southerners to a national perspective. At this, Emma was stunned, since she had been working to regain her previous expertise in mathematics by assisting in a school of black adults in Atlanta. She had no intention of changing her course, and she reminded her husband, who was on a jaunt to Boston at the time, "You cannot plan for me at all at your present distance from me."

Furthermore, when John suggested that teaching the children might be good for her health, Emma explained what would improve her health: "To have my husband remember that God has given me brains and judgement and the feeling of responsibility as well as to himself, and to cease to *distress* and *chafe* me by opposing every plan I make, and by attempting to think for me." She also asserted, "I was born with a respect for the inherent rights of *every person*" and "for the right of each person to judge for him or herself what God requires of them, and do you suppose that I grant all this to you, as you know and the Father knows I have, and feel within me none of those rights?" She felt that

20. Emma Bryant to John Bryant, September 23, 1866, n.d. [July, 1868?], in Bryant Papers.
21. Emma Bryant to John Bryant, July 26, 1878, March 28, 1883, *ibid.*

she had previously proved her sympathy for his work by her "willing-ness to help in it without any assured feeling of its success in your lifetime or mine."[22]

Sentenced to indigence by her husband's struggle, Emma Bryant questioned the code by which he required that she seek no meaningful work beyond occasional sewing at home or volunteer work with chil-dren. The humiliation and resultant defeat of that dependency finally became apparent to her: "I do not know whether to call it providential and unavoidable or whether by more courage and resolution I could have broken through the barriers that seemed to forbid me to become a bread winner and have accomplished something before this ill health came upon me and perhaps have avoided the ill health by the very peace of mind that would have probably come with regular occupa-tion." Concerning her husband's political career, she had once said, "Dependency on the whim and caprice of others" was "not healthy"; now she saw that that statement applied to herself as well. "I know that it is only the general and large view which you take of it," she wrote the ever absent Bryant. "I am troubled both for [Alice] and for you and for our future. God help us."[23]

Further, Emma saw the futility of trailing behind John and seeking the elusive ideal of family, hearth, and home. "Ever since we were married we have looked forward to some golden Eldorado when we should be able to live habitually together," she commented. "I hope that we may live long enough to realize our dreams in this respect." Realistically, however, she was learning to rely more on her own re-sources and decisions. In a dramatic move contrary to her husband's wishes, she decided to rent a small house where she could cook her own food. John had insisted that she board with a colleague of his; the money he sent for rent would therefore sustain his wife and friend at the same time. But Emma thought the food served was unnutritious. The ruin of her health was a cost "too high" to pay in order to help them. "I think if you knew the added strength, moral, mental, and

22. Currie-McDaniel, *Carpetbagger of Conscience*, 169–71. Bryant's school sought out poor, unschooled children. Only 63 percent of white children were enrolled in public schools in Georgia in 1880. See Jones, *Soldiers of Light and Love*, 199.
23. Emma Bryant to John Bryant, December 25, 1882, September 20, 1880, in Bryant Papers. On the taboos against middle-class women working, as reflected in Emma Bryant's words, see Smith-Rosenberg, "Hearing Women's Words," 33.

physical, that I should derive from [the move] you would at least *ask* God to enlighten you" as to the wisdom of it, she wrote. "You must," she added, "leave me to act according to my best judgement."[24]

The agony of learning independence was well worth the effort. Emma Bryant made a home for herself and her daughter on the outskirts of Atlanta and by 1883 noted a change in southern attitudes. She remarked on a measure of acceptance in a nearby church. As for Alice, she wrote, "I do not think she suffers at all [at school] from political consideration or is in any way slighted or ostracized."[25]

In 1884 John Emory Bryant received a political appointment to the highest office he held in the South, that of United States marshal for northern Georgia. He held the position for only a few months, because it was a lame-duck appointment, but his daughter remembered it as a happy period when the family was together. At the end of the term, in November, 1884, Bryant left the South for the last time. In New York he devoted himself to business, the National Union League, and the lecture circuit.

Emma concentrated on obtaining an education for her daughter. Believing that college was "essential to confidence and thoroughness," she was determined that Alice would have that experience. Emma now took on the teaching assignment for which she had prepared in Atlanta. By 1887 both mother and daughter had moved into the East Tennessee Wesleyan University community, Emma as a teacher and Alice as a student. Free at last from the grinding poverty and dependency of "body and spirit," Emma Bryant spent a little money on laces and ribbons and rode horseback several times a week, her health regained. After Alice graduated from college, they joined John in New York, where Alice lived with her parents until her marriage.[26]

Emma Spaulding Bryant grew through adversity to be an independent thinker and a person on her own terms. Sensitive to the entire fabric of inequality, she seemed to have a remarkable insight into the oneness of the reform impulse. In 1881, having just read Helen Hunt Jackson's book *A Century of Dishonor*, she expressed her views on the

24. Emma Bryant to John Bryant, August 28, 1881, April 1, February 11, 1883, in Bryant Papers.

25. Emma Bryant to John Bryant, May 3, 1883, *ibid.*

26. Emma Bryant to John Bryant, January 29, 1884, *ibid.*; Currie-McDaniel, *Carpetbagger of Conscience*, 176, 178.

plight of American Indians. "I trust that it will not be followed by a dreadful retribution [such as that] which baptized this land in blood before slavery was destroyed," she said. Because of the treatment of these Native Americans, she was ashamed to be an American citizen. In parentheses she added, "I believe even women are citizens." The extent of her involvement is unclear, but according to her daughter's account, Emma was a suffragist, which is not surprising considering the lines of reasoning the dialogue with her husband took. Moreover, she demanded the same respect for all persons. In one revealing letter, occasioned by a report of a negative northern reaction to abolitionist sentiment in 1883, Emma noted: "When we remember that we claim the north as at least fifty years in advance on the south in almost everything, it is certainly not surprising that republicans have met a like treatment here [in the South]. I have for many years believed that the germs of human nature, the essentials of it I may say, are the same everywhere, and all experience and observation confirms that view." Moving easily to join this to the issue of equality, she continued, "As with the sexes . . . all the essentials of human nature" are the same. "What would be a galling chain to a man is no less so to a woman."[27]

Blanche Butler Ames

Blanche Butler, daughter of Union general Benjamin Butler of Massachusetts, had the finest finishing-school education possible for a girl. She attended the fashionable Academy of the Visitation in Georgetown to become, as her mother wished, not only an "agreeable companion" but also a "highly educated and accomplished woman." Homesick and lonesome for their home in Lowell, the young Blanche, by her own admission, did not excel in her studies and sometimes wished "they would have Civil War, if I could go home."[28]

A more keenly developed sensibility to national affairs came with some maturity and her father's election to the United States House of Representatives in 1867. Beautiful and assertive, Blanche was at home

27. Emma Bryant to John Bryant, August 19, 1881, Alice Bryant Zeller Autobiographical Sketch, and Emma Bryant to John Bryant, April 1, 1883, in Bryant Papers.
28. Sarah Butler to Blanche Butler, September 15, 1860, Blanche Butler to Sarah Butler, February 4, 1861, in Ames (comp.), *Chronicles from the Nineteenth Century,* I, 51, 65.

in Washington society but conscious of the Butler family and tradition in Massachusetts when she met Adelbert ("Del") Ames, who represented Mississippi in the United States Senate. Ames, a West Point graduate and Union army officer from Maine, had been appointed provisional governor for Mississippi in 1868 and military commander there in 1869. After serving in the Senate in the early 1870s, he would be elected governor of Mississippi in 1873.

A handsome couple, Blanche and Del attracted newspaper gossip as they courted in 1870. Their marriage in Lowell, on July 20, 1870, was perhaps the most dazzling society wedding of the Reconstruction years, with six hundred guests inside the church by invitation and ten thousand outside. For a time, setting the date had revolved around whether President Grant would be able to attend. Finally, Blanche herself determined that they must plan a schedule that suited them. "It is to be your wedding and mine," she wrote. "If *people* wish to come to it—very well, we shall be glad to see them. But I cannot arrange the time, in order to catch them en paussant." Accustomed to having her wishes carried out, she deliberately omitted "obey" from her vows in the wedding ceremony. After asking Del if he objected, she stated that whatever his answer, she had "not the least intention of making that promise." After the wedding, she preferred to be addressed as Blanche Butler Ames rather than Mrs. Adelbert Ames. The latter she sometimes used in playful deference, but only with her husband.[29]

Ames had married into a different situation from the one he had known. With Blanche, he married the Butler name, wealth, and national recognition and gained access to major political figures on the national scene. Although he claimed to fear that he was intellectually inferior to his wife's associates, Senator Ames seems to have relished his association with Representative Butler, as the two of them talked politics and plotted strategy for Republican ascendancy in the South as well as the North.[30]

With his northern connections, Ames literally epitomized the foremost connotation associated with the word *carpetbagger:* his roots were in Maine, his parents and family business were in Minnesota, and his wife remained first and foremost a Butler from Massachusetts.

29. Blanche Butler to Adelbert Ames, May 18, June 26, 1870, *ibid.*, I, 30, 177.
30. Adelbert Ames to Blanche Butler, June 22, 1870, *ibid.*, I, 172; William S. McFeely, *Grant: A Biography* (New York: Norton, 1981), 362–64.

Blanche's mother, Sarah Hildreth Butler, a close confidant to her only daughter, apparently was not displeased with the match, but her perception seems to have been that Blanche had married someone beneath the family's social class. Sarah Butler resolutely made it clear to Blanche that she must not move west. Her horror of the "frontier" surely colored the new wife's expectations when she met Del's family in Northfield, Minnesota. Blanche reported with surprise that they "set a nice table" with "silver and white damask." Plates were changed and courses served through dinner "as well as they are at home."[31]

Impressed but not persuaded, Blanche informed her husband that she would visit Minnesota but could never consider it as a permanent home. She would have a similar judgment for the South. Unable to lure his wife south for more than short visits, Del found personal as well as political reasons for long stays out of the state, a fact of which Mississippians were well aware. He literally lived with his carpetbag a more constant companion than his wife, though the visits were frequent enough to result in six Ames children. The correspondence between Blanche and Del reveals a deep and loving relationship throughout their marriage.

Blanche Butler Ames felt little but disdain for the South. She had confessed even before her marriage to Adelbert: "I don't know that I look forward with great delight to 'working for the interests of Mississippi.' I am fearful I have not that love for my state that I ought to have as its Representative." Then, with the thought of a new option, she added, "If you let me run at the next election I may get up a little more interest."[32]

In fact, Blanche had no intention of either running for office or involving herself with the people of the South. On her first visit, a southern woman on shipboard tried to engage her sympathies regarding the South's plight. Blanche was clearly annoyed and complained that "the dreadful little woman" had "whined" for no cause, since "we care little or nothing about her sorrows and troubles."[33]

This carpetbagger's wife intended to stay in Mississippi no longer than seemed "decent." She was content either to board or to visit on

31. Blanche Ames to Sarah Butler, September 10, 1870, in Ames (comp.), *Chronicles from the Nineteenth Century*, I, 195.

32. Blanche Ames to Adelbert Ames, n.d. [June, 1870], *ibid.*, I, 162.

33. Blanche Ames Diary, November 10, 1870, *ibid.*, I, 216. Who Blanche meant by "we" is unclear; perhaps she meant Del, perhaps her travel companions.

her infrequent sojourns there. She considered the mild winters in the state its one advantage, whereas the food was steadfastly a source of dismay. "True Southern style" cooking, as the Ameses perceived it, included "lard and flour for bread—lard and ham for bacon—lard and beef for steak. Lard was the basis of everything." Her first impression of Mississippi, and the houses that were reputed to have been the "most beautiful and aristocratic" before the war, was that none compared with "her father's place in Lowell." To Blanche, southern "plantations" were no more than "rude cabins."[34]

Adelbert Ames had been criticized as a senator because he owned no property in Mississippi and because he did not live there. Seeking to answer both charges, he purchased a house in Natchez and tried to entice Blanche to move south. Her immediate response was that he should rent the house at once. "We shall not be likely to go down there to keep house," she said, since "you have so little time to spend in the state." Her visit to Natchez was more pleasant than expected, but the neighbors were "very bitter southerners" and did little to change her first reaction.[35]

Once Del was elected governor of Mississippi in 1873, Blanche might have considered longer stays in the state, but the generous contours of the governor's mansion were unsatisfactory. She found it a "great barn of a house"; it was "dirty" and "shabby" on first view. After a thorough cleaning by servants and convicts, who worked under Blanche's watchful eye, a second appraisal found the dwelling "very spacious and pleasant, but like a hotel," and she "hardly felt at home in it." (In fact, she spent only six months there during the first year and four months during the second year of Del's term in office.) Her husband soon came to the same conclusion. "This is not a home and never can be," he decided. "Where our own vine and fig tree are to grow I know not, but it is true that in imagination I plant them *not* here."[36]

As in Natchez, their reception in Jackson underlined the fact that the carpetbagger and his family were aliens. Blanche, admitting that "every white person in the city is inclined to be prejudiced against us,"

34. Blanche Ames Diary, November, 1870, *ibid.*, I, 213–15.
35. Blanche Ames to Adelbert Ames, November 19, 1872, Blanche Ames to Sarah Butler, May 21, 1873, *ibid.*, I, 420, 456.
36. Blanche Ames to Sarah Butler, February 16, 1874, Adelbert Ames to Blanche Ames, August 2, 1874, *ibid.*, I, 650, 694–95.

stayed within the confines of the governor's mansion. Neither did she allow her children to stray beyond the gates. The insect world was no less inhospitable. Huge mosquitoes were hungry and persistent in both the official residence and in a second home on the Gulf. An unforgettable portrait, symbolic of a besieged carpetbagger, was Del's account of becoming a virtual prisoner behind the mosquito netting in his gubernatorial bed.[37]

In the summer of 1875 widespread racial unrest and violence threatened stability in Mississippi. After failing to strengthen his tenuous hold on the legislature, Del's future seemed to rest on President Grant's willingness to send federal soldiers into the state. But Grant, not wishing to detach troops to Mississippi and increasingly bored with the "southern question," resisted requests for more troops to bolster the Republican regimes in the South. Del, fearing all-out warfare between whites and the former slaves, declined to raise black militia to meet the increasing volume of violence. In an effort to assist him, Blanche allowed her father to read Del's desperate letters to the president, a strategy to which the beleaguered governor did not consent and one that proved ineffectual in any case.[38]

After the state elections of 1875, in which the Conservatives recaptured the Mississippi legislature, the southern intention to restore "home rule" could not be denied, despite the time remaining in the term to which Del had been elected. Democrats attacked the governor's record more loudly, accusing him of malfeasance because of his budgetary priorities and threatening impeachment.[39]

When she was not with him, Blanche remained a confidant and adviser to her husband through correspondence. Events moved so quickly as Del's position in Mississippi deteriorated, however, that his letters could not keep her up to date. Furthermore, Blanche viewed her husband's work primarily as a political avenue to power and status, even though the vehicle was what she perceived to be the degraded state of Mississippi. As Adelbert's grasp on the political situation slipped and the state was threatened with racial war in 1875, from

37. Blanche Ames to Sarah Butler, March 4, 26, 1874, Adelbert Ames to Blanche Ames, August 2, 1874, *ibid.*, I, 657, 667, 695.

38. Harris, *Day of the Carpetbagger*, 658–73; Blanche Ames to Adelbert Ames, September 7, October 20, 1875, in Ames (comp.), *Chronicles from the Nineteenth Century*, II, 166–67, 228–29.

39. Harris, *Day of the Carpetbagger*, 684–94.

Massachusetts Blanche concerned herself with his holding on in order to return to the Senate. Their plan had been for Del to give up his place as governor in exchange for his old Senate seat from Mississippi. At one time this feat had seemed manageable, and Blanche was loathe to relinquish the idea. She and Del and the children would look back with pleasure, she wrote, "on account of the name you have won, and the position. . . . Please bear my remarks in mind and gratify my ambition if possible. I care so little for the opinion of the people of Mississippi."[40]

Later, as Adelbert expressed less and less interest in Mississippi politics and little confidence in his ability to grant his wife's request, it changed to a demand: "I asked you before for your own sake, Dearie— now I *demand it* as *my* right that you should take the Senator's position and then resign. I have a great deal of pride in this, Del, and surely if you can gratify it as well as not, it is your duty to do so." He should do it for his son, she said, so that one day he could say, "My father was a senator." To her credit, when the gravity of the situation was finally made plain to her, it was Blanche who suggested the compromise that allowed Del to resign in 1876 and avoid impeachment. By that time, the coveted senatorship was not even a remote possibility.[41]

After Reconstruction, Blanche and Adelbert Ames did not concern themselves with the South. They left Mississippi believing that slavery and then Reconstruction "had destroyed the mind" of southern people or "at least impaired their judgement and consciousness to the extent that we cannot live among them." Having paid his dues to the idealism of the Republican dream, Del returned to the consuming issue of where his family would live. Blanche, confidently claiming her "right to share in your plans and deliberations," resisted his idea that they "could carpet-bag" in Minnesota as they had in Mississippi. After her mother's death in 1876, she seemed determined to take her place in the family residence at Lowell and "keep house" for her father and brothers, despite the fact that they were seldom at home for any length of time and her husband protested that "their own home" would be best for their family, preferably one near his business. Confirmed in her own mind as a matriarch at age twenty-nine, she remained convinced

40. Blanche Ames to Adelbert Ames, September 5, October 22, 1875, in Ames (comp.), *Chronicles from the Nineteenth Century*, II, 161, 231.
41. Blanche Ames to Adelbert Ames, March, 1876, *ibid.*, II, 353; Harris, *Day of the Carpetbagger*, 695–98; Current, *Those Terrible Carpetbaggers*, 325.

that her place was in Massachusetts. As she wrote to Del, persuading him that her decision was wise, she teased, "I believe with a little experience you will be very fond of money-making" in some worthy venture nearby. She urged him to think of himself as "one of [the] three masters" of the Butler homestead, since she intended to be its mistress.[42]

It is doubtful that Adelbert ever succeeded in feeling himself master in Lowell, but he did continue to spend long visits there and also to pursue his own interests in the family sawmill business in Minnesota and in his practical inventions, for which he regularly sought patents. Eventually, he accumulated enough wealth to make a comfortable living. Blanche, throughout, continued to be helpful with advice, encouragement, and practical help, such as monitoring their business records. In one of his more discouraging periods of financial trouble, she wrote warm wifely advice: "Don't worry. Do what is before you day by day with no thought of tomorrow." The daily letters, so much a part of their married life, continued unabated. It was Blanche herself who arranged for their publication, to ensure that she would be remembered "as a personality."[43]

In fact, the strong personality of Mrs. Ames was evidenced throughout the correspondence that chronicled her life. As a girl she had been aware that she was special and felt, with the pampered determination of a child of wealthy parents, that she could have whatever she wanted. As a young bride she had predicted that marriage would never bring "that awe and reverence which some wives feel for [husbands], the 'Lords of Creation.'" On the contrary, she wrote her fiancé, "there will be things about which you must be a child, and it will be useless for you to try to impose upon me with grand airs, and long words."[44]

Yet, despite this flair for independence, seen also in the omission of

42. Adelbert Ames to Blanche Ames, August 7, 1874, October 1, 1875, Blanche Ames to Adelbert Ames, November 5, 1875, June 3, 1876, May, 1876, in Ames (comp.), *Chronicles from the Nineteenth Century*, I, 702–703, II, 202, 252, 387–88, 376. The other two masters presumably were Blanche's father, Benjamin Butler, and her brother, Ben.

43. Harris, *Day of the Carpetbagger*, 721; Current, *Those Terrible Carpetbaggers*, 414–15; Blanche Ames to Adelbert Ames, September 26, 1886, in Ames (comp.), *Chronicles from the Nineteenth Century*, II, 559; Jessie Ames Marshall's note, in Ames (comp.), *Chronicles from the Nineteenth Century*, II, 681.

44. Blanche Ames to Adelbert Ames, June 9, 1870, in Ames (comp.), *Chronicles from the Nineteenth Century*, I, 158–59.

"obey" from her marriage vows and her insistence that she be called Blanche Butler Ames, Blanche was oddly exhilarated by the restrictions of the marriage bond. "What a glorious sense of freedom," she averred, to be married. No longer would she have doubts and hesitations about what is "best or proper for a girl to do." Her self-consciousness was gone, and "determination, self-possession," and self-reliance were hers. She had been married almost two years when a single young man visited the Butler home while Adelbert was away. She wrote to him that he need have no fears, for her flirting days were over. She had "no zest for such amusement," she said. "Life is more filled with richness and promise now, and there are no uncertainties or regrets to trouble one."[45]

The inconsistencies between what her abilities and personality demanded and what the role of wife prescribed, however, returned to disturb her. "Men always seem to have the advantage," she observed, "in dress, in law, in politics—everything. Will the time ever come when it will be equally easy for women to exist?" Another time, when she felt her opinion was being taken lightly, she complained that if she were a voter, Del could not afford to ignore her views. "Ergo, women should hold office and vote," she added. Seeking some avenue for individual accomplishment, Blanche turned to painting. She showed promise as an artist and became hopeful that she truly could achieve some renown. "What glorious satisfaction" it would be, she declared, "to be absolute master of one art, or profession." To know oneself "so gifted" as to be able to carry an art to the "highest human perfection" would be wonderful, she believed. In another letter, after commenting with pride on her husband's work, she again revealed her ambition: "I must accomplish something equally grand," she promised him and herself.[46]

As the pressures of rearing six children encompassed her, Mrs. Ames did not find the opportunity for grandeur. She developed instead a sense of despair and frustration that her life was made up merely of "trifles." "I am occupied from morning to night," she wailed, yet there was "so little accomplished." After describing one day of

45. Blanche Ames Diary, October 31, 1870, Blanche Ames to Adelbert Ames, July 20, 1872, ibid., I, 212, 364.

46. Blanche Ames to Adelbert Ames, December 10, 1870, November 3, 1873, April 26, 1871, ibid., I, 222, 626, 265.

routine domestic duties that included some child care but mostly decisions about meals, family, and household, she concluded: "This brings me up to the present time when I am writing to you and feeling cross that you are not here, and that I am what I am and that the world is what it is." Combating her feeling of helplessness that she was "the one left behind," Blanche tried, in addition to painting, sculpting and reading "amusing novels." It was not that her days were unpleasant; she had countless servants to keep her from drudgery. It was rather a dissatisfaction, an "eager restless yearning after I don't know what," as she expressed it.[47]

The youthful Blanche Butler had stated with confidence that for her "there is no bend to head or knee." The matronly Blanche Ames espoused instead "adaptability, [which] smoothes the rough places in life immensely."[48] Blanche Butler Ames was talented and resourceful but could find no way to impel herself beyond the traditional mold of the cultured upper-class female. As for Reconstruction, it had barely touched her.

Emma Kilborn Tourgée

Emma Kilborn's home was in Ashtabula County, Ohio, before the Civil War. She grew up in a climate of liberal reform, attended a coeducational school, and was keenly aware of politics and social issues as a teenager. Emma was not particularly drawn to religion, and she worried in the "secret chamber" of her heart that she did not feel guilty enough to please a righteous God. At age nineteen she admitted that when she was younger, she had considered conversion but had decided it was "perfectly useless" to be a Christian when "there was time for that in the years to come." Instead of trying to be a Christian, she "plunged deeply" into the innocent pleasures of youth, adored danc-

47. Blanche Ames to Adelbert Ames, October 14, 1873, May 14, 1878, October 3, 1876, *ibid.*, I, 600, II, 493, 437. Jones also mentions the "trifles" from which middle- and upper-class women in New England fled. Jones, *Soldiers of Light and Love,* 40–42, 207. See also Clinton, *The Other Civil War,* 40–53; Scott, *The Southern Lady,* 32–35.

48. Blanche Butler to Adelbert Ames, June 26, 1870, Blanche Ames to "Dear children," December 2, 1899, in Ames (comp.), *Chronicles from the Nineteenth Century,* I, 177, II, 680.

ing, and enjoyed friends and family in equal measure. Nevertheless, she claimed, "*I do love God* and hope to reach heaven."[49]

Albion Winegar Tourgée, Emma's schoolmate at the Kingsfield Academy in Ohio, had a reputation of being a strong intellect, though obstinate. His letters reveal that he was rather self-righteous as well. Immediately attracted to each other as they watched a sunset together, probably at a school function, they began their friendship with the familiar guise of "sister" and "brother." As they spent more and more time together, the relationship easily led to intimate moments and talk of marriage. Albion coached Emma's religious sensibilities but did not encourage her reform-minded conscience. When he left Ohio for college at the University of Rochester, he wrote of his regard for her but teased her, even in 1860, when she wrote that she had become "quite a rabid little petticoated Black Republican of late." From his ivory tower and involvement with his studies, Albion claimed, "I pursue the even tenor of my way entirely undisturbed by the political tumult around me." On another occasion he declared, "The fact is I haven't time to read politics and I don't care a copper which [side] whips." As for Emma's desire to aid the Republican cause, he said: "Pray more earnestly . . . that you may be the mother of a *dozen boys* . . . that your old age may be consoled with the reflection that you have added twelve voters to the strength of the Republican party. I think myself that this last is the most sensible method for your aiding the cause."[50]

In her own studies at the Female Seminary in Gainesville, New York, Emma concentrated on history and the arts, since Albion strongly resisted the idea of her studying geometry and science, thinking those subjects "unwomanly" and inappropriate for a female. "I don't want a triangulated mono-maniac for my wife; so just throw aside your mathematical longings and when you study anything *study modern languages* and *music*. Will you not my love, for *my sake?*" Emma did his bidding, reveled in the subjects open to her, and became "so happy" with the challenge that she sometimes forgot to write him. "I believe," she confessed, "that were I allowed to do just as I pleased and *could,* I would forget home, friends, *love,* everything for my books—sometimes it seems as if *forty years* would be all too short a time for me to

49. Emma Kilborn to Albion Tourgée, July 16, 1859, in Tourgée Papers.
50. Currie-McDaniel, "Courtship and Marriage," 287–89; Albion Tourgée to Emma Kilborn, February 4, September 26, 1860, in Tourgée Papers.

learn all I wish." She continued her interest and involvement in politics and in that regard warned that by the time she had finished school, "I may have given up entirely the idea of getting married *ever.*" But she hastened to add that she was only half serious.[51]

The time between Emma and Albion's engagement in April, 1859, and their marriage in May, 1863, was a long four years. Their courtship was marked with difficulties that several times came close to ending their relationship. At least two major problems carried over into and continued throughout their entire married life. First, Albion enlisted in the Union army in June, 1861. Discounting a back injury acquired while skating and then inflamed by a fall during training, he glorified war as a "sweet and noble" cause and expected to serve a full term. But another blow to his back from a runaway battery cut short his tenure in the army and, in the long run, condemned him to a lifetime of intermittent pain. In the short run, it caused slow recovery, black moods, and discouragement. Emma vowed to remain faithful to him, but she wondered if he would regain his courage. He seemed to her to be "floating out upon the ocean of life without chart or compass, a plaything of the winds, a sport of the waves."[52]

The second factor that marred their courtship was the "natural outgushing" of Albion's "affectionate nature." While their engagement effectively took her out of circulation, her fiancé felt no compunction about evenings of hugging and kissing with his favorite "sisters," always assuring Emma that he could distinguish between this and the "love-caress" he saved for her. Emma learned to endure his detailed accounts of these relationships rather stoically, encouraged by Albion's firm definition that he had chosen other females to be his friends but her "for a wife."

Nevertheless, embroiled in one such "sister" relationship, Albion clearly was torn between two loves. The women solved his problem by becoming friends themselves and sharing their mutual hurt, that one had been betrayed and the other served as "second best." Albion was not happy with the resulting change in the atmosphere when his "brotherly kisses" were not welcomed as before. His anger at "Miss

---

51. Albion Tourgée to Emma Kilborn, January, 1860, Emma Kilborn to Albion Tourgée, April 4, 1861, October 6, 1860, in Tourgée Papers.

52. Currie-McDaniel, "Courtship and Marriage," 295–96; Emma Kilborn Diary, November 9, 1862, in Tourgée Papers.

Impertinence" (Emma) for interfering made him rage that if he could, he would "go to war" and "not write until his body was scattered over the plains of Secession."[53]

Emma outlasted the bleak, sarcastic moods, and Albion eventually cleared his head of the other involvement, though it is likely that similar attachments occurred later. They were happily married in 1863 and began planning for Albion's future career. As early as 1862, a "southern scheme" had surfaced, but without clear definition. In the summer of 1865, after working on a newspaper and reading law in Erie, Pennsylvania, Albion moved with Emma to Greensboro, North Carolina. They sought a warm climate, which was believed to be beneficial for his back, but they also wanted a fresh start and economic opportunity as well. Their early identification with black rights suggests that the Tourgées also expected to find a cause in which they could believe.

Tourgée's initial business efforts as newspaper editor and part owner in a horticultural nursery and plantation failed. His family, which included Emma's parents, were forced to live in a rude log cabin and suffered long months of poverty, cold, and hunger. Before her marriage, Emma Kilborn had expressed a "dread and terror" that "evil and poverty [will] be our lot in life." Now it seemed that her worst fears had been realized. In addition to having economic difficulties, the family quickly aroused southern hostility by advocating better treatment of former slaves by whites. Emma's parents conducted a school for blacks, and Albion openly worked with the Union League and the Republican party. Emma attempted to meet whatever needs that arose. Once, she recounted, at a time when they could least afford it, she had given two dollars to a former slave who needed shoes.[54]

Albion, who had claimed as a student, "I rather dislike, yes hate, detest, the tedium of business," was more successful as a carpetbagger.

53. Lizzie Everitt to Emma Kilborn, December 3, 1861, Albion Tourgée to Emma Kilborn, August 7, 1859, March 10, 1860, Emma Kilborn to Albion Tourgée, October 2, November 27, 1861, Lizzie Everitt to Emma Kilborn, October 9, 24, 1861, Albion Tourgée to Emma Kilborn, December 3, 1861, in Tourgée Papers. The relationship of Lizzie and Emma confirms the evidence of female friendships seen in Smith-Rosenberg, "The Female World of Love and Ritual."

54. Currie-McDaniel, "Courtship and Marriage," 298–99; Olsen, Carpetbagger's Crusade, 28–75; Emma Kilborn to Albion Tourgée, October 5, 1859, Emma Tourgée to Albion Tourgée, October 7, 1877, in Tourgée Papers.

He served in the North Carolina Constitutional Convention of 1868 and used his limited legal training to advantage. Having been admitted to the Ohio bar in 1867, he was appointed as one of three commissioners to revise North Carolina's law code in 1868. His election to a judgeship in the state superior court improved finances considerably and allowed for the purchase of a fine team of horses and a large, rambling house in Greensboro.[55]

The temporary affluence did not allay the tension of southern resentment, which only increased with Albion's political activity. Threatening letters, which Emma included among the "wearisome vexations" of their situation, were sometimes addressed to her. "A friend of all loyal people," clearly a southern lady, addressed Mrs. Tourgée with a friendly warning that "even ladies (and I blush to write it) are saying [Albion] ought to be served to a suit of tar and feathers." Her modest, anonymous adversary hoped Emma would receive the warning in the spirit with which it was written.[56]

Emma, who assisted Albion during their first years in the South, gradually became less and less active in his work. Although he sometimes asked her to join him in his travels, she found sufficient reasons to stay at home. The trips were frequent and included journeys to the North to attend Union League conventions and other political meetings, as well as routine in-state rounds with the circuit court. Extensive correspondence was the mainstay of their relationship, but Emma was increasingly isolated and lonely. (In 1868 she mentioned "such kind friends" as Miss Sarah and Miss Mary, but they could not substitute for an absent husband. And other southern women provided only the usual insults.) Albion thrived on his political success and won the reputation, among friends in the North at least, of being distinct from the "mere political adventurers . . . who care nothing for the interests of the people they represent . . . but are simply 'on the make.'" But sensitive natives saw him as exactly that, and the hostility against him continued. As a judge, his visibility and his outspoken criticism of

55. Albion Tourgée to Emma Kilborn, June 9, 1859; Currie-McDaniel, "Courtship and Marriage," 298–99; Olsen, *Carpetbagger's Crusade*, 143–44. Bryant also was admitted to the bar through his home state (Maine).

56. Emma Tourgée to Albion Tourgée, October 7, 1866, "A Friend of All Loyal People" to "Mrs. Tourgée," October 16, 1866, in Tourgée Papers.

racial attitudes and violence associated with the Ku Klux Klan made him a likely target.[57]

The extent of Emma's unhappiness with her situation may be glimpsed in her actions in 1870. Having suffered two earlier miscarriages, she survived a difficult pregnancy and gave birth to her only child, Aimée Lodoilska ("Lodie"), in November of that year. Immediately after the birth, she traveled with her newborn daughter to Erie, Pennsylvania, for an extended visit and family nurturing from her sisters. How long she intended to stay is unclear, but Albion clearly was troubled by the action. He had an "inclination to blame you, ever since you went away," feeling that "you wanted to be *away* from me." He urged her to return, promising "a brighter and less selfish heart than you have known lately." Apparently responding to her request that he leave the South, he urged her to be patient and not "downhearted." He maintained that "the battle is over, the victory won." There may be "harsh times" again, he said, but they could anticipate "happiness and success." In a more practical vein, and with a show of impatience again, Albion informed his wife, "I am afraid you took more than your share of the furnishings, etc., as you generally do."[58]

Albion did succeed in coaxing Emma's return to Greensboro after several months, but she quickly discovered the unjustified optimism in his prediction. Little changed, except for the worse, as the time of Republican ascendancy in the state neared an end. Her husband would remark in time that her face had "gathered a fixed patient look as if you were all the time carrying some burden." As for the concern he had promised, Albion admitted in 1873 that he had been "engrossed and careless." He wanted to be less "cross and hasty" and believed he did not "talk as harsh and get angry about business matters so often as I used to." But Emma looked "as if the sickness of hope deferred had made you heartsick indeed."[59]

Emma Tourgée saw the political realities. In 1870 the Conservatives had taken control of the North Carolina legislature. In 1874, when

57. Emma Tourgée to Albion Tourgée, March 11, 1868, July 14, 1867 [1868], R. M. Tuttle to Albion Tourgée, November 26, 1869, *ibid.* In correspondence, the presence of Emma's mother in the South never was reflected as a comfort, even to her daughter. On the other hand, because of his strong aversion to his mother-in-law, Albion frequently mentioned her as a source of conflict.

58. Albion Tourgée to Emma Tourgée, December 20, 1870, *ibid.*

59. Albion Tourgée to Emma Tourgée, January 5, 1873, *ibid.*

Albion's term as judge ended, he lost a second attempt to win a congressional seat. New problems of financial solvency plagued the Tourgées from this time on. Correspondence during a state convention in 1875, as southerners tried to undo the Reconstruction constitution of 1868, indicated that Emma still followed her husband's efforts and urged him not to despair. Republicanism "is the cause of Right and must be triumphant at the end," she wrote. Still, she felt "sorry that you have to waste your time there when you can do no good." Also, while he struggled for "Right" in Raleigh, she had no money in Greensboro, and their milk cow was not giving enough milk. "I hope Darling this won't trouble you," she quietly implored. "I would not say anything about it if I knew any other way. . . . If I had but $5.00 it would relieve the present necessity."[60]

Emma lasted another four years in North Carolina, though neither the political prognosis nor her situation improved. A letter written by Albion to a certain "My dear Mary" during this time may indicate that another woman was close to him. In the letter he excused himself for not writing her and pleaded: "Do not blame me for my silence till I see you and explain it in full. I have no opportunity to write to you except at night when I happen to be alone for a few minutes in my office and *then* I *cannot* do it. It is like thinking of a lost pleasure so sweet that I cannot endure to contemplate its loss." He signed the letter "Yours."[61]

Whatever the case in that regard, in 1878, as Albion attempted another futile campaign for a congressional seat, and perhaps because of it, Emma had reached the limit of her endurance. She again fled to Erie with her daughter, leaving her mother and husband behind. (Her father had died and been buried in North Carolina.) From the safety of Erie she wrote, entreating Albion to join her there. Throughout the fall campaign, he answered in some letters that he wanted nothing more than to leave "this weary land of strife and hate. . . . Why did I ever bring you here to experience sorrow. . . . I do think it was the very greatest mistake of my mistaken life." But in other correspondence he sounded hopeful of winning and confident that "I am right." Throughout, the familiar, moody Albion dramatized their separation and claimed that he feared he would never see her again. "Forgive my weakness and if I never see you—if I do not write you again—forgive

60. Emma Tourgée to Albion Tourgée, September 8, 25, 1875, *ibid.*
61. Albion Tourgée to "My dear Mary," July 16, 1877, *ibid.*

me and love me still. May God bless you, dearest and sweetest and noblest of wives."[62] When the election finally came, Albion was crushed. "Everything," he despaired, "has gone against me by tremendous majorities. I do not understand it." He went on, "I can see nothing before me now but the most pinching & hopeless poverty." He was "utterly cast down," with "nothing to hope for." He was "dead politically." Worst of all, he wrote his wife, he had "linked your life with mine in my downfall." But then, after reflection, as he tried to explain the overwhelming proportions of the defeat, he became less charitable and blamed Emma for her desertion: "I was very sorry that you felt it necessary to go when you did. . . . I was confident that it would injure my campaign and the result was even more than I anticipated. It was made a constant theme all over the district."[63]

Still Tourgée tarried in the South, anguished that he could think of nothing else to do, reluctant to leave. "I do like the old region and I have strung so many sweet hopes on bright dreams here that I seem almost to have knit my heart into the land," he reflected. Ironically, because he was perceived by North Carolinians as having chosen to remain without his wife even in the face of his election defeat, he received a measure of acceptance and was treated with new respect— at least in Raleigh. The "current rumor," Albion reported, was that Emma "left . . . in a rage" to get a divorce in the North because "I will not abandon dear, ole N.C."[64]

His spirits began to lift with the "beautiful . . . dress" of the piedmont spring weather and another of his sexual "temptations," an encounter with a friendly widow who wanted them to "comfort" each other in their loneliness. Albion used the details of this liaison to remind his wife of her conjugal duties and urge her to rejoin him. After all, he counseled, she "brooded over fanciful sufferings." The South had not "been a wholly bad foster mother to us."[65]

Emma was not convinced. Their marriage seemed at an impasse. "I

62. Albion Tourgée to Emma Tourgée, September 15, 22, October 1, September 29, 1878, *ibid.* Enmity between Albion and Emma's mother added to his troubles during the fall campaign. Mrs. Kilborn soon returned to Erie.
63. Albion Tourgée to Emma Tourgée November 6, 9, December 12, 1878, *ibid.*
64. Albion Tourgée to Emma Tourgée, April 13, January 20, February 1, 13, 1879, *ibid.*
65. Albion Tourgée to Emma Tourgée, April 13, 16, 1879, *ibid.;* Currie-McDaniel, "Courtship and Marriage," 303; Albion Tourgée to Emma Tourgée, March 2, April 16, 1879, in Tourgée Papers.

hate Erie about as bad as you do N.C.," Albion asserted in December, 1878, and must "get the South out of me." He also wrote: "I am free to confess that I do not understand you. . . . I have never understood why you went—why you came from Raleigh or why you lost interest in what I was engaged upon. I suppose it was because you had lost confidence in me, faith in my judgment and trust in my capacity, and felt that you must act upon your own." By the following April, how-ever, anxious to be reunited and be "of one mind," they agreed to compromise by finding a new, neutral location for their home. "I think nothing short of death can separate us very long hereafter darling," Albion wrote optimistically. "We are not made to live alone."[66]

This plan was made easier by the success of Albion's novel about Reconstruction, *A Fool's Errand*, which he had completed during the hard winter of their separation. In the novel the author left little doubt about his own frustrations with southern racism and resistance to change. Not only did the book allow for their move to New York, where publishers wanted him to write another novel, but it necessi-tated his leaving the South because of the outcry over his story. Albion became an instant celebrity in the North, but his career as a carpetbag-ger was over.

The novel's success transformed the life of the Tourgées but did not totally erase the specter of poverty. Additional books brought fame and prestige, but an ill-fated attempt at publishing a literary weekly ended in debt and discouragement. The effort, nevertheless, afforded Emma the opportunity to exercise her business acumen and organizational skills. It was she who managed the publication office and corre-sponded with his publishers and the sponsors of his lectures.[67]

Emma Tourgée was continually disappointed by her husband's in-ability to handle business matters, but she never doubted his genius. Even after his death in 1905, she devoted herself to protecting and enhancing his reputation. The South and its pain had provided Albion a mission and, as it turned out, the grist for his literary talent. But Emma's cause had remained her husband. It is a measure of the diffi-culties she faced in the South that she had jeopardized her marriage to escape them. Despite her own strong feelings and considerable per-

66. Albion Tourgée to Emma Tourgée, December 11, 29, 1878, March 2, April 16, 1879, in Tourgée Papers.
67. Currie-McDaniel, "Courtship and Marriage," 305–307.

sonal resources, she had accepted Albion's definition of her role: to "enable, to prompt, to encourage me to do all that which I must." As a mature woman, she confirmed that view. "I have no self," she declared. "I belong to [my husband and daughter] and am content with either." In the end he would say of her, "You have been the one perfect wife."[68]

Etta Stearns

The details of Etta Stearns's story come indirectly, through the account that her husband, Charles Stearns, wrote of his venture into Georgia. Etta had met Charles aboard a ship en route to the South in 1866. She was a schoolteacher, and he, recently widowed, was a self-appointed missionary and would-be planter from Massachusetts and Colorado. They planned to purchase a plantation, "divide its products among those who perform the labor," and engage in "the important undertaking of elevating the freedmen."[69] Stearns lived near Augusta, Georgia, from 1866 to 1872, attempting to manage his farm with a residue of the former plantation's freed slaves. His involvement with politics came through the elected office of judge of ordinary (probate judge) in 1868.

Upon her marriage, Etta relinquished her career, presumably thinking their work would encompass teaching, which it did. As in the case of many other Yankees, the first hostility they experienced from neighbors surfaced over the issue of their teaching blacks. Charles and Etta conducted a Sunday school each sabbath in the largest of the former slave cabins on the plantation, and the native Georgians feared they would "teach political and social equality" to their students. Admittedly, the lessons were both "general and religious."[70]

Etta and Charles continued their school, primarily for adults at first, because of their strong sense of commitment, but they were disappointed in the progress made by their students. After a year, stunned by the "terrible effect" of slavery on its victims, they were "less enthusiastic" in reference to the "immediate elevation" of the former slaves,

68. *Ibid.*, 308–309; Albion Tourgée to Emma Kilborn, May 20, 1860, Emma Tourgée to Albion Tourgée, May 19, 1890, in Tourgée Papers; Olsen, *Carpetbagger's Crusade*, 349.
69. Stearns, *The Black Man of the South*, 30–31.
70. *Ibid.*, 57–69.

because of their "total ignorance." The need "cannot be imagined," Charles commented, when even the simplest information, such as the days of the week, the months of the year, and the difference between left and right, had to be learned.[71]

Etta's frustration extended beyond the school to the daily routine of the household. She was appalled at the "systematic disobedience" of former slaves to her instructions concerning how to do things. Having expected to use only kindness in "managing" the servants, both Etta and Charles yielded to a "mixture" of gentle prodding and "force," though neither tactic alone nor both in combination were remarkably effective. Etta's every tenet of cleanliness and efficiency seemed to clash with the customary patterns of cooking and housekeeping.[72]

Their new home, a typical plantation "big house," was a crude, two-storied structure: "During the fifty years it had maintained its grim position, it had remained wholly innocent of paint." It was made of "hard pine, and in the massive style peculiar to the South," it had three brick chimneys, a brick foundation, and several separate buildings, including the "smoke-house," the "meal-house," and the "milk-house." Etta immediately brought the kitchen inside the main structure. She returned from her first trip North with a new stove and tried to instruct the reluctant black servants in its use.[73]

In addition to finding the former slaves resistant to change, Etta thought them ignorant, mendacious, and "the worst thieves that the Lord ever permitted to live." It was impossible "to find an honest one. . . . I do not believe there is one in this cursed land." She felt "deeper and more thorough disgust" every day; there was "nothing to like" in that "hateful abode." It was "hateful from beginning to end." Her husband confessed that "while my wife detested slavery, she was not an extravagant lover of the colored race."[74]

It seemed that there would be no end to the trials of this carpetbagger's wife. A flea infestation, which "tormented all," but especially Etta, with her "delicate female flesh," almost drove them to burn down the plantation's big house. The "frigid manner" with which their neighbors greeted them created additional anxiety. "Not half dozen"

71. *Ibid.*, 153–59.
72. *Ibid.*, 45, 49.
73. *Ibid.*, 37–38, 42–43, 144–46.
74. *Ibid.*, 181, 54–55.

southern ladies ever called, and one informed Etta that it was not the custom for southern ladies to call on Yankees. Etta replied that she would welcome visitors, "but they may rest assured I shall not lament their absence."[75]

Etta Stearns did not live to endure the extent of her husband's stay in Georgia, much less the whole period of Reconstruction. Having found little joy in her new home, she became ill and died in the fall of 1867. Her husband explained that she was "accustomed to a more fertile soil, and a less tropical heat." In this "land of misery" she "drooped and pined away." He went on to say that, "quick and energetic in her temperament" and accustomed as she was to a "pattern of neatness and refinement," she "could not endure the slow and slovenly motions of the people around her." Charles buried his wife's body in what had been to her a "cursed" and "hateful" foreign land. The next year, when he turned to politics, he claimed to feel her presence and guidance. To pick up the burden of teaching the black children on the farm, he enlisted his sister from the North. Eventually, his mother came to assist him as well, and she also died in Georgia.[76]

Stearns did not last long as a carpetbagger. He had received his commission only a month after Republican governor Rufus Bullock was inaugurated in July, 1868. But after federal troops were withdrawn, there was little protection for a county official. At first he discounted threats against his life, but he decided to take them seriously when an unruly mob attempted to intimidate him one day and pushed him down the steps the next. When an "ugly crowd" urged him to resign his office, he determined that was the only judicious thing to do. Although the memory made him a "little ashamed," he concluded that it was best to live and write his story from a northern refuge.[77]

Conclusion

The wives of carpetbaggers must have anticipated travel to the "barbarous" South with a combination of hopeful expectation and dread. Well

75. *Ibid.*, 57, 172.
76. *Ibid.*, 180, 238, 305.
77. *Ibid.*, 214–27.

schooled by abolitionist and wartime propaganda in contempt for the southern "slave culture," they anticipated a lazy and decadent people, easily their social inferiors. Slavery had somehow "blighted the Southern people," the carpetbaggers said so often. The regional and class consciousness, exemplified by Blanche Ames's account of meeting her in-laws in Minnesota, was compounded in North-South relations by decades of mistrust and residual wartime tensions. After the war, the newcomers saw southerners as defeated rebels. Blanche Ames refused to attend church in Mississippi, because to her, all the ministers had been disloyal (though she had often missed Sunday worship in Lowell as well).[78]

Indeed, for Blanche, "the only redeeming feature of the South [was] the climate." By this she meant the mild winter months, which she compared with the bleak New England cold, but the heat of summer in the South was another matter. During the two springs, 1873 and 1875, when Blanche actually lived in Mississippi, her mother began her repetitive warning in April that her daughter should retreat from what Blanche herself termed the "malarious atmosphere" of the lower Mississippi. Blanche endured until mid-June, when she returned to Lowell and the Butler summer home at Bayview. Emma Bryant also sought the cooler climes of the North to escape the Georgia heat in summer.[79]

With mild winters perceived as the region's greatest advantage, reaction to other characteristics of the South tended to be censorious. The food was steadfastly a source of dismay to Blanche Ames and Emma Bryant. Emma noted with chagrin that "the meat used here is largely pork, and the vegetables, even potatoes, are all cooked with pork." Blanche fretted that with a new cook she would have to teach her "that lard is not the staff of life." Charles and Etta Stearns believed that "greasy pork [was] the delight of every Southerner." Emma Tourgée

---

78. Overy, *Wisconsin Carpetbaggers,* 8–10; Swint, *The Northern Teacher in the South,* 56; Blanche Ames Diary, November, 1870, in Ames (comp.), *Chronicles from the Nineteenth Century,* I, 216.

79. Blanche Ames Diary, November 10, 1870, in Ames (comp.), *Chronicles from the Nineteenth Century,* I, 216; correspondence between Sarah Butler and Blanche Ames from 1873 and 1875 in Ames (comp.), *Chronicles from the Nineteenth Century;* Emma Bryant to John Bryant, August 25, 1866, in Bryant Papers.

rarely complained about the southern palate, but she avoided the problem by tending a garden and cooking her own food.[80]

Perceptions of the southern people and life-style were seldom more positive than of the food. Preconceived notions of the planters of the region often did not jibe with the "plantations" that new owners were shown. Southern plantations were to Blanche Ames no more than "rude cabins." When Etta and Charles Stearns beheld their dwelling, their first "impulse was to have it razed." Further, they disliked the unfamiliar design of having the kitchen separate from the primary living quarters. Initially oblivious to the advantages of this division, which shielded the house from the cooking heat in summer and isolated it from the perennial danger of fire, Etta saw only the disadvantages of the arrangement, based on her experience in cold Massachusetts. Also, her sense of order and efficiency constantly clashed with what to her was the laziness of those around her. (This reaction was identical to that of the missionary teachers as a group, one of whom Etta had been initially.) The pace of southern life in general seemed slow and dull to the northerners.[81]

The attitude of southerners toward these visible, human reminders of their defeat was no more accommodating than the clash of values. Each side in the drama of "southern hostility versus northern arrogance" expressed fierce loyalty to the familiar and to "home." The southern elite exhibited a pride in their culture that mirrored the class and regional consciousness of New Englanders. And the concern of Sarah Butler that Blanche might marry someone from outside Massachusetts and her social circle reflected the anxiety of southern parents that daughters might marry similar interlopers, termed "damn Yankees." It was not unusual for carpetbaggers to marry teachers who shared their goals, but they did not always marry northerners. Adelbert Ames recorded several marriages of Union officers and officials to southern women, one of whom he complimented as "the handsomest

80. Emma Bryant to John Bryant, February 11, 1883, in Bryant Papers; Blanche Ames to Sarah Butler, January 30, 1874, in Ames (comp.), *Chronicles from the Nineteenth Century,* I, 643; Stearns, *The Black Man of the South,* 191; Emma Tourgée to Albion Tourgée, July 20, 1870, in Tourgée Papers.

81. Powell, *New Masters,* 124–25; Blanche Ames Diary, November 10, 1870, in Ames (comp.), *Chronicles from the Nineteenth Century,* I, 215; Stearns, *The Black Man of the South,* 37, 42–44, 144, 180; Swint, *The Northern Teacher in the South,* 61; Jones, *Soldiers of Light and Love,* 23, 47.

and most ladylike I have ever seen." Ames sympathized with the in-law problems of such a marriage, though his were of a different sort. Reporting one case in which the bride's parents were furious at their daughter for marrying a Yankee, Ames advised the groom to avoid the family fray and move northward. Other examples abound. Emma Bryant had hoped that their neighbors would like them better, but she would not risk her principles to gain the favor of southerners. Yet each side thought that it was protecting principles.[82]

Ironically, the reception of haughty hostility only confirmed the northerners' view that the southerners were only "half civilized" at best. The Yankees had not anticipated social rejection by their perceived inferiors; the incongruity was ludicrous. Ames stated with exasperation to his wife that a northern couple of his acquaintance, "the most elegant people [in Mississippi,] are ostracized by [those] who, [in the] North, could take no place in Society." Etta Stearns expressed her "conscious superiority" over the neighbors who shunned her but still coveted their social recognition. Her husband explained the contradiction. After all, he wrote, "everyone craves human society," and if one's equals or superiors were not available, "we are sometimes glad of that of our inferiors."[83]

The solution of the carpetbagger wives was to ignore the closed doors and to seek the solace of companions from the North. In the cities this choice was more satisfactory than in the countryside. Etta Stearns, on a farm in rural Georgia, did not have the resources or persons easily available to alter her daily routine. She bravely claimed that she would not lament the absence of company, but she was lonely and was "wildly delighted" when six or eight white missionary teachers, "the only ones of our color" she had seen in months, visited from Augusta for several days and broke her isolation. The women "talked

82. Wyatt-Brown, *Southern Honor*, 207; Current, *Three Carpetbag Governors*, 23; Daniels, *Prince of Carpetbaggers*, 82; Adelbert Ames to Blanche Ames, September 23, 1871, October, 1872, August 15, 1873, in Ames (comp.), *Chronicles from the Nineteenth Century*, I, 315, 410, 522; Pessen, *Riches, Class, and Power*, 205, 218; Emma Bryant to John Bryant, December 30, 1866, in Bryant Papers.

83. Jones, *Soldiers of Light and Love*, 83. According to Jones, the teachers anticipated hostility to their work. Powell shows that attitudes toward planters from the North varied, with the need for economic cooperation tempered by political considerations. Powell, *New Masters*, 62–63, 129–32. The letters of the wives show shock and dismay at social rejection. Adelbert Ames to Blanche Ames, October 20, 1871, in Ames (comp.), *Chronicles from the Nineteenth Century*, I, 339; Stearns, *The Black Man of the South*, 172.

in a familiar way" and a grand "strawberry festival" celebrated the occasion. Blanche Ames, conscious of the sentiment against her, remained behind the gates of the governor's mansion. There she invited "all carpetbaggers [in] to eat" and, to avert boredom, organized "little croquet parties of which they are very fond."[84]

The missionary teachers, some of whom rescued Etta Stearns from loneliness from time to time, found a similar way to console themselves. Within the walls of their dwellings, which were furnished by the American Missionary Association, they created small enclaves of northern culture, organizing events such as ice cream and strawberry socials. They duplicated northern pleasures rather than risk contamination by southern diversions or hurt by southern slights.[85]

Although the teachers rarely experienced the threat of physical violence, the wives of carpetbaggers found that the political realities of Reconstruction affected their lives as much as did the social circumstances. Southerners had no intention of allowing carpetbaggers the luxury of honest elections, appeal to reason in persuading public opinion, or attempts at new solutions to old problems. Insults gave way to physical danger and threats to actual attack and sometimes even murder. Terrorist groups, such as the Ku Klux Klan, made life unpredictable and filled it with anxiety. Emma Bryant always had a freedman guard in the house when her husband was away, and she took a gun when she answered the door. Emma and Albion Tourgée also had pistols in the house to ensure their safety. Mrs. Tourgée's hair reportedly turned completely white in one night of terror when "midnight marauders" surrounded their home in 1867. Blanche Ames wrote from Mississippi, "We pull down the shades and close the blinds at night, lest some foolish person might think it well to fire in." She added, "This is a strange community."[86]

The danger was even less tolerable when endured alone, and long separations between husband and wife were typical. Blanche Ames

84. Stearns, *The Black Man of the South*, 181, 172; Blanche Ames to Adelbert Ames, March 4, 26, 1874, in Ames (comp.), *Chronicles from the Nineteenth Century*, I, 657, 667.
85. Jones, *Soldiers of Light and Love*, 168, 182–83.
86. *Ibid.*, 82, 169, 188; Rable, *But There Was No Peace*; Otto H. Olsen, "Southern Reconstruction and the Question of Self-Determination," in George M. Fredrickson (ed.), *A Nation Divided: Problems and Issues of the Civil War and Reconstruction* (Minneapolis: Burgess, 1965), 113–41; Olsen, *Carpetbagger's Crusade*, 55; clipping from Philadelphia *Press*, n.d., in Tourgée Papers; Blanche Ames to Sarah Butler, December 14, 1874, in Ames (comp.), *Chronicles from the Nineteenth Century*, II, 70.

chose for the most part to stay with her family in Massachusetts while Del sought his political future in Mississippi. She preferred to do her "duty" by writing letters to encourage him and keep him abreast of the lives of their children and kin. To assuage her conscience, she wrote daily, though she confessed: "I *don't* love to write you. But I believe that you like to have my letters. Therefore I send them." Emma Bryant and Emma Tourgée also made correspondence the mainstay of their relationship with their husbands. The lives of these two wives also illustrate the isolation of married northern women who endured the "female rituals" of pregnancy and childbirth alone, deprived of the support they might have had from females at home.[87]

The disruption of family life and the long separations raise the question of fidelity. Predictably, there is little evidence to indicate that the husbands were unfaithful, though they certainly had opportunity enough. One of Bryant's enemies accused him of a sexual liaison with a black woman in Augusta, a charge Bryant vehemently denied. Tourgée, admittedly a ladies' man as a youth, continued as a married man to confess his "temptations," as he labeled them, or at least he confessed some of them.

Sexual fidelity is a difficult subject to assess from the perspective of the twentieth century, so different were the mores for wives and lovers of the carpetbaggers' time. Both Bryant and Ames wrote to their wives in terms that reflected faithfulness, and their concern for "righteousness" would tend to buttress that action. But this is quite an unreliable measure. As Blanche herself couched the question, why should she trust Del, when she would trust "no other man alive"? Was he really better than the others, she queried, or "am I blinded by my own affection?" Although professional advice from physicians and clergy in the North leaned toward constancy for the male spouse, there was clearly a double standard. The husbands enjoyed considerable freedom compared with their wives, who had to tolerate many restrictions. Despite his own license to enjoy intimate encounters with female friends, Tourgée shamed Emma Kilborn for the passion she exhibited for dancing before their marriage. She was contrite in asking, "Did I do wrong" if "I kept time with my feet and moved with the

---

87. Blanche Ames to Adelbert Ames, June 19, 1870, in Ames (comp.), *Chronicles from the Nineteenth Century,* I, 169; Smith-Rosenberg, "Hearing Women's Words," 28.

music?" In answer, he asked if she felt "any better, any purer," after dancing. He urged her to "exalt and purify your mind and heart." Del Ames belittled and accused his wife of conceit and vanity when she went to dances without an escort and enjoyed the attention of various men in her social circle. John Bryant's concern for "free love" if "the wife" enjoyed some freedom of male companionship reveals an anxiety about altering female roles.[88]

The correspondence of the carpetbagger wives reflects a certain awareness of women's rights as an issue, but the actuality of change seemed remote. Emma Bryant is the exception, as shown in her suffragist activity and struggle for self-sufficiency. She sensed the "irrationality and 'unnaturalness' of a world ordered around male definitions of gender and sexuality."[89] Once married, each wife relinquished her career goals, thereby modifying the contours of her southern experience and the relationship within her marriage. Whereas the female missionary teachers saw the South as a field for their own development and an escape from societal trivia, for the wives it was a secondary cause with few personal satisfactions and many frustrations. Of more concern for the wives was their association with white society, but their relationship to it was not geared toward finding solutions to the region's problems. Ironically, they experienced the South through the former slaves' culture but judged it by the white. The implications of this for measuring the overriding power of class consciousness are enormous.

The husbands' careers and causes took on a different meaning for each wife. Emma Tourgée worked closely with Albion in their first economic ventures and efforts at teaching blacks. But when he was made judge, she did not continue teaching, and his work more and more took him away from home and her companionship. Albion, after precluding his wife's assistance by his choice of career, blamed her for not being there on his terms when he felt she might be useful to his political plans. Emma Bryant expressed concern for the former slaves

88. Blanche Ames to Adelbert Ames, September 7, 1873, in Ames (comp.), *Chronicles from the Nineteenth Century,* I, 554; Wyatt-Brown, *Southern Honor,* 295; Emma Kilborn to Albion Tourgée, September 14, 24, 1859, in Tourgée Papers; Adelbert Ames to Blanche Ames, Blanche Ames to Adelbert Ames, October, 1875, in Ames (comp.), *Chronicles from the Nineteenth Century,* II, 236–42; John Bryant to Emma Bryant, August 19, 1873, in Bryant Papers.
89. Smith-Rosenberg, "Hearing Women's Words," 41.

and taught black adults for a time, but primarily as a path to her own goals. She assisted John in publishing his newspapers and would have campaigned by his side had the summons come. The elusive prize of subsistence and a livelihood for the Bryants was not the major goal for Blanche Butler Ames, who looked for status.

Despite the differences in location and circumstances, as well as in the reasons that brought their husbands to the South, the experiences of these wives of carpetbaggers reflect a striking similarity. The wives, expecting the region to be inferior, found hostility, heat, and unacceptable living conditions. Further, they were unable to establish a nurturing homelife or community among southerners. For varying reasons, including stark poverty, danger, absent husbands, and their own choices, the wives could not assist in the one essential thing the carpetbaggers needed to change the image of their name, that is, creation of a stable home in the South. One could say that the quality of woman found in these wives—intelligent, talented, and strong willed—was the very characteristic that made them less tolerant of the dreadful situation, as well as unable to be the agents for positive change they might have been. Blanche Ames simply refused association with the "vulgar" Mississippians any more than would "seem decent," and she clung to her Butler name and tradition. Emma Bryant saw the opportunity for growth in diversity and chose her own path to educate and thus free her daughter and herself. Even Emma Tourgée, devoted to her husband, envisioned a more sanguine future for her cause outside the strife of the South. She insisted that Albion leave.

The carpetbagger wives identified with the perspective of their husbands and saw themselves as superior victors over the South. In this they reinforced the historical difficulty of making gender roles a target for reform.[90] Had the wives only realized it, southern women shared more of their travails than they knew. The tedium with which Blanche Ames described her long days of domesticity was duplicated in the years before the war by the plantation mistress. The life of the "southern lady" was much like that of her northern sister. Further, researchers have documented a growing dissatisfaction among southern wom-

90. Gerda Lerner, *The Creation of Patriarchy* (New York: Oxford University Press, 1986). Lerner's discussion of the participation of women in the class structure of the men who both define and protect them is instructive on this point. See especially pp. 139–40, 213–14, 217–18.

en. The sarcastic expression "Lords of Creation," used by Blanche Ames to describe men, was the very phrase repeated over and over in southern diaries as wives spoke of their patriarchal husbands. For strong women such as Emma Bryant, the independence born of painful experiences in the South would mirror the effect of the Civil War and Reconstruction on southern women, though the latter did not fully perceive their independence as yet. Women without men had already risen to wartime emergencies. After Reconstruction, a generation of women alone would, of necessity, seek employment for the first time.[91]

A final word regarding the husbands, those confident, ambitious men who represented society's apogee of class, race, and gender: A diverse lot at the outset, they are classified as a group by their involvement in southern politics. No matter what the reason they came south—duty in the military for Ames and in the Freedmen's Bureau for Bryant, business opportunity and health for Tourgée, a mixture of religious and economic ventures for Stearns—all quickly tangled with the key social and political issue of the era, the freed slaves. One should applaud their idealism, optimism, and significant achievements, but they overestimated their ability to solve quickly the problems they faced. Universally, they met with disappointment, frustration, and failure in the face of southern racism, resistance to change, and violence. Albion Tourgée titled his account of his efforts *A Fool's Errand, by One of the Fools,* and John Bryant called the southern civilization "totally different from the northern." Bryant and Tourgée, who had contemplated cooperation in newspaper work at the outset of Reconstruction, had gone separate ways, but they found similar experiences. Well into the 1890s each continued on the lecture circuit in the North, expounding on "the southern problem" and condemning southern intransigence. Charles Stearns later said, "Little did I dream of the nature of evil I had to contend with." As one focuses on the forces of class and gender, the impossibility of the carpetbaggers' task should not be forgotten. And as Richard Current has pointed out, one "should refrain from comparing a realistic representation" of the carpetbaggers "with an idealized picture of their Southern white oppo-

91. Clinton, *The Other Civil War,* 38–39; Scott, *The Southern Lady,* 31–35, 78–90, 106–11; Wyatt-Brown, *Southern Honor,* 201.

nents . . . defenders and practitioners of racism in some of its ugliest forms."[92]

Still, in their relationship with their wives, these carpetbaggers reflected no reform leadership and were scarcely different from their southern counterparts. Although the wives found some self-awareness and independence, it was largely through necessity rather than through the support of their husbands. The men contemplated only how the women might serve their interests: "to enable, to prompt, to encourage me to do all that which I must," as Albion Tour-gée explained it to Emma Kilborn, instructing her that she must also become an "accomplished and attractive lady." Adelbert Ames desper-ately wanted Blanche with him in Mississippi, but he opposed political rights for women. In later life, both Tourgée and Bryant were solicited by feminists to lend their support to the suffrage movement, but they gave the cause little assistance. As abolitionists and reformers, the carpetbaggers condemned the patriarchal society of slavery, but they were blind to the repercussions that undoing that hierarchy had upon family structure. Although they chose strong women to share their lives, they were unable or unwilling to make their wives equal part-ners, perhaps fearing, as Bryant said, that freedom for "the wife" might subvert the husband's authority.[93]

Despite the obvious opportunism of some, clearly the carpetbaggers were not universally corrupt or immoral. Still, by regional arrogance and shortsighted allegiance to stereotypes of behavior, they unwit-tingly limited their own success. Furthermore, the gender roles they supported and reinforced by the treatment of their wives revealed the

92. D. Hodgin to Albion Tourgée, October 8, 1866, in Tourgée Papers; Stearns, *The Black Man of the South*, 28; Current, *Those Terrible Carpetbaggers*, 425.

93. Albion Tourgée to Emma Kilborn, May 20, 1860, August 7, 1863, in Tourgée Papers; Harris, *Day of the Carpetbagger*, 581; Susan B. Anthony to Albion Tourgée, June 22, 1892, in Tourgée Papers; John Bryant to Emma Bryant, August 19, 1873, in Bryant Papers. Current, *Those Terrible Carpetbaggers*, 415, states that Del and Blanche Ames supported their children's causes of suffrage and birth control but he does not reveal the source for that information. Albion and Emma Tourgée corresponded with Frances Willard and Ida Wells-Barnett. See Frances Willard to Albion Tourgée, December 21, 1894, Ida B. Wells to Albion Tourgée, August 26, 1895, in Tourgée Papers. According to his daughter, John Bryant once attended a suffrage convention with his wife. Alice Bryant Zeller Auto-biographical Sketch, in Bryant Papers. See Ellen Carol DuBois, *Feminism and Suffrage: The Emergence of an Independent Women's Movement in America, 1848–1869* (Ithaca, N.Y.: Cor-nell University Press, 1978), 53–78, for a discussion of the Radicals' willingness to aban-don feminist goals.

limitations of their reform motive. The naïveté with which they approached the South was but another side of the chauvinism with which they saw women and not so different from the racism of which they accused the southerners and shared in themselves. They represented the powerful in a society that was replete with elitism, racism, and sexism, illustrating how class status and power, human-made, can force biologically determined sex and race to serve hegemonic purposes. The corrupting influence of these ideologies—indeed, the complicated and interconnecting forces of race, class, and gender brought to bear on politics—may be uniquely observed in the wives of the carpetbaggers and their husbands.

Part II

The Racial and Class Dimensions of the Populist Challenge

3 / CHARLES L. FLYNN, JR.

Procrustean Bedfellows and Populists: An Alternative Hypothesis

For over thirty years the standard interpretation of late nineteenth-century southern politics has been built upon the masterly work of C. Vann Woodward. First sketched in *Tom Watson, Agrarian Rebel* and then painted in broader strokes from the same palate in *Origins of the New South,* this interpretation has been supported by most historians and modified by only a few, though virtually all have employed its conceptual framework as the foundation of their own work.[1] In doing so, most if not all have accepted Woodward's major premises: The Democratic party, both state and national, was a collection of what he called "procrustean bedfellows." Anachronistic sectionalism and racist demagoguery unified the southern Democracy while stifling debate on the problems and direction of the New South. The Populist party offered an effective critique of New South industrialism and an alternative to racist demagoguery, but it was crushed by Democratic violence and fraud on one side and by the betrayal of those who supported fusion behind William Jennings Bryan on the other.

Woodward's interpretation of southern politics is based primarily on his research in Georgia, but a recent reappraisal of Populism in that state casts more than a little doubt on Woodward's Georgia-based view.

1. C. Vann Woodward, *Tom Watson, Agrarian Rebel* (1938; rpr. New York: Oxford University Press, 1970); C. Vann Woodward, *Origins of the New South, 1877–1913* (Baton Rouge: Louisiana State University Press, 1951).

In *The Wool-Hat Boys*, Barton Shaw showed that the Populists and Democrats in Georgia were remarkably similar in their views; that they wrote remarkably similar, at times even identical, platforms on state and national issues; that Populists embraced commercial values; that they increasingly tailored their appeal in efforts to win middle-class votes in towns and cities and readily discounted working-class support; that they were anything but racial liberals and Tom Watson's twentieth-century bigotry had long nineteenth-century roots; that black support for the Democrats was well-founded; and that Progressivism in Georgia was by and large rooted in Democratic, not Populist, party leadership of the 1890s.[2] In his award-winning work, Shaw convincingly portrayed a Populist party that was, if anything, quite conventional—hardly a radical challenge to the commercial or racial values of the New South.

Although Shaw refreshingly undercuts the morality-play drama of *Tom Watson* and other accounts, he does not replace traditional interpretations with an alternative explanation for the passionate conflict between Democrats and Populists. He points out that landowning Populists tended to be somewhat more economically hard-pressed than their landowning Democratic rivals, that Populists were hostile to the courthouse rings that controlled much of the Democratic party, and that they drew upon local traditions of dissent. But by themselves, these marginal differences in wealth and local rivalries seem inadequate to explain a movement that engendered such devotion among its supporters and such fear among its opponents that men risked their lives and livelihoods for the cause. Indeed, Shaw's description of the racially and ideologically conventional qualities of Populism in Georgia makes the 1880s and 1890s seem more paradoxical than ever and demonstrates the need for yet one more major reappraisal of Populism.

A reexamination of primary sources suggests a new hypothesis about the relationship between ideology and partisan conflict in late nineteenth-century Georgia and, as was implied in both *Tom Watson* and *The Wool-Hat Boys*, across the South. Populism in Georgia can be understood only in terms of the Democratic party politics out of which it grew. During the 1880s the Democratic party was held together not only by the New South creed of agricultural and, to a lesser extent,

2. Barton C. Shaw, *The Wool-Hat Boys: Georgia's Populist Party* (Baton Rouge: Louisiana State University Press, 1984).

industrial development but also by a conspiracy theory of national politics that was, in fact, an evocative critique of national policies and the special burdens that they placed upon the South. The Populists and other so-called "Independents" shared the belief in this conspiracy theory and in the Democratic critique of policies associated with the national Republican party. But the Populists came to believe that hope for the success of Democratic principles in the federal government lay in building a new party system for the nation. The one-party system within the state helped to intensify differences over tactics in national politics into differences of principle. The hostility of state and local Democratic leaders to the third-party effort, their use of illegal methods to ensure Democratic victories, and their continued loyalty to a national party organization that seemed destructive of farming interests led Populists to doubt the sincerity of the commitment of Democratic leaders to the views that nearly all espoused. In one sense, party organization became the issue dividing Georgia Democrats and Populists, but at stake for Populists was the right of political participation itself. A division over political tactics thus became a fight over the substance of democracy, and the result was the especial bitterness of the agrarian revolt within Georgia and the one-party South.

Throughout the 1880s and, for that matter, the 1890s, the appeal of the Democratic party in Georgia was based upon both a program of economic development and a conspiracy theory of national politics. The party within Georgia was not a collection of "procrustean bedfellows," for both those within it and those who left it agreed with both parts of party dogma. Historians have traditionally overstated the emphasis on industrial development and underestimated the heavy emphasis on agricultural interests in the New South creed, but Democrats, Independents, and Populists all promoted diversified farming, raising home supplies, and home manufacture. As the depression of the 1890s deepened, Populists may have deemphasized the importance of that program as a solution to the farmer's problems, but it had been an integral part of the program of the Farmers' Alliance, and many Populist leaders were among its most prominent proponents.[3] Historians have similarly failed to recognize the power of the conspiracy theory espoused by Georgia Democrats in the late nineteenth cen-

3. Charles L. Flynn, Jr., *White Land, Black Labor: Caste and Class in Late Nineteenth-Century Georgia* (Baton Rouge: Louisiana State University Press, 1983), Chapter 6.

tury, though it served as a basis not only of the political agenda of the state Democratic party but also of the positions espoused by Independents and Populists.

During the eighteenth and nineteenth centuries, conspiracy theories served not only as a source of party identity and unity but also as a sincere and effective critique of government policy. American revolutionaries believed that King George III and others conspired against their liberty. Jeffersonian Republicans thought that those who disagreed with them were monarchists. Jacksonian Democrats thought that they saw a conspiracy among aristocratic interests. So, too, did Republicans see a conspiracy in the "Slave Power" and its influence in the federal government.[4] The conspiracies may have been imaginary, but the differences over values and policy that they reflected were profound.

The sincerity and potency of the conspiracy theory propounded by the Democratic party in late nineteenth-century Georgia have not been acknowledged, perhaps because historians have not been attuned to the issues that the South's Democrats thought were central. Corruption in government, tariffs, and pensions for Union veterans of the Civil War, for example, hold different and far less meaning for historians than for the politicians and the common folk who railed against them with religious fervor. To historians these issues have meant simply differences over policies and interests. To southern Democrats they were evidence of an ongoing conspiracy by the leaders of the Republican party to enrich themselves and to maintain political power at the expense of "the people" and, quite literally, at the expense of representative government.

The conspiracy theory had its origins in Reconstruction, which became to most southern whites a compelling symbol of Republican venality for decades thereafter. The clichés that are so familiar and that are so readily dismissed as ill-founded and deep-rooted in racism all reflected and affirmed the conspiracy theory. Across the political spec-

4. Bernard Bailyn, *The Ideological Origins of the American Revolution* (Cambridge, Mass.: Belknap Press, 1967); Gordon S. Wood, *The Creation of the American Republic, 1776–1787* (Chapel Hill: University of North Carolina Press, 1969); Richard Hofstadter, *The Paranoid Style in American Politics* (New York: Knopf, 1966); J. Mills Thornton III, *Politics and Power in a Slave Society: Alabama, 1800–1860* (Baton Rouge: Louisiana State University Press, 1978); Larry Gara, "Slavery and the Slave Power: A Crucial Distinction," *Civil War History,* XV (1969), 5–18.

trum of white Georgians, for example, the accepted interpretation of Reconstruction was the same. Whether Democratic party regular, Independent, or Populist, the canon did not vary. In 1883, John Dent, a farmer in Floyd County in northwest Georgia, recorded it in his journal as he wrote an essay entitled "Politics and Politicians Since the War": "To the North it was a war to hold [on] to the South for the wealth that it contributed to the north, and during the war it was the object of every Northern man out of the army, to become rich by the War. . . . The South was conquered . . . [and] unjustly robbed of four billions of property and left a howling waste." Politicians repeated, of course, the conventional wisdom. James C. C. Black, a decade before he became the reluctant opponent of Thomas E. Watson, remembered that during Reconstruction "law no longer held its benign sway, but gave place to the mandate of petty dictators enforced by the bayonet. What little property remained was held by no tenure but by the capricious will of the plunderer." Watson's view and words were identical: "Our laws [were] made by our slaves and enforced by the bayonet. Our rulers aliens and plunderers." Augustus O. Bacon, the man Tom Watson supported for governor in 1886 and a future United States senator, summarized the guiding principle of the Republican party as "desire for plunder." And William H. Felton, the foremost Independent in the 1870s and 1880s and a Populist in the 1890s, shared all these beliefs with equal bitterness. This unanimity should be no surprise, nor should the power and sincerity of these ill-founded beliefs. For among scholars, as well as in popular wisdom, they remained a standard view of Republican motivations well into the twentieth century.[5]

The belief in an ongoing Republican conspiracy after Reconstruction

5. Gerald Ray Mathis, Mary Mathis, and Douglas Clare Purcell (eds.), *John Hory Dent Farm Journals and Account Books, 1840–1892*, Microfilm (University, Ala.: University of Alabama Press, 1977), Vol. XV, undated entry following December, 1884; James C. C. Black, Speech at Atlanta, Georgia, unascribed newspaper clipping, May 2, 1886, Scrapbook Vol. IV, in James Conquest Cross Black Papers, Southern Historical Collection, University of North Carolina, Chapel Hill; Thomas E. Watson, Speech at Greensboro School, July 4, 1883, Scrapbook Vol. V, 317–18, in Thomas E. Watson Papers, Southern Historical Collection, University of North Carolina, Chapel Hill; Augustus O. Bacon, Manuscript Journal, 1868, p. 101, cited in Lala Carr Steelman, "The Public Career of Augustus Octavius Bacon" (Ph.D. dissertation, University of North Carolina at Chapel Hill, 1950), 24; Rebecca Latimer Felton, *My Memoirs of Georgia Politics* (Atlanta: Index Publishing Co., 1911), 47, 435; Frank Lawrence Owsley, "The Irrepressible Conflict," in Twelve Southerners, *I'll Take My Stand: The South and the Agrarian Tradition* (New York: Harper and Brothers, 1930), 61–91.

was equally powerful. Democrats did not think that Republicans had been born again with Redemption. Republicans had plundered during Reconstruction; they plundered still in the 1880s. As John Dent wrote in 1883, the Republicans sought to "keep up the war taxes, for twenty years after the war [in spite of surplus revenues], and [to keep] stealing all they could lay their hands upon, in short the policy was and is to rob the people and keep them poor by taxation so as to create a moneyed aristocracy as rulers of the government. Their plan is to change the Government from a Republic to one of a money power aristocracy creating a class of Rulers and Imperialists to be supported and maintained by the Government." Dent called this "the *European policy*, to make the Rich richer, and the Poor poorer. Our government," he claimed, "has been completely changed." Robert Toombs, a Democratic party hero and former Confederate cabinet officer and general, agreed: "Their system always was to plunder everybody." And these beliefs were conventional in Georgia. Just as, according to one historian, Augustus Bacon "came to associate the Republican party with plunder, corruption, lawlessness and tyranny," so, too, did his fellow partisans.[6]

To Democrats, the devastation of the war, coupled with Republican policies after it, explained the persistence of southern poverty. "The South rendered to the torch and sword three billions of property," said Henry Grady, who was a living textbook of southern political clichés. "That thirty million dollars a year, or six hundred million dollars in twenty years, has been given willingly of our poverty as pensions for Northern soldiers, the wonder is that we are here at all." The Lumpkin *Independent* and the Americus *Weekly Recorder* praised Representative Charles Crisp from southwest Georgia, later Speaker of the House of Representatives, for his fight to limit pensions, saying, "The pension bureau is a favorite channel through which to rob the treasury." And William H. Felton bitterly complained that pensions "saddled" an "enormous burden on the down trodden South." The tariff, too, was

6. John Dent, "Politics and Politicians Since the War," December 19, 1883, in Mathis, Mathis, and Purcell (eds.), *Dent Farm Journals*, Vol. XV, undated entry following February, 1884; *ibid.*, Vol. XV, August 12, 1882; Robert Toombs, Address, January 19, 1874, quoted in Milledgeville *Union and Recorder*, January 28, 1874; Steelman, "The Public Career of Augustus Octavius Bacon," 31.

"tribute" paid. In fact, it was the most burdensome of all Republican exactions, so that, in Grady's words, "under artificial conditions other sections might reach a prosperity impossible under natural laws."[7] Hundreds of articles and speeches repeated the litany.

From such a perspective, the corruption that plagued Republican administrations seemed less a series of isolated incidents than another symptom of the systematic abuse of government for personal gain. John Sherman of Ohio might say, "We are republicans . . . because we believe the success of our party will best promote the interests and advance the prosperity of the people." But campaign slogans such as "TURN OUT THE RASCALS" and "DOWN WITH THE THIEVES" seemed only too appropriate when, as one newspaper said, Democrats knew that "neither he [John Sherman] nor any other politician is a republican for any such reason. Mr. Sherman and his colleagues are republicans because that party has been the means of introducing them to the flesh-pots and swill-tubs of the Nation." And by one Democratic estimate, the swill-tubs yielded much: "The Republican party, through its officials, have robbed the government of from 40 to 45 million dollars in the last 20 years . . . and the Republican protective tariff party has robbed the people of 1 billion dollars every one of those 20 years."[8]

Complaints about the treatment of labor, complaints that Populists in Georgia later repeated and upon which they, like regular Democrats, halfheartedly appealed to urban laborers, were rooted in the conspiracy theory as well. Neither Democrats nor Populists favored any basic change in labor law or the capitalist system in Georgia; rather, they described industrial poverty and labor conflict in the North as an additional confirmation of the devastation wrought by the Republican conspiracy. "Did it ever occur to you that the numerous strikes of workmen in the North . . . were mainly due to the protective tariff?" asked one newspaper. "Is it any wonder . . . that men should lose all faith in corporations and capitalists, and should be ready to imbibe

7. Henry Grady, "The South and Her Problems," in *The New South: Writings and Speeches of Henry Grady* (Savannah: Beehive Press, 1971), 26; Lumpkin *Independent*, quoted in Americus *Weekly Recorder*, February 11, 1886; William H. Felton, "Who Is Responsible for Pensions?" Taxes Folder 1, in Rebecca Latimer Felton Papers, University of Georgia Library, Athens; Grady, "The South and Her Problems," 30.

8. Atlanta *Constitution*, June 7, 29, 1884; Milledgeville *Union and Recorder*, October 14, 1884. See also Americus *Weekly Recorder*, December 7, 14, 1883, August 29, 1884.

some of the communist teachings of foreign demagogues?"[9] In 1891, Tom Watson repeated this common argument as he explained poverty in New York tenement houses, Pennsylvania coal fields, and New England factory towns to the Brotherhood of Locomotive Firemen of Augusta: "Capital is protected by law from outside competition. Labor is not." Indeed, Watson knew that the tariff issue was a powerful one. "This gigantic system of fraud has born heavily upon the whole country," he said in 1886. "But its hardship has been peculiar to us." He and the *Southern Alliance Farmer* used it in 1891 to justify his drift toward the Populist party and his refusal to vote for Charles Crisp as Speaker of the House.[10]

Throughout the 1870s and 1880s, the money issue, which focused on the coinage of silver and the special privileges of national banks, was also part of the conspiracy theory. "Nothing is more remarkable than the persistency with which the leading national banks at the north and their newspaper organs have fought silver," proclaimed the Atlanta *Constitution* in 1883 as it attacked "the money power." Those demanding a currency based solely on gold were called "unscrupulous speculators, who hope to control the finances of the country" for their own benefit. "The greed of coin surreptitiously procured the passage of a law by Congress demonetizing silver," claimed the Americus *Weekly Recorder* in 1885. This episode was one more instance of Republican corruption: "It is greed of gold that for the past twenty-five years has attempted, and too often been successful, to use the machinery of government for the benefit of the favored few." As in the case of the tariff, Republicans passed laws "to rob their constituents . . . [and to] concentrate into the hands of the few the wealth of the country."[11] Among Georgia Democrats, these complaints became more intense and more frequent as time passed and the farm economy grew worse.

9. Americus *Weekly Recorder*, July 28, 1887. See also Americus *Weekly Recorder*, February 22, 1884; Waynesboro *True Citizen*, September 15, 1882; Atlanta *Constitution*, January 16, May 3, 4, 1883.

10. Unascribed newspaper clipping, June, 1891, Scrapbook, 1887–1891, pp. 142–44, in William J. Northen Personal Papers, Georgia State Archives, Atlanta; Thomas E. Watson, Speech at Hephzibah, June 16, 1886, Scrapbook Vol. V, 360, in Watson Papers; Thomas E. Watson to Charles F. Crisp, March 31, 1891, unascribed newspaper clipping of a reprint from the *Southern Alliance Farmer*, Scrapbook Vol. V, 13, in Black Papers.

11. Atlanta *Constitution*, April 19, 1883; Americus *Weekly Recorder*, June 5, 1885, December 31, 1885. See also Dawson *Weekly Journal*, January 17, February 14, 1878.

Georgia Democrats recognized, therefore, what Woodward called the South's colonial economy, and they believed that their economic subordination was a result not only of chance but also of policy. Their complaints about the burdens of Republican-backed policies were both accurate and justified. Taxation was inequitable. The tariff was unjust. Pensions often served as a kind of Republican party patronage and, as such, a source of Republican popularity and support. The New South program of regional economic development—of "hog and hominy at home," improved agricultural techniques, and industrial development—was a well-conceived effort to expand the cycle of trade and, therefore, of prosperity within the South. Its corollary, the conspiracy theory, was a politically potent critique of national politics and policies that contributed to the region's problems.

If the difference between the national Republican and the national Democratic parties in the 1880s seems elusive in retrospect, it was not elusive to Georgia Democrats at the time. Democrats were committed to the Jeffersonian and Jacksonian traditions of laissez-faire and localism, and their critique of Republican policies shows that, as had been the case with Jefferson and Jackson, these positions were rooted in more than racism alone. "Under Republican administration, business interests have been fostered until they now assume to control the government," Democrats complained, and they claimed that their party believed "the government should be so administered as to afford the greatest good to the greatest number . . . the farmers, mechanics and tradesmen." They believed that the Democratic party was the party of "honesty, frugality, simplicity and the rights of the States," whereas the Republicans fostered "the growth of monopolies, reckless extravagance, [and] gigantic rings to plunder the people, and . . . to destroy the rights of the States, and establish a splendid and paternal government."[12] A quick review of standard textbooks for their characterization of the Republican party and national economic development in the late nineteenth century confirms that many historians have come to a similar conclusion in the late twentieth century.

Georgia Democrats recognized that northern Democrats might differ with them over some policies. During 1885 and 1886, for example,

12. Americus *Weekly Recorder*, December 7, 1883; Charles F. Crisp, quoted in Americus *Weekly Recorder*, August 29, 1884.

Grover Cleveland was severely criticized for his opposition to silver.[13] But the Georgians remembered that northern Democrats had opposed Republican policies during Reconstruction, and they believed that, in doing so, the northerners had proved their loyalty to the Constitution.

On this point, too, Democrats in Georgia and across the South could make a convincing case. From the perspective of the late twentieth century, all Americans may be gratified that during Reconstruction the Republicans added the promise of legal equality for all to the Constitution, but it is nonetheless true that the actions they took to impose those changes were of dubious constitutionality at the time. Republicans contended that no state could leave the Union. They justified the Civil War on precisely those grounds. Yet the Republicans required the southern states to ratify constitutional amendments dramatically reducing their own powers and increasing the power of the federal government before they were allowed back into the Union (the same Union that they had not left). If the constitutional amendments that resulted from these Republican policies were noble, the procedures with which they were forced upon the the southern states were hardly legally sound or logically consistent. And as Republicans required the former Confederate states to grant to blacks rights that northern states controlled by the Republicans refused to concede, they at least raised questions about their own motivations.

To southern Democrats there was no question. The federal impositions were unconstitutional, indeed tyrannical. Whatever the shortcomings of some northern Democrats, they had proven their commitment to legitimate, honest government by their opposition to the Republicans. For that reason the national Democratic party became synonymous with a belief in democratic principles themselves and with a protection against the reimposition of the supposed horrors of Reconstruction. Robert Toombs asked, after years of "turmoil, trouble, revolution, slavery [to the Republicans], robbery, and plunder, how can you best protect society against a recurrence of these evils?" To white Georgians the answer was through the unity of all those committed to democratic government at home and across the nation: the "Solid South" and its northern allies facing the Republican threat. To

13. *Ibid.*, December 10, 17, 1885; Milledgeville *Union and Recorder*, January 26, December 9, 1886.

most white Georgians, the Democratic party meant all those devoted to democracy. "We are all Democrats," chimed the Milledgeville *Union and Recorder* in 1886.[14]

The "Independent movement" in Georgia during the 1870s and 1880s reflected the pervasiveness of these beliefs. Historians have frequently and accurately pointed to Independent candidates as evidence of a nascent two-party system in the state and as precursors of the Populists.[15] In many ways they were. Historians also have considered Independents to be evidence of hostility to Democratic party doctrine, but in this historians have been quite mistaken. The Independent movement was the result not of differences over the New South creed or the conspiracy theory's critique of federal policies but of a one-party political system that left insufficient room for the competing ambitions of its members.

Independent candidates appeared in the 1870s in sections of Georgia where there were large Democratic majorities and where a candidate for a Democratic nomination felt that he had been cheated of it by a nominating convention or caucus. William H. Felton was the most prominent and representative example. He felt that a congressional nomination had been stolen from him by party bosses, so he challenged the official nominee in the general election in 1874. Felton was successful, but as he said in 1875: "The question in the canvass was not one of political faith. It is centered around the fact that the people were alarmed at the growing tendency to centralize power in the hands of a few men. . . . I am a Democrat." Emory Speer, another prominent Independent, justified his campaign for Congress on similar grounds. Independents commonly explained their cause in those terms. One calling himself "Georgia" wrote to a newspaper to explain that an Independent was "simply a Democrat who refuses to submit to machine politics." Indeed, he claimed, the Independent candidate was

14. Robert Toombs, Address, Atlanta, January 19, 1874, quoted in Milledgeville *Union and Recorder*, January 28, 1874; Atlanta *Constitution*, January 29, 1884; Americus *Weekly Recorder*, December 21, 1883; Milledgeville *Union and Recorder*, May 25, 1886.

15. Alex M. Arnett, *The Populist Movement in Georgia: A View of the "Agrarian Crusade" in the Light of Solid-South Politics* (New York: Columbia University, 1922), 33; Woodward, *Origins of the New South*, 77–78; J. Morgan Kousser, *The Shaping of Southern Politics: Suffrage Restriction and the Establishment of the One-Party South, 1880–1910* (New Haven: Yale University Press, 1974), 214–21; Vincent P. De Santis, *Republicans Face the Southern Question: The New Departure Years, 1877–1897* (Baltimore: Johns Hopkins University Press, 1959), 163–64.

often "a better Democrat and man than the one who has received the nomination." In 1877 no less a Democratic organ than the Atlanta *Constitution* agreed. Even in criticizing Independent candidates, regular Democrats sometimes confirmed this view. While Independents called themselves Independent Democrats, unorganized Democrats, and true Democrats, regular party men called them "the disorganizers . . . the 'sore-head Democrats' " and charged that they acted out of "petty feeling of spite or vaulting ambition that o'erleaps itself, to the serious detriment of their own party." As the New York *Times* reported in 1878: "Democrats and Independents were identical in principle. . . . Their hatred of Republicans and their determination that Negroes would have no political power found them as united." The *Times* declared that the Independent "movement in Georgia was nothing less than a family struggle for power and the desire for office."[16]

The Independents' claim that they were loyal Democrats was not rhetorical flourish. Felton and others stayed loyal to the New South creed and to the conspiracy theory about the national Republican party. In their hearts they were still faithful to the Democratic party and to the Solid South. But the response of regular Democrats to Independent candidacies was often wickedly severe; party discipline, the Democrats believed, was essential. "Every person should be independent in the exercise of his rights and liberties . . . so long as his actions are not antagonistic to the well-being of society and good order," wrote one regular-party organ about the Independents. "But when he enters into a premeditated . . . conspiracy to subvert the best interests of society, then his principles cease to be respected." A letter to the editor of another journal was also representative when it argued against Independent candidacies: "Without organization the demo-

16. George L. Jones, "William H. Felton and the Independent Democratic Movement in Georgia, 1870–1890" (M.A. thesis, University of Georgia, 1971), 98; Judson C. Ward, "Georgia Under the Bourbon Democrats, 1872–1890" (Ph.D. dissertation, University of North Carolina at Chapel Hill, 1947), 79–83; William H. Felton, Address, January 19, 1875, quoted in Jones, "William H. Felton and the Independent Democratic Movement," 54–55; Jim Alan Furgeson, "Power Politics and Populism: Jackson County, Georgia, as a Case Study" (M.A. thesis, University of Georgia, 1975), 23, 24, 28; Atlanta *Constitution*, December 21, 1877, quoted in Jones, "William H. Felton and the Independent Democratic Movement," 98; Felton, *Memoirs, passim;* clipping from Dalton *Citizen,* n.d., Scrapbook I, in Rebecca Latimer Felton Papers; Dawson *Weekly Journal,* July 5, 1877; New York *Times,* October 29, 1878, quoted in Jones, "William H. Felton and the Independent Democratic Movement," 120.

cratic party of Georgia can accomplish nothing." Many Democrats thought they saw in the Independent movement a "scheme . . . for the benefit of the Republican party," and in light of the dangers that held in their minds, their attacks on Independents were wide-ranging and vicious.[17]

The Independents, unjustly charged with disloyalty and confident of their own righteousness, gradually changed their stance toward the Democratic party. Subject to harsh attacks and suspicious that elections as well as nominations had been stolen by their rivals, Felton and other prominent Independents came to believe that the Democratic party organization in Georgia, like the Republican party nationally, had fallen into the hands of dishonest men who conspired against "the people" and subverted democracy. Felton and other Independents who lost elections became fully convinced that leading Democrats, including James M. Smith, Joseph E. Brown, John B. Gordon, Alfred Colquitt, and countless others, were corrupt conspirators and not true democrats. "[Rufus] Bullock was selected to hold up the old battle-scarred carcass of Georgia in its poverty and desolation while many of the present headlights of Bourbon Democracy did the '*skinning*,' " Felton charged. "In my opinion the coalition continues until the present, the skinning process has never been concluded."[18] Independents claimed to have the purer records of loyalty to their section and to Democratic principles, and they attacked every possible target with charges of dishonesty and corruption. Democratic politicians resented the attacks. "To hear him [Felton] talk," said former governor James M. Smith, "he has all the purity in his own heart and everyone else is a villain. Nothing is too sacred for his defiling tongue. No character too high for his infamous abuse."[19]

The bitterness of the Independents was understandable. They had, in the words of one, "a right to liberty of speech and of action as well as any other. . . . The vengeance of the 'organized,' " he continued,

17. Dawson *Weekly Journal*, April 27, 1882; "A Democrat" to Editor, clipping from Atlanta *Constitution*, marked September 7, [1882], in Scrapbook, 1882–83, in Joseph E. and Elizabeth G. Brown Papers, University of Georgia, Athens; Ben H. Hill interview with Henry Grady, January 2, 1882, quoted in Felton, *Memoirs*, 407–409. See also Felton, *Memoirs*, 429.

18. William H. Felton to Editor, Atlanta *Constitution*, February 13, 1882, quoted in Felton, *Memoirs*, 435.

19. Felton, *Memoirs*, *passim*; Atlanta *Constitution*, June 13, 1886.

proved that regular Democratic leaders were not faithful to democratic principles. The party organization seemed to suffer not from isolated instances of corruption but from a chronic, systemic case of the disease. After Felton lost a bid for reelection to Congress in 1880, a friend described the change that Felton had undergone as an explanation for his defeat: "When, in 1874, you made war on what you believed to be a corrupt *ring* in the democratic party—a ring that was using the organization for their own ends, your position was entirely defensible. But when after that you made war on the *organization itself* you made your great mistake."[20]

The harshness of the debate and the belief that elections had been stolen not only embittered Felton and other prominent Independents but also changed their posture toward the Democratic party. Emory Speer, for example, began his career as a Democrat but, angered and alienated by his experience as an Independent, became a Republican. Felton denied that he ever thought of becoming a Republican. "Thank God my Democracy is not *smirched with such a crime*," he wrote. But he did toy with the possibility of a Republican-Independent coalition in 1882. He even wrote a platform on which a fusion ticket might run. One prominent plank called for "a free ballot and a fair count," a traditional Republican demand rooted in the experience of the rights of suffrage denied. What had started as a family fight among Democrats seemed increasingly threatening to the Democratic party. "I have always feared the Independent Democracy," Ben Hill told Henry Grady in 1882. "[Felton] told me repeatedly nothing could ever drive him from the democratic party." Yet it seemed to Hill that the Democrats had lost Felton.[21]

The fusion effort failed before it became serious. In all likelihood it was destined to be frail and short-lived. Independent candidacies were fueled by the grievances of individual politicians and sustained by their personal popularity. Few Democrats gave any indication that they

20. J. B. Hargrove to William H. Felton, May 19, 1880, in Rebecca Latimer Felton Papers; Ben H. Hill to William H. Felton, November 10, 1880, in Rebecca Latimer Felton and William Harrell Felton Papers, University of Georgia, Athens.

21. Furgeson, "Power Politics and Populism," 20; Ward, "Georgia Under the Bourbon Democrats," 166; William H. Felton to Ben H. Hill, February 21, 1882, quoted in Felton, *Memoirs*, 415; John M. Matthews, "The Negro in Georgia Politics, 1865–1880" (Ph.D. dissertation, Duke University, 1967), 132–33; Ward, "Georgia Under the Bourbon Democrats," 124; Ben H. Hill interview with Henry Grady, January 2, 1882, quoted in Felton *Memoirs*, 407–409.

were prepared to leave the party of Redemption. The Democratic party and democratic principles remained synonymous in the minds of most white southerners.

Nonetheless, the changes in Speer and Felton, and in other prominent Independents who felt most aggrieved, illustrated the way in which loyal Democrats might respond when they believed that their right to participate in politics on their own terms—their democratic rights—had been denied. Because of the rigidity of the South's one-party system, mutual trust had been broken. A conflict among those who shared the same Democratic party platform had, in the minds of prominent Independents, become a conflict of principles—the principles of democratic participation: the right of dissent, the right to vote, and the right to an unfettered voice in their own affairs.

Independent candidacies became less common during the 1880s, apparently because of changes in the systems by which the Democratic party chose candidates. Beginning in 1876, a two-thirds rule governed nominating conventions, making grievances born in close contests less likely than before. More important, during the 1880s, Democrats started using primaries, sometimes to select local candidates, sometimes to choose delegates to conventions. Independent candidacies continued to appear from time to time in places that still used caucuses, but the gradual move from caucuses to primaries seems to have accomplished two things. It allowed for greater competition among rivals, and rival ambitions, within the structure of the Democratic party, and in broadening participation, it lent to Democratic nominations the legitimacy of democratic participation.[22] Within state politics, the use of primaries enabled the one-party system to acquire some of the flexibility of a two-party state.

Like the controversy surrounding the Independent movement, the progress, intensity, and bitterness of the Populist revolt can be explained better as a consequence of this party structure and the broadly shared conspiracy theory of national politics than by any ideological construct. The battle between Democrats and Populists in Georgia was neither initially nor ultimately over federal policy on silver or over banks or railroads or labor. As Barton Shaw showed, Democrats and Populists in Georgia shared similar or identical positions on the policy issues of the 1890s. Instead, the Populist revolt in Georgia began as a division over state and regional strategy in national politics—over whether the national Democratic party or a new national Populist party offered the best hope for the triumph in the federal government of the views that Georgia Democrats and Populists shared. The conspiracy theory of national politics and the equation of the Democratic party with democratic rights kept many, perhaps most, white Georgians faithful to both the local and the national Democratic organizations. However, many farmers nearest to bankruptcy moved into the third party with a desperate urgency. Faced with what they called Cleve-landism, they felt betrayed by the national Democratic party. And led by Tom Watson, they asked their fellow Democrats "to believe in principles more strongly than . . . in party names" and to join the members of Georgia's Democratic party to a new national political alliance, the People's party.[23]

At the close of the 1880s, no one anticipated the conflict that was to come. There were issues, of course. Discontent among farmers in Georgia was increasingly formidable, and the appeal of the Farmers' Alliance was great. Under growing financial pressure, dirt farmers demanded relief from the federal policies that they thought were responsible for their fate. But in Georgia they did not expect to be forced to choose between their loyalty to the Alliance and its platform on one hand and to the Democratic party on the other. One nervous and self-styled prominent Democrat described the self-confidence of the farmers. In place after place the Alliance, he complained, "declares . . . that it is the 'democratic party' and boldly asserts that every man who will not endorse it and the candidates which it puts forward is not true 'democrat.'" Clearly many long-active members of the Democratic party were suspicious of the Alliance, perhaps because of its secrecy but more likely because many men they knew well and had supported in the past were being replaced by unknowns. Yet the Democratic party, often with local primaries, accommodated the increasing discontent with relative ease. Tom Watson's primary victory over the incumbent Democrat in 1890 was a case in point. Even Woodward found little

23. Unascribed newspaper clipping, 1892, Scrapbook Vol. V, 501, in Watson Papers.

difference between their views to parallel the great difference between their styles. Watson's style appealed to the impatience, frustration, and anger among hard-pressed farmers, while the incumbent expressed the same positions in less satisfying, more moderate tones.[24]

The similarity between the two candidates should not be surprising, for in outlining the Alliance yardstick for candidates, the state executive committee listed criteria consistent with long-standing Democratic party positions in Georgia. Three state issues led the list: increased power for the state railroad commission, improved public schools, and improvements in the penitentiary system. Four national issues followed: the reduction of taxes and "an economical and judicious administration" of the government, "the revision of the protective tariff . . . to the greatest extent possible," the restriction of "speculation and combines, that seek to interfere with [the] price of prime necessities," and the expansion of the money supply. Finally, the committee listed the subtreasury plan, but it worded this plank in such a way that Democrats with reservations about it could endorse the entire package. The Alliance called for a subtreasury "or some better system for the relief of the struggling masses." The subtreasury was an important issue, but apparently to endorse it "or something better" served more as an emblem of deep commitment to action on behalf of farmers than as a commitment to a particular course of action. Alliancemen in Georgia were themselves divided and unsure on the subtreasury proposal, and in the wake of the election of 1890, interest in it dwindled quickly. By early 1891 attention had already focused on silver, and by 1893 the subtreasury had been dropped completely.[25] In fact, in 1890 the Georgia Alliance and Alliance candidates endorsed and promoted the New South creed. They embraced the state Democratic party dogma with vigor.

In 1890, Alliancemen were not unhappy with the Democratic party of Georgia; they controlled it. The Atlanta *Constitution* acknowledged as much.[26] And Alliancemen differed with other Democrats in the

24. M. V. B. Ake to William H. Felton, August 23, 1890, in Rebecca Latimer Felton Papers; Woodward, *Tom Watson*, 148–51.

25. Athens *Weekly Banner*, April 8, 1890, quoted in Lewis N. Wynne, "The Alliance Legislature of 1890" (M.A. thesis, University of Georgia, 1970), 58–59; Shaw, *The Wool-Hat Boys*, 100, 108. For a description of the subtreasury proposal see Woodward, *Origins of the New South*, 199.

26. Atlanta *Constitution*, June 6, 7, July 4, 1890.

state not over government policies but over whether to attempt to forge a new party system allying the South and the West.

It is in this case, if any, that there is validity to the notion that the Democratic party was a gathering of procrustean bedfellows. The identification of the state party with the national organization was, according to the conspiracy theory born during Reconstruction, a source of protection. But it was also a problem, and in 1891, as Georgia Democrats turned their attention toward the federal government and the upcoming presidential election in 1892, they knew it. As early as February, prominent Democrats were worrying publicly about Grover Cleveland's desire to return to the White House as a well-known opponent of the free coinage of silver. Even Senator Joseph E. Brown, the prominent politician least in tune with the agrarian revolt, expressed his concern, saying, "Mr. Cleveland [is] . . . clearly at variance with the position of the democratic party on the free coinage matter." In private, expressions of concern were greater. Former governor Henry D. McDaniel, an astute observer of politics in the state, wrote to a friend: "I regret to see the persistent efforts to press Cleveland's nomination. . . . He is not a favorite with the Southern farmers, and the prospect of his nomination would . . . encourage the advocates of the third party." McDaniel thought that most farmers in Georgia did not want to join the Populist party, but as early as June, he wrote that he feared the supporters of Cleveland would "force them out of the Democratic party on the silver issue. . . . Nothing is more certain than that practically all the elements out of which the new party would spring favor free coinage of silver."[27] The case in favor of a third party rested entirely upon the conviction that easterners in the Democratic party would subvert the policies and reforms long embraced by quite nearly all Democrats in Georgia.

Tom Watson agreed. He did not reject Democratic dogma. He gradually came to believe that a new national coalition uniting southern and western farmers would be essential for the old faith to triumph. During 1891 he and others reluctantly came to the conviction that, in his words, "both our present parties are dominated by the money power. The gold bug policy is as offensive to men when it comes from

27. *Ibid.*, February 22, 1891, clipping in Scrapbook, 1890–92, in Brown Papers; Henry D. McDaniel to Judge, June 27, 10, 1891, in Letter Book, May 28, 1891–January 14, 1892, in Henry D. McDaniel Personal Papers, Georgia State Archives, Atlanta.

Cleveland as when it comes from [Republicans]." But Watson moved slowly. He wanted "to reform" the national Democratic party, "not to desert it." He worried, however, that "if the Democratic leaders wish to disrupt the party by driving us out, they will have the name of Democracy, while we still preserve its principles." That spring, Leonidas L. Polk, president of the National Farmers' Alliance, described the situation in North Carolina similarly: "All want the next Congress to [reform] . . . the financial system of this government. . . . I can speak for my own State, and I think that they have been true and loyal to the Democratic party as any men in the south. They will certainly not support Mr. Cleveland . . . [or] any man who comes from the Eastern States. We are afraid of Wall street power."[28]

Reform did not come. To the contrary, evidence seemed to multiply that the national party was in alien hands, and the Populist party in Georgia was born. By the end of the year, McDaniel lamented that "Cleveland's nomination [was] assured and free silver ignored." Only if Congress fulfilled old Democratic promises and enacted "free silver and such reforms as . . . decided tariff reduction" would the growing movement toward a new party be arrested.[29]

Thus, in the early 1890s, Populists and Democrats in Georgia were faced with the incongruity between the national and state Democratic parties. Like Independents and party regulars a decade before, they argued not so much over policy but over which national party and which individual Georgians were most faithful to the same political agenda. The argument consumed most of 1891 and 1892.

Before Cleveland's election in 1892, Democratic party regulars claimed that the beliefs shared by Georgia Democrats and Populists would be best served by the national Democratic party. Leaders in Tom Watson's district were representative when they wrote that farmers "in Georgia have always controlled the Democratic party and can still control it if they remain within its ranks." Repeating the standard charge that Republican policies on the tariff, the coinage of silver, and pensions had combined to keep the South poor, they argued that the

28. Thomas E. Watson, Speech in Jefferson County, July 4, 1891, quoted in Atlanta *Journal*, clipping marked July 10, 1891, Scrapbook Vol. V, 22, in Black Papers; unidentified newspaper clipping, July 26, 1891, Scrapbook Vol. V, in Black Papers, cited in Shaw, *The Wool-Hat Boys*, 38; Milledgeville *Union-Recorder*, May 13, 1891.

29. Henry D. McDaniel to Heard, December 23, 1891, Letter Book, May 28, 1891–January 14, 1892, in McDaniel Papers.

Democrats, not the Populists, offered "the earliest and most substantial relief if it is to be had at all." On the coinage of silver, the positions of both parties were the same. "A large majority of the [national] Democratic party is openly in favor of" silver, these Democratic leaders said. "Georgia's full Democratic vote went for the free coinage bill in Congress. The Third party cannot gain any more votes for silver in Georgia." But because of former Republicans in its ranks, the national Populist party failed the test on the tariff and pensions: "The word 'tariff' is not in the platform [of 1892]," and Populists from the Great Plains states had ensured that their party favored increasing the burden of pensions by "paying to Federal soldiers of the late war the difference between the value of the paper money they received and gold."[30]

To Democrats, the danger of the third-party effort was in the opportunity if offered to the national Republican party. "The reformers (so called) are only riveting more firmly the shackles of monetary slavery upon the Southern People," wrote Henry McDaniel to a friend in 1892. And consistent with the belief in an ongoing Republican conspiracy, McDaniel thought the Force Bill, which would have permitted federal supervision of elections in the South, made the upcoming election especially ominous: "Nothing in human power will be left undone to take control of our elections," he warned. Indeed, since Democrats had not simultaneously controlled the presidency and both houses of Congress since 1860, it was common for Democratic leaders to claim the party was completely unresponsible for federal policies and to celebrate the overwhelming Democratic victory expected in November as "the restoration of our wise System of government somewhere within its Constitutional limits."[31]

Those who favored the third party argued that they were promoting the principles of the Democratic party of Georgia within a national

30. Clipping from Columbus *Enquirer-Sun*, marked April 1, 1892, and June 1, 1892, Scrapbook Vol. II, 84, in Northen Papers. See also unascribed newspaper clipping, September 13, 1892, *ibid.*, 137–38. Milledgeville *Union-Recorder*, May 26, 1891; unascribed newspaper clipping, September 21, [1891], Scrapbook, 1890–92, in Brown Papers.

31. Henry D. McDaniel to Heard, July 28, 1892, Letter Book, January 20, 1892–April 11, 1893, in McDaniel Papers; Milledgeville *Union-Recorder*, June 14, 1892; Robert N. Gourdin to William Porcher Miles, December 3, 1892, in William Porcher Miles Papers, Southern Historical Collection, University of North Carolina, Chapel Hill.

organization that promised greater chance of success. The problems with the Democratic party lay not in Georgia but in the national organization. "The alliance between the eastern and southern democrats is unnatural and ruinous. That between east and west is alike unnatural, insincere, and artificial," wrote one farmer. "But a political alliance between the West and South under a new name with identical interests is the natural alliance. . . . Do men tell us that we disrupt the South and threaten negro domination? Tell them that our principles are the true democracy and that we are returning to the faith of our fathers."[32]

Georgia Populists also showed their belief in state Democratic party dogma, since they claimed that Cleveland and other leaders of the national Democratic party were leaving democratic principles behind. They charged that the national Democratic party was not pure enough on the issue of the tariff. Similarly, they charged: "Northern democrats are just as eager to oppress the South as Northern republicans. They vote for every pension bill." Cleveland was no different from a Republican, they said, for he had even "appointed more negroes to office than any other President."[33]

Following the election of 1892, the content of this debate changed little. However, the agricultural depression deepened, and the policies of Cleveland betrayed the hopes of Georgia Democrats and confirmed the Populists' worst fears. The number of Populists grew, and the conflict became more and more bitter. The continued loyalty of many Georgia Democrats to the national party organization made them appear either foolish or dishonest to many Populists. William H. Felton explained his conversion to the third party: "I am obliged to say, the People's Party understood the situation better than I did [in 1892]. . . . I *know there is no relief*, for me or for you, in following clevelandism any longer." While loyal Democrats complained of the "stupidity of certain Eastern Democrats" and the president's policies, Tom Watson taunted:

32. Milledgeville *Union-Recorder*, May 24, 1892.
33. Thomas E. Watson, Speech in Baldwin County, quoted in Milledgeville *Union and Recorder*, August 11, 1891; Thomas E. Watson to Charles F. Crisp, March 31, 1891, reprinted from *Southern Alliance Farmer*, unascribed newspaper clipping, n.d., Scrapbook Vol. V, 13, in Black Papers. See also entry dated June 6, 1891, in Crawfordsville (Taliaferro Co.) Farmers' Alliance No. 1437, Minutes Book, 1888–1893, Georgia State Archives, Atlanta; William H. Felton, "Who Is Responsible for Pensions?" Taxes Folder 1, in Rebecca Latimer Felton Papers.

"One year ago this country was being fed on the ambrosia of Democratic expectations. Today it is gnawing the cobs of Democratic reality."[34]

As the Populist revolt grew, it appeared increasingly threatening to Democrats, for the conspiracy theory and its Solid South corollary led regular-party men to view it as a threat to democracy itself. The story of the increasing strength and crusading passion of southern Populism in the face of the deepening depression and Cleveland's policies has been repeatedly and well told. So has that of the dishonest elections and threats of violence to which Democratic regulars in Georgia subjected their Populist neighbors.[35] But it is important to recognize that regular-party men were not simply protecting class privilege. They accepted substantial dissent and rivalry for control within the Democratic party of Georgia. They had shown as much in the election of 1890. They were, however, unable to conceive of legitimate dissent outside of their party. The conspiracy theory that defined their party's organization and purpose precluded the possibility of legitimate political action outside of it. With convoluted and self-justifying logic, they believed Democratic control to be synonymous with honest and legitimate government. With perverse sincerity, they used all the tactics of Redemption to suppress the Populist challenge. "We had to do it!" pled one Democrat.[36]

To the Populists, who were similarly steeped in the conspiracy theory of national politics, the Democratic tactics seemed as corrupt and self-serving as they in fact were. But those tactics were also something more. They were evidence that the state's Democrats, like Republicans and like Cleveland Democrats in the North, were quite literally serving undemocratic purposes.

When Populists in Georgia began their party movement, they were exercising political rights that they had always assumed they enjoyed.

34. William H. Felton, "Why I Vote with People's Party" (MS in Dr. Felton Manuscripts, Folder 3, in Rebecca Latimer Felton Papers); Henry D. McDaniel to William Reese, April 21, 1894, Letter Book, April 17, 1893–November 15, 1894, in McDaniel Papers. See also unascribed newspaper clipping, 1893, Scrapbook Vol. V, 40–49, in William H. Fleming Papers, University of Georgia, Athens; Woodward, *Tom Watson*, 264.

35. Arnett, *The Populist Movement in Georgia;* Woodward, *Tom Watson;* Shaw, *The Wool-Hat Boys.*

36. Arnett, *The Populist Movement in Georgia,* 184. See also Sparta *Ishmaelite,* October 27, 1893.

They knew they were not Republicans. They were committed to the ideals of their state Democratic party. They assumed they had the right to run for office, to vote, and to have their votes counted. Like Independents before them, they believed and they consistently said that they were promoting Democratic party principles. But like the Independents before them, they were also changed when Democratic party regulars repeatedly and systematically violated their legal rights of democratic participation. Populists gradually came to fight not only against Clevelandism but also against the subversion of democracy, against those who would not play by the rules. They came to view the leaders of the Democratic party as they viewed the Republicans, not only as political rivals but also as undemocratic agents of self-serving corruption. "If we had a Democratic party with any democracy in it," declared the *People's Party Paper*, there would be no need for a People's party.[37]

In 1896, as agrarians took control of the national Democratic party, repudiated Cleveland, and nominated William Jennings Bryan for president, "middle-of-the-road" Populists (those who did not want their young party to join the Bryan crusade) showed that maintaining their party's separate identity had become an issue of democratic principle, an issue even more fundamental than silver. Middle-of-the-road Populism was strongest in Georgia and the one-party South, where the ill-treatment of Populists was greatest. That ill-treatment, the repeated violations of democratic rights, explains the reluctance of Georgia Populists to rejoin the Democratic party.

The state platform of the Populist party showed as much. In fact, in 1896 the Populist and Democratic platforms in Georgia remained nearly identical except for planks that revealed the Populist equation of democratic rights with their party's purpose. The most-detailed provisions of the Populist platform all concerned protection for the rights of suffrage and popular participation. Georgia Populists demanded that "all public officers be elected by the people." They denounced the power of the legislature to select judges and solicitors, because "rings and cliques and . . . corrupt politicians" traded and bartered for political office. "The price of office in Georgia under Democratic rule," they

37. Clipping from *People's Party Paper*, December 1, 1893, Scrapbook Vol. XXVI, 27, in Watson Papers.

said, "is obedience to party masters." And they pled at length "for a free ballot and a fair count."[38]

In Georgia the progress of the Independent movement and that of Populism closely paralleled each other. Neither movement entailed substantial dissent from standard Democratic party positions on either state or federal policy. Both shared in the state Democratic party's conspiracy theory of national politics and its powerful critique of federal policies. Both had their origin in organizational questions. Independent candidacies arose because local party organizations had trouble accommodating competition within their ranks until the two-thirds rule and primary elections added flexibility to the party. Populism became formidable because Georgia's Democratic party was part of a national party alliance with which it was at odds.

It is not surprising that those white Georgians who were hardest pressed financially came to doubt that the national Democratic party was a source of protection in the 1890s. The conspiracy theory of national politics not only helped Georgians to explain their financial woes but led them to suspect that the national Democratic party had fallen into the hands of self-serving manipulators. Populists, therefore, thought of themselves as part of the Democratic party tradition as they sought a new national alliance for Georgia Democrats.

Perhaps those who agree about much are prone to the bitterest battles about their differences, but Independents in the 1870s and Populists in the 1890s were shocked to learn that even those who believed in state Democratic party dogma were not free to promote their views outside the confines of the one true catholic and (in the fervor of political faith) apostolic party. Sincerely sharing in Democratic party dogma, Independents and Populists found it more than embittering to be burned for heresy. They knew that they were not Republicans. They were not "illegitimate." They did not question the racist division of society. They promoted the New South creed. So the experience of battle changed them. The repeated and systematic violation of their rights led them to associate the leaders of the Democratic party in Georgia with those distant and conspiratorial forces that they had long been taught were at work in the nation. The mutual trust upon which

38. Milledgeville *Union-Recorder*, August 8, 1896.

democracy depends had been broken. In their eyes, therefore, they fought for democracy itself.

This view of the Independent candidacies and Populism of late nineteenth-century Georgia may seem to some less inspirational than the more standard portrait of a challenge to commercial values and corporate interests. To recognize the organizational roots of these battles should not, however, diminish an appreciation of something that Independents and Populists knew: As has been so frequently the case, democratic rights, universally celebrated in the abstract, were denied to many in practice by men who claimed to be defenders of democratic virtue. Nothing less than democracy itself was at stake in the political struggles of late nineteenth-century Georgia.

4 / ERIC ANDERSON

The Populists and Capitalist America: The Case of Edgecombe County, North Carolina

In 1965, Robert F. Durden characterized the Populists as "angry agrarian capitalists." Caricatured by their opponents as dangerous radicals, most Populists were in fact unmoved by the socialism of Henry Demarest Lloyd and other unrepresentative reformers. According to Durden, free silver and William Jennings Bryan constituted "the climax of Populism," not its betrayal.[1]

Such views are somewhat out of fashion today. Several influential neo-Marxist historians have argued that the Populists presented a "radical alternative" to America's social and political structure. Appearing "at almost the very last moment before the values implicit in the corporate state" captured the nation, Populism, real Populism, was built on a vision of cooperation that was neither capitalist nor strictly socialist. The Populists expressed a "producer ideology" at odds with "bourgeois individualism and the free market," according to Steven Hahn. "Blaming the concentration of wealth and power on the corruption of the political process, Populists did not wish to unfetter the 'invisible hand' of the marketplace," Hahn asserted. "They wished to protect a 'liberty tree' rooted in petty ownership of productive re-

1. Robert Durden, *The Climax of Populism: The Election of 1896* (Lexington: University of Kentucky Press, 1965), 3–6 *passim*. See also Durden, "The 'Cow-Bird' Grounded: The Populist Nomination of Bryan and Tom Watson in 1896," *Mississippi Valley Historical Review*, L (1963), 397–423.

sources." Unradical Populists, by this interpretation, were not genuine Populists but "trimmers," selfishly promoting "a superficial shadow movement of the agrarian revolt." As Lawrence Goodwyn put it, politicians such as North Carolina's Marion Butler and Nebraska's William V. Allen and William Jennings Bryan were "essentially men without ideas" who participated in "a reform movement whose sources they did not grasp and whose interior energy did not become part of their own political consciousness."[2]

The new view of Populism is remarkably flexible, able to incorporate research that might seem to refute it. Goodwyn enthusiastically endorsed, for example, Bruce Palmer's careful study of the Populist "attack on capitalism," even though Palmer concluded that most Populists shared "a commitment to a competitive, private property– and profit-oriented market economy." The Populists, Palmer wrote, "did not . . . question the fundamental tenets of the American economic system as they understood them—the market, supply and demand, private ownership and profit, and the beneficence of economic competition between small economic units." Far from rejecting industrial society, the Populists were like many other southerners in their expectation that railroads and manufacturing would produce an economically improved "New South."[3]

Perhaps the essence of the new view is merely admiration for the farmers' movement, a conviction that its program was rational and practical, and the conclusion that compromise destroyed a promising democratic movement (or moment). Thus, even if Palmer's Populists are not far from Durden's "angry agrarian capitalists," Durden, according to this view, was still wrong in seeing the triumph of fusion and free silver as sensible, perhaps even inevitable in America's consensus polity. At any rate Durden's scholarship has been assiduously ignored by many of the recent students of Populism, including Palmer.

Local history might offer a reliable way to test Durden's analysis of two decades ago. Were the ordinary Populists radically disenchanted with America's political system and market-oriented economy? What

2. Lawrence Goodwyn, *Democratic Promise: The Populist Moment in America* (New York: Oxford University Press, 1976), xii–xiv, 590–91; Steven Hahn, *The Roots of Southern Populism: Yeoman Farmers and the Transformation of the Georgia Upcountry, 1850–1890* (New York: Oxford University Press, 1983), 282.

3. Bruce Palmer, *"Man over Money": The Southern Populist Critique of American Capitalism* (Chapel Hill: University of North Carolina Press, 1980), xvii–xviii, 205, 208.

was the political consciousness of small political leaders, whose arena was the county or the township? For what ideas were isolated Populist voters willing to risk social ostracism? Did the free-silver issue represent a practical way to express their vision?

The answers depend, perhaps, on where one looks. The historian could study a Populist stronghold in "antimonopoly," Greenback Texas or in "fusionist" North Carolina. One might even study the People's party where it was weak and perhaps uncorrupted by dreams of victory.

Edgecombe County, North Carolina, is an intriguing, if unlikely, place to study Populism. A major cotton-producing county in eastern North Carolina, Edgecombe was a county in which blacks outnumbered whites two to one. Overwhelmingly Democratic before the Civil War (and enthusiastically secessionist in the crisis of 1861), Edgecombe became reliably Republican after 1868. Plantation agriculture persisted in Edgecombe long after emancipation, with land in many cases remaining in large parcels owned by a powerful planter, though farmed by sharecroppers. By 1900 less than a third of the county's farms were cultivated by their owners, and many whites had joined the largely black ranks of renters and sharecroppers.[4]

A center of power of the Farmers' Alliance, Edgecombe was not a Populist stronghold of any kind. The county never elected a single Populist legislator or congressman. In five elections, no Populist candidate for president or governor ever carried the county. The best the Populists could do was to wrest several county offices from the Democrats, but this was only possible with the aid of hundreds of black Republican votes. (These victories came in 1896, the point at which most recent students of Populism drop their investigations.) Even so, Edgecombe provided several key leaders to the farmers' movement, including North Carolina Alliance president Elias Carr (governor from 1893 to 1897), William E. Fountain (Populist state chairman in 1897),

4. Blacks were a declining proportion of Edgecombe's population, falling from 69.6 percent in 1880 to 62.4 percent two decades later. For population statistics and Edgecombe's social and economic context see Eric Anderson, *Race and Politics in North Carolina, 1872–1901: The Black Second* (Baton Rouge: Louisiana State University Press, 1981), 8–33. The tenancy rates are from *Twelfth Census, 1900: Agriculture*, Pt. 1, pp. 108–109. On Edgecombe's prewar politics, see Marc W. Kruman, *Parties and Politics in North Carolina, 1836–1865* (Baton Rouge: Louisiana State University Press, 1983), 16, 273–78.

and editor-politician James B. Lloyd, a close associate of Senator Marion Butler.

Near the end of the brief life of Edgecombe Populism, one party member lamented, "Our party in Edgecombe was made up by some men who stood well socially, financially and every other way." These community leaders had the influence and resources, apparently, to enable them to withstand "the vilification and abuse of Democrats for all these years."[5]

The available evidence supports this description of Edgecombe's Populist activists. The candidates, the letter writers, and the party officials were indeed among the county's "best men," the sort likely to preside as magistrates or to pioneer civic improvements and new business ventures. In general they accepted their community's conventional wisdom. Many of them were fervently religious, but none seemed to have more than a superficial interest in interracial cooperation. They denounced the follies of the federal government but offered no comprehensive socialist program to change it, though they might occasionally quote socialist analysis. Many Edgecombe Populists accepted third-party action reluctantly and only as a tactic for achieving reform. Their first allegiance was to ideas, not to a party or a set of politicians.

Using Democratic sources, one could easily prove that the Populist leaders were extreme radicals. For example, two of the "charter members" of the county's third party, J. M. Cutchin and Marcus J. Battle, were denounced as anarchists by the Tarboro *Southerner*. "With Messers. Cutchin and Battle, whatever is is wrong," declared the staunchly Democratic newspaper in 1892. "To pull down without building up is anarchy, nihilism. A man does not have to preach murder and arson to be an anarchist."[6]

Despite the anger of their opponents, men such as Battle and Cutchin were far from anarchism, nihilism, or even socialism. Marcus J. Battle, "the original free silver man of Edgecombe county," belonged to

5. J. M. Cutchin to Marion Butler, September 19, 1898, in Marion Butler Papers, Southern Historical Collection, University of North Carolina, Chapel Hill. A 1920 county history made a similar comment. J. Kelly Turner and John L. Bridgers, Jr., *History of Edgecombe County, North Carolina* (Raleigh: Edwards & Broughton Printing Company, 1920), 303–304.
6. Tarboro *Southerner*, November 3, 1892.

a large and influential clan in the county. One of nine children, a kinsman of the well-known educator Kemp P. Battle, he was not yet ten years old when a slave killed his father. Later he served in the Confederate army and lost a brother in the Civil War. Battle was a devout Methodist and a farmer, and he served as a justice of the peace for many years before he became involved in third-party politics. When North Carolina's Populist party was born in 1892, he was fifty-five years old and the father of seven children.[7]

Battle became a supporter of the new party for a variety of reasons. In particular he blamed the farmers' hard times on the gold standard and came to see Democratic candidate Grover Cleveland as little different from Republican president Benjamin Harrison. At first his social position in the community gained him a hearing even in the Democratic press. In a letter to the editor of the *Southerner*, he sketched a comprehensive vision of the Democrats' failure: "Will [a Democratic administration] give greater impetus to the development of the South?—the extension of our railroad mileage—the opening up of our mining interests, the increase of manufacturing plants, the building up of villages, towns and cities? Will it infuse new life in the rural districts, by enhancing the value of realty and personalty? Will the price of our products be enhanced? Will labor command better prices? Will the average man realize the difference?"[8]

For Battle the promise of Populism was practical and thoroughly capitalistic. The editor of the *Southerner* responded in orthodox, laissez-faire language: "It is not the mission of the Democratic party or any other party to build railroads, to enhance values, to boom prices, or to engage in manufacturing and mining." Battle had not, of course, advocated government ownership of industry in general, but he had assumed that government was responsible for creating a healthy environment for economic growth. The Democratic editor denied this assumption, insisting that the only legitimate function of the state was to secure

7. Thomas H. Battle to William Battle, December 23, 1897, in Battle Family Papers, Southern Historical Collection, University of North Carolina, Chapel Hill; Herbert B. Battle and Lois Yelverton, *The Battle Book: A Genealogy of the Battle Family in America* (Montgomery: Paragon Press, 1930), 595, 598, 602–603; *North Carolina House Journal,* 1876–77, p. 921; *North Carolina House Journal,* 1881, p. 764; *North Carolina House Journal,* 1887, p. 785.
8. Tarboro *Southerner,* September 22, 1892.

individual liberty "consistent with collective security."[9] In this concept of the state's role lay the most important difference between the two men, and colorful words about arson and anarchy merely obscured matters.

Battle's view of government was rooted in a profoundly religious concern about inequality. "My sympathies go out to the poor—the oppressed," he wrote to a Democratic relative, banker Thomas H. Battle. Denying any envy of the rich, he said: "I certainly respect honest thrift. But I would like to see a more equitable distribution of the products of labor—the products of agriculture, particularly." The problem, as he saw it, was not overproduction but "under consumption." Citing English social critic John Ruskin and the Golden Rule, he expressed a longing for a day of restitution. "Gods [sic] laws are just and His care is over his people. He will even things up in due time, tho' the days of miracles are past, and God works through human instrumentalities."[10]

Late converts to Populism in Edgecombe joined for the same reasons, apparently, as the "charter members." Tarboro mayor William E. Fountain renounced the Democratic party early in 1896, nearly four years after Marcus J. Battle lost confidence in the old party, yet his profession of faith had a familiar ring. A popular and public-spirited businessman, Fountain had served eight terms as mayor. "Father of the Bank of Tarboro," promoter of cotton mills, and booster of the town's new tobacco market, he shared Battle's belief that Populism would create a healthy business environment, affirming "that business prosperity is more or less dependent on legislation affecting business." Like Battle, he saw politics in religious terms. "Both of the old political parties have shown that they are on the side of Mammon," he declared. The People's party had the "mission" of implementing "the reforms demanded by the multitude." It had been "ridiculed, misrepresented and spit upon by politicians and gold-worshippers," said Fountain. "Did they do less to Christ?" The state's leading Populist newspaper praised the decision of this "busy business man" and

9. *Ibid.*
10. Marcus Josiah Battle to Thomas H. Battle, December 20, 1897, in Battle Family Papers.

urged other entrepreneurs to imitate his example: "Mr. Fountain is a man who takes no step unadvisedly, and if there are business men anywhere who think they have no time to give to the investigation of legislation affecting business, the best they can do is to follow the lead of this representative business man who HAS TAKEN time for that purpose, and try to help him restore prosperity to this country and people."[11]

The Climax of Edgecombe Populism

Fountain joined a party that was, if Durden is correct, close to its peak in early 1896. On the national level Populism was so strong that it was contributing to a revolution in one of the major parties: the repudiation of an incumbent president by his own party. On the local level, however, Populism's strength was less clear.

By some measurements, Edgecombe Populism was fading rapidly by 1896. On the basis of simple voting aggregates, the Populists were at their strongest in 1892 and 1894 and were declining well before the violence and fraud of the "white-supremacy campaign" of 1898. For example, the Populist congressional vote rose from 508 votes (13 percent) in 1892 to 709 votes (19 percent) in 1894, only to fall to 370 votes (7.6 percent) in 1896 and 87 votes (1.7 percent) two years later.[12]

Such statistics are, by themselves, quite misleading. In terms of real political power, Edgecombe's Populists were at their strongest point in the summer of 1898, when they were poised to elect a legislator, sheriff, county treasurer, and two members of the board of county commissioners. The difference between 1892 and 1898 was largely a difference in the technique of cooperation between Populists and Negro voters.

From the beginning, the People's party in Edgecombe had been built upon a small core of white voters. In a county with 1,726 registered

11. Raleigh *Caucasian*, January 21, 1897, January 23, 1896. For biographical information on Fountain, see Tarboro *Southerner*, November 7, 1901, April 26, 1900.
12. For the congressional election returns, see Anderson, *Race and Politics in North Carolina*, 348–50. For other returns, see Edgecombe County Record of Elections, 1880–1894, 1896–1900, in North Carolina State Archives, Division of Archives and History, Raleigh; Tarboro *Southerner*, October 18, November 15, 1894.

white voters in 1894, about 400 white men, many with ties to the Alliance movement, constituted the basic strength of Populism.[13] Obviously, this small group could not win without significant black support. At first, the Populists appealed directly to black voters. In 1892, for example, Edgecombe Populists took the remarkable step of including on their electoral slate an important black nominee—Miles Williams, a candidate for the legislature. But most Negroes chose to remain faithful to the Republican party, even though the local organization was enfeebled by corruption and factionalism. Most white Populists were halfhearted in their appeals for black votes, and many quietly "scratched" Williams' name on election day.[14] The black Populist ran at the bottom of his ticket, nearly 200 votes behind presidential aspirant James B. Weaver.

The Populists had modest success in attracting what might be called black "protest votes." When a Republican nominee was unpopular, such as Negro congressional candidate Henry P. Cheatham in 1894, hundreds of blacks supported the Populist nominee to register their discontent but not necessarily their affirmation of Populist principles. In two black-majority townships (numbers 11 and 13), the Populist candidate for Congress, Howard F. Freeman, ran ahead of both Cheatham and Democratic congressman Frederick A. Woodard.

A far more effective procedure, in the face of the prejudices of both black and white voters, was fusion. By this means, Populists were able to take advantage of black political strength, without converting blacks to their ideology or confronting their own Negrophobic tendencies. The logic of coalition was irresistible to any Populist studying the election returns. In 1892 a Democrat won the county's senate seat, even though the uncoordinated Republican-Populist opposition together polled 355 votes more than he did. In 1894 a Populist running for sheriff with Republican support garnered 1,794 votes while James B. Lloyd, the Populist candidate in a three-way state senate race, received only 603 votes.

13. U.S. Congress, House, *Contested Election Case of Henry P. Cheatham v. Frederick A. Woodard from the Second Congressional District of the State of North Carolina* (1896), 147. The estimate of four hundred white Populists in the county is consistent with election returns and the judgment of Frank L. Battle, a well-informed contemporary politician. See *Contested Election Case of Cheatham v. Woodard,* 167.
14. Tarboro *Southerner,* October 18, 1894.

The fusion approach was used as early as 1892, when Populists and Republicans supported the same candidate for sheriff, though they could not agree on candidates for register of deeds or the legislative positions. Two years later the two parties that were out of office worked together on both the sheriff's race and the campaign for register of deeds. In 1896, after the fusion-controlled legislature rewrote the state's unfair election laws, coalition candidates captured Edgecombe by huge margins—margins reflective of the actual black voting strength, undiluted by vote fraud.[15] With more than 60 percent of the vote, William E. Fountain ousted the incumbent Democratic treasurer, while fusion associates defeated the Democratic sheriff and register of deeds. At the same time, the Populists could disavow, they thought, direct responsibility for the three black legislators and thirty-one black magistrates elected in the county, since these offices were not covered by fusion agreements.

By 1898, Edgecombe Democrats were thoroughly discouraged. "Politics is more of a side line this year than ever," commented the *Southerner* late in July, predicting the quietest election in years. About the same time, James B. Lloyd reported to Senator Butler: "There is no enthusiasm among Dems here now. Politically they are lifeless and hopeless." Emboldened perhaps by these circumstances, Edgecombe Populists pushed cooperation even further, persuading the numerically superior Republicans to give them a member of the state house of representatives and two of the three elected county commissioners, as well as the previously agreed-upon county offices. Although the Populists did not formally endorse the two Republican nominees for the legislature (both black "gold bugs"), some Populists feared that the policy of tacit, indirect support for these black candidates was unwise. "I feel that we have almost committed political suicide," was J. M. Cutchin's private comment. A fusion slate that included Negroes would "drive away so many of our best men," he warned.[16]

In the end, the misgivings of ordinary Populists helped make Democratic appeals for white supremacy particularly effective. At the moment of its greatest influence, Edgecombe Populism suddenly col-

15. For information on the election law changes, see Anderson, *Race and Politics in North Carolina*, 227–28.
16. Tarboro *Southerner*, July 21, 1898; James B. Lloyd to Marion Butler, July 22, 1898, Cutchin to Butler, September 19, 1898, in Butler Papers.

lapsed, helpless and confused in the face of accusations that party leaders were dependent upon Negroes.

Principles and Opportunity

Despite the appearance of opportunism suggested by their complex maneuvering, Edgecombe's Populist leaders were not mere "pie eaters"—unprincipled men hungry for office at any cost. They understood the agrarian reform movement and yearned for its success. In fact, some of them were particularly bold in negotiations with black politicians because they believed blacks would soon be disfranchised. They hoped disfranchisement would open the way for honest debates among white men and a grand coalition of "the reform element in the three parties."[17]

Even William Fountain, the Edgecombe Populist who appeared most flagrantly opportunistic, was not primarily inspired by greed or political ambition. Indeed, if he had been more of a politician, he might have taken greater care to appear consistent. Like the maneuvering of Edgecombe County Populists in general, Fountain's twists and turns illustrate not opportunism but rather an awkward adherence to both conventional Democratic principles and Populist reform.

Elected mayor of Tarboro as a Democrat in 1895, he renounced the Democratic party in 1896 and won election as country treasurer under the Populist banner. In 1897 he was elected chairman of the North Carolina People's party. In the white-supremacy campaign he first led Edgecombe Populists into a risky alliance with blacks and then, at the last moment, publicly endorsed the Democratic campaign against "Negro domination" and declared his candidacy for Congress, running against both the black incumbent, George H. White, and the regular Populist nominee, his former friend James Lloyd.[18]

"I am not a politician," Fountain asserted as he embraced white supremacy in 1898, and in some ways he never was. He had become a Populist because he was profoundly opposed to politicians and ordi-

17. William E. Fountain to Marion Butler, August 9, 1898, J. M. Cutchin to Butler, January 14, 1897, in Butler Papers.
18. Raleigh *Caucasian*, January 21, 1897; Anderson, *Race and Politics in North Carolina*, 274–76.

nary partisanship. He explained his decision of 1896 to join the new party in remarkably antipolitical terms. "Party platforms," he said, "with double meaning, have been used for the purpose of obtaining power. None of the pledges were fulfilled, and the honest party adherents have been betrayed." Fountain believed that "partisanship should no longer control men when great principles, tending to the relief of the people are at stake." Urging "the people" to rise above party, he denounced the "selfishness, greed, and bitter political intolerance" that had corrupted the old parties and prevented effective action in favor of free silver.[19]

A few months after joining the Populists, Fountain was warning his new comrades about the dangers of sacrificing principle for political gain. In a letter to Butler's *Caucasian* in April, 1896, he declared that office seekers must not be allowed to pervert the People's party as they had the Republicans and Democrats. He opposed cooperation with the old parties unless an alliance would really "unite all reform forces" and "put Country above party."[20]

Fountain never offered a simple class-conflict analysis of the nation's problems—an outlook associated with radical antimonopoly Populists. He assumed that the enlightened self-interest of businessmen coincided with the interests of farmers. Businessmen had a duty "to cast their ballots so that relief may come, and their business interests may advance and prosper with the prosperity of the farmers and every productive industry around them." The Democratic party, he told businessmen, was really "antagonistic to our interests" and "the welfare of the country."[21]

He sounded similar themes when he turned against Populist leadership in the waning days of the 1898 campaign. Speaking at an immense mass meeting of white citizens in Goldsboro, Fountain declared, "I am no politician, but a plain business man, and I have no ambition for office." A man who had recently been negotiating with black politicians, he now asserted that eastern North Carolina was facing a "Negro domination" that threatened the general prosperity. The conditions existing in North Carolina, he said, were "paralyzing the business interests of the state" and driving away outside invest-

19. Raleigh *Caucasian*, January 23, 1896.
20. *Ibid.*, April 2, 1896.
21. *Ibid.*

ment, and "white men, without regard to party, ought to come together and change it."[22] In short, Fountain's brief foray into politics ended much as it had commenced, with the Tarboro merchant calling for the restoration of good business conditions by citizens rising above politics.

After the election, the Populist *Caucasian* issued a blistering editorial: "The most contemptible and infamous conduct that any man in this State has ever been guilty of is that of W. E. Fountain."[23] But the available evidence suggests that Fountain believed his actions would promote the cause of free silver and reform. He was also, no doubt, frightened.

Fountain was precisely the sort of person that white supremacy was designed to silence—or convert. As Democratic leaders saw it, the antidote to "Negro domination" was white solidarity, and the primary targets of their overheated rhetoric were those white men who had made possible the renaissance of black politics after 1894. Democrats relentlessly repeated the message that Negro domination had been "brought about through a division of the white men at the ballot box" and that if white men had remained united, "these things could not have been."[24]

As the white-supremacy campaign intensified in the late summer of 1898, many of Fountain's neighbors saw him in a new light. His dealings with black Republicans changed him from a benefactor and respectable citizen to a traitor. The *Southerner* called him the "coon candidate for treasurer" and published a hymn parody:

> There is a Fountain filled with greed
> Drawn from Cy Thompson's head
> Where Repops go to drink and feed
> And white men fear to tread.[25]

A correspondent from the Charlotte *Observer*, taking a firsthand look at black power in the eastern part of the state, described Fountain as "the most unprincipled, mean white man in this section of the state."

22. Raleigh *News and Observer*, October 29, 1898; Kinston *Daily Free Press*, November 1, 1898.
23. Raleigh *Caucasian*, November 17, 1898.
24. Goldsboro *Daily Argus*, October 28, 1898.
25. Tarboro *Southerner*, September 29, 1898. Cyrus Thompson was North Carolina's Populist secretary of state.

According to this report, "the decent white people here look upon him as they would a midnight houseburner, and should a riot ever occur he would be the first man to suffer. He has made himself a menace to the welfare of the community in which he dwells." At first, Fountain's friends came to his defense, and forty-two Democrats, including the chairman of the board of county commissioners and the president of the Bank of Tarboro, wrote to the *Observer* repudiating the attack on him. But the pressure for white solidarity quickly overwhelmed these voices. The *Southerner* published an editorial expressing surprise that any Democrat would defend Fountain from the *Observer*'s charges. Ignoring the accuracy of the accusation (which it termed a "matter for individual decision"), the *Southerner* asserted, "It is bad policy for white men to give aid to their political enemies." A few days later a public meeting in Tarboro unanimously endorsed the *Observer*'s attack on Fountain, with "quite a number of those who had signed the statement for Fountain" offering no dissent. In mid-October a Populist leader warned Senator Butler not to speak in Edgecombe "or any of the 'black' counties." He wrote: "Threats are daily made here of trouble. They are saying Mr. Fountain will be killed. . . . The feeling here is intense." The next day he added: "So many threats have been made against him that I fear some fiend may assassinate him. Yesterday I heard that a certain Dem said that he did not think Mr. Fountain would be living at the election."[26]

The Democrats' fury was ironic, for Fountain secretly welcomed the prospect of black disfranchisement. "We have nothing to fear with the negro out of the way," he had told Senator Butler early in the campaign. Writing in the strictest confidence, Fountain argued that the Populists would benefit from their opponents' racial rhetoric. The Democrats had kept Negroes a factor in politics even when the Democracy was in control "for the sole purpose of demoralizing and corrupting them" and using them as a "bug bear to scare ignorant white men, thereby solidifying them in the perpetuation of Democratic machine rule." Populists, he said, ought to call the Democrats' bluff: "I believe the time has come to force the white man idea in such a way as to

26. Charlotte *Observer*, September 20, October 1, 11, 1898; Tarboro *Southerner*, September 29, 1898; James B. Lloyd to Marion Butler, October 14, 15, 1898, in Butler Papers.

compel the Democrats, should they be successful in securing the next legislature, to disfranchise the negro as Tilghman [*sic*] has done in South Carolina." Although he owed his office to substantial Negro support, Fountain concluded, "If it is to be a fight between white men, we can next time . . . beat the gold men, leaving us the dominent [*sic*] party in the state."[27]

The "mean, unprincipled" white man who was allegedly promoting "Negro domination" was actually a believer in white supremacy all along. No doubt he rationalized his actions as a prudent way to promote "reform" and outwit the gold men—though Populist leaders saw more treachery than shrewdness in this strategy. There is no evidence that in endorsing white supremacy, Fountain meant to repudiate any part of the Populist platform.

Two Kinds of Alliancemen

The tangled details of local history often undermine broad, satisfying generalizations. William Fountain, promoter of cotton mills and owner of a telegraph line, certainly envisioned no radical alternative to the American economic system. His willingness to bargain with blacks reflected no fundamental break with southern racial traditions, no plan to substitute the "reality" of economic class interests for the "illusions" of racial conflict. From one perspective, he could be an example of an "angry agrarian capitalist." From another viewpoint, he would be, no doubt, an example of a "trimmer," a "man without ideas" who was a late convert to Populism without really understanding it. Fountain's performance might be offered as support for Bruce Palmer's description of North Carolina Populism. The party was weakened, according to Palmer, by an "influx of free silver Democrats" who relished intense free-silver imagery but not "substantive discussions of any reform demand."[28]

Political parties are not usually weakened, of course, by gaining

27. Fountain to Butler, August 9, 1898, in Butler Papers.
28. Palmer, *"Man over Money,"* 141–51.

more adherents, and some historians may be uncomfortable with the task of distinguishing "true" and "false" Populists.[29] It may be more useful, and less tendentious, to compare the People's party in the 1890s with the Republican party in the 1850s. In each case a new, minor party was trying to become a major party by "broadening its base" (in modern jargon), or, to put it bluntly, by emphasizing the popular planks in its platform and playing down the more controversial or sectarian. Thus, by what Stanley Elkins has called the "fellow-traveler principle," citizens were brought to endorse "free soil," though they were unwilling to support radical abolitionism.[30] The winning Republican platform of 1860 was vaguer, less strident than the platform of 1856. In a similar way, the Populists muted their demands for the subtreasury scheme, for example, in hopes of exploiting more attractive issues, such as free silver. And if President Cleveland had retained control of the Democratic party, the free-silver strategy would have made the Populists a major party.

It is important to remember that in the South most members of the Farmers' Alliance stayed in the Democratic party. Those who took the drastic step of leaving the "white man's party" were primarily identified by their rebellion. To the majority of voters outside the People's party, the disputes of Populist factions were secondary, for as noisy as their quarrels were, a general Populist consensus united them. Only a curious sort of factional arrogance could pretend that the differences between Tom Watson and Marion Butler were more important than the differences between either one and Cleveland.

In Edgecombe the majority of Alliancemen who stayed within the Democratic party was well represented by Elias Carr. Born into the county's "planter aristocracy," Carr was an influential gentleman farmer when he became involved in agrarian protest in 1886. After serving as president of a local Alliance and the Edgecombe County Alliance, he won two terms as president of the state organization,

29. Unlike Goodwyn, Palmer "does not excommunicate anybody who claimed to have been a Populist," as Walter Nugent has noted. But he also points out that Palmer clearly prefers the more radical Populists, though he does not make their position normative. Nugent, "The Disappearance of the Producing Classes," *Reviews in American History*, IX (1981), 197.

30. Stanley M. Elkins, *Slavery: A Problem in American Institutional and Intellectual Life* (Chicago: University of Chicago Press, 1968), 185–89.

serving from 1889 to 1891.[31] Then, in 1892, North Carolina Democrats selected him as their candidate for governor, hoping to hold Alliance voters tempted by the third-party option.

Carr ran on a platform largely borrowed from the Alliance except for its first section denouncing the McKinley tariff and the Force Bill. The paragraph demanding the abolition of national banks "and the substitution of legal tender treasury notes in lieu of national bank notes" was copied word for word from the Alliance's demands of 1889. Also plagiarized from the St. Louis document were the demands for free silver, economy in government, an end to futures speculation, and the prohibition of alien landownership. Although the Alliance appeals for the subtreasury plan and government ownership of railroads were omitted from the platform, some conservative Democrats were unenthusiastic. The editor of the Tarboro *Southerner* described the free-silver and fiat-money planks as unwise, though he was willing to submit to the judgment of the party.[32]

Clearly, North Carolina Democrats were prepared to concede a great deal to the agrarian movement in order to defeat the third party. Although their strategy succeeded in 1892, Carr won the governorship with only 48 percent of the vote.[33] If Republicans and Populists could combine their strength next time, the Democrats would be doomed.

Some of the most important leaders in Carr's home county, including the president and secretary of the Edgecombe Alliance, joined the third party in 1892. The key issue for such men was the reliability of the Democratic party. Regardless of the rhetoric of the Democratic platform, these Alliance members doubted that the state and national Democratic party was a fit instrument of reform. The radicalism of third party men consisted not in their political creed—after all, a man could demand free silver, fiat money, the subtreasury plan, and all the rest and still be a good Democrat—but in their firm conviction that the

31. Lala Carr Steelman, *The North Carolina Farmers' Alliance: A Political History, 1887–1893* (Greenville, N.C.: East Carolina University Publications, 1985), 55. See also Steelman, "The Role of Elias Carr in the North Carolina Farmers' Alliance," *North Carolina Historical Review*, LVII (1980), 133–58.

32. Tarboro *Southerner*, June 9, May 26, 1892; John D. Hicks, *The Populist Revolt: A History of the Farmers' Alliance and the People's Party* (Minneapolis: University of Minnesota Press, 1931), 427–30.

33. Donald R. Matthews (ed.), *North Carolina Votes* (Chapel Hill: University of North Carolina Press, 1962), 111.

Democratic party was hopelessly corrupt and deserved to be defeated. As agrarian editor A. L. Swinson of Goldsboro put it, there was "no possible hope for the reform demands through a Democratic chanel [sic]." Not until the Democrats were defeated would the Alliance agenda be achieved.[34]

James B. Lloyd, editor of the Alliance newspaper the *Farmers' Advocate* and president of the Tarboro Alliance, is a good example of Edgecombe's Populist Alliancemen, citizens who were not appeased by the nomination of Carr. "A straight and typical young Populist—one of that class of young men who are determined that American systems shall prevail in America," Lloyd was probably the most important People's party activist in the county. At various times he served as chairman of the party's county executive committee, secretary of the county Alliance, member of the Populists' state central committee, candidate for the state senate, and nominee for Congress. Too young for Civil War experience, he bore the title Captain Lloyd for his work as commander of the local militia company, the socially prestigious but militarily insignificant Edgecombe Guards.[35]

On many subjects Lloyd agreed with Carr and other Alliance Democrats. Although he was often described as a conservative, Carr did support the subtreasury plan and the rest of the Alliance's 1890 Ocala platform.[36] Lloyd and Carr agreed on the need for monetary expansion and the value of free silver. Although neither man was a Negro-baiter, neither had any interest in challenging the system of race relations prevailing in eastern North Carolina. Both men favored the graduated income tax as a way of diminishing inequality. (Even the Tarboro *Southerner* supported this idea, arguing that the graduated income tax

34. Tarboro *Southerner*, July 21, 1892; James L. Hunt, "The Making of a Populist: Marion Butler, 1863–1895," *North Carolina Historical Review*, LXII (1985), 194. See also J. M. Cutchin's letter, under the headline "Principles not parties," in Tarboro *Farmers' Advocate*, June 15, 1892.

35. Raleigh *Caucasian*, March 5, July 23, 1896, August 11, 1898; Tarboro *Southerner*, July 21, September 8, 1892, April 5, 1894. Lloyd ceased publishing the *Farmers' Advocate* in December, 1892, citing his deteriorating eyesight. Tarboro *Southerner*, December 15, 1892. On Lloyd's militia service, see Tarboro *Southerner*, August 25, September 22, November 3, 24, 1892; Tarboro *Farmers' Advocate*, September 21, 1892.

36. Steelman, *The North Carolina Farmers' Alliance*, 241–42, 193–95. For Lloyd's political views, see his letters in the Raleigh *Caucasian*, May 3, 1894, May 9, 23, June 4, 27, 1895. See also his editorials in the Alliance (not Populist) organ, the Tarboro *Farmers' Advocate*.

as a remedy "to the acquisition of undue wealth" was good Democratic doctrine, not a third-party innovation.)[37]

Carr differed from Lloyd on the St. Louis platform of 1892, a document Carr rejected because it advocated government ownership of the railroads and generous pensions for Union veterans. Unlike some Alliancemen, Carr considered the protective tariff a real, not a sham, issue, and he objected to the St. Louis platform's silence on the subject.

The most important difference between Lloyd and Carr was that Lloyd would not support Grover Cleveland again. Lloyd was disenchanted with the central political institution of North Carolina—the Democratic party—and he could not love Cleveland for the enemies he had made. For Carr, Cleveland's stands on the tariff and the Force Bill made him a satisfactory friend of the southern farmer. For Lloyd, Cleveland was the most important obstacle to really significant reform.

Carr's way and Lloyd's way each entailed awkwardness, if not worse, for the conscientious Allianceman. Staying within the Democratic party meant accepting, somehow, the nation's most prominent opponent of soft money, Grover Cleveland. It meant coexisting with Senator Matt W. Ransom, an old-fashioned "rebel brigadier" thoroughly out of sympathy with the farmers' movement, and working with his associates, such as former congressman Furnifold M. Simmons, state Democratic chairman in 1892 and 1898. Walking out of the Democratic party, on the other hand, might only strengthen the non-Alliance, antireform elements remaining in the party. Even outside the Democratic party, Populist Alliancemen would be required to work with a different set of "gold bugs" (the Republicans) to have any real hope of winning the state.

In the course of partisan struggle with the Democrats, some Populists came to believe that defeating the Democratic "machine" was the most important of all reforms. They affirmed this without denying any of the old issues and familiar demands, just as Carr continued to invoke agrarian solidarity, refusing to recant the subtreasury heresy, as he supported Cleveland. A longtime participant in the agrarian movement, farmer and lumber-mill owner J. M. Cutchin, expressed this conviction a few weeks before the 1894 election. Writing to the

37. Tarboro *Southerner,* May 25, 1893.

Caucasian, Cutchin affirmed his strong support for the Populist national platform. But the main issue was now fair elections: "There is no
use in further talk about dead silver, the tariff, and broken promises,
but the one living issue confronting us is to have an honest election or
none at all."[38]

In the climactic showdown of 1898, Lloyd could well have been
elected to Congress, as a Populist, if he had been willing to endorse
white supremacy. Second-district Democrats knew there was no
chance of defeating Negro incumbent George H. White in a three-way
race, but they were unwilling to support Lloyd merely because he was
a white admirer of William Jennings Bryan and a believer in free silver.
To win, Lloyd would have to accept the Democrats' issue, repudiating
all those Populists who considered the white-supremacy campaign a
cunning distraction, and undermining fusion arrangements throughout the district. The Tarboro *Southerner* advised Lloyd, "You must either renounce your promise to vote for negro legislators in Edgecombe
or sit in silence and see White walk away with the pie." Lloyd refused
to endorse white supremacy, not because he was interested in black
rights or because any plank in the Omaha platform was directly threatened, but because he was committed to keeping North Carolina out of
Democratic control.[39]

Conclusion

The history of Edgecombe Populism suggests several tentative conclusions. First, the standard litmus tests for Populism, or "true reformers," prove misleading in the actual circumstances of Edgecombe. The
loyal Democrat Carr supported the divisive, "radical" subtreasury
plan. The fusionist Populists in Edgecombe continued to support the
Omaha platform and preach antimonopoly ideals, though such language and such commitments supposedly vanished in Marion Butler's
crafty pursuit of winning coalitions. According to Palmer, "Reference
to and defense of the Omaha platform had disappeared almost entirely" among North Carolina Populists by 1896. Yet that year the par-

38. Raleigh *Caucasian,* October 4, 1894.
39. Tarboro *Southerner,* September 15, 1898. On attempts to get Democratic support
for Lloyd without endorsing white supremacy, see Lloyd's letters to Senator Butler,
September 24 and October 21, 1898, in Butler Papers.

ty's county convention declared that if Populism were successful, "we solemnly pledge that this great county shall be redeemed from the corporate, monopoly, English and banking influences that now dominate it."[40]

Second, Edgecombe Populists were essentially heretical Democrats. Like lapsed fundamentalists or ex-Communists, they were furious about the old party's "betrayal" and determined to free others from its thrall. Yet they also hoped to salvage something good from the Democracy and restlessly searched for ways to unite all reform elements. Some of them, like William Fountain, may have been relieved to find an issue so urgent—racial solidarity—that unity on a new basis was possible.

Certainly Edgecombe's history shows that white supremacy was always present in the political calculations of both Populists and Democrats. In 1892 as well as 1898 it was an issue. The genius of Furnifold Simmons and Josephus Daniels made it the only issue in 1898, whereas in 1892 Marion Butler (and James Lloyd and Marcus Battle) were successful in subordinating—though not repudiating—white supremacy and promoting a package of agrarian reforms.

Last of all, there is little evidence that the Populists were spokesmen for Edgecombe County's have-nots. Edgecombe was a county where nearly half the white farmers were renters, not to mention the black farmers, nine-tenths of whom were landless. It is possible to imagine a political movement led by poor men defending their interests by attacking landlords and merchants and gentlemen farmers.[41] Edgecombe Populism was not such a movement. Its focus was on distant national abuses, and it offered little immediate, practical, local relief for farmers who tilled someone else's acres.

Edgecombe County's experience with Populism raises as many questions, perhaps, as it answers. None of the historiographical explanations of the People's party fits perfectly the home county of Fountain, Carr, and Lloyd. But if the county's Populists are at all representative of the state and region, Robert Durden's analysis of Populism is worthy of renewed attention.

40. Palmer, "Man over Money," 143; Raleigh Caucasian, July 23, 1896.
41. The census of 1900 counted 2,284 farms in Edgecombe, of which 1,156 were operated by whites. There were 536 farms operated by white tenants and 1,035 by black tenants. Twelfth Census, 1900: Agriculture, Pt. 1, pp. 108–109.

Furnifold M. Simmons and the Politics of White Supremacy

During the late nineteenth century, Democrats concocted a picture of Reconstruction that colored the minds of most white North Carolinians—and most history books—for half a century. It was a period, according to this mythology, of Negro domination, Republican extravagance and corruption, and the humiliation and degradation of white men and women. Despite those myths, however, the period from 1876 to 1894 was one of uneasy Democratic dominance in North Carolina. The balance of voters between Republicans and Democrats was closer than in other southern states. According to J. Morgan Kousser's ingenious calculation, the Democrats never exceeded 54 percent of the vote. By 1892 the Democrats were far from united, and they faced serious new problems. The state's two United States senators—Zebulon Vance and Matt W. Ransom—seemed always at swords' points over party policy and patronage, and their differences were becoming increasingly ideological. Democratic leaders had noticed earlier "an alarming disintegration" of the party in the west. Now they were facing rebellion in the rural areas throughout the state, where the Farmers' Alliance was making sounds about a third party that would endorse the free coinage of silver to achieve monetary inflation, the subtreasury scheme as a means of supporting farm prices, and government regulation—perhaps ownership—of the railroads. Such a program was anathema to the supporters of President Grover Cleveland, and so a substantial number of Democrats in North Carolina were threatening a bolt to a third party. Marion Butler, for example, was suggesting that Populists and "reform-minded" Democrats combine to destroy the power of entrenched Democrats.[1]

Although Republican leaders thought of taking advantage of Democratic differences, they had troubles of their own. One question was strategic—how to deal with the fact of a third party. Some Republicans assumed that the Populist upheaval would so weaken the Democratic party that the Republicans could maintain ideological integrity and win on their own. Others argued that the immediate goal should be to win the next election, which they thought could be more surely accomplished by a calculated cooperation with the Populists.

Among Republicans, the issue of race was particularly divisive. Out of about one hundred thousand Republican voters in 1892, perhaps thirty thousand were black. Black politicians sensed that the political convulsion of the time might give them an opportunity to bargain for places of ever greater influence, and they did so with vigor. Some in the Republican party, such as its chairman, John B. Eaves, favored winning the support of the blacks; others, such as Daniel L. Russell, soon to be governor, feared that close association with blacks might be suicidal in the racist climate of the nineteenth century, might lead to white flight from the party, and would certainly create an opportunity for the Democrats to accuse the Republican party in North Carolina of being dominated by Negroes.[2]

1. J. Morgan Kousser, *The Shaping of Southern Politics: Suffrage Restriction and the Establishment of the One-Party South, 1880–1910* (New Haven: Yale University Press, 1974), 55; Raleigh *News and Observer*, February 3, 1889; Joseph F. Steelman, "Republican Party Strategists and the Issue of Fusion with Populists in North Carolina, 1893–1894," *North Carolina Historical Review*, XLVII (1970), 247; Dwight B. Billings, Jr., *Planters and the Making of a "New South": Class, Politics, and Development in North Carolina, 1865–1900* (Chapel Hill: University of North Carolina Press, 1979), 158–59; Jeffrey J. Crow, "Cracking the Solid South: Populism and the Fusionist Interlude," in Lindley S. Butler and Alan D. Watson (eds.), *The North Carolina Experience: An Interpretive and Documentary History* (Chapel Hill: University of North Carolina Press, 1984).

2. Joseph F. Steelman, "Vicissitudes of Republican Party Politics: The Campaign of 1892 in North Carolina," *North Carolina Historical Review*, XLIII (1966), 430ff. See also Raleigh *News and Observer*, March 19, 1891; H. Leon Prather, Sr., *Resurgent Politics and Educational Progressivism in the New South: North Carolina, 1890–1913* (Rutherford, N.J.: Fairleigh Dickinson University Press, 1979), 381. The *News and Observer* stated on September 2, 1892, that there were 109,000 black men over twenty-one years of age, and it estimated that there were about 95,000 black voters. Perhaps the best source states that 94,684 persons voted Republican for governor (33.8 percent of the total vote) and 100,675

Despite divisions among Republicans, differences among the Democrats seemed so acute as the election of 1892 approached that they became increasingly pessimistic about their chances of winning in the state. Indeed, when they met in state convention in July, the atmosphere was gloomy, but after some preliminary maneuverings in which the chairman of the state executive committee resigned, they elected Furnifold McLendel Simmons as his replacement. This choice was of unusual significance because for the next thirty-eight years Simmons was to be one of the most powerful, and for part of that time *the* most powerful, politician in North Carolina.[3]

A thirty-eight-year-old lawyer from New Bern, Simmons had grown up in the slave culture of the Old South on his father's plantation of a thousand acres or more in Jones County in eastern North Carolina. During the Civil War he heard the guns of the Union navy and of invading Union troops. He lived through Reconstruction and, from the time he was ten years old, was indoctrinated with the white southern Democrats' view of that period. He studied briefly at Wake Forest College and in 1873 graduated from Trinity College (then located in Randolph County, some sixty miles west of its present location in Durham). He read law and in 1875 began to practice. In time he developed a lucrative practice and acquired extensive landholdings.[4]

His interest in politics began early. At the age of twenty-one he ran for the state legislature unsuccessfully. He ran again several years later and was again defeated—largely because of the number of black Republicans in eastern North Carolina. In spite of these defeats, Simmons was chosen chairman of the Democratic executive committee of

---

voted Republican for president (36.2 percent). Donald R. Matthews (ed.), *North Carolina Votes* (Chapel Hill: University of North Carolina Press, 1962), 111, 6. To calculate the number of black voters with precision is impossible. According to the eleventh census, there were slightly over 109,000 black males of voting age in 1890. Kousser estimated that 27 percent of adult males voted Democratic in 1892. *Eleventh Census, 1890: Population,* Pt. 1, p. 751; Kousser, *The Shaping of Southern Politics,* 183.

3. Richard L. Watson, Jr., "Furnifold M. Simmons, 'Jehovah of the Tar Heels'?" *North Carolina Historical Review,* XLIV (1967), 166–87.

4. See Josiah W. Bailey, *Simmons—Organizer of Victory* (N.p., n.d.), 2, in Pamphlet Collection, Duke University Library, Durham, N.C., a pamphlet based on an article that appeared in the *Carolina Democrat* during the senatorial campaign of 1912; J. Fred Rippy (ed.) *F. M. Simmons, Statesman of the New South . . .* (Durham, N.C.: Duke University Press, 1936), 2–10. On Simmons' work in a particular case, the Browning trial, see Raleigh *News and Observer,* July 17, 1898.

his congressional district—the second—in 1884, a district that had a substantial majority of black voters. In 1886, however, probably as a result of Democratic shenanigans, two blacks in the district were nominated by Republicans for United States congressman; the Democrats took advantage of the divided loyalties of the blacks and elected the thirty-one-year-old Simmons to the post. His term as congressman was not eventful, but he gained the respect of his agrarian constituency by fighting the jute-bagging trust. In 1888, however, blacks were reunited, and Simmons lost his seat in Congress and returned to his practice in east Carolina, more experienced and increasingly respected by fellow Democrats. In 1890 he gained further respect among party bigwigs, but lost the affection of many farmers and a second nomination for Congress by refusing to support some of the principles of the Farmers' Alliance, which he considered "unconstitutional . . . unwise, and even dangerous."[5]

In 1892 the position of chairman of the Democratic state executive committee seemed a thankless one, and Simmons considered turning it down. But he was energetic and ambitious, and politics and the Democratic party had already become a very important part of his life. So he accepted the challenge and organized the Democratic forces so successfully that they gained a clear-cut victory in the state. Democrats gave North Carolina's electoral vote to Cleveland, elected Elias Carr governor, and won a workable majority in the legislature. Simmons received considerable credit for the victory, though there were those who had the discourtesy to point out that the combined vote of the Republicans and the newly formed Populists was larger than that of the Democrats. Regardless, large, cheering crowds greeted him on the return to his home in New Bern after the election, and he was rewarded by being appointed collector of internal revenue for the Fourth District of North Carolina.[6]

For the next four years, Simmons, as a federal officeholder, was less actively involved in state politics. Those years were not happy times

5. Raleigh News and Observer, January 16, 1938; Eric Anderson, Race and Politics in North Carolina, 1872–1901: The Black Second (Baton Rouge: Louisiana State University Press, 1981), 134ff., esp. 175; Rippy (ed.), F. M. Simmons, 16–18.

6. Rippy (ed.), F. M. Simmons, 19–20; Raleigh News and Observer, July 16, 20, November 6, 11, 13, 1892; Wilmington Messenger, quoted in Raleigh News and Observer, February 2, 1894; Raleigh News and Observer, June 20, November 25, 1893, March 15, 1896.

for North Carolina's professional Democrats. In spite of widely reported differences within the Republican and Populist parties in 1894,
the great majority of members of the two parties swallowed their differences and combined forces to defeat the Democrats. The result of
this fusion in 1894 was overwhelming. In races for the state's congressional delegation, only 3 of 10 Democratic candidates were elected; in
the state house of representatives, only 46 out of 120 Democrats won;
and in the state senate, only 8 of 50. Such decisive control of the
legislature by the fusionists led to the election of Marion Butler, the
Populist leader, to replace Senator Matt Ransom, Democrat, and Jeter
Pritchard, Republican, to replace Senator Zebulon Vance, who had
died in office on April 14, 1894.[7]

In the period from 1893 to 1896, some Democratic leaders seemed to
be attempting to sell the party to North Carolina voters as a happy
medium between radical Populists and reactionary Republicans. This
attempt failed. The Democratic convention in 1895, with some of the
leading Democrats figuratively holding their noses, even endorsed
the free coinage of silver at 16 to 1—no doubt as an attempt to lure back
the Populists. Such moves did lead to vigorous negotiations over a
two-year period as to whether Democrats should fuse with Populists,
whether Populists should fuse with Republicans, or whether there
should be any fusion at all. These differences were reflected in the state
conventions of 1896, when the Democratic assemblage was described
as being in an uproar and a man from Massachusetts allegedly considered the Republican gathering a "howling, sulking, cursing mob."
Confusion and accusations of treachery characterized the campaign,
with the issue of gold and silver serving to dominate the rhetoric until
mid-October. Then it became clear that Daniel L. Russell, the Republican nominee for governor, was far ahead of the Democratic candidate, Cyrus Watson, and in desperation the Democrats, led by Sim-

7. J. G. de Roulhac Hamilton, *History of North Carolina Since 1860* (Chicago: Lewis
Publishing Company, 1919), 244–50, vol. III of *History of North Carolina*, 3 vols.; Steelman,
"Republican Party Strategists," 267–69; Allen W. Trelease, "The Fusion Legislatures of
1895 and 1897: A Roll-Call Analysis of the North Carolina House of Representatives,"
North Carolina Historical Review, LVII (1980), 281; Kousser, *The Shaping of Southern Politics,*
186. Actually, Pritchard replaced Thomas J. Jarvis, whom Governor Elias Carr appointed
to replace Vance in April, but that appointment exacerbated the differences in the Democratic party, since Jarvis tried to persuade Ransom to resign. James L. Hunt, "The Making
of a Populist: Marion Butler, 1863–1895," *North Carolina Historical Review,* LXII (1985),
324–32.

mons and the Raleigh *News and Observer*, conducted a racist campaign prophesying that a Russell victory would lead to Negro domination.[8]

The results, as in 1894, were decisive, but in 1896 a national election added excitement—and confusion. William Jennings Bryan, the free-silver advocate who won the Democratic presidential nomination, received North Carolina's electoral vote, while the rest of the Democratic slate went down to defeat. Hal W. Ayer, the Populist state chairman, could write to Butler and boast that the campaign had no parallel: "We took our hand and carried the state for Bryan (under the name Democrat) and then faced the state Democrats and carried the state against their gang and all the tricks, cunning, fraud, and rascality that they could devise." The excitement of the election had brought out an unusually high percentage of voters, perhaps 85 percent of the eligible electorate and perhaps 87 percent of the eligible blacks. Russell was easily elected governor, and the Democrats were reduced to only 30 out of 120 seats in the lower house of the assembly and 7 out of 50 in the state senate.[9]

The Republicans and Populists who were elected to the state legislature in 1894 and in 1896 lost no time in approving a program of what they considered reform. The fusion legislature "became the first to deal constructively with public education . . . since Reconstruction."[10] It also "augmented the expenditures for charitable and correctional in-

8. Raleigh *News and Observer*, May 26, 1895; Jeffrey J. Crow and Robert F. Durden, *Maverick Republican in the Old North State: A Political Biography of Daniel L. Russell* (Baton Rouge: Louisiana State University Press, 1977), 71–72. The confusion about what the parties stood for and for whom to vote is clear from the press, letters to the editor, and private correspondence of the time. See, for example, Raleigh *News and Observer*, February 23, October 10, 13, 15, 1896; T. J. Jones to Marion Butler, May 18, 1896, Tyler C. Cox to Butler, September 1, 1896, Hal Ayer to Butler, September 11, 1896, W. A. Guthrie to Butler, September 13, 26, October 16, 1896, and Thomas E. Watson to Butler, October 28, 1896, in Marion Butler Papers, Southern Historical Collection, University of North Carolina, Chapel Hill. See also Anderson, *Race and Politics in North Carolina*, 235.

9. Raleigh *News and Observer*, November, 1896; Ayer to Butler, November 7, 1896, in Butler Papers; Kousser, *The Shaping of Southern Politics*, 41, 183; Crow and Durden, *Maverick Republican*, 73. Kousser credits the Democrats with twenty-six members of the House. Kousser, *The Shaping of Southern Politics*, 186. Trelease states that thirty were elected and two unseated. Trelease, "The Fusion Legislatures," 281.

10. For details, see Prather, *Resurgent Politics and Educational Progressivism*, 124–31. In the two fusion sessions, the Democrats in the House opposed raising the school tax almost unanimously. On other legislation involving public schools, however, though Republican and Populist support was generally stronger, a majority of Democrats also supported it. At the same time, "the Democrats consistently indicated the greatest support for higher education," including strong support for the black institutions. Trelease, "The Fusion Legislatures," 287–91.

stitutions and intensified taxation of railroads and businesses."[11] What infuriated the Democrats, however, were the changes made in political practices. The County Government Act of 1889, by which Democrats who controlled the state legislature had manipulated local office holding, was repealed, and the selection of local officials was taken from the legislature and returned to the voters in the counties. The fusion legislature attempted to assure fairness at the polls by requiring a judge and registrar from the three parties at every precinct. It simplified voting for illiterates by allowing different-colored ballots, and it established safeguards against the common practice of arbitrarily disqualifying voters.[12]

These electoral changes, made in 1895, had immediate effects. Perhaps the most important was the increased participation of black voters from about 63 percent in the election of 1892 to about 87 percent in 1896. The legislature in 1897 included eleven blacks, matching the total number of Negroes in the three previous sessions.[13] With the victory of fusion and the passage of the new laws, blacks received numerous appointments to such positions as sheriff, magistrate, school committeeman, and register of deeds. Republican victory in the nation, moreover, meant the certainty of federal appointments of postmen, customs officials, and federal marshals. President William McKinley appointed twenty blacks as postmasters in the Second Congressional District alone.[14]

11. Kousser, *The Shaping of Southern Politics*, 186–87. Billings suggests that Kousser exaggerated the extent of the differences between the fusion and Democratic legislatures and shows how differences within the Populist and Republican parties limited the extent of their "reform" program. Billings, *Planters and the Making of a "New South,"* 140, 177, 183. In fact, it appears that the Democrats gave substantially stronger support to welfare institutions than either Republicans or Populists, and even on taxing measures, the parties were frequently divided. Trelease, "The Fusion Legislatures," 291–308.

12. Anderson, *Race and Politics in North Carolina*, 227–28; Kousser, *The Shaping of Southern Politics*, 186–87; Crow, "Cracking the Solid South," 337–38. The new election procedures were opposed by every Democrat in the House. Trelease, "The Fusion Legislatures," 282.

13. Anderson names seven blacks from the Second Congressional District alone. Prather lists only three blacks, but one of them is not listed by Anderson. Anderson, *Race and Politics in North Carolina*, 238, 247. Cf. Prather, *Resurgent Politics and Educational Progressivism*, 101–107. Trelease lists nine blacks in the House in 1897. Trelease, "The Fusion Legislatures," 281.

14. T. J. Jarvis to Cyrus Thompson, August 24, 1898, in Cyrus Thompson Papers, Southern Historical Collection, University of North Carolina, Chapel Hill; Democratic Executive Committee of North Carolina, *Democratic Handbook* (1898), 45; Raleigh *News and Observer*, May 8, 1897; F. M. Simmons to J. C. Pritchard, in Raleigh *News and Observer*, November 6, 1898.

The scene was now set for two of the most fateful campaigns in the history of North Carolina. Facing the electorate and the state's leadership were many significant questions involving the future of the three political parties and the economic and social challenges of the New South. The remainder of this essay will examine the roles of race, class, and party in these campaigns, with particular emphasis on the contribution of Furnifold M. Simmons, the political leader perhaps most responsible for the return of the Democrats to power in North Carolina in 1898 and for the disfranchisement of black people in 1900.

In 1898, hungry for victory, the Democratic party turned once more to Simmons, the architect of the last Democratic victory in 1892, and made him head of the Democratic state executive committee. Simmons revived his organization of 1892 and launched a virulent white-supremacy campaign marked by corruption and intimidation. This campaign resulted in a legislative turnover. Although the voting was close in terms of ballots counted, the Democrats won 94 seats in the state house of representatives, the Republicans held 23, and the Populists only 3; in the state senate the ratio was 40 Democrats, 7 Republicans, and 3 Populists. The immediate aftermath in Wilmington, the largest city in North Carolina, was a bloody coup d'etat, in which highly respectable Democrats massacred an unknown number of blacks and overthrew the duly elected city officials.[15]

Despite unequivocal denials by Simmons and other Democratic campaigners in 1898 that they had plans to disfranchise any voters, black or white, they claimed in 1899 that the overwhelming victory for white supremacy required black disfranchisement. Indeed, many upright white southerners seriously believed that ridding the electoral process of the ignorant black was a reform. Other southern states—Louisiana, Mississippi, and South Carolina—had already adopted legislation designed to disfranchise blacks, and a special legislative committee debated for hours over which model to follow. The committee and Simmons finally decided to push for an amendment to the state constitution modeled after the Louisiana plan that would have to be

15. Hamilton, *History of North Carolina Since 1860*, 299; Kousser, *The Shaping of Southern Politics*, 186; Raleigh *News and Observer*, November 18, 1898; H. Leon Prather, *We Have Taken a City: Wilmington Racial Massacre and Coup of 1898* (Rutherford, N.J.: Fairleigh Dickinson University Press, 1984).

ratified by state referendum. On February 18, 1899, the House approved the measure by a vote of 81 to 27, and the next day the Senate followed suit by a vote of 42 to 6. All the Republicans opposed it. All the Democrats voted for it except six who had promised not to vote for disfranchisement. Three Populists voted for it, they claimed, because it was to be submitted to the people.[16]

The main provisions of the amendment were Sections 4 and 5.

Section 4: Every person presenting himself for registration shall be able to read and write any section of the Constitution in the English language; and in addition thereto, shall have paid on or before the first of March of the year in which he proposes to vote, his poll tax, as prescribed by law, for the previous year, and he shall exhibit his receipt therefor when he offers to vote. Poll taxes shall be a lien only on assessed property, and no process shall issue to enforce the collection of the same except as against assessed property.

Section 5: No male person who was on January 1, 1867, or at any time prior thereto, entitled to vote under the laws of the state in the United States wherein he then resided, and no lineal descendant of such person, shall be denied the right to register and vote at any election in this State by reason of his failure to pass the educational qualification prescribed in Section 4 of this article: provided he shall have registered in accordance with the terms of this article prior to December 1, 1908, and no person shall be entitled to register under this section after that date.[17]

Although Simmons was reasonably confident that the amendment would be approved, he realized that a strong campaign could be organized against it because of a widespread fear of disfranchisement among illiterate whites. Indeed, Populist leaders were convinced that the amendment was designed to "remove the lower classes of whites" from politics, thus transferring all political power from "the plain honest masses in the country to the town ringster who would perpetuate his rule by the use of the 'educated' town nigger." Almost 20 percent of the white adult males and more than 40 percent of black adult males

16. William A. Mabry, *The Negro in North Carolina Politics Since Reconstruction*, Trinity College Historical Society Papers (Durham, N.C.: Trinity College Historical Society, 1940), 57; Dewey W. Grantham, *Southern Progressivism: The Reconciliation of Progress and Tradition* (Knoxville: University of Tennessee Press, 1983), 112–13; Rippy (ed.), F. M. *Simmons*, 27; Josephus Daniels, *Editor in Politics* (Chapel Hill: University of North Carolina Press, 1941), 324–25; Hamilton, *History of North Carolina Since 1860*, 299; Raleigh *News and Observer*, November 18, 1898; *North Carolina House Journal*, 1899, pp. 654–55; *North Carolina Senate Journal*, 1899, pp. 494–95.

17. *North Carolina Laws*, 1899, p. 218; Mabry, *The Negro in North Carolina Politics*, 59; Raleigh *News and Observer*, February 18, 1898.

were illiterate in 1900. Simmons feared that a statewide referendum might unite these illiterate voters with those Republicans and Populists who saw the amendment as a Democratic power play.[18] The amendment would then be in trouble.

Simmons concluded that the repeal of the electoral laws passed by the fusionists would help to ensure ratification of the amendment, and the repeal of these laws became the immediate goal of the new Democratic majority. By the end of January, 1899, the legislature had repealed the fusion law that had placed the election machinery in the control of the local voter and had assured all political parties representation by poll watchers, and a legislative committee was hard at work on a substitute. Although Simmons was not a member of the legislature, he worked closely with the committee and went over "the proposed new law point by point."[19]

That law established a somewhat modified version of the prefusionist system. The General Assembly would elect a state board of elections, which in turn would choose a county board of three "discreet persons" who would choose all registrars and judges, thus effectively depriving Republicans of possible control of local elections. Registrars were given the power to limit registration by the questions they were permitted to ask, and illiterate voters were handicapped by provisions that required an ability to read if ballots were to be deposited correctly. Moreover, the notorious "Simmons Bull Pens"—screened-off areas where votes were privately counted—were authorized once more. Understandably, local Republicans were outraged.[20]

Simmons had promised that the Democratic legislature of 1899 would carry out all the promises of the Democratic platform, and when that legislature adjourned in early March, he could boast that every promise had been kept. The legislature had repealed or neutralized every significant act of its fusionist predecessors. It had almost destroyed Negro political power by changing the charters of towns, increasing the number of commissioners in counties, and conferring on

18. Kousser, *The Shaping of Southern Politics*, 55. The Raleigh *Caucasian*, June 28, 1900, based its suspicions on an article in the Charlotte *Observer*, June 6, 1900.

19. *North Carolina Laws*, 1899, Chapter 16; Mabry, *The Negro in North Carolina Politics*, 62; Raleigh *News and Observer*, January 21, 1899.

20. Prather, *Resurgent Politics and Educational Progressivism*, 174; Winston *Union-Republican*, March 23, 1899; Davis *Record*, quoted in Winston *Union-Republican*, October 26, 1899; W. P. Bynum, Jr., to Marion Butler, January 16, 1900, in Butler Papers.

justices of the peace (who were appointed by the legislature) the authority for the election of commissioners; the school law was modified to prevent the possibility that Negro committeemen might serve white schools and to set higher salaries for white than for black schoolteachers. Josephus Daniels, the strongly partisan editor of the *News and Observer*, emphasized that the legislature had authorized county commissioners to levy a special tax if, without such a tax, the schools could not be kept open four months of the year; he also underlined an "epoch-making event"—an appropriation of a hundred thousand dollars (actually an insignificant sum) to the public schools of the state. Gestures were made to the Populists by prohibiting the gifts of free passes on railroads and by making elective the offices of corporation commissioners and commissioners of agriculture and labor. Moreover, in spite of opposition from the railroads, the legislature required "all railway and steamboat companies" to "provide separate but equal accommodations for the white and colored races on all passenger trains and steamboats."[21]

The legislative successes of the Democrats were merely a prelude to 1900—a year in which a presidential election would take place, once more involving Bryan and McKinley in a battle over silver and gold and, more prominently, over overseas expansion; in which the governor and other state and local officials would be chosen; in which the state would for the first time try out a statewide primary for United States senator; and in which the referendum on the constitutional amendment for disfranchisement would be held. Normally all of these activities would have taken place in November, but one provision of the new election law attempted to sort out these various elements by moving the state elections, including the referendum, to August, thus making it more difficult for the fusionists to call for federal protection of the polls when the state voted on the amendment.

Party lines, confused at first on the amendment, became clearer as the campaign heated up. The Democrats were enthusiastically for it. When the question of its constitutionality arose, Simmons defended it on the grounds that an across-the-board literacy test was certainly constitutional, and that since the grandfather clause would not protect

21. Raleigh *News and Observer*, March 10, 1899. See criticism of Daniels' celebration of the legislature in, for example, Winston *Union-Republican*, March 30, 1899.

white immigrants or deny free Negroes or descendants of free Negroes their voting rights, it should not be considered discriminatory against blacks and so was not unconstitutional either. Simmons estimated that twenty-five thousand to thirty thousand blacks would vote because they were literate; that an additional two thousand might vote because they were lineal descendants of free Negroes who had been entitled to vote in North Carolina before 1835; and that there were several hundred more blacks who had moved from other states where they or their ancestors had had the right to vote before 1867. A. J. McKelway, editor of the *Presbyterian Standard,* among many others, endorsed this position. Simmons marshaled about 150 knowledgeable North Carolinians, mostly lawyers, to support his position and accused some Republican lawyers and newspapers of having been bribed to argue its unconstitutionality. Simmons' position was tricky, however, since even free Negroes had been disfranchised between 1835 and 1867. But from 1743 to 1835, there had been no racial restriction on voting in North Carolina, and free Negroes had indeed voted. Their lineal descendants, therefore, could theoretically vote after 1901.[22]

Although a few Republicans came out publicly in favor of the amendment, the Republican party formally opposed it. The Populist party did not take an official position on it. It had powerful support, however, from some Populists, including Charles H. Mebane, the superintendent of public instruction, who argued that the amendment would force white people to spend more money for education and for sending their children to school.[23]

Marion Butler was slow to take a position on the amendment. He had hoped that one Democratic claim might actually work out—that the amendment, by disfranchising most black people, would essentially remove them from the political process and thus make it more difficult for the demagogue to use race to obscure more substantive issues. By January, 1900, however, his reasoning led him to the op-

22. Raleigh *News and Observer*, May 21, September 5, 1899; A. J. McKelway, "The North Carolina Suffrage Amendment," *Independent*, LII (1900), 1955–57; Simmons to Alan K. Smith, October 24, 1900, in Raleigh *News and Observer*, October 29, 1899; John Hope Franklin, *The Free Negro in North Carolina, 1790–1860* (Chapel Hill: University of North Carolina Press, 1943), 105–20. The classic defense of the amendment was that of one of its authors, George Rountree. Raleigh *News and Observer*, February 18, May 14, 1899.

23. Raleigh *News and Observer*, September 3, December 28, 1899; Charlotte *Observer*, April 8, 1900.

posite conclusion: that the amendment would disfranchise the "good old country darky who was as faithful and true as steel to our mothers, wives, and sisters during the late war"; that about fifty thousand literate Negroes would still be able to vote; and that these would include "the trifling town Negro who walks the streets of our towns with eye glasses and with hat cocked on the side of his head, who talks loud and takes up all the sidewalk." Butler argued that the cry against Negro domination had been aimed at blacks' holding office rather than at their right to vote, and hence he had urged Democratic legislators to support an amendment that would deny black people the right to hold office, an amendment, he said, that would be clearly constitutional. The Democrats had refused, even though under the suffrage amendment that they proposed, the Negro might still hold office. Clearly, he said, the "Negro-howling" Democratic machine is "preserving the race issue for use in future campaigns." Butler pointed out that the grandfather clause, even if declared constitutional, would expire in 1908. How many boys are there, he asked, "who are twelve years of age and under, who are just beginning to be able to help their poverty-stricken fathers and mothers in farm or factory"? These boys, he said, because they had not been able to go to school, were sure to be disfranchised and "put on a plane lower than the town darky."[24]

Butler insisted that only Democratic lawyers "who are backing the Simmons Red Shirt Machine" were willing to support the amendment's constitutionality. Most constitutional lawyers, he asserted, considered the grandfather clause unconstitutional. The only question was whether the whole amendment would fall with the grandfather clause. If the grandfather clause should fall, he calculated, "the result will be to disfranchise fifty to sixty thousand white voters of the state, many of them old men and Confederate soldiers, many of them too old to start to school . . . while the town negro . . . would still vote." Butler, in short, became convinced that the Democrats had designed the amendment as a political device to gain power and retain it.[25]

The campaign that followed was a confused mixture of organiza-

24. Marion Butler to George Wilcox, January 1, 1900, in Raleigh *Caucasian*, January 4, 1900.
25. Thurman Sutton to Marion Butler, January 30, 1900, in Butler Papers. See also Raleigh *Caucasian*, February 22, April 26, 1900; Butler to Wilcox, January 1, 1900, in Raleigh *Caucasian*, January 4, 1900.

tional politics, emotional outbursts, intimidation, corruption, and pageantry. Although national issues, such as free silver and overseas expansion, and state issues, such as the regulation of railroads and of corporations and support for education, were occasionally discussed, the focus was on the amendment and the gubernatorial election. By the time the Democratic convention met on April 10, 1900, the party had found its folk hero in Charles B. Aycock, and it nominated him for governor amid "wild scenes of enthusiasm." Delegates to this convention shouted themselves almost speechless at his appearance.[26]

Recognizing that opponents were arguing persuasively that the amendment was unconstitutional, Simmons and the Democratic leadership attempted to turn the attention of the electorate away from that question and toward the amendment's desirability. As the campaign wore on, however, the fusionists seemed to have increasing success in convincing some voters that at least the grandfather clause was unconstitutional and that the United States Supreme Court would strike down that section of the amendment, leaving those sections intact that would disfranchise all illiterate voters. Simmons, seeing the effectiveness of the argument in persuading illiterate whites to oppose the amendment, supported a move to rewrite the amendment to state that it should "be taken as a whole" and that, if any section of it should be declared invalid, the entire amendment would fall. The General Assembly was called into session, and the revision of the amendment was approved by the assembly and by the Democratic caucus on June 11. Although the Raleigh *Caucasian* laughed at these actions, fusion leaders feared that the change might gain support for the amendment among illiterate whites.[27]

Voters went to the polls on August 2. Aycock won impressively, 186,650 votes to 126,296, and so did the amendment, which voters ratified, 182,217 to 128,285. Republican spokesmen quickly asserted,

26. Oliver H. Orr, Jr., *Charles Brantley Aycock* (Chapel Hill: University of North Carolina Press, 1961), 144, 156–60, 165–68; Charlotte *Observer*, March 31, June 26, 23, 1900; New Bern *Democrat*, April 20, 1900; Raleigh *News and Observer*, June 28, 30, 1900; Prather, *Resurgent Politics and Educational Progressivism*, 191.

27. Raleigh *News and Observer*, January 11, 1900; Rippy (ed.), *F. M. Simmons*, 28; Charlotte *Observer*, February 2, 1900. Both Judge George H. Brown and Simmons claimed the "paternity" of the revised amendment. Raleigh *Caucasian*, February 8, 1900. The Raleigh *Progressive Farmer*, July 24, 1900, argued that there was "danger of the elimination of the grandfather clause, leaving in force an educational test for whites and blacks alike."

however, that Democratic boasting that North Carolina had gone for "white government" by a majority of fifty thousand to sixty thousand votes was an oversimplification. The Asheville *Gazette* averred that though Simmons claimed substantial success in the west, the twenty-nine counties farthest west actually gave a majority of 4,190 against the amendment, and the large majorities for the amendment, strangely enough, came from the eastern counties where black voters, who had presumably voted against the amendment, were most numerous. Indeed, votes against the amendment in the east had been few, probably because of massive fraud and ballot-box stuffing.[28]

In spite of the rumblings of the fusionists, Simmons was jubilant. All in all, he concluded, Aycock's campaign was "the most wonderful ever made in the state." Simmons could feel a sense of satisfaction, for both friend and foe gave him much of the credit for the victory. "What leader can compare to him," the hostile Asheville *Gazette* editorialized sarcastically, "who led to victory . . . the black hosts and white, and marshalled under negro poll holders the votes of republicans and populists and democrats in one grand array of democratic majorities." According to his friends, who considered him "the most efficient organizer the state has ever known . . . and a man of the highest personal character," no political reward was too great.[29]

Simmons decided to apply for the reward of United States senator, an office that he considered to be the "acme of a Southern man's ambition."[30] In 1900 the Democratic nominee for United States senator was to be chosen in North Carolina's first statewide primary, which was to be held simultaneously with the presidential election.[31] By the

28. Crow and Durden, *Maverick Republican*, 156; Wilmington *Messenger*, August 5, 1900; Asheville *Gazette*, August 26, 1900. Statistical sources on the extent of fraud vary. See Anderson, *Race and Politics in North Carolina*, 4–5, 306–307; J. Wiley Shook to Editor, Asheville *Gazette*, August 28, September 13, 1900.

29. Wilmington *Messenger*, August 9, 1900; Asheville *Gazette*, September 21, 1900; statement of Judge Womack to the Raleigh *Post*, quoted in *Webster's Weekly* (Reidsville, N.C.), September 13, 1900. For numerous letters reiterating Womack's views, see Raleigh *News and Observer*, October 14, 1900.

30. Raleigh *News and Observer*, January 24, 1901.

31. The origins of the movement for this primary in North Carolina are obscure, but it was supported by the more populistic elements in the Democratic party. See Grantham, *Southern Progressivism*, 119–21; Raleigh *News and Observer*, December 12, 1899, April 13, 1900; Charlotte *Observer*, October 4, 1900; Daniels, *Editor in Politics*, 365; Josephus Daniels to H. G. Connor, January 16, 1900, in H. G. Connor Papers, Southern Historical Collection, University of North Carolina, Chapel Hill.

time the amendment was ratified in August, 1900, three other distinguished Democrats had announced that they would be available for
the office: Alfred M. Waddell, mayor of Wilmington, former congressman, Civil War veteran, and hero of the Wilmington coup d'etat
in 1898, who had threatened black people with death if they should
vote in 1900; the highly respected Thomas J. Jarvis, a former governor
who had succeeded Vance as senator; and Julian S. Carr, Confederate
veteran and wealthy Durham industrialist and philanthropist. All four
of these candidates, as good party men, agreed not to jeopardize the
passage of the amendment by launching potentially divisive senatorial
campaigns before the amendment had passed.[32]

With the amendment approved, however, the candidates were off
and running, and before long the fears of the critics seemed to be
coming true. "Fellow party members are flying at each other's throats,"
chortled the Charlotte *Observer*, which had opposed the primary. And a
pleased Populist commented that he felt like "saying to all our people:
'hush, be still and do not disturb the kil-kinney cat-fight.'" By mid-
October the contest had become too hot for Jarvis and Waddell, and the
primary, for the last month, became a bitter battle between Simmons
and Carr.[33]

Simmons, in the meantime, had been assuming the posture of the
loyal party worker. He promised that, as chairman of the state executive committee, he would not let his personal ambitions interfere with
his obligations to William Jennings Bryan and the national campaign.
Throughout the campaign, moreover, he never mentioned the name of
his opponent and professed to be concentrating only on national issues rather than his own election. His critics would have none of this.
"Away with such hypocrisy!" complained John Webster, editor of a
Reidsville weekly. "Does not every sensible man . . . know that
Mr. Simmons is making a campaign ostensibly for the ticket but in
reality for himself? . . . Mr. Simmons is going about the State to exhibit

32. Raleigh *News and Observer*, October 18, 1899; Orr, *Charles Brantley Aycock*, 368;
Wilmington *Messenger*, September 11, October 13, 16, 1900; Rippy (ed.), *F. M. Simmons*,
30; Wilmington *Messenger*, September 19, October 17, 1900; Raleigh *News and Observer*,
September 25, 1900; Simmons to Editor of the Asheville *Citizen*, in Raleigh *News and
Observer*, October 17, 1899; Daniels, *Editor in Politics*, 333–34.

33. [A. S. Peace?] to Butler, 1900, Box 13, Folder 115S, in Butler Papers; Raleigh *News
and Observer*, October 25, 1900; Raleigh *Caucasian*, November 1, 1900; Raleigh *News and
Observer*, October 2, 13, 23, 1900.

himself and incidentally to promote his own candidacy." Indeed, in the final three days of the campaign, Simmons traveled continuously, repeating essentially the same speech but making "many happy hits" with "fervent eloquence."[34]

In the last analysis, the campaign revolved around whether Simmons should be rewarded for the work that he had done for his party. His friends insisted that unless there were good reasons to the contrary, he should be so rewarded. Carr and his friends argued that Simmons had an unfair advantage because of his influence with the party machine, that the machine was corrupt, and that Simmons as chairman must be held responsible. Regardless, the results were decisive. While Bryan carried the state but lost in the nation, Simmons defeated Carr by a margin of about fifty-five thousand votes, and as the party had decided, the Democrats sent Simmons' nomination to the state legislature. The legislature, safely Democratic, elected him over the Republican nominee, Richmond Pearson, in January, 1901, by a straight party vote, thus launching a senatorial career of thirty years, a record for a North Carolinian.[35] The blacks had been disfranchised, and the principal actor had received his reward.

Historians have not come to the same conclusions about what motivated either the principal actors in the drama of disfranchisement or the 300,000 or so voters who divided their loyalties among the Democratic, Republican, and Populist parties between the years 1892 and 1900. Some historians have stressed the ideology of white supremacy.[36] Others have emphasized economic factors and in some

34. *Webster's Weekly* (Reidsville, N.C.), November 1, 1900; *Raleigh News and Observer*, November 4, 1900; Wilmington *Messenger*, November 2, 1900.

35. Raleigh *News and Observer*, November 7, 1900, January 22, 23, 24, 1901.

36. Favorably disposed toward the white-supremacy argument are Hamilton, *History of North Carolina Since 1860*; Samuel A. Ashe, *History of North Carolina* (2 vols.; Raleigh: Edwards and Broughton, 1908–25), II, 1205–1207, 1214; R. D. W. Connor, *North Carolina: Rebuilding an Ancient Commonwealth, 1584–1925* (4 vols., New York: American Historical Association, 1928–29); Archibald Henderson, *North Carolina: The Old North State and the New* (Chicago: Lewis Publishing Co., 1941). Sharing the emphasis upon the motivation of white supremacy but critical of it is Mabry, *The Negro in North Carolina Politics*. On the complexity of the concept of white supremacy in this context, see Guion Griffis Johnson, "The Ideology of White Supremacy, 1876–1910," in Fletcher Green (ed.), *Essays in Southern History Presented to J. G. de Roulhac Hamilton* (Chapel Hill: University of North Carolina Press, 1949), 31, 127–56; Paul M. Gaston, *The New South Creed: A Study in Southern Mythmaking* (New York: Alfred A. Knopf, 1970), 125, 132–33, 138; Lawrence J. Friedman, *The White Savage: Racial Fantasies in the Postbellum South* (Englewood Cliffs, N.J.: Prentice-

instances developed the idea that the era's conflicts were a modified form of the class struggle.[37] Still others have pointed to partisan rivalries and personal ambitions.[38] All of these factors were involved in the white-supremacy campaign of 1898 and in the disfranchisement campaign of 1900, and the safest approach would probably be to stop there. But the case of F. M. Simmons, a key actor in these events, is unique and deserves a separate treatment in depth.

Simmons was the principal campaigner for the Democrats in 1898 and 1900, and in spite of a successful law practice, he thought of the Democratic party, public service, and his family as his first loves. He knew all the tricks of the political trade, including ballot-box stuffing, disallowance of ballots, and intimidation. With regard to the election of 1898, he later recalled that as Marion Butler returned from Raleigh to his home in Sampson County, "he was met on the way by some of our boys who scared him . . . to death but did not harm him." Confessed Simmons: "I had sent them to do this." He would bend the truth for political purposes. The most notorious example of such prevarication was his assurance during the campaign of 1898 that the Democrats would not disfranchise any man, black or white. Then, as soon as the campaign was over, he threw his full support to the suffrage amendment, claiming that "the demands of the people overrode any promises made by individuals in the election."[39]

Hall, 1970), 98, 150; Joel Williamson, *The Crucible of Race: Black and White Relations in the American South Since Reconstruction* (New York: Oxford University Press, 1984). A careful, in-depth study is Robert H. Wooley, "Race and Politics: The Evolution of the White Supremacy Campaign of 1898 in North Carolina" (Ph.D. dissertation, University of North Carolina, 1977).

37. Helen G. Edmonds, *The Negro and Fusion Politics in North Carolina, 1894–1901* (Chapel Hill: University of North Carolina Press, 1951), 140–41, 151, 153, 187; Joseph F. Steelman, "The Progressive Era in North Carolina" (Ph.D. dissertation, University of North Carolina, 1955), 158, 212, 216–17. Recent debate on this interpretation is in Kousser, *The Shaping of Southern Politics;* Billings, *Planters and the Making of a "New South";* John W. Cell, *The Highest Stage of White Supremacy: The Origins of Segregation in South Africa and the American South* (New York: Cambridge University Press, 1982); Paul D. Escott, *Many Excellent People: Power and Privilege in North Carolina, 1850–1900* (Chapel Hill: University of North Carolina Press, 1985).

38. The political motivation is highlighted in a number of works emphasizing white supremacy, the possible disfranchisement of illiterate white Republicans, and the roles of individual prominent politicians. See, for example, Williamson, *The Crucible of Race,* 231; Prather, *Resurgent Politics and Educational Progressivism;* Orr, *Charles Brantley Aycock,* 56.

39. Rippy (ed.), *F. M. Simmons,* 46; Raleigh *News and Observer,* September 24, 25, 1898; Rippy (ed.), *F. M. Simmons,* 25; Democratic Executive Committee of North Carolina, *Democratic Handbook* (1900), 4–5.

Although he denied that he was responsible for the amendment, there was little question whom the Republicans and Populists considered responsible. "The breaking of such a pledge," editorialized the *Caucasian*, "was sufficient ground for repudiating Simmons and his red-shirt-ballot-box-stuffing machine." Thirty years after this campaign, one observer thought back and complimented Simmons on having "put the nigger out of politics in North Carolina by passing a constitutional amendment." Indeed, Populists and Republicans, in the emotional atmosphere of the campaign, tended to credit Simmons for almost everything that happened. They talked about Simmons' role and the Simmons machine; they claimed that Simmons would "blackmail every business in the state, promising legislation in return for campaign funds." He was told that he had "ever been a thorn in the side of good government and decency," and in western North Carolina, children were taught to utter his name in horror. He was accused of working "on the passions and prejudices of people" and riding "into office on the back of the poor negro for the last twenty-five years." He was blamed for organizing "his red shirt brigades" and ordering them "to frighten and intimidate voters, and prevent them from registering and . . . voting." Simmons was not insensitive to such accusations and sometimes took as much as an hour of a two-and-a-half-hour speech to defend himself against what he described as vilification and slander.[40]

How much of this give-and-take was simply a part of the game of politics it is impossible to say, but there was no question that Simmons was largely responsible for what the fusionists called "the Simmons Election Law" of 1899 and that Simmons and the Democratic election officials made skillful use of that law in 1900 to disfranchise those blacks who might have voted against the amendment designed to eliminate their political presence. The Democrats, to be sure, staunchly defended the enactment as a means of preventing convicts and wandering or deliberately imported Negroes from voting. Daniels claimed that

40. Raleigh *Caucasian*, March 29, January 25, February 22, April 26, 1900; George E. Jones to Simmons, February 20, 1930, in Furnifold M. Simmons Papers, Manuscript Department, Duke University Library, Durham, N.C.; J. F. Newell to Butler, February 21, 1900, in Butler Papers; Charles A. Jonas to Simmons, June 12, 1900, in Raleigh *Caucasian*, June 21, 1900; Raleigh *Caucasian*, July 26, 1900; Asheville *Gazette*, July 10, 1900; Thomas B. Fowler to Simmons, June 4, 1900, in Winston *Union-Republican*, July 5, 1900; Charlotte *Observer*, May 27, 1900; Winston *Union-Republican*, May 31, 1900.

at least ten thousand such illegal votes were cast in 1896—enough to elect Russell governor. Each side argued interminably over which election law—the fusionist or the Democratic—was the fairer.[41]

It is important to realize that politics may well have been the greatest of games for many nineteenth-century Americans, that Simmons was a professional playing that game, and that winning was important—by legal means preferably, but by force or fraud if necessary. Most Americans, particularly in the South, lived in rural areas, without benefit of the sports and theater available in the metropolitan areas. Before the days of radio, television, good roads, and automobiles, isolation was a fact of life for most North Carolinians. By the late 1890s, it is true, rural free delivery was beginning to bring mail to these isolated places. However, since almost 20 percent of the whites and more than 50 percent of the blacks had had little if any schooling and since many of those with some schooling were nevertheless illiterate, it is obvious that newspapers and periodicals had few subscribers in rural North Carolina.[42]

Although meticulous organization of every precinct, rural and urban, was undoubtedly the key to Simmons' success in electioneering, he always included in his planning large doses of picnic and spectator sport. In 1898, for example, aware of the differences still dividing the Democrats and of the pessimism resulting from the losses of 1894 and 1896, he planned a series of galas for August 3. These rallies were designed to clear up the "estrangements" and to restore "the state to the rule of intelligence, virtue, and decency." An estimated twenty thousand people attended these meetings. They listened to town bands and to speakers—two or three speeches in the morning, two or three in the afternoon until "the evening shadows fall." On October 21 between three thousand and four thousand people gathered at Fayetteville, traveling "from the swamps of Beaver Dam to the sandhills of Quewhipple and Little River" in the "old family carryall, the farm wagon and the two-seated go cart." Trains brought delegations from Wilmington and other towns, detachments of Confederate veterans, and the Wilmington Cornet Band, which played at stations along the way. In Fayetteville the procession marched to the fairground

41. Raleigh *News and Observer*, August 6, 1898; Raleigh *Caucasian*, August 11, 1898.
42. Kousser, *The Shaping of Southern Politics*, 55.

at noon, led by the band, which was followed by a "scarlet brigade" of hundreds of red-shirted horsemen waiting in column to escort an ornate float containing sixteen pretty girls. The exercises were opened by "a fervent prayer to God . . . followed by a union choir's stirring rendition of the state anthem, 'Carolina! Carolina!'" Then, "with throbbing hearts," men and women joined in singing "The Old North State." In late afternoon "the hospitable doors of the fair building were thrown open and the toothsome refreshment of the barbecued pig, the roast of beef, chickens and hams, and all the other good things" were provided to the assembled hundreds.[43]

Some of these rallies were designed as public debates. Future governors Robert Glenn and Charles Aycock emerged as Democratic champions. Marion Butler and Cyrus Thompson defended the Populist side, while Republican spokesmen included two distinguished blacks, John C. Dancy, collector of customs at Wilmington, and James H. Young, a state legislator from Raleigh. (Blacks, however, rarely if ever participated in direct debates with white politicians.) The partisan press usually attempted to declare victory in these encounters. In an Aycock-Thompson debate at Concord on September 12, 1898, for example, the *Caucasian* reported that "when the smoke of battle cleared away it was a study to observe the faces of local Democratic leaders. Never since the people of Washington rode down in their carriages to observe the flight of the Confederates at Bull Run has there been anything approaching the spectacle presented by the Cabarrus Democrats." Aycock, in other words, was only to be pitied. On the other hand, when the same two speakers met at Goldsboro ten days later, the *News and Observer* told a different story: "Dr. Cyrus Thompson, the Napoleon of fusion, is no doubt today hearing the lashing of the waves that break on the shores of his political St. Helena." At this meeting apparently Thompson had met his Waterloo.[44]

Celebrations of final victory in these games were even more dramatic. They were held throughout the state, but Josephus Daniels and others planned one to take place in Raleigh on November 15, 1898, the

43. Charlotte *Observer*, July 20, 1898; Raleigh *News and Observer*, August 4, 1898; Wilmington *Messenger*, October 22, 1898; Charlotte *Observer*, October 22, 1898; Wooley, "Race and Politics," 271–72, 280.

44. Raleigh *Caucasian*, September 22, 1898; Raleigh *News and Observer*, September 24, 1898. For a comprehensive coverage of such "speakings," see Prather, *Insurgent Politics and Educational Progressivism*, 147–50.

like of which the city had "never witnessed before." Two thousand torches and five hundred barrels of tar were prepared to illuminate the principal streets; "a mile or more of transparencies" were readied; the fireworks included "one thousand of the biggest bombs that can be made; one thousand of the biggest sky rockets and one thousand roman candles shooting fifty times each." Railroads provided lower rates, as they usually did for special occasions. From 7 P.M. to midnight, thousands of people moved on foot, on horseback, on bicycles, and in carriages. Noise was so great from bands, tinhorns, and shouting Democrats carrying brooms, pitchforks, banners, torchlights, and transparencies that it was impossible to hear some of the speeches. Simmons received an ovation that "rose above the boom of the explosives and the strains of the bands."[45]

Simmons felt even more triumphant after the ratification of the amendment and the election of Aycock in 1900. "Never before in any campaign in the history of the State has so much literature been distributed," he claimed—some five million documents and papers had gone out. In addition to the daily correspondence, "which was the largest ever known," seventy-five thousand personal letters were mailed "from headquarters directly to the voters." This literature was designed to provide background for the speakings from the stump that would begin in June. Simmons recalled that earlier in the year the speakings had been "desultory," but starting in June, "people flocked to our meetings." He also claimed that "a notable feature" had been the number and interest of ladies attending. "They came to our meetings," he assured his party members, "with the full consent of their fathers and husbands and brothers, because the questions involved in the campaign touched the home and fireside."[46]

The triumphant Simmons piled on the superlatives. The Democratic convention had been enthusiastic over the nomination not only of Aycock but of the entire state ticket. Indeed, the ticket, from the candidate for lieutenant governor to the candidate for attorney general, was a strong one, consisting of two lawyers, a prosperous tobacco farmer hostile to the tobacco trusts, a member of the Brotherhood of Locomotive Engineers, a physician, and a railroad employee. Recognizing

45. Raleigh *News and Observer*, November 11, 16, 1898. A colorful account is in Prather, *Resurgent Politics and Educational Progressivism*, 167–68.

46. Interview with Simmons, Raleigh *News and Observer*, August 7, 1900.

the collective abilities of the Democratic candidates, Simmons and Aycock agreed on a probably unprecedented tactic. All candidates would go on the campaign trail together and speak from the same platform. The ticket blanketed the state with speeches (well over a hundred of them), traveling, according to the *News and Observer,* four thousand miles by train and more than one thousand by buggy. Aycock was usually the star. At least seventy-five thousand persons heard him. His initial speech included a pledge to improve education, but then he began to emphasize white supremacy and Negro disfranchisement. Later in the campaign, when Simmons recognized that the equally vigorous arguments of Marion Butler were convincing illiterate whites that they might be disfranchised, Aycock campaigned for improving education and wiping out illiteracy in an attempt to quiet the fears of illiterate parents that their children were also doomed. Aycock's mystique was magnified by his usual entourage: hundreds of armed men on horseback wearing red shirts, women dressed in pure white, and men, women, and children in bicycle brigades accompanied by marching bands from nearby towns. "Never before in North Carolina has such an army of great campaign orators appeared before the stump," Simmons declared, "and never before were such crowds assembled in the State to hear political speeches." He estimated that at the end of the campaign "a thousand speeches were being made in the State daily."[47]

The game that was being played, while it provided entertainment for the faithful, had a deadly serious intent when the Democrats confronted the Republican enemy. To the Democrat of the 1890s, the Republicans had been responsible for the "horrors" of Reconstruction. A later generation of Democrats considered the Democratic triumph of 1876 a victory for "peace, order . . . good government," and "righteousness."[48] Fusionist success in 1894, according to the Democrats, launched another period of "extravagance and corruption." The fusionists made changes in election procedures, which even though fairer than the Democratic system, were undoubtedly designed to protect Republican majorities in the western counties and to protect black

47. *Ibid.*
48. Hamilton, *History of North Carolina Since 1860,* 194; Democratic Executive Committee of North Carolina, *Democratic Handbook* (1900), 7–8.

Republican voters in the east so that, combined with white Republicans and perhaps white Populists, Negro Republicans could gain control of county and city governments in the east.

Fusion successes in the east, which did put an unprecedented number of black people into office, convinced the Democratic leadership that they had to resort to an old ploy to restore their party's supremacy, which was under threat because a substantial number of voters were being lured away by the People's party. In 1896, for example, there were 175,216 Democratic votes for president and 155,446 Republican votes. But for governor, there were only 145,266 Democratic votes, as opposed to 153,787 Republican votes and 50,302 Populist votes. About 75,000 of these Republican voters were black.[49] Since the Republican party was so dependent upon black voters, an obvious Democratic prescription was to call for white unity against "black domination." The Democrats had followed such a strategy before, and the Populists in 1898 feared that the Democrats would again "launch the hypocritical negro crusade" and thus "seduce the Populists to come back to the Democratic party." This junction of white voters would then capture the legislature, which, Judge Thomas H. Sutton warned Butler, would pass some kind of educational qualification for voting that would secure Democratic supremacy.[50]

By mid-1897, the Democrats were admitting that white supremacy would be their rallying cry, but they refused to acknowledge that the theme was racist. "The paramount issue everywhere and at all times," preached the *News and Observer* "is good government[;] white supremacy is but the synonym in this state for good government." In other words, fusion between Populists and black and white Republicans had led to Negro "radicalism," and now there was a need for white unity to combat bad government. "The fight here," wrote Alfred Moore Waddell of Wilmington, "is one between barbarism and civilization—between white men and Negroes manipulated by unprincipled demagogues." The highly respected A. J. McKelway, editor of the

49. Matthews (ed.), *North Carolina Votes*, 6, 111; Mabry, *The Negro in North Carolina*, 15. I have used Kousser's estimate of the percentage of Republican voters who were black to calculate the number in 1896. See *Twelfth Census, 1900: Population*, Vol. I, Pt. 1, p. 992; Kousser, *The Shaping of Southern Politics*, 183.

50. T. H. Sutton to Marion Butler, January 31, 1898, R. B. Davis to Butler, March 7, 1898, in Butler Papers. See also Raleigh *Progressive Farmer*, August 30, 1898.

Presbyterian Standard, also developed the themes of Negro domination and bad government in a widely read article in the *Independent.*[51] For its part, the Democratic state executive committee, at its meeting in December, 1897, called for "honest white people" to end "corrupt, incompetent, and scandalous rule" in North Carolina, and these sentiments were written into the Democratic platform in May, 1898.[52]

The same kind of political motivation—whereby white people would combine to defeat the Negro-dominated Republican party— was undoubtedly at work in the Democratic push for the constitutional amendment. Marion Butler, an astute though not an unbiased witness, decided reluctantly to oppose the amendment almost entirely on political grounds. The amendment, he insisted, was a means used by the "Ransom-Simmons Democratic machine" to keep itself in power. This machine, claimed Butler, had deluded the people for thirty years by obscuring the economic issues and "riding the negro scarecrow into office." Indeed, Butler made the motivation even more conspiratorial. As Butler saw it, Simmons knew that he had won out by only a few votes over the followers of Zebulon Vance—that is, those Democrats oriented toward the Populists—in the last Democratic convention. So, Butler hypothesized, since the poor and illiterate were largely the followers of Vance, Simmons would disfranchise them in order to secure his power in the party. Then, through the election law, he could control the ballot boxes and thus in effect disfranchise the Populists who could read. With blacks, illiterate whites, and Populists taken care of, he could perpetuate his machine's control in the state.[53]

Looking at the South as a whole, Kousser has pointed out that "direct Democratic assertions of the partisan purposes of restriction were somewhat rare," but he also found that "the indirect evidence of partisan interest is overwhelming." He showed that legislative action on

51. Raleigh *News and Observer,* July 13, 14, August 12, 20, September 18, 1897; Wilmington *Messenger,* September 11, 1898; A. M. Waddell to James K. Jones, April 20, 1898, in Wilmington *Messenger,* April 25, 1898; A. J. McKelway, "The North Carolina Suffrage Movement," *Independent,* LII (1900), 1955–57. See also Wilmington *Messenger,* May 17, 1898; Raleigh *News and Observer,* April 20, 1898.

52. Raleigh *News and Observer,* February 23, March 20, 1898; Democratic Executive Committee of North Carolina, *Democratic Handbook* (1898), 188–90; Democratic Executive Committee of North Carolina, *Democratic Handbook* (1900), 8–9.

53. Marion Butler to George Wilcox, January 1, 1900, in Raleigh *Caucasian,* January 4, 1900.

disfranchisement was highly partisan: In North Carolina the Democratic caucus put the amendment in its final form, and the final tally in the legislature that formulated the amendment showed the Republicans unanimously opposed and the Democrats overwhelmingly in favor. The "Simmons Election Law" of 1899 was approved by an equally partisan vote and was worded in such a way that the predominantly Democratic legislature could manipulate elections in predominantly Republican counties.[54]

Partisanship was stimulated by the fact that victory meant jobs to some and the loss of jobs to others. Simmons, it will be recalled, received as his reward for chairing the Democratic state executive committee in 1892 the federal appointment as commissioner of internal revenue for the Fourth District of North Carolina. That job paid from $3,500 to $6,000 per year and gave him considerable power through his right to appoint deputy collectors and workers in the distilleries. There were many other federal workers—postmasters and mailmen, census takers, marshals and deputy marshals, tax collectors and deputy tax collectors, and, in the customshouses, collectors, storekeepers, and gaugers. On the state and local level, there was also a great variety of jobs: state printers, fertilizer inspectors, and magistrates, and jobs in the prisons, the asylums, and institutions for the deaf, dumb, and blind. All these jobs were available to worthy Democrats when there were Democratic victories in state or nation.[55]

Although partisanship was certainly an important factor in the white-supremacy campaigns, any extensive analysis of such partisanship inevitably leads to the question of class. The Republicans and Populists were certainly convinced, for example, that the white-supremacy rhetoric in 1898 was merely a cloak to defeat the Populists. "A vote for the 'Democratic Negro calamity howling machine,'" warned the *Caucasian* just before the election of 1898, "is a vote to turn the legislature over to railroads and monopolies." Alfred Eugene Holton, chairman of the Republican state committee, in assessing the defeat of

54. Kousser, *The Shaping of Southern Politics*, 258–59; Raleigh *News and Observer*, February 18, 1899; Hamilton, *History of North Carolina Since 1860*, 299–300.

55. Raleigh *News and Observer*, June 20, November 25, 1893, March 15, 1896; U.S. Department of the Treasury, Office of Internal Revenue, *Reports of the Commissioner of Internal Revenue*, 1894–95.

the Republicans in 1898, declared that bankers, businessmen, and railway interests alienated by the fiscal program of the fusion legislature
had poured unlimited funds into the campaign to defeat the fusionists
behind the unifying creed of white supremacy.[56]

On the matter of disfranchisement, the fusionists were equally convinced that the Democrats planned to disfranchise both Negroes and
illiterate whites. Democrats knew, according to the fusionist argument, that the Supreme Court would declare the grandfather clause
unconstitutional while leaving the disfranchisement clause in effect; or
if, as the legislation finally read, the grandfather clause and the disfranchisement clause must stand or fall together, other provisions of
the amendment, such as the poll tax, would effectively disfranchise the
illiterate and the poor. Moreover, since after 1908 the literacy test
would apply to everyone, how, they asked, could a thirteen-year-old
son of an illiterate in 1901 who must work to support his family be
expected to learn to read by 1909?[57]

The accusations of the Republicans and Populists ignored the underlying differences within the Democratic party. The Farmers' Alliance
had attracted rural members of that party, and not all of those so
influenced had either deserted the Democrats or joined the Populists.
Those Alliancemen and their sympathizers who remained formed the
nucleus of Democrats who were enthusiastic for Bryan and Bryan's
platform, particularly that section that demanded the coinage of silver
at the ratio of 16 to 1. These Democrats were not unsympathetic to
cooperating with the Populists, and they detested Grover Cleveland.
W. H. ("Buck") Kitchin put it succinctly: "I would prefer the Devil
himself for President to Cleveland, provided he was not a Republican."
In 1898 a substantial element in the Democratic party probably favored
fusing with the Populists when Marion Butler invited them to do so.
The platform committee of the Democratic party turned fusion down
by a vote of six to three. Josephus Daniels claimed to have fought

56. Raleigh *Caucasian*, October 27, November 3, 1898; Raleigh *Progressive Farmer*,
October 25, 1898; A. E. Holton and Cyrus Thompson to the People of North Carolina,
October 25, 1898, in Thompson Papers; D. M. Hobbs to Butler, November 10, 1898, George
Jones to Butler, December 10, 1898, in Butler Papers; Charlotte *Observer*, November 19,
1898.

57. Letter from "Mr. X" of Stokes County, Winston *Union-Republican*, June 22, 1899.
See also Winston *Union-Republican*, July 6, 13, October 26, 1899; Butler to J. S. Mitchell,
November 15, 1898, in Butler Papers.

"heroically" for fusion, and he might have won had it not been for the personal hostility to Butler among the Democrats.[58]

Tension among Democrats over this episode nearly tore the party apart. W. H. Kitchin considered Butler "devoid of principle, honor, or manhood," yet he favored cooperation with the Populists under the banner of silver and flagellated himself for not having fought for his principles more vigorously on the floor of the state Democratic convention of 1900. He believed that the convention had sold out to the "gold bugs." From his point of view, the villains were the Raleigh *Morning Post*, closely associated with the Southern Railway and A. B. Andrews, the Southern's vice president; the Charlotte *Observer* and its able editor, Joseph P. Caldwell; and Senator Matt Ransom and Ransom's henchmen. Kitchin believed that they had co-opted the Democratic party by "nefarious, treasonable plans to destroy the silver forces in favor of the corporation and money aristocracy."[59]

The silver forces were upset by the unwillingness to fuse, and Simmons' appointment as chairman made it worse because some considered him Matt Ransom's henchman. As Kitchin saw it, Simmons' election "sent a thrill of joy in the hearts of all gold bugs." Simmons, Kitchin wrote confidentially to his son, "is the tool of Andrews, Ransom and Company." So great was the despair of the silver Democrats, warned Kitchin, that they might either stay at home on election day or vote for the Populists. Joseph Steelman, after extensive research into these internal controversies of the Democratic party, concluded, as had the Populists, that "economic factors outweighed the race issue" and that "the race issue was not of paramount importance" in 1898.[60]

One piece of evidence that has been used to show that economic factors were involved is a deal made by Simmons in 1898 with the railroad interests. He promised that, if the Democrats controlled the

58. W. H. Kitchin to Z. B. Vance, [December, 1887], quoted in Anderson, *Race and Politics in North Carolina*, 194; James A. Lockhart, Sr., to Josephus Daniels, May 28, 1898, in Raleigh *News and Observer*, May 31, 1898. Those for fusion were Daniels, W. W. Kitchin, and R. A. Doughton. Daniels, *Editor in Politics*, 566; Raleigh *News and Observer*, May 27, 1898. Helen Edmonds questions whether Daniels was sincere and suggests that he favored making a counterproposal to the Populists so objectionable that they would refuse it. Edmonds, *The Negro and Fusion Politics*, 137.

59. W. H. Kitchin to W. W. Kitchin, two undated letters apparently written after the Democratic state convention in 1898, in Folder 4018, W. H. Kitchin Papers, Southern Historical Collection, University of North Carolina, Chapel Hill.

60. *Ibid.* Steelman cites newspapers and letters of Walter Clark, associate justice of the state supreme court. Steelman, "The Progressive Era in North Carolina," 158–65.

next legislature, railway taxes would not be increased during the next biennium. Apparently the promise worked because he later said that from "the Corporate leaders and from various Democrats of moderate means, I obtained all the campaign funds I needed." Indeed, most industrialists and businessmen undoubtedly favored the Democrats. Toward the end of the campaign, however, Simmons felt less secure. He wrote to Matt Ransom that he had "had much trouble" in getting financial support to carry on the campaign, and that he was "in need of funds." Moreover, after the campaign, having relied on contributions that he did not get, Simmons found that he was personally a thousand dollars in debt and called on friends to help him out. It appears that business interests were subsequently unhappy about the Democratic legislature's actions in 1899, and so they did not come through as generously in 1900. At the same time, of course, Populists and Republicans were also making plays for business support.[61]

Simmons' deal with the railroads in 1898 may show that economic interests were at stake, but it does not show that they were the motivating factor. There was no foreordained process or pattern in this story. Simmons, a very practical man, had decided that the Democrats needed business and industrial votes and financial support to turn out the "rascals" who were in power. He made a deal, which he later had difficulty in defending, to get that support, and business elements, clearly unhappy with what the fusionists had done and fearful of what they might do, cooperated when and to what extent the spirit moved them.[62]

Class divisions in the Democratic party also played a role among the motives behind the disfranchising amendment. There is some evi-

61. Rippy (ed.), *F. M. Simmons*, 23, 29; Escott, *Many Excellent People*, 258–59; Simmons to Matt Ransom, October 26, November 3, 1898, in Matt W. Ransom Papers, Southern Historical Collection, University of North Carolina, Chapel Hill; Orr, *Charles Brantley Aycock*, 161–62.

62. Rippy (ed.), *F. M. Simmons*, 29. Simmons was accused of lobbying on the floor of the state senate for favorable tax rates for the railroads. He denied that he was a paid agent of the Southern and insisted that his "conferences" with legislators were efforts as chairman of the Democratic state committee to obtain campaign pledges. He pointed out that he had appeared as counsel against the Southern Railway on numerous occasions. *Webster's Weekly* (Reidsville, N.C.), September 20, October 18, 1900; Simmons to W. R. Allen, in Charlotte *Observer*, September 18, 1900; Raleigh *Caucasian*, September 27, 1900; *Webster's Weekly* (Reidsville, N.C.), October 4, 1900; Broadside, W. R. Allen to Editor, in *Webster's Weekly*, October 10, 18, 1900.

dence that the purpose was to disfranchise poor and illiterate whites as well as black people. A widely cited editorial from the Charlotte *Observer*, a paper so ardently for Cleveland that its editor, Joseph Caldwell, announced after Bryan's nomination that it would support McKinley, described the campaign as an effort on the part of "the white people of North Carolina to rid themselves of the danger of the rule of negroes and the lower class of whites." Moreover, the fact that the Simmons election law of 1899 put the Democratic legislature in control of state elections not only in black counties but also in predominantly Republican counties that were relatively poor suggests that more than disfranchising black people was involved.[63]

Precise motives, however, are not clear. If Joseph Caldwell or A. B. Andrews or other "Gold Democrats" had written the amendment, that would probably be incontrovertible evidence of a class struggle. But since Daniels, Aycock, Simmons, and the Kitchins—Black Belt Democrats—had a hand in it, the motivation might seem logically to have been political—to disfranchise the Republicans who happened to be poor.

It is not at all certain, however, that Democrats of their persuasion wished to disfranchise any whites. Although Aycock's conversion into a crusader for education may have come later in the campaign, his reiterated pledge not to disfranchise white voters had a growing note of sincerity and conviction in it. Simmons' position was more ambivalent. Although some liberal members of the party, such as the Kitchins and John Webster, editor of the outspoken *Webster's Weekly*, distrusted him, he was the premier party man. He came out for silver, perhaps somewhat belatedly, in 1896 and fought loyally for Bryan in 1900. There is but slim direct evidence that he wanted to disfranchise white voters because of their economic or social class, but knowledge of Simmons' political views and methods might be used as indirect evidence to suggest that he would have been extremely happy to disfranchise white Republicans. The contrary evidence at the time was his speeches and interviews, which consistently denied any intent to disfranchise whites. Indeed, in his speech to the Democratic convention in 1900, he called for unity of *all* whites in support of white supremacy

63. Steelman, "The Progressive Era in North Carolina," 215–16; Kousser, *The Shaping of Southern Politics*, 191; Edmonds, *The Negro and Fusion Politics*, 187.

but added that whites would not always stand together and that the mountain whites might continue to vote Republican. In a democracy, he concluded, such differences were a good thing.[64]

Perhaps the best evidence against the notion that class was the primary motive behind the amendment is the grandfather clause, even given its expiration date of 1908. According to the law, all whites registered at the time of the amendment's ratification and all whites who registered as they came of age between that time and 1908 would be permanently registered. In those eight years, moreover, as Aycock saw it, the drive to educate all North Carolinians should have had its effect in reducing illiteracy. And as the campaign went on, emphasis was increasingly placed on the importance of the amendment in persuading people to learn to read.[65]

But finally, though personal ambition, political partisanship, and economic factors were involved in the white-supremacy campaigns, race was the umbrella under which the campaigns were run. White supremacy was an issue that served the frankly political goal of bringing prodigal Populists back into their Democratic home under a banner designed to unify all white people, and the concept of white supremacy was an offshoot of the racism that was epidemic in the country at that time. It appeared in the treatment of Native Americans and even more pervasively in fears that Anglo-Saxons in the United States would be overwhelmed by inferior immigrants from Asia and southern and eastern Europe. Indeed, the intellectual superiority of Anglo-Saxons was widely accepted even in distinguished universities, and that belief infiltrated the literature of eugenics and of immigration restriction. Southern white culture simply took Anglo-Saxon supremacy for granted, and North Carolina took particular pride in its Anglo-Saxonism.[66] "Anybody can get out of North Carolina," said

64. Edmonds, The Negro and Fusion Politics, 205; Prather, Resurgent Politics and Educational Progressivism, 191; Orr, Charles Brantley Aycock, 158, 171; Rippy (ed.), F. M. Simmons, 90–91.

65. Kousser argued that 1908 was politically the earliest possible date that the Democrats could have abandoned the grandfather clause. Kousser, The Shaping of Southern Politics, 192; Orr, Charles Brantley Aycock, 168–74; Hugh T. Lefler and Alfred Ray Newsome, North Carolina: The History of a Southern State (3rd ed.; Chapel Hill: University of North Carolina Press, 1973), 560; Anderson, Race and Politics in North Carolina, 296, n. 2; Prather, Resurgent Politics and Educational Progressivism, 190–91.

66. For a brief summary, see Glenn C. Altschuler, Race, Ethnicity, and Class in American Thought, 1865–1919 (Arlington Heights, Ill.: Harlan Davidson, Inc., 1982).

George Winston, president of the North Carolina Society of New York, "but it requires a great deal of talent and character to get into the State. Less than one half of one percent of our population is foreign born. . . . We are the purest-bred Anglo-Saxon Community on the globe." Josephus Daniels wrote: "The day is not come when the white people of North Carolina will permit the Colored man to rule over them. The Anglo-Saxon neck has never bended to such yoke." In 1898 the Wilmington *Messenger*, in urging support for the war against Spain, pointed out that Spaniards were not Anglo-Saxon.[67]

The "Negro problem," a respected public servant complained, would lead to "a most miserable and degraded civilization" caused by "the recession of the white and the development of the black." This change would have no "redeeming quality," he added, since that race is "vile, degraded, full of lust and lying."[68]

Historian Edward L. Ayers has suggested a complicated explanation for the intensification of racial distrust in the 1890s. A fundamental factor, he argued, was that "a new generation of blacks and whites faced each other across an ever-widening chasm." Unlike in the period of slavery, both races withdrew "into their own neighborhoods and churches." In the late 1880s and 1890s there was a serious economic depression leading to the loss of jobs and the increase of poverty, particularly black poverty. Even W. E. B. Du Bois charged that conditions and economic depression had resulted in "a class of black criminals, loafers, and n'er-do-wells" who roamed the countryside. Few though these unfortunates might be, Ayers suggested, they strengthened the stereotype of the bad Negro inspired by sexual lust. Even the most extreme statements, it should be noted, were made by men of intelligence, education, and social status and were frequently accompanied by assurances that "the white men—the true men of their noble race—are not hostile to the Negroes." Yet in the next breath they would say, "This putting Sambo and Sanky and Pompey in office is just what the white man will not have." As the Wilmington *Messenger* saw it, Booker T. Washington was right in stressing industrial education, but "Mr. Sambo had the ballot and the offices . . . too soon." The

67. Raleigh *News and Observer*, September 27, 1903, October 15, 1896, August 20, 1897, September 27, 1903; Wilmington *Messenger*, February 22, 1898. See also Williamson, *The Crucible of Race*, 119ff.
68. George Howard to Henry G. Connor, November 6, 1895, in Connor Papers.

Charlotte *Observer* expressed itself as being "fond of the colored race" but criticized blacks for being brash and boisterous and for taking charge when in a majority. Daniels once declared that he was "shamed and sickened" at the assassination of the family of a recently appointed Negro postmaster in South Carolina. The blame, he added, should not be upon the black but upon those who appointed him.[69]

Obviously the question of race relations was extremely sensitive in North Carolina. It had been held beneath the surface in the years of Democratic control. Even in 1896, campaigning stressed issues that were primarily economic or political. The fusion victory at home and the Republican victory in the nation, however, even worried white members of the coalition because they knew that blacks who had contributed to the victory would demand their rewards, and white fusionists feared that if blacks received offices, the results would be disastrous.[70]

Republican blacks did receive important appointments. Indeed, several hundred federal and local offices were filled by blacks. Although the Republicans seem to have exercised some care to see that blacks were not put in important executive positions, Congressman George White, the leading black officeholder, had seen to it that at least twenty black postmasters were appointed in the Second Congressional District. Simmons insisted that in New Hanover County there were forty black magistrates, fourteen black policemen, "a score" of black constables, and numerous deputies and other officials. He also listed sixteen black magistrates in Bertie County, thirty-one in Edgecombe, and twenty-nine in Halifax, and there were undoubtedly more in Warren and Northampton, where blacks were in the majority. There were black county commissioners in Craven, Warren, and Halifax counties. The *News and Observer* listed by name twenty-seven black magistrates, five deputy sheriffs, and twelve school committeemen in Craven County and five black policemen in the county seat of New Bern.

---

69. Edward L. Ayers, *Vengeance and Justice: Crime and Punishment in the Nineteenth-Century American South* (New York: Oxford University Press, 1984), 237–38, 241–44, 250–52; Wilmington *Messenger*, August 19, February 22, 1898; Charlotte *Observer*, August 26, 1898; Raleigh *News and Observer*, February 25, 1898.

70. A. J. Moye to Marion Butler, April 30, 1896, in Butler Papers; W. B. Fleming to Marion Butler, quoted in Anderson, *Race and Politics in North Carolina*, 240–41. Joel Williamson makes a particular point of the impact of Republican appointments. Williamson, *The Crucible of Race*, 191–92. See also Wooley, "Race and Politics," 206–13.

Halifax had twenty black school committeemen. These minor officials came in "close and daily contact" with whites, male and female, and created explosive resentment. Some of these black officeholders were well-educated lawyers, teachers, and preachers who filled their offices with distinction. Others were unqualified: some were corrupt or ignorant.[71]

The Democratic press delighted in accentuating the negative. The *News and Observer* quoted a man from New Bern who complained:

that we have twenty-seven ignorant, incompetent, and in most instances un-principled magistrates in Craven County . . . that we have not a single white deputy sheriff in Craven County . . . that the next treasurer from Craven County will be a negro bar-room keeper . . . that a white girl—and God has given them to us as sweet, as pure and as beautiful as ever stood in the twinkle of a star—cannot even for sweet sentiment obtain a license to marry . . . by one of her race . . . that the City attorney for New Bern is a negro . . . that five guardians of the homes and liberties of the people of New Bern are incompetent, ignorant, and, in most instances . . . corrupt negroes.

Former governor Thomas Jarvis claimed that there actually was "negro domination" in Greenville, since there were apparently four black and two white city councilmen.[72]

Such figures are difficult to verify, but in any event the accusation that office holding for blacks in North Carolina constituted Negro domination was ridiculous. Yet there were probably more Negro officeholders in North Carolina than anywhere else in the United States, and it is reasonably certain that the reaction would have been much the same in Massachusetts if blacks had held as large a percentage of offices there as they did in North Carolina.

71. Williamson, *The Crucible of Race*, 191–92; Prather, *Resurgent Politics and Educational Progressivism*, 110–15. Some out-of-state newspapers, such as the Washington *Post*, the Baltimore *Sun*, and the *Manufacturers' Record* (Baltimore), accepted the statistics on "Negro domination" quoted in the Raleigh *News and Observer*, September 15, November 4, 8, 1898. See also Thomas Jarvis to Cyrus Thompson, August 24, 1898, in Thompson Papers; Anderson, *Race and Politics in North Carolina*, 242, 245; Mabry, *The Negro in North Carolina*, 40.

72. Raleigh *News and Observer*, August 25, 1898. See also Raleigh *News and Observer*, December 3, 1897, March 18, 1898; letter from Bertie County, July 24, 1898, in Wilmington *Messenger*, August 11, 1898; Wilmington *Messenger*, August 12, 1898; Charlotte *Observer*, August 26, 1898; Atlanta *Constitution*, quoted in Charlotte *Observer*, August 30, 1898; Cyrus Thompson to Thomas Jarvis, August 23, 1898, Jarvis to Thompson, August 24, 1898, in Thompson Papers. James W. Pelham, a former Republican mayor of Greenville, insisted that Jarvis exaggerated the extent of Negro influence. Wooley, "Race and Politics," 314.

Rage at Negro office holding, moreover, was not limited to the Democratic party. The Populist constituents of Senator Marion Butler begged him to get rid of Negro appointees: From Rocky Mount came a plea to "relieve the people of the present management of the post-office." From Scotland Neck came the wail that there are "no places where the negro is so objectionable as in the post offices." And a Craven County Populist warned that his Populist friends were "qualing" under the affliction of "a surplus of negroes holding office and more negro candidates who are sure of election." Nonetheless both Republicans and Populists made numerous efforts to refute charges of "Negro domination."[73]

As the campaign of 1898 drew to a close, Simmons directed his campaigners to concentrate almost entirely on the issue of white supremacy. A highlight was a rally at Goldsboro on October 28 organized by Simmons, "the brave and manly general of North Carolina's white forces," to consider "the political and social conditions in the East." He arranged for special schedules and half fares for those traveling on the railroads to the rally, and thousands came, perhaps as many as ten thousand, on the trains, on horseback, in wagons, and in carriages. The goals of the meeting were to prove Negro domination in the east and to unite all white men regardless of party under the banner of white supremacy. In opening the meeting, Simmons recited a list of black officeholders and said that there were nearly a thousand of them in North Carolina. As chairman of the state Democratic organization, he "solemnly asserted that there is negro rule and domination in eastern North Carolina."

After the Reverend N. M. Jurney prayed "fervently and devoutly," Simmons scored a real coup in introducing Major William A. Guthrie of Durham and William E. Fountain of Tarboro. Guthrie had been the Populist candidate for governor in 1896 and still claimed to be a member of the Populist party, which, he asserted, boasted of its Anglo-

73. John R. Underwood to Butler, December 15, 1897, W. A. Dunn to Butler, March 16, 1898, G. L. Hardison to Butler, August 3, 1898, in Butler Papers; Thomas Jarvis to Cyrus Thompson, August 22, 1898, in Thompson Papers; Raleigh *News and Observer*, September 15, 1898; Wooley, "Race and Politics," 313–14. Helen Edmonds made a careful study of Negro office holding. She found that whites objected to it not because of the number of black officials, but because there were any at all. Edmonds, *The Negro and Fusion Politics*, 84, 94, 111–12, 121–23, 132. Eric Anderson pointed out that Edmonds underestimated the number of black officeholders. Anderson, *Race and Politics in North Carolina*, 247.

Saxon blood and denied membership to Negroes. He questioned whether there "was a good white man in North Carolina who loves his state, who loves his race, and who would desire to perpetuate Negro domination." Fountain, recent chairman of the Populist executive committee, confirmed Simmons' description of conditions in the east and assured his listeners that he was "ready to exert his best efforts in favor of white supremacy."[74]

The issue of white supremacy dominated the news columns and obscured more substantive issues. As the Republicans and Populists rather plaintively put it, "Every question of national or state importance has, by our opponents, been ignored or subordinated to their single issue." Even the Spanish-American War, declared in April, 1898, became involved with Anglo-Saxon supremacy by the demeaning of Spaniards, of Cubans, and of the conduct of black troops. Simmons persuaded Josiah W. Bailey, editor of the Raleigh *Biblical Recorder*, the leading Baptist journal in the state, to raise his editorial voice in favor of white supremacy. Bailey had been crusading for a four-month school term in the public schools and against state support for higher education. Simmons agreed to see that the legislature would appropriate funds for public schools but not increase support for higher education.[75]

On November 2, Simmons addressed a campaign document, which he considered his masterpiece, "to men of Anglo-Saxon blood against the disgrace of negro domination." He printed 100,000 copies and distributed them by train and horseback throughout the state. The

74. Raleigh *News and Observer*, October 15, 26, 29; Wilmington *Messenger*, October 28, 1898. Fountain had been the recipient of "Villifying and Slanderous" statements in the Charlotte *Observer* because of his Populist associations. Raleigh *Caucasian*, October 6, 1898. Fountain may well have been playing a complicated game here. He certainly favored white supremacy, even to the point of disfranchising blacks, but he probably considered Simmons a part of "the Ransom Machine," which he described as the gold element and wanted to break by rallying "the true silver rank and file Democrats to our banner." W. E. Fountain to Marion Butler, August 9, 1898, in Butler Papers. Fountain's actions confused other Populists. J. M. Cutchin to Butler, September 19, 1898, James B. Lloyd to Butler, August 11, 23, 1898, in Butler papers. Rallies continued in the eastern communities.

75. George Graham to A. W. Graham, May 12, 1898, in A. W. Graham Papers, Southern Historical Collection, University of North Carolina, Chapel Hill; Raleigh *News and Observer*, August 17, 19, 26, 1898; John R. Moore, *Senator Josiah W. Bailey of North Carolina: A Political Biography* (Durham, N.C.: Duke University Press, 1968) 9–11; Raleigh *News and Observer*, July 31, 1898; John E. Ray to J. W. Bailey, August 3, 1898, in Josiah W. Bailey Papers, Manuscript Department, Duke University Library, Durham, N.C.

issues, as he put it, were clean, honest government and white supremacy against extravagant, corrupt government and Negro domination. He charged the Republicans with venality sometimes "too foul to be described," and his charges later brought countercharges, denials, and counterdenials. He went on: "In the midst of all this din and conflict, there came a voice from the East, like the wail of Egypt's midnight cry. . . . A proud race . . . which had never bent the neck to the yoke of any other race, by the irresistible power of fusion laws and fusion legislation had been placed under the control and dominance of that race which ranks lowest, save one, in the human family." He itemized charges of Negro office holding and insults to white womanhood and highlighted a notorious editorial written on August 18 by one Alexander L. Manly, editor of the Wilmington *Record,* a black newspaper. Particularly infuriating was Manly's statement, taken out of context, that "our [blacks'] experience among the poor white people in the country teaches us that the women of that race are not any more particular in the matter of clandestine meetings with colored men, than are the white men with colored women." This editorial, as Simmons saw it, had caused other issues to "pass out of the public mind," and "in a swirl of indignation, which burnt forth like the lava from a pent-up volcano, there was thrust to the forefront the all-absorbing and paramount question of white supremacy." Then came the last straw, he said. Instead of giving in to the "calm, fixed determination of the brave and chivalrous white men of the state," the fusionists had called on the federal government to send in federal troops to force white people "to submit to the continuation of conditions, which to the Anglo-Saxon are worse than death."[76]

Simmons hailed the victory of 1898, which brought overwhelming Democratic control of the state legislature, as a victory for white supremacy and also as one leading inevitably to the disfranchising amendment. According to Simmons, that amendment "simply recog-

76. Rippy (ed.), *F. M. Simmons,* 26, 80–87. For a piece of the original editorial, see fragment of Wilmington *Record,* August 18, 1898, in North Carolina Collection, University of North Carolina, Chapel Hill. See also Wilmington *Messenger,* August 21, 1898; Raleigh *News and Observer,* August 24, 28, 1898. Republicans and Populists also condemned this editorial, which had probably led to a further deterioration of their white support. Crow and Durden, *Maverick Republican,* 129ff. Some reports later stated that the editorial was written by William J. Jeffries, the associate editor, without consulting Manly. Raleigh *News and Observer,* December 11, 1898. See also Raleigh *News and Observer,* May 3, 1898.

nizes a difference in hereditary intelligence—a difference which is well known by every well informed student of racial qualities and characteristics."[77]

When the General Assembly of 1899 convened in January, George Rountree led supporters of the amendment in the House. He claimed that enfranchising black people had been proved an "egregious mistake," that "even the heartiest enthusiast had seen his hopes wither in the previous 30 years, and that numerous states had now imposed limitations." He justified excusing whites from the provisions of the literacy test by a complicated argument based upon heredity and inheritance. Quoting a contemporary authority on constitutional law, he asserted that "the art of self-government must be acquired through the accumulated experience of generations handed down traditionally." He insisted that the law was constitutional. The amendment would not discriminate against black people as a race, he averred, since all Negroes would not be disfranchised. Descendants of free blacks who had been able to vote before 1867 could still exercise the franchise, he pointed out, as could literate blacks, while recent white immigrants who were illiterate would not be permitted to vote. A similar law in Massachusetts, he added, was designed to prevent foreigners from voting. On May 13, Rountree made an even stronger speech supporting the constitutionality of the amendment, citing Edmund Burke, John Stuart Mill, and several Supreme Court decisions. He denied explicitly that the motive of the amendment was "to disfranchise negroes as such," but then went on to say that in any case "it is beyond the province of the courts to inquire into the motives of the legislature." Rountree later stated that he had become convinced of the need to disfranchise black people one day in 1894 when he had observed a "queue 100 yards long" of blacks waiting to vote for Thomas W. Strange and one H. McClammy for the legislature. At the last minute, word came from Judge Daniel Russell to vote for McClammy and G. Z. French. So all the blacks switched from Strange to French.[78]

Much as Populists and Republicans tried to divert attention from the racial issue, many voters believed unequivocally that the basic issue of the campaign was the effect of perhaps 100,000 ignorant black voters

77. Raleigh *News and Observer*, February 12, 1899.
78. *Ibid.*, February 18, May 14, 1899; George Rountree, "Memorandum of My Personal Reasons for the Passage of the Suffrage Amendment," in Connor Papers.

on the body politic. "There is no other issue" said Josiah W. Bailey, Baptist editor and future United States senator. Disfranchisers reasoned that the Negro was incompetent and that the amendment would take him out of politics, thus removing the need for corruption at the polls and also providing for greater security for white womanhood. The issue thus became quite simple. "Centuries of unlimited opportunity," wrote General Andrew D. Cowles, a Republican of Statesville, "have endowed the White Man" with the divine right to rule, while "God had never chosen the negro to lead any great movement, make a discovery, invent anything." In February, Simmons set out to organize two thousand white-supremacy clubs "to make permanent in North Carolina the supremacy of the white race."[79]

As the election of 1900 approached, the Democratic cries of "negro domination in the East" became hysterical. The fusionists attempted to prove that such claims were hypocritical. They pointed out that western North Carolina had heard nothing about Negro domination until the Democrats had lost control of the state; that until that time, the Democrats "had done everything in their power to secure the negro vote"; that, in fact, Simmons himself had once "boasted of receiving thousands of negro votes." Moreover, the fusionists insisted, under the "Simmons Election Law," when the Democratic election board of Craven County was to choose the local election officials, the Republicans and Populists recommended "intelligent white men of high character," but the election board chose Negroes who had supported the Democratic party in recent elections. The fusionists publicized the names of the blacks appointed by Democrats elsewhere and insisted that there were between three hundred and four hundred of them, "in several instances the same old pet negroes known to be unprincipled." When Simmons apparently denied that any Negro had been "appointed judge of an election in North Carolina," the *Caucasian* com-

79. George E. Hunt to Marion Butler, January 18, 1900, in Butler Papers; Raleigh *Caucasian*, March 29, 1900. See also Raleigh *Caucasian*, January 25, February 22, April 26, 1900; Winston *Union-Republican*, May 31, 1900; Asheville *Gazette*, July 6, 17, 28, 1900; Raleigh *News and Observer*, July 29, 1900. Although the *News and Observer* used the figure of 80,000 black voters, the number of potential voters was greater. According to the census of 1900, there were 127,000 black males twenty-one years old or older in the state. *Twelfth Census, 1900: Population*, Vol. I, Pt. 1, 992. See also A. D. Cowles to Solomon Doyle, May 26, 1899, in Raleigh *News and Observer*, June 11, 1899; Charlotte *Observer*, April 8, February 22, 1900.

mented that the people of the state were "shocked not only by Mr. Simmons' brazen hypocrisy, but also by the fact that these negro judges have been placed by Mr. Simmons in a position where they will have autocratic and unlimited power in passing upon the right of every white voter in the precinct to vote." The *Populist Handbook* for the campaign formally charged the Democrats with hypocrisy on the white-supremacy issue and claimed that the Democrats were continuing to appoint blacks to office in certain counties. Simmons then sponsored *Populist Handbook Answered*, a pamphlet specifically refuting this and other charges made by the Populists.[80]

The overwhelming victory for the amendment in 1900, and incidentally for Aycock in his campaign for governor, was achieved, as in 1898, by fraud and intimidation and by calling for the unity of white men against the Negro domination allegedly brought about by the fusion of Republicans and Populists. Highly respected and thoughtful men had responded to this call. Henry G. Connor seemed convinced that "certain political evils . . . would . . . continue to sap the strength out of our political life and character and, to a large extent, our social and individual life and character . . . until we had removed from politics the first cause, the negro or the race question." With the Negro eliminated from politics, Connor assumed, subsequent campaigns would not be fought on the color line. "The best possible vindication of your position in regard to the amendment," Connor wrote to Josiah Bailey, "is to say nothing about the negro . . . [in future campaigns] and go to the people on the real issues."[81]

Simmons did not feel quite that way. He reminded his fellow North Carolinians that the disfranchising amendment did not go into effect until 1902, and thus that eighty thousand Negroes would still be qualified to vote in November, 1900. "If the Republicans attempt to organize and vote the 80,000 ignorant Negroes whom the constitutional amendment disfranchises but who will still be entitled to vote in November," he warned, "this course of conduct will inject the race

80. A. Z. to Asheville *Gazette*, July 3, 7, 11, 1900; Winston *Union-Republican*, July 26, 1900; Asheville *Gazette*, July 14, 21, 1900; Raleigh *Caucasian*, July 12, 19, 26, 1900; Edward T. Clark to Marion Butler, July, 1900, H. G. Alexander to Butler, July 23, 1900, in Butler Papers; *Populist Handbook Answered* (1900) in Pamphlet Collection, Duke University Library, Durham, N.C.

81. Anderson, *Race and Politics in North Carolina*, 4–5, 306–307; H. G. Connor to Josiah W. Bailey, August 7, 1900, in Bailey Papers.

issue in its worst form into politics." Josephus Daniels was even more specific. "The man who votes for McKinley in November," he trumpeted, "votes for negro collectors of customs, negro postmasters, and negro revenue officers." The Wilmington *Messenger* echoed this sentiment: "The whites in North Carolina must not lose sight of McKinley's course as to the negro[;] the way he treated North Carolina white people is one of infamy and detestation." Republicans were quick to point out that the Democrats did not consider the Negro issue settled and warned that they probably would not drop it so long as there was any opposition to the Democratic organization in North Carolina.[82]

The religious press joined in a plea to eliminate the racial issue. The *Presbyterian Standard*, commenting that Negro rule was no longer a threat to the state, warned that blacks were "in need of protection from hoodlums of our own race." Josiah W. Bailey, who had effectively supported the amendment, denounced what he considered the dishonesty of Simmons, Aycock, and others in breaking their pledge to abandon the racial issue with the passage of the amendment. "The colored people are our fellow men," he wrote. "All races are of one blood, are derived from one man, and he from God. . . . We must be kindly to our colored fellow men." Bailey apparently went so far as to warn Simmons that if a racist campaign were waged, he would "cast his vote for McKinley as a Protest." Daniels promptly denied that pledges had been made to drop the racial issue as soon as the amendment was passed. He was infuriated at Bailey, whom he described as thinking that he had "carried the amendment all by himself" but was "now protesting against the mention of McKinley's negro postmasters in the national campaign." Exchanges were frequent and bitter between Daniels and Bailey on this issue.[83]

These exchanges again exposed differences within the Democratic party. Henry G. Connor, though a personal friend of Daniels, considered the latter's "views injurious to the State and to the party." The Charlotte *Observer* quoted approvingly the Greensboro *Telegram*,

---

82. Charlotte *Observer*, August 12, 1900; Raleigh *News and Observer*, August 7, 1900, quoted in Wilmington *Messenger*, August 8, 1900.

83. Winston *Union-Republican*, August 9, 1900, quoted in Charlotte *Observer*, August 14, 1900; *Biblical Recorder*, quoted in Raleigh *Progressive Farmer*, August 14, 1900. The Raleigh *Christian Advocate* took a somewhat similar position. Asheville *Gazette*, August 30, 1900; Winston *Union-Republican*, August 9, 1900; Raleigh *News and Observer*, August 19, 1900. See also Daniels, *Editor in Politics*, 358–60.

which had said that "the cringing soul of the *News and Observer* is too small to understand an argument pitched upon the grounds of humanity, justice, and forbearance," and a friend of Bailey's characterized the *News and Observer* as "a caricature of respectable journalism" and its editor as "the shallowest demagogue ever produced in North Carolina in the last fifteen years." The Charlotte *Observer* admitted that if the "negro cry is to be raised . . . those of us who urged the adoption of the amendment upon the grounds that it would eliminate the issue, lied to the people."[84]

Largely as a reward for Simmons' effectiveness as a political organizer, he was nominated for senator in 1900 in the first statewide primary held in North Carolina. In his campaign for the Senate, too, he repeatedly gave evidence that race was a principal force in his mind. He refused to apologize for the intimidation and corruption that had characterized recent campaigns in which he had been involved. He explained that "Anglo-Saxons had to be free," and he denounced Republicans for appointing blacks to federal offices. When he was formally elected by the General Assembly, speakers in both houses praised him for having developed a "superb organization" and by "untiring efforts" leading "the battle of the white people of North Carolina for the protection of the white womanhood and white mankind of the state."[85]

In trying to make sense out of complicated political campaigning, it is usually possible to find evidence for a variety of hypotheses. In the two campaigns discussed in this essay, the relative weight of motivating factors cannot be precisely fixed. For a majority of those who voted Democratic or for the amendment in 1898 and 1900, the racist appeal of white supremacy combined with extreme partisanship was determining. To detect the conscious or unconscious motivations of the leaders who either devised the campaign strategy or provided the financial support is more difficult. Clearly the Populists' program seemed a threat to the business and railroad interests, and clearly, too, Simmons

84. Charlotte *Observer*, August 22, 1900; H. G. Connor to J. W. Bailey, August 7, 1900, Charles A. Thomas to [Josiah Bailey], in Bailey Papers; Charlotte *Observer*, September 3, 1900.

85. Asheville *Gazette*, October 4, 1900; Charlotte *Observer*, October 7, 1900; Wilmington *Messenger*, November 2, 1900; Raleigh *News and Observer*, January 23, 1901.

and Jarvis sought financial support from these business interests and were successful in getting it. Economic issues were, therefore, obviously involved in this campaign, but evidence suggesting a class conflict is obscured by the differences within the Democratic party, by the ambiguities of the Populist and Republican positions on business issues, and by the fact that many Populists joined the Democrats in supporting white supremacy and disfranchisement.

Indeed, the problem of detecting class conflict in the 1880s and 1890s, as Lawrence Goodwyn has warned, is difficult, and though it can be useful as "an interpretive device," it can also be "a treacherous tool." Goodwyn was referring to agricultural societies with their "landowners, smallholders, and landless laborers." Referring to the Populists, he pointed out, "The agrarian movement was created by landed and landless people." Industrialization added further elements to the complex picture by creating a new gentry, sometimes from the old gentry, and a working class that rarely cooperated with the agrarians. To top it all off, in North Carolina there were regional differences.[86]

The complexities were highlighted in the battle over the amendment in 1900. In that campaign the evidence of business support for the Democrats is not so clear as in 1898. There were Democrats who distrusted the poor and illiterate regardless of race, but there were also Democrats who were sympathetic to "the lower classes." Some, such as Josephus Daniels, the Kitchins, and John Webster of *Webster's Weekly*, approved of particular aspects of the Populist program, especially the free coinage of silver, and never favored disfranchising the poor white; others, such as Joseph Caldwell, editor of the Charlotte *Observer*, and Colonel A. B. Andrews, a vice president of the Southern Railway, were Cleveland Democrats and seemed to favor disfranchisement of all illiterates. Still others, such as Aycock and Simmons, were political operators, pragmatic in their approach, who consistently denied any plan

86. Lawrence Goodwyn, *The Populist Moment: A Short History of the Agrarian Revolt in America* (New York: Oxford University Press, 1978), xv–xvi, 101–102, 177–79. Robert C. McMath deprecated Norman Pollack's class theory, concluding that the Farmers' Alliance "was woven too deeply into the social fabric" and its members "were too consciously farm owners to become near proletarians." Robert C. McMath, *The Populist Vanguard: A History of the Southern Farmers' Alliance* (Chapel Hill: University of North Carolina Press, 1975), 156. Wooley noted Simmons' success in rallying Democrats of every point of view to the white-supremacy cause. Wooley, "Race and Politics," 260.

for disfranchising white people.[87] Unlike in other states, where disfranchisement was accompanied by a considerable amount of antidemocratic theorizing that attacked manhood suffrage, in North Carolina, Simmons, Daniels, Aycock *et al.* argued vigorously for the basic intelligence and educability of the poor white.[88] As both Eric Anderson and Hugh Lefler have pointed out, an *enfranchising* clause guaranteed illiterates the right to register until 1908, a provision that would mean that thousands of illiterates would be able to vote long after that date, and in the meantime other thousands might be able to learn to read and become eligible.

Although racism colored the rhetoric of thousands of white North Carolina citizens in 1898 and 1900, the partisan motive is almost equally clear. Regardless as to whether the illiterates were black or white, the majority of them were likely to vote against the Democrats. Most blacks were Republican, and most illiterate whites lived in western counties and voted strongly Republican. Thus, from the point of view of the Democrats, disfranchisement was a good thing. It could be justified as a purification of the voting system that would eliminate somewhat disreputable and ignorant voters and also reduce the need to prevent their voting by intimidation or fraud. The ultimate objective, however, was to eliminate opposition parties and enthrone the Democrats.

It is almost impossible to factor out the economic and political from the racial motive. What happened in North Carolina fit the pattern of a fundamentally racist society uneasily adjusting itself to the Fourteenth and Fifteenth amendments and suddenly confronting a new generation of ambitious, politically conscious blacks who were infiltrating the political and government infrastructure at a time of economic crisis. Political, social, economic, and ideological positions were threatened, and the result was a series of explosions of which the Wilmington riot

87. It may be argued, of course, that in 1898 Simmons and Aycock essentially promised that no one would be disfranchised after that year's election; that as soon as the election was won, they broke that promise; and that there was no reason to think that they were any more honest in 1900 in their intents. Kousser calculated that voting participation of whites, as well as of blacks, declined significantly after disfranchisement, and argued that it was a class matter because voting for disfranchisement was higher in counties where wealth was substantial than in counties of poor whites in the hills. Kousser, *The Shaping of Southern Politics,* 244–45, 248.

88. Cf. Kousser, *The Shaping of Southern Politics,* 250–57.

was perhaps the most tragic. Indeed, it is at least possible that, in spite of the unifying effect of the racial issue, the fusionists would have won in 1898 and prevented disfranchisement had it not been for blatant fraud, intimidation, and actual violence on the part of the Democrats.[89]

Men of political ambition profited. Aycock became governor, two of the Kitchins became governor and congressman, and Simmons became senator, an office that he thought was the highest a southerner could achieve. Throughout his career, the terms *white supremacy* and *Negro domination* were effective slogans, but they also had real meaning for him. Like Daniels, Aycock, and the Kitchins, he had grown up in the Second Congressional District, where blacks outnumbered whites and held numerous offices. Although Simmons himself was relatively moderate on the racial issue in the 1880s, the rhetoric of white supremacy was all around him, and his own moderation received a blow when, in spite of Democratic fraud, Henry P. Cheatham, a well-educated, black school principal, defeated him for reelection to Congress in 1888. Simmons, however, had demonstrated such skill in organization and partisan sleight of hand in these early campaigns that he was called to the party chairmanship in 1892 and again in 1898. The organization that Simmons created in 1898 provided the basis for his political power for the next thirty years. It had been formed to defeat a coalition of Populists and Republicans in two violent, emotional campaigns in which white supremacy was a prevailing theme.[90]

Simmons continued to boast about those campaigns throughout his political career, even in the election of 1928, when he bolted from the party that had been his political home since the 1880s and, to all intents and purposes, supported Herbert Hoover for the presidency. On October 25, 1928, over a statewide radio hookup, "Our Old Chieftain of White Supremacy" spoke for three hours. His opening remarks re-

89. Eastern North Carolina, particularly the Second Congressional District, provides the setting for what Joel Williamson called "Radicalism." "Where Radicalism lived," he wrote, "it throve and it ruled with force and fire but it did need a special kind of food to survive—the vision of the menacing black male." Williamson, *The Crucible of Race*, 182. The trouble with trying to fit North Carolina's political leaders into Williamson's categories is that the fit is not precise. At times the rhetoric seems to be saying that blacks were beasts and could not be salvaged, but then in the next breath would come redeeming features and assurances that they had their place. Wooley insists that there is no conclusive proof that a majority of eligible voters favored disfranchisement. Wooley, "Race and Class," 349–50.

90. Raleigh *News and Observer*, January 24, 1901; Anderson, *Race and Politics in North Carolina*, 159–67. Cf. Williamson, *The Crucible of Race*, 194–95.

viewed his career. He mentioned his first major state fight in 1892 against Populists and Republicans, in which, "when I got through with them . . . their backs were sore and bloody." He described the government of the fusionists as characterized by corruption and "negroes in office"; he claimed that in 1898 he had raised the question of "black or white supremacy for North Carolina." In 1900, Simmons continued, "Aycock . . . and I decided that the Democratic Party must go forward educationally, industrially, and morally, but in order to do [that,] what we had first to make certain [was] that the negro can never come back into politics again."[91]

* * *

In September, 1903, Simmons' father, seventy-eight-year-old Furnifold Greene Simmons, a highly respected landowner and public servant, was murdered on his farm near Trenton in Jones County. A black man, Alfred Daniels, was arrested for the murder. The neighbors and friends were "deeply indignant at the brutal assassination, and their feelings were aroused to put a quick end to the life of the wretch." At this point Simmons, "his heart overflowing with deep grief," came "from the house of mourning," pleaded with his neighbors to "let the law take its course," and begged that "there be no lynching." The pleas of the son "saved the wretch's life." Even so, the accused was immediately moved secretly by night from the Trenton jail to New Bern for "safekeeping."

On November 4, Daniels was brought to trial at Trenton, seat of Jones County. The afternoon of that first day was taken up with the question of whether the county commissioners had fraudulently discriminated against Negroes in drawing the jurors from the county lists, but the trial took place. The jury deliberated for thirty minutes and rendered a verdict of guilty on the basis of an alleged confession. Daniels was condemned to be hanged on December 11. His lawyers appealed. The case was argued before the state supreme court on February 26, 1904. Daniels' lawyer argued that there had been discrimination in the selection of the jury and that Daniels' confession was made under "mortal dread of being lynched."

On March 8, the supreme court affirmed the decision of the lower

91. Richard L. Watson, Jr., "A Political Leader Bolts: F. M. Simmons in the Presidential Election of 1928," *North Carolina Historical Review,* XXXVII (1960), 534.

court that "negro Alfred Daniels" would be hanged for the murder of Simmons. Daniels' attorney, J. C. L. Harris, however, did not accept this verdict. On April 15 he went to Washington and made the final plea. He applied to United States Supreme Court Justice John M. Harlan for a writ of error on the ground that the commissioners of Jones County had no names of Negroes in the jury box. He was not successful. Daniels, who in the meantime had been moved to Goldsboro for "safekeeping," was returned to Trenton, and on May 19, 1904, at 1:36 P.M. he was hanged. He said on the scaffold that he had been forgiven. At the time, newspaper accounts indicated that the murder had occurred when the elder Simmons had intercepted Daniels poaching on his property. Years later, however, Simmons hypothesized that the assassin "was perhaps seeking vengeance for what I had done."[92]

92. Raleigh *News and Observer*, September 15, 16, 17, November 3, 5, 6, 7, 8, 1903, February 27, March 9, 1904; Rippy (ed.), *F. M. Simmons*, 29; Wilmington *Messenger*, April 16, May 18, 20, 1904; Raleigh *News and Observer*, September 15, 1903; Rippy (ed.), *F. M. Simmons*, 28–29. It should be recalled that Justice Harlan was the lone dissenter in the *Plessy* v. *Ferguson* case of 1896.

Part III

Racial Bonds and Class Divisions in the Post-Reconstruction South

The Meaning of Freedom: Black North Carolina in the Nadir, 1880–1900

"As a people and especially as a free people, we are to-day on trial," declared Frederick Douglass in an address to the Second Annual Exposition of the Colored People of North Carolina in 1880. "The question is asked by friends and by foes, and should be asked by ourselves, what is to become of the colored race in America? Will they advance or recede, will they rise or fall, survive or perish, die out as the Indians are dying out? It is a great question, and no body can answer, but ourselves." Douglass believed that emancipation had given black people the power to determine their own future, but two decades later that power was being stripped away. In 1900, in "An Address to the White People of North Carolina," a group of black Tar Heels protested the impending passage of a constitutional amendment that would disfranchise the vast majority of the state's blacks. "It is already urged by an influential portion of the . . . leading men that these amendments to the State constitution are temporary expedients," the address charged. "That the thirteenth, fourteenth and fifteenth amendments to the constitution of the United States must be repealed. Repeal them and slavery again becomes lawful. . . . In view of these facts, it is natural that we should feel the greatest anxiety as to the outcome of efforts now being made not only to restrict our right to vote, but to deny that right altogether."[1]

Fear of impending disfranchisement and loss of other rights, fear even of extinction—these fears reflect either extreme paranoia or unconscionable oppression. But they offer random testimony to the vigilance of former slaves during a period that has been called the nadir of Afro-American history. "From the end of Reconstruction to the end of the nineteenth century . . . marked the lowest point in the quest for equal rights," the late Rayford W. Logan maintained. "Second-class citizenship for Negroes was accepted by Presidents, the Supreme Court, Congress, organized labor, the General Federation of Women's Clubs—indeed by the vast majority of Americans, North and South, and by the 'leader' of the Negro race."[2] Afro-Americans, nonetheless, were able to remain legally free men and women.

Their experience of obtaining and retaining freedom, so integral to understanding the social history of "the postbellum South," is an area of Afro-American studies needing more attention from scholars. Over the past fifteen years many excellent monographs set in the Civil War and Reconstruction periods have appeared. These works have treated either the role of slaves in emancipating themselves or of freedpeople in sustaining themselves. But studies about southern blacks of the post-Reconstruction age remain few. Although the era has been impressively analyzed by econometricians and political historians interested in race relations, the historiography of the postbellum South lacks major studies of black institutional and intellectual life. A great deal is known about leaders, namely their racial ideologies, their participation in politics, their protests against injustices such as lynching, and their self-help endeavors in the economic, educational, and religious spheres. Yet a broader and clearer portrait is needed of the Negro community, including the contributions of its rank and file, if historians are to understand how it fared in "the contest over the meaning of freedom."[3]

1. Clipping from Raleigh *Journal of Industry,* October 9, 1880, Scrapbook, 1880–86, clipping from Raleigh *Morning Post,* January 2, 1900, Scrapbook, 1900–1902, in Charles N. Hunter Papers, Manuscript Department, Duke University Library, Durham, N.C.

2. Rayford W. Logan, *The Betrayal of the Negro: From Rutherford B. Hayes to Woodrow Wilson* (Rev. ed.; New York: Collier Books, 1965), 9, 11.

3. Harold D. Woodman, "Sequel to Slavery: The New History Views the Postbellum South," *Journal of Southern History,* XLIII (1977), 523; Barbara Jeanne Fields, *Slavery and*

During the 1880s and 1890s the institutions intended to secure blacks' independence were tested to the limit. These decades offer important evidence for assessing what freedom meant in the generation after slavery. To the extent that sources permit, the assessment should stress black perspectives, such as that of Douglass as he spoke before the exposition and that of the authors of the address protesting disfranchisement. Racism, of course, must not be forgotten. Circumscribing the Negro by custom and by law, racism was pervasive in the New South. "Emancipation settled that the slaveowner no longer stood between state and citizen but left open to dispute what the relationship between the two would become," historian Barbara Jeanne Fields has written. The push for equal status—indeed, freedom's significance in its entirety—evolved in a context of continuing discrimination. How might the oppressed respond to the contemporary situation? Did they think of freedom as whites did? Would they be crippled by cowardice or fear in a white-dominated world? Was institution building a more or less viable option for them than it had been for ex-slaves of the 1860s and 1870s? Would core traditions and values of race pride and self-help be sufficient to sustain hope for the future? Could philosophies and tactics of accommodation and protest be employed to achieve equality? Within the broad boundaries of these questions, this essay will discuss North Carolina black history in the nadir. Focusing on major trends, I will examine blacks' shared aspirations, ideas, and struggles as they tried, in the spirit of the earlier freedpeople, "to enlarge their liberty and ensure their independence."[4]

Freedom to earn, though usually begrudged by bosses and land-

---

Freedom on the Middle Ground: Maryland During the Nineteenth Century (New Haven: Yale University Press, 1985), xiii. For the years 1865–1877, cf. Leon F. Litwack, Been in the Storm So Long: The Aftermath of Slavery (New York: Alfred A. Knopf, 1979), and Peter Kolchin, First Freedom: The Responses of Alabama Blacks to Emancipation and Reconstruction (Westport, Conn.: Greenwood Press, 1971). On economic and racial developments, ca. 1865–1900, cf. Robert Higgs, Competition and Coercion: Blacks in the American Economy, 1865–1914 (New York: Cambridge University Press, 1977), with Roger L. Ransom and Richard Sutch, One Kind of Freedom: The Economic Consequences of Emancipation (New York: Cambridge University Press, 1977), and Howard N. Rabinowitz, Race Relations in the Urban South, 1865–1890 (New York: Oxford University Press, 1978). To grasp the breadth of late-nineteenth-century black history, see Logan, The Betrayal of the Negro, and August Meier, Negro Thought in America, 1880–1915: Racial Ideologies in the Age of Booker T. Washington (Ann Arbor: University of Michigan Press, 1963).

4. Fields, Slavery and Freedom on the Middle Ground, 206; Orville Vernon Burton, In My Father's House Are Many Mansions: Family and Community in Edgefield, South Carolina

lords, was a primary concern of black North Carolinians, the sine qua non of their subsistence. The transition from slavery to a free labor market, which occurred during Reconstruction, had given them a start, albeit lowly, toward an improved livelihood. But poverty rather than prosperity would be the lot of the vast majority. Those who resented the new order asked, Will the Negro work? And the stereotype persisted, as a white North Carolinian put it, that a "nigger hated work, and had no ambition." If, with labor to barter, Negro workers engaged in economic competition for higher shares or wages, their options were limited by white coercion, including "recurring episodes of violence, intimidation, and fraud." Thus they became mostly renters, sharecroppers, and propertyless toilers. In 1876 the United States Department of Agriculture estimated that 4 to 5 percent of North Carolina's freedmen owned land, compared with 4 percent in Tennessee and Alabama, 5 percent in South Carolina and Texas, 5 to 6 percent in Mississippi, Louisiana, and Arkansas, and 8 percent in Florida. These minuscule percentages reveal not only "the roots of black and white southern poverty" but also flaws in congressional policy, such as the failure to distribute land to freedmen and the insufficiency of federal aid to the postwar South. As if it were a folk response to this policy, nearly 20,000 poor black southerners made an exodus to Kansas in 1879, stimulating a migration from North Carolina to Indiana of between 2,500 and 3,000 blacks.[5]

Economic aspirations clearly underlay the Carolina event, but opponents denied that, deploring it in testimony taken before a United States Senate investigating committee whose predominantly Democratic membership was determined to blame the entire southern exodus on a Republican conspiracy to import Negro voters to the North. That was not so, said thirty-year-old Samuel L. Perry of Chatham

(Chapel Hill: University of North Carolina Press, 1985), 230; Ira Berlin, Joseph P. Reidy, and Leslie S. Rowland (eds.), *Freedom: A Documentary History of Emancipation, 1861–1867*, Ser. 2 (New York: Cambridge University Press, 1982), xxi.

5. Higgs, *Competition and Coercion*, 37–38, 45, 51–52; Gerald D. Jaynes, *Branches Without Roots: Genesis of the Black Working Class in the American South, 1862–1882* (New York: Oxford University Press, 1986), 14–15; C. Vann Woodward, *Origins of the New South, 1877–1913* (Baton Rouge: Louisiana State University Press, 1951), 205; Nell Irvin Painter, *Exodusters: Black Migration to Kansas After Reconstruction* (New York: Alfred A. Knopf, 1976), 251–52, 256; Frenise A. Logan, *The Negro in North Carolina, 1876–1894* (Chapel Hill: University of North Carolina Press, 1964); Joseph H. Taylor, "The Great Migration from North Carolina in 1879," *North Carolina Historical Review*, XXXI (1954), 31.

County, an ex-slave, a sometime farm laborer, and the leader of the trek to Indiana. Perry testified that the exodus began with ordinary people's desire for betterment: "We would meet and talk about it Sunday evenings—that is, the laboring class of people—the only ones I knew anything about; I had not much to do with the big professional negroes, the rich men. I did not associate with them much, but I got among the workingmen." Phrases of desperation and hope—"having labored hard for several years, under disadvantages," "our progress has been so retarded," and "emigration is the only way in which we can elevate ourselves"—filled Perry's petition to solicit financial help, though little was forthcoming. Indiana Republicans contributed toward migrants' fares, he admitted, but he swore that no drawbacks from railroad companies were given to him. The movement's immediate cause was the Landlord and Tenant Act passed by the North Carolina General Assembly in 1877. "The part of it where we think it is most severe is where it gives the landlord the right to be the court, sheriff, and jury, and say when the rents shall be paid," Perry stated. "It bears heavily on all the poor people."

Hearing about wages of "two or three dollars a day out there," one debt-ridden tenant insisted under cross-examination that he "started there to make a living." But James E. O'Hara, a black lawyer and politician from Halifax County and a powerful opponent of the migration, dismissed it as "induced by a class of persons who come and tell the people they will get better wages by going to Indiana." He added, "So far as I can tell, it is just the floating population that are leaving." Playing down stories of racial unfairness in the state, O'Hara instead believed that "industrious colored men" could and would make progress in North Carolina. A black farmer from Wilson County, though he did not approve of the migration, tried to explain what prompted many of his poorest neighbors to leave: "Some, I think, were going for better wages, and some were complaining that they could not get their rights under the law," he said. Others, presumably, went along for whiskey and "a big ride." Rejecting tenants' complaints, a Negro landowner from Goldsboro stated that he liked the Landlord and Tenant Act, which granted him a lien on everything on his land. He declared, "I think I am entitled to that."

Notwithstanding all the opposition, the Exodusters' action spoke for itself. Senator Daniel W. Voorhees' question to O. S. B. Wall, president of the black-run Emigrant Aid Society, established one significant point about the migration. "What proportion of them were able to and did pay their own way from North Carolina to Indiana?" Voorhees asked. Wall responded, "I should say one-half at least; more likely two-thirds." The Exodusters assumed the initiative in migrating, despite limited means and criticism from the professional and propertied elements. Expecting to improve their welfare, the downtrodden moved on. Bearing witness to human courage, their actions were an indictment of the Negro's entrapment in the society of the Tar Heel State in the years right after Reconstruction.[6]

Those black Carolinians who stayed managed to eke out opportunities only in the face of oppression, forcing even the bravest black spokesmen to be pragmatic. "GOD WILL HELP THOSE WHO TRY TO HELP THEMSELVES" was the motto on the maiden issue of the Raleigh-based *Journal of Industry* in 1879. As organ of the infant North Carolina Industrial Association, chartered by the legislature to hold annual expositions, it would publicize "colored . . . progress—under the broad aegis of freedom—in agriculture, mechanism, invention, education, science, etc." "We propose to steer clear of politics, sectarianism, personalities, and the like," announced coeditors Charles N. Hunter and Osborne Hunter, Jr., brothers, former slaves, and educators. Tactfully, then, an editorial on the "exodus fever" called attention to those "with a hope of bettering their condition" who "are going by the hundreds." To keep others like them "within the borders of the Old North State," the editorial advised, "let us put a premium on labor." A letter to the editor attempted to do just that: "The war is over, and we must go to work for ourselves." The correspondent explained that freedom without advancing knowledge along a variety of lines "in this enlightened day" might be as despicable as slavery, "and if we ever expect to enjoy our freedom like white men . . . we must at once go to work." Exhortations to get busy rather than denunciations of whites, these statements echoed the driving sense of independence that was evident in the Exodusters' testimonies. It was as if the black community had looked

6. *Report and Testimony of the Select Committee of the United States Senate to Investigate the Causes of the Removal of the Negroes from the Southern States to the Northern States,* 46th Cong., 2nd Sess. (3 vols.; 1880), I, ix, 36, 49–57, 61–63, 254–57, 261, 280–82, 290–98, 393–97; Taylor, "Great Migration from North Carolina," 23–31.

away from demands for reparations or "forty acres and a mule" toward an idealization of free enterprise and labor. "Work is the secret of success in every department of human affairs," counseled the *Journal of Industry*. "If we wish to rise," readers were told, "we must not only make general efforts, but above all things we must put forth individual efforts."[7]

The bootstrap motif, reflecting mainstream assumptions about success in the Gilded Age, could mean underemphasizing formidable obstacles and, to foster pride, overemphasizing modest achievements. The keynote speaker certainly did this at the First Annual Exposition of the North Carolina Industrial Association. Negroes "with scarcely sixteen years of national life vie with their brethren of centuries," James E. O'Hara asserted, but, he continued, "I shall not attempt to enumerate the trials and hardships endured by the Negro during the last decade." Instead he painted a bright picture, happily reporting that over thirteen thousand acres in Halifax County, eight thousand in Warren County, plus thousands more in Nash, Wilson, Edgecombe, Wake, Franklin, Granville, Craven, Northampton, and Wayne counties, "called the Negro master." The reality was that most blacks were landless and black landowners held proportionately little acreage. But for men committed to the accumulation of wealth, and not just to assailing the oppressor, orating on prosperity was a practical means of admonishment and uplift.[8]

The impulse to rise, whether evoked in O'Hara's prophecy that "we shall be a great and prosperous people" or expressed metaphorically in the popular hymn "Higher Ground," enabled Negroes to endure economically. In 1880 the state's essentially rural population (867,000 white, 531,000 Negro, 1,000 Indian) was feeling the pressure of economic and social forces. Most of the gainfully employed received inadequate prices for crops and extremely low wages for labor. In 1898, the first year that information was obtained on farm wages by race and state, blacks received 59 cents and whites 63 cents a day for routine

7. Clippings from Raleigh *Journal of Industry,* April, November 19, 1879, Scrapbook, 1833–79, in Hunter Papers; Claude F. Oubre, *Forty Acres and a Mule: The Freedmen's Bureau and Black Land Ownership* (Baton Rouge: Louisiana State University Press, 1978), xi.

8. Clipping from Raleigh *Journal of Industry,* November 19, 1879, Scrapbook, 1833–79, in Hunter Papers.

farm work—figures that ranked thirteenth and fourteenth, respectively, in the "census South" of fifteen states. Meanwhile, employers' growing power over their employees added insult to injury. A North Carolina act of 1883 stipulated "that any tenant or lessee of lands who shall . . . with intent to defraud the landlord or lessor, give up the possession of the rented or leased premises to any person other than his landlord or lessor shall be guilty of a misdemeanor." This law meant in effect that a poor man, even if protected by a law that forbade a farm owner from seizing "the crop of his tenant when there is nothing due him," could be forced to stay on the land—locked into an unfair contract or burdened by chronic debt. Such coercion took a high toll on the road to the New South, even as a Negro newspaper, the Fayetteville *Sun*, which favored raising everyone's standard of living, welcomed "the current of trade, the statistics of business, the busy hum of the engine and the wheel, the merchant's bustle and the farmer's thrift."[9]

Upward mobility invariably followed a color line. Ordinarily, while blacks sharecropped and hired out for cash, whites owned and managed farms. In the expanding industrial sector, except in customarily all-white cotton mills, the numbers of black operatives and unskilled laborers dwarfed those of white owners, foremen, and skilled mechanics. Between 1880 and 1890, Negro businesses increased from 80 firms worth $79,500 to 175 worth $129,000 (very modest valuations), but most Negroes contended against abject poverty. During the decade, approximately 38,400 blacks (compared with 19,800 whites) left the state. Some 60 percent of blacks, as opposed to 23 percent of whites, were illiterate in 1890. That year blacks, who constituted 40 percent of the total work force, held 38 percent of all jobs in agriculture, fisheries, and mining; 18 percent in professional service; 73 percent in domestic and personal service; 27 percent in trade and transportation; and 29 percent in manufacturing and mechanical industries. Hardly idle, they worked most typically as farmhands and servants. Heeding Booker T. Washington's call to "cast down your bucket where you are," the mass of them stayed in North Carolina and survived, numbering 624,000, or

9. Clipping from Raleigh *Journal of Industry*, November 19, 1879, Scrapbook, 1833–79, clipping from Fayetteville *Sun*, September 26, 1883, Scrapbook, 1880–86, in Hunter Papers; *Songs of Zion* (Nashville: Abingdon Press, 1981), 39; U.S. Bureau of the Census, *Historical Statistics of the United States: Colonial Times to 1970* (2 vols.; 1975), I, 32, 94, 95; *Tenth Census, 1880: Compendium*, I, 364; Higgs, *Competition and Coercion*, 64; North Carolina *Laws and Resolutions*, 1883, pp. 134, 216.

33 percent of the populace, by 1900. Illiteracy by then had been reduced to five of every ten, but eight in ten did farm and domestic work.[10]

The experiences underlying this demographic and occupational summary are conveyed dramatically by the narratives of the North Carolina ex-slaves who were interviewed by the Federal Writers' Project in the 1930s. Like the Exodusters, they were among the hard-pressed of "the Freedom Generation," scrapping to make ends meet but exemplifying responses that either complemented or contradicted those of the Negro intelligentsia. Looking at a random sample of 34 former slaves (14 males and 20 females), one finds that their average age in 1890 was thirty-six. Slightly over half, or 18 (9 men and 9 women), mentioned occupations. The men consisted of 1 drayman, 1 factory laborer, 1 stevedore, and 6 farmers; the women consisted of 5 domestics and 4 farmhands. Of 5 who could read and write as young adults, 1 was male. A total of 17 (8 of them men) said they had married at least once between 1870 and 1900, and 6 (only 2 men) had become interstate migrants between those years.[11]

This is the profile of a rural peasantry for whom freedom and work were inseparable. Assertions such as "I farmed around from one plantation to another" and "Sometimes we worked as hirelings and den as share croppers" belie stereotypes of idleness and evince individual and family initiative. Some who found the right farm, moreover, were loyal to the owner. "We didn' leave Marse Paul 'til he died," remembered Cy Hart, a lifelong tenant on Stagville plantation near Durham, owned by Paul C. Cameron, one of the state's richest and most powerful men.

10. *Eleventh Census, 1890: Occupations*, 58–63; *Twelfth Census, 1900: Occupations*, 352, 354, 356; *Twelfth Census, 1900: Agriculture*, I, 12; *Thirteenth Census, 1910: Agriculture*, VII, 222–23; *Eleventh Census, 1890: Population*, II, xli, xxxv; North Carolina Bureau of Labor Statistics, *First Annual Report, 1887* (Raleigh: State Printer and Binder, 1887), 11–14; Logan, *The Negro in North Carolina*, 112–13; Frenise A. Logan, "The Economic Status of the Town Negro in Post-Reconstruction North Carolina," *North Carolina Historical Review*, XXXV (1958), 452; Paul D. Escott, *Many Excellent People: Power and Privilege in North Carolina, 1850–1900* (Chapel Hill: University of North Carolina Press, 1985), 171, 172, 180; Higgs, *Competition and Coercion*, 64; Louis R. Harlan and Raymond W. Smock (eds.), *The Booker T. Washington Papers* (13 vols.; Urbana: University of Illinois Press, 1972–84), III, 584.

11. Paul D. Escott, *Slavery Remembered: A Record of Twentieth-Century Slave Narratives* (Chapel Hill: University of North Carolina Press, 1979), 159, 163, 165; George P. Rawick (ed.), *The American Slave: A Composite Autobiography* (19 vols.; Westport, Conn.: Greenwood, 1972), Ser. 1, XIV, 17–18, 31, 57, 68–69, 80–81, 146, 214–15, 234–35, 252–53, 262, 276–77, 306, 326–27, 338–39, 348–49, 360–62, 380–81, 444–45, 448–49, XV, 10–11, 22, 36, 86–87, 98–99, 104, 122–23, 182, 236–38, 282–83, 350–51, 354, 362, 382–84, 418–19.

Others remained bitterly aware of their own powerlessness. "He charged de same thing three times and I had it to pay. I stayed two years an made nothin'," snapped ex-tenant Addy Gill of Raleigh. "I members payin' for a middlin of meat twice." Another woman who hated farming, though she did it in order to eat, proudly explained: "I wuzn' no fiel' hand. I was a hand maid trained to wait on de ladies." Moments of opportunity did come, as can be seen in the statement "He had a job at a sawmill near Dunn, so dar we went ter live in a new shanty." But security eluded most. Insecurity forced the bulk of the ex-slave underclass to seek refuge ultimately in a subeconomy of extended families, kinship obligations, and mutual-aid organizations, all of which contributed to black survival.[12]

Viewed against the background of folk experience, the formal statements of leaders on "a fair chance to make a living" provide further insight into the Negro community's material striving. In their pronouncements were insistent but tactful complaints about deprivation. Renowned visitor Frederick Douglass, addressing the second state exposition of the North Carolina Industrial Association, was aware of black progress in places such as the Republican-dominated Second Congressional District. But he lamented that "we are poor, very poor—especially the newly emancipated"—and charged that this destitution was due to a "sentiment of hostility, I am sorry to say, [which] has not disappeared even from this most liberal of the Southern States." Acceptance of the former slave as fellow citizen and free worker, he maintained, could mean future peace and prosperity for all. "Emancipation was not the destruction, but the salvation of North Carolina," Douglass told "the old master class, some of whom may hear me to-day." Perhaps the former slaveholders heard James W. Hood, outspoken resident, activist, and bishop of the African Methodist Episcopal Zion church, whose speech two days later condemned the color bar in the job market. "Take away the hedge, and give the black man an open field," demanded Hood, "and he will everywhere exhibit qualities of the first order." Other prominent blacks, including John C. Dancy, editor of the Salisbury *Star of Zion* and later of Charlotte's *A.M.E. Zion Church Quarterly*, protested similarly. Afro-American leaders complained that blacks were "unceremoniously

12. Rawick (ed.), *The American Slave*, XIV, 253–326, 381, 445, XV, 351.

lynched," paid "far less a month than many . . . workmen get in a day," and told "that we must go to Africa to solve the 'Negro problem.'" Scapegoats of "the race-baiting proclivities of the trade unions," Negroes also became targets of Jim Crow cars and the disfranchising amendment. Might these "cruel discriminations . . . continue with impunity?" asked Joseph C. Price, president of Livingstone College and probably the most important southern black leader prior to Booker T. Washington. Rejecting the belief that the Negro was "inherently different" or inferior, Price wanted to change "this attitude of the white man" by means of blacks' mental improvement and "progress in the accumulation of material wealth."[13] Yet changing white attitudes through demonstrated achievement would be no easy task for a race recently up from slavery.

It is significant that black leadership did not retreat from such a task. Douglass prescribed what amounted to a simple formula: "Save your money for a rainy day," "combine and insist upon living wages for honest work," and "remain in North Carolina." Hood went on record in favor of thrift, improved pay, and nonmigration, but emphasized most strongly that "we must pay strict attention to our habits," avoid waste, fast living, and making "too many" excursions. "We, of all people, have no time to play cards and other games, even for amusement," he chided, proposing a kind of Christian moral economy. "We have too much important work on our hands." Condescending, and perhaps ill-timed, was the position of visiting Virginia educator Robert Kelser, who, at the 1885 exposition and in the presence of state officials, stressed "that the trouble the Negro now has is because of the trifling, shiftless, members of the race." Dancy, by contrast, declined to make charges of improvidence and instead pitied poor folk, especially "the luckless, colored peasantry" who were confronted with "disappointment and hardship." He urged only that they appreciate the drawbacks of migration and that, whenever deciding to "strike tents," they pursue "industry, economy and morality." Less sympathetic, one *Star of Zion* columnist argued "that an emigration from America to Africa

13. Clippings from Raleigh *Journal of Industry*, October 9, 1880, October 8, 1881, Scrapbook, 1880–86, in Hunter Papers; Salisbury *Star of Zion*, January 8, 1886, March 9, 1893, September 17, November 1, 1900; "The Contention Between Capital and Labor," *A.M.E. Zion Church Quarterly*, II (1892), 412; J. C. Price, "The Race Question in the South" and "Our Struggle for Industrial Opportunity," both in *A.M.E. Zion Church Quarterly*, III (1893), 314–15, 319–20, 529; Meier, *Negro Thought in America*, 80–82.

would be damaging to our very best interests, moral, religious and financial."[14]

The man who probably popularized and spoke up for those interests more than anyone else in North Carolina, Charles N. Hunter, coeditor of the *Journal of Industry*, clipped, filed, and distributed items on uplift appearing in publications all over the state. For example, an article from the Raleigh *Appeal* in 1886 denounced black dependency and acclaimed "self development," noting, "We must cease looking beyond for those forces which must come from within." Other articles recognized men such as John S. Leary, a Fayetteville lawyer and president of the Industrial Association, and Warren C. Coleman, a successful Concord businessman and treasurer of the association, both members of a petite bourgeoisie—"the ruling element in Negro society." Their perseverance against the odds was used rhetorically to encourage the large working class below them. For when a Duplin County millowner could write in 1888 that "many colored people have, by work and economy, got good homes of their own, and are looking up, while I do not think the whites are doing so well according to their chance," it gave substance to Hunter's faith. It also substantiated the antiemigrationist line at a time when back-to-Africa advocates, chiefly Bishop Henry M. Turner of the African Methodist Episcopal church, had become conspicuous and loud. "We are further removed from slavery here in America than are the negroes of Brazil, many of whom are still in manacles," Dancy declared, criticizing a proposal to colonize one million blacks in South America. "We may be at a disadvantage here, but have we trustworthy assurance that we will be less so there?"[15]

Despite a hardening color line and escalating emigrationist rhetoric in the 1890s, optimists took their stand on hope for progress. One of the cleverest endorsements of domestic migration came from Bishop C. R. Harris, who, seeing it as a chance to profit and proselytize,

14. Clippings from Raleigh *Journal of Industry*, October 9, 1880, October 8, 1881, Richmond *Criterion*, November 17, 1885, Scrapbook, 1880–86, in Hunter Papers; Salisbury *Star of Zion*, January 29, February 26, 1886.

15. Clippings from Raleigh *Appeal*, March, 1886, Raleigh *Evening Visitor*, November 10, 1886, Charlotte *Daily Chronicle*, November 16, 1886, Scrapbook, 1880–86, in Hunter Papers; John H. Haley, *Charles N. Hunter and Race Relations in North Carolina* (Chapel Hill: University of North Carolina Press, 1987), vii–x; North Carolina Bureau of Labor Statistics, *Second Annual Report, 1888* (Raleigh: State Printer and Binder, 1888), 184; Edwin S. Redkey, *Black Exodus: Black Nationalist and Back to Africa Movements, 1890–1910* (New Haven: Yale University Press, 1969), 28, 32–36; Salisbury *Star of Zion*, February 16, 1888.

inquired: "Why not go where, while earning a living you may preach the gospel to the poor, and extend the borders of Zion?" Most Negro businessmen, however, wished that black people would stay put and buy black. Appeals to "be proud . . . go and give them [black businessmen] your support, they need it" soared on behalf of group enterprises, as did an entrepreneurial vision: "Every town of four thousand and upward can well support two Negro physicians, one good drug store, one dentist, two lawyers, six teachers, ten dressmakers, one milliner, twelve carpenters, eight brickmasons, six painters; and then . . . cooks, nurses, washerwomen, etc." This community effort, which meant employment and income for everyone, stimulated efforts "to help ourselves" in business and labor. Next to the A.M.E. Zion Publication House (Charlotte), the Coleman Cotton Manufacturing Company (Concord), and the North Carolina Mutual and Provident Association (Durham)—the most outstanding businesses—stood the state's Colored Alliance of fifty-five thousand farmers and the Negro workers' assemblies of the Knights of Labor in fifty counties.[16]

Accolades for advancing black people usually went to businessmen, notably Coleman, "wealthiest colored man in the state"; Richard B. Fitzgerald, a Durham brick manufacturer; and John H. Williamson, publisher and editor of the Raleigh *Gazette,* who personified "the enterprise and the accumulative genius of the race." With the Negro's achievements in the twenty-five years since bondage, predicted an ultraoptimist, "in one century God will advance him beyond the present powers that be and his capability will give him the presidential chair of this great country of ours." Some black leaders thought that to doubt any tenet of this racial faith, as President D. J. Saunders of Biddle University did when he dubbed the planned black display at the 1895 Atlanta Exposition a Jim Crow exhibit, undermined the Negro's "capacity for the highest mental and material development." No doubt Washington's economic optimism and accommodationist stance to-

16. Clippings from Salisbury *Star of Zion,* July 24, 1890, February 21, 1895, Raleigh *Gazette,* May 28, 1893, Scrapbook, 1887–99, in Hunter Papers; Maggie W. Hypsher, *The Negro Eldorado* (Wilmington, N.C.: Daily Review Job Print, 1893), 14, pamphlet in North Carolina Collection, University of North Carolina, Chapel Hill; Helen G. Edmonds, *The Negro and Fusion Politics in North Carolina, 1894–1901* (Chapel Hill: University of North Carolina Press, 1951), 110; Logan, *The Negro in North Carolina,* 103, 111; Sidney H. Kessler, "Organization of Negroes in the Knights of Labor," *Journal of Negro History,* XXXVII (1952), 262–63.

ward the white community made it easier for journalists to overlook problems such as the Negro death rate, which the *A.M.E. Zion Church Quarterly* once described as "appalling," and instead to stress new "lines of enterprise." Washington himself was the patron saint of black North Carolina and the race's "Philosopher Economist." Sounding much like Washington and virtually closing his eyes to North Carolina's impending disfranchisement of the Negro, Bishop Hood announced in 1900, "We are going to have improved opportunities in the near future."[17] He was too optimistic.

Freedom to learn, the unabridged right to pursue an education, tapped streams of racial endeavor as no other undertaking did. Emerging from the darkness of slavery, freedpeople contracted what a Raleigh journal termed "a disease for learning" and hence sought enlightenment in literacy. This rage to read and write received concrete direction from the Freedmen's Bureau and northern missionary associations, which by 1867 maintained more than 237 schools for over 22,788 blacks. Schooling provided blacks a formal culture of aspiration. Black state senator Thomas O. Fuller remembered: "The three 'R's' had the right of way. Friday afternoons were spent in drills, marching, speeches and singing. Often we had our spelling match, using Webster's Blue Back Speller." In 1876, a year after the state constitution mandated equal but segregated schools, black children were 38 percent of total enrollment. Still, only two in ten of the minority school-age population attended classes, compared with four in ten for the majority. The Negro community inherited the unfinished agenda of Reconstruction. "I think our first great need is education," admonished Hood, who until 1872 had been assistant state superintendent of public instruction. "No matter what the pursuit education is necessary to make it safe and profitable."[18] A synthesis of experience and vision, his statement summed up a generation's fondest hope.

As the journey "through the wilderness to the promised land of

17. Clippings from Raleigh *Gazette*, May 16, 1891, Wilmington *Record*, September 28, 1895, Scrapbook, 1887–99, clipping from Washington, D.C., *Colored American*, January 13, 1900, Scrapbook, 1900–1902, in Hunter Papers; Salisbury *Star of Zion*, January 15, 1892, January 24, 1895, March 1, May 10, August 2, 1900. See editorials in *A.M.E. Zion Church Quarterly*, III (1893), 386–87, 533, VII (1897), 51–52, IX and X (1899–1900), 79–80.

18. Roberta Sue Alexander, *North Carolina Faces the Freedmen: Race Relations During Presidential Reconstruction* (Durham, N.C.: Duke University Press, 1985), 152, 161, 163, 168; Logan, *The Negro in North Carolina*, 139; clipping from Raleigh *Journal of Industry,*

knowledge" met with extreme prejudice, minimal movement was made toward educational equality. It was emblematic that Sidney M. Finger, the Democratic superintendent of public instruction, in 1886 referred to Negroes as "the most barbarous people on the face of the earth, and perhaps the most ignorant." North Carolina reported 161,262 white and 95,160 black pupils in 1880. Their rates of illiteracy for ages ten to fourteen were 45 and 76 percent, respectively; the average school terms were six and four months. Statewide racism as well as poverty plainly produced such troubling conditions. Nine of the fifteen states in the census South had a smaller illiterate adult population than North Carolina, twelve exceeded North Carolina's "total value of school property," and eleven surpassed it in expenditures for teachers' salaries. Although North Carolina's total of 2,146 "separate schools for colored children" was bested only by Mississippi's 2,147, backwardness and segregation affected youths of both races. Yet, Negro youths had fewer teachers, experienced shorter terms, attended classes in worse buildings, and received poorer instructional supplies than did white youths. School funds were grossly unequal. Negro communities in Goldsboro, Tarboro, and elsewhere consistently fought against a movement to fund "separate schools from separated tax revenues." In 1883 that funding approach, despite Negro protest, was authorized for all school districts by the legislature. The state supreme court declared this flagrant measure unconstitutional in 1886, but blacks still had to face noncompliant boards of education and other effective forms of discrimination. Racism clouded their educational horizon. Only a minuscule proportion of students entered the five state-run and thirteen denominational academies and colleges for Negroes in North Carolina. In 1890 some 46 percent of blacks ten to fourteen years of age attended school, compared with 66 percent for whites. By 1900 the percentages increased to 55 and 68, disclosing four times more black gain but in a system of ongoing disparity. In 1900 the monthly teacher salary for white males was $24.16; for white females, $22.96; for black males, $21.64; for black females, $19.85.[19]

October 8, 1881, Scrapbook, 1880–86, in Hunter Papers; Thomas O. Fuller, *Twenty Years in Public Life, 1890–1910: North Carolina–Tennessee* (Nashville: National Baptist Publishing Board, 1910), 14.

19. Clipping from Raleigh *Journal of Industry*, October 8, 1881, Scrapbook, 1880–86, clipping from Raleigh *News and Observer*, June 4, 1902, Scrapbook, 1900–1902, in Hunter

What permitted blacks to persevere was a psychology of service and striving that had as its goal the elevation of "a race which has lately come from bondage." Part of this psychology was the desire to excel, which could be encouraged both by individual examples and by institutional objectives. Rural educator Robert G. Fitzgerald, brother of the brickmaker and formerly a sailor in the Union navy, exuded a commitment to excellence in Orange County, where "indifference and hostility marked the attitude of officials." But he inspired a zeal for learning in the young, including in his daughter Mary Pauline, who attended St. Augustine Normal School. Walking "in proud shoes," she began a teaching career in 1885 that would span a half century. Thomas O. Fuller, Shaw University Class of '90, Baptist minister and state senator, recalled that he received "no little inspiration" from an erudite white professor who "had been a slave-owner, and [was] now engaged to emancipate the minds of the descendants of former slaves." Roanoke Academy, the lower division of Plymouth State Normal School, employed a faculty with similar goals, "who will aim to both morally and educationally qualify students" for a useful life, its catalog stated. Parents were invited to send their children because "the more you educate [them] the better citizens you will make, and [they] may gradually rise to wealth and position." Plymouth's normal department, listing other requisites for success, pledged "to instill into young minds a love of order, respect for proper authority, and a desire to shun every kind of vice."[20]

Papers; S. M. Finger, *Educational and Religious Interests of the Colored People of the South, February 24, 1886,* printed address in North Carolina Collection, University of North Carolina, Chapel Hill; Escott, *Many Excellent People,* 184–85; *North Carolina Laws and Resolutions,* 1883, pp. 407–408; Logan, *The Negro in North Carolina,* 147, 151–52; U.S. Bureau of Education, *Negro Education: A Study of the Private and Higher Schools for Colored People in the United States* (2 vols.; 1917), II, 393–459; *Tenth Census, 1880: Population,* 916, 925; *Eleventh Census, 1890: Population,* I, 733; *Twelfth Census, 1900: Abstract,* 71; U.S. Bureau of the Census, *Negro Population, 1790–1915* (1918), 398; Hugh V. Brown, *E-Quality Education in North Carolina Among Negroes* (Raleigh: Irving-Swain Press, 1964), 78.

20. Clipping from Raleigh *Journal of Industry,* October 8, 1881, Scrapbook, 1880–86, in Hunter Papers; Pauli Murray, *Proud Shoes: The Story of an American Family* (New York: Harper & Row, 1978), 234–36, 238–40, 276; Fuller, *Twenty Years in Public Life,* 18; flyer from Roanoke Non-Sectarian Male and Female Academy (1881), and State Colored Normal Schools, *Annual Catalogue, 1896 and 1897,* p. 7, both in North Carolina Collection, University of North Carolina, Chapel Hill. See also Ken Chujo, "The Black Struggle for Education in North Carolina, 1877–1900" (Ph.D. dissertation, Duke University, 1988), 126–44, and James D. Anderson, *The Education of Blacks in the South, 1860–1935* (Chapel Hill: University of North Carolina Press, 1988), 33–78.

The stress put on character and conduct as building blocks of black manhood and womanhood reflected a strong religious orientation, even in tax-supported schools. In their church-oriented and community atmosphere, core group values of "cleanliness, self-sufficiency, and hard work" could be reinforced. Black schools not only bore the burden of combating illiteracy; they inculcated behavior designed to disprove racial stereotypes of dirtiness, dependency, laziness, and immorality. On the devout campus of Zion Wesley Institute (later Livingstone College), "a recommendation of good moral character" was required for admission, though persons were admitted "without regard to sex or denomination." If nondenominational Rankin-Richards Institute of Bertie County screened applicants less scrupulously, it explained in 1891 that its "course of instruction . . . is practical, moral and religious, supplemented by industrial training."[21] A blend of sacred and secular emphases would prepare the next generation; discipline of both heart and mind would be necessary.

To "educate the head as thoroughly as possible," schools generally taught both scholastic and manual skills, supposedly the keys to knowledge and security. Teachers faithfully followed the practice everywhere—from the Princeville Graded School, established by residents of this all-black Edgecombe County town in 1883, to Biddle University of Charlotte. Known for its biblical and classical orientation, Biddle also boasted an "industrial department" second to none. A student who was an apprentice printer there told the state commissioner of labor in 1893 that the best thing for "my people to better themselves financially," in addition to being saved "from the saloon and other low places of vice," was "to learn some useful trade." At Henderson Normal Institute, men learned printing and women took cooking or sewing, along with language, literature, mathematics, and natural and social science. The school strictly forbade "games of chance, profane or indecent language; the use or possession of tobacco, snuff, intoxicating liquor, or weapons of any kind." The four state-run normals offered courses in seven subject areas. To history "should be relegated abstract questions relating to slavery . . . as well as many of the more difficult topics of our State," the bulletin of the

21. Salisbury *Star of Zion*, October 31, November 7, 1884; Burton, *In My Father's House*, 254–55; flyer from Rankin-Richards Institute (1891), in North Carolina Collection, University of North Carolina, Chapel Hill.

Colored State Normal Schools delineated, whereas the subjects of agriculture and domestic science would "fit pupils to be more efficient in such industrial work as they will . . . pursue in later life." De-emphasizing the manual sphere and endeavoring to meet the "earnest demands of a rising class" in society, Livingstone College tilted its curriculum toward the ministerial, legal, and teaching professions. "There were few books in the library then," reminisced W. F. Fonvielle, class of '90. The ordinary student "had no money and few friends, but he was anxious to get up in the world."[22]

That ambition to reach the top was cultivated especially by black teachers, who succeeded the northern missionaries as caretakers of Negro education, becoming the state's first corps of college-trained black educators. "One of the best educated young men we have ever had," the Enfield *Progress* acclaimed a Greensboro professor, and the Raleigh *Outlook,* applauding another's "eloquent extempore appeal," urged "parents to take advantage of the Graded Schools." According to the census, "teachers and professors in colleges, etc.," numbered only 1,490 in a black work force of 266,317 in 1900, but as racial models they loomed larger than their numbers might suggest. The characteristics of a sample of 25 of them, selected on the basis of their state-wide influence, make their stature and significance clearer. The sample comprises 20 men and 5 women. Years of birth are known for 19 of the men and 2 of the women, and for these 21 the average age in 1890 was thirty-four. Two of the 5 women were born free, and of the 16 men whose status at birth is known, only 1 was born free. Of the 18 teachers whose college background is known, 13 attended college in North Carolina. These mostly indigenous achievers earned 24 academic and received 7 honorary degrees. Three-fourths of the group combined teaching with other pursuits: 4 doubled as attorneys, 2 as businessmen, 3 as journalists, 2 as legislators, 7 as ministers, and 1 as a physician.

22. Clipping from Raleigh *Journal of Industry,* October 8, 1881, Scrapbook, 1880–86, in Hunter Papers; Joe A. Mobley, "In the Shadow of White Society: Princeville, a Black Town in North Carolina, 1865–1915," *North Carolina Historical Review,* LXIII (1986), 363–65; North Carolina Bureau of Labor Statistics, *Seventh Annual Report, 1893* (Raleigh: State Printer, 1894), 89–90; Henderson Normal Institute, *Annual Catalogue, 1904,* pp. 8–9, 12, 14–15, and *Course of Study of the Colored State Normal Schools* (Raleigh: State Board of Education, 1904), 2–7, both in North Carolina Collection, University of North Carolina, Chapel Hill; W. F. Fonvielle, *Reminiscences of College Days* (Raleigh: Edwards and Broughton, 1904), 26, 60.

According to the Raleigh *Gazette,* Charles N. Hunter, "as editor, educator and orator," had "but few equals in the Negro race." It also stated that "no colored man in the State, perhaps in the South, stood higher in his profession, or enjoyed a more universal esteem both among white and colored people, than Prof. James A. Whitted," a Durham principal. James W. Hood and Joseph C. Price, for their part, won national recognition for educational statesmanship. Simon G. Atkins of Slater Academy and James B. Dudley of Agricultural and Mechanical College in Greensboro, as well as Peter W. Moore of Elizabeth City Colored Normal School and Ezekiel E. Smith of the State Colored Normal School at Fayetteville, headed growing institutions. Smith served as United States minister to Liberia, James E. O'Hara as a congressman, and William P. Mabson as a state senator. Edward A. Johnson, a Raleigh alderman, attorney, and professor, authored *A School History of the Negro Race in the United States* (1890) and *History of Negro Soldiers in the Spanish-American War* (1899). Charles W. Chestnutt, "a young man of tremendous natural powers," resigned as principal of the normal school at Fayetteville in 1883 to go north, but his future writings, especially his fiction, would contain frank portrayals of race relations in the Cape Fear region. Anna J. Cooper, a languages instructor at St. Augustine and "figure of public interest," went north in 1887 and then completed *A Voice from the South, by a Black Woman of the South* (1892). Sanctioned by this record of accomplishment in a day when education's doors were barely ajar, black teachers' influence on students must have been enormous.[23]

23. Salisbury *Star of Zion,* December 3, 1891, March 17, 1898; clipping from Charlotte *Messenger,* June 30, 1883, Scrapbook, 1880–86, clippings from Enfield *Progress,* August 12, 1887, Raleigh *Outlook,* June 24, 1887, January 23, 1888, Raleigh *Gazette,* October 29, November 26, 1892, Scrapbook, 1887–99, in Hunter Papers; *Twelfth Census, 1900: Occupations,* 352, 356. The freeborn were Charles W. Chestnutt (b. 1858), born in Ohio; Sadie A. Fitzgerald (1875); James W. Hood (1831), Pennsylvania; James E. O'Hara (1844), New York; and Ezekiel E. Smith (1878). The slave-born were Simon G. Atkins (1863); Calvin S. Brown (1859); Anna J. Cooper (1859); John C. Dancy, Sr. (1857); James B. Dudley (1859); John R. Hawkins (1862); Charles N. Hunter (1851); Edward A. Johnson (1860); William P. Mabson (1846); Peter W. Moore (1858); William G. Pearson (1859); Joseph C. Price (1854); Nicholas F. Roberts (1849); Lawson A. Scruggs (1857), Virginia; George C. Shaw (1863); and James A. Whitted (1847). The four teachers whose birth dates and statuses are not known were Sadie Ellison of Henderson, Mary E. Fonvielle of Goldsboro, Lizzie B. Searcy of Reidsville, and Robert S. Taylor of Princeville. *Who's Who in Colored America,* 1927, pp. 7, 60, 182, 187; *Who's Who in Colored America,* 1928–1929, pp. 50, 74, 77, 86, 89, 97, 208, 287; *Who's Who in Colored America,* 1941–1944, 239; Eric Anderson, *Race and Politics in North Carolina, 1872–1901: The Black Second* (Baton Rouge: Louisiana State University

Teacher organizations confronted important issues and, purporting to be democratic rather than elitist, advocated programs to educate every segment of the black community. Encouraged by the establishment in 1877 of a state normal school and tax-funded graded schools, which the Raleigh *Monthly Elevator* labeled "rounds . . . in the ladder of our freedom," the North Carolina State Teachers' Educational Association, brainchild of black educators and politicians, asked for even more. James O'Hara, Henry P. Cheatham, and George H. White, all future congressmen, were members. Charter member Charles N. Hunter, opposing the Clinton *Caucasian*'s argument that "the State in educating negroes is acting contrary to her best interests," believed North Carolina was "bound by the Constitution" to provide "its colored citizens a means of . . . education." Not prepared to force the issue, however, he proposed, "Let us do something for ourselves, and urge upon the State its duty to assist us." That dual emphasis pervaded the association's fourth annual meeting in 1885, where informal fellowship and devotional services preceded spirited presentations on the necessity of "teaching color in the public schools" and "inciting our people to self-help." Despite a condescending address by state superintendent S. M. Finger, other speakers implored teachers to "form associations everywhere for your own defence" and to "beware of ruts. Keep up with the times." Another spokesman, who criticized the fact that the tax funds were racially separate, urged "a tax on the whole property" that would upgrade all public schools. Later annual meetings hosted Senator Henry W. Blair of New Hampshire and recommended passage of the $77,000,000 Blair educational bill "as [the] best means of preparing the masses for the patriotic exercise of an intelligent citizenship"; named the Raleigh *Outlook* official organ while commending "more practical work" as well as "mental and moral education"; toasted black Wilmington for its "unbounded hospitality" for the meeting of 1891; and at the twentieth session, not only reaffirmed stressing to students "the practice of thrift" but resolved that

Press, 1981), 62–63; Mobley, "In the Shadow of White Society," 349; *Paths Toward Freedom: A Biographical History of Blacks and Indians in North Carolina* (Raleigh: Center for Urban Affairs, North Carolina State University, 1976), 131, 145, 148, 159, 176, 179, 182, 187; N. C. Newbold, *Five North Carolina Negro Educators* (Chapel Hill: University of North Carolina Press, 1939), 4, 38, 89, 118; Murray, *Proud Shoes*, 11; Penelope L. Bullock, *The Afro-American Periodical Press, 1838–1909* (Baton Rouge: Louisiana State University Press, 1981), 73–74, 99–102; *A.M.E. Zion Church Quarterly*, III (1893), 546–51.

"encouragement should be given to the few who are able to take the higher training." Echoes and endorsements of these views were in editorials by J. C. Dancy and columns by Simon Atkins, Charles Hunter, and others, among them a teenage female who scored the neglect "of educating our girls."[24]

Black Carolina was also active and influential in the American Association of Educators of Colored Youth. When the organization held its fourth convention at Wilmington in 1892, Atkins, Price, expatriate Anna Cooper, and D. J. Saunders, president of Biddle University, were nominated for offices, with Dancy slated for the board of directors. Atkins' paper explained that southern whites needed effective schooling, too, "if the nation is to be safe"; Cooper's explored the relationship between learning and work. Saunders, a known opponent of the vocational approach, issued a challenge: "The capacity of the race . . . is conceded, but it remains to be demonstrated that in respectable numbers we can walk more independently in the highways of art, science and literature." The same conclave adopted Dancy's resolution "that we do condemn lynching, in the most positive terms, as the crowning evil of the age." Urging "the preparation of text-books by colored educators" in 1893, Virginia professor D. B. Williams told delegates that Edward A. Johnson's history text was "much needed and highly appreciated. . . . It is a boon to the race, and should be placed into the hands of every colored boy and girl." Condensed from George Washington Williams' pioneering two-volume *History of the Negro Race in America* (1883), Johnson's *School History of the Negro Race* was published in 1890. A teacher who combined pedagogy and pride, Johnson wrote the book because, as he stated, "the children of the race ought to study some work that would give them a little information on the many brave deeds and noble characters of their own race." In reality it presented a

24. Clipping from Raleigh *Monthly Elevator*, May, 1877, Scrapbook, 1833–79, clippings from Clinton *Caucasian*, February 1, 1883, Charlotte *Africo-American Presbyterian*, July 9, 1885, Scrapbook, 1880–86, clippings from Raleigh *Outlook*, January 15, April 29, August 5, 1887, Scrapbook, 1887–99, clipping from Raleigh *Baptist Sentinel*, June 30, 1900, Scrapbook, 1900–1902, in Hunter Papers; *Journal of the Fourth Annual North Carolina State Teachers' Educational Association, 1885* (Raleigh: A. Williams and Co., 1886), 6, 18, 20–21, 25, 31; *Proceedings of the Twentieth Annual North Carolina Teachers' Association, 1901* (Elizabeth City, N.C.: E. F. Snakenberg, Printer, 1901), 25–26; Percy Murray, *History of the North Carolina Teachers Association* (Washington, D.C.: NEA, 1984), 16, 20–21, 23–24, 27; Salisbury *Star of Zion*, May 21, June 25, December 3, 1886, January 21, 1887, June 7, July 19, March 12, June 25, 1891, October 29, 1896.

lot of information, using biographical sketches, historical calendars, summaries of events, documentary excerpts, and illustrations. Several of the thirty-five brief chapters covered the Negro in North Carolina, and all traced the journey from slavery to freedom. By 1894 this textbook was printed in a third edition and introduced into many schools in the Carolinas and Virginia. Thus, Johnson and his fellow Tar Heel educators were attracting regional and national acclaim.[25]

Noted as practitioners, these men and women also deserve credit as thinkers, for their philosophical and theoretical observations illumine the contemporary black conviction that education meant liberation. That education should also have an ethical purpose was rarely questioned, mainly because of the broad sweep of Christianity and democratic idealism in private and public schools. Without "a moral as well as a literal training," Bishop Hood exclaimed, "we are more likely to have educated rascals than useful citizens." He would discipline head and heart together toward the end of building character, which might help Negroes, in the words of more devout pedagogues, to shun the "use of alcoholic drinks" and to "give freely to others." As though to enhance temperance and sharing, race and gender entered into the discussion. Education "on an abstract basis" appealed "to Caucasians, Jews or Greeks," Anna J. Cooper reasoned. "The fact is, however, that Race devotion with us is not merely a choice but a necessity, and . . . our only hope." Such a people, "just twenty-one years removed from the conception and experience of a chattel," should cherish both manhood and womanhood, she thought. "Let us insist then on special encouragement for the education of our women and special care in their training." Simon Atkins, while not dissenting on objectives of racial identity and genuine coeducation, stressed teacher preparation and professionalism and educational foundations. Could anyone build competence and pride better than "a body of teachers who have consecrated themselves to teaching as a life-work"? He believed future progress rested on this "the greatest of all professions—except, perhaps, the ministry." Theory on pedagogy varied from instruction in

25. See "Proceedings of the Fourth Annual American Association of Educators of Colored Youth, 1892," in *A.M.E. Zion Church Quarterly*, III (1893), 348, 349, 352, 385, 491, 495; and Raymond Gavins, "A 'Sin of Omission': Black Historiography in North Carolina," in Jeffrey J. Crow and Flora J. Hatley (eds.), *Black Americans in North Carolina and the South* (Chapel Hill: University of North Carolina Press, 1984), 3–6.

"industrial pursuit" and "that which best prepares for life" to that stressing development of the "power of the mind." But eclecticism and pragmatism about content or what to teach gave way to consensus on the transcendent value of black education. It would mean freedom from "oppression and insult," deliver the race "from its night of darkness into the pure sunlight of a grander era," and prove the Negro's "ability and enterprise." It would make blacks "more useful and honorable in our sphere of life," serve as a "panoply that protects us against the assaults of ignorance," and "quicken the currents of a healthful moral life." Education was indispensable.[26]

Freedom of religion, a constitutional liberty denied to slaves and given grudgingly to freedmen, empowered the Negro to "worship God under his own vine" and enabled black churches to become "the most vital centers of group activity." Blacks greeted emancipation with "religious and hysterical fervor. This was the coming of the Lord," pioneer scholar W. E. B. Du Bois wrote—a bit pejoratively. "It was all foolish, bizarre and tawdry. Gangs of dirty Negroes howling and dancing . . . yet to these black folk it was the Apocalypse." Their religiosity achieved coherence and direction in a multipurpose church—concurrently a house of prayer, "an agency of social control, a source of economic cooperation, an arena of political activity, a sponsor of education, and a refuge in a hostile white world." Like a mother, it would nurture the spirit of independence that quickened Afro-American institutional life in the post-Reconstruction era.[27]

The church's presence may be seen partly in statistics on its principal followings, which were overwhelmingly Protestant and rural. Nearly a third of black Carolinians (150,166) belonged to five denominations in

26. Letter from Charles N. Hunter to editor of unidentified newspaper, March 17, 1877, unascribed clipping, Scrapbook, 1833–79, clipping from Raleigh *Journal of Industry,* October 8, 1881, letter from Hunter to editor of unidentified newspaper, unascribed clipping, July 7, 1882, Scrapbook, 1880–86, clippings from New York *Age,* March 9, 1889, Raleigh *Gazette,* April 30, 1892, Scrapbook, 1887–99, clipping from Raleigh *Progressive Educator,* December, 1902, Scrapbook, 1900–1902, in Hunter Papers; Salisbury *Star of Zion,* March 13, August 28, 1885, January 7, November 3, 1887, March 15, 1888, July 13, 1893, December 23, 1897, September 13, 1900; Anna J. Cooper, *A Voice from the South, by a Black Woman of the South* (Xenia, Ohio: Aldine Printing House, 1892), 26, 28, 78.

27. Clipping from Raleigh *Journal of Industry,* November 19, 1879, Scrapbook, 1833–79, in Hunter Papers; Escott, *Many Excellent People,* 180; W. E. B. Du Bois, *Black Reconstruction in America, 1860–1880* (1935; rpr. New York: Atheneum, 1970), 122–24; Albert J. Raboteau, *Slave Religion: The "Invisible Institution" in the Antebellum South* (New York: Oxford University Press, 1978), ix; Alexander, *North Carolina Faces the Freedmen,* 77.

1882, the first date for which there are comparative estimates. Sixty-three percent of these belonged to the Baptist denomination, 19 percent to the African Methodist Episcopal Zion church, 7 percent to the African Methodist Episcopal church, 6 percent to the Colored Methodist Episcopal church, and 3 percent to the Presbyterian church. Catholics, Congregationalists, Episcopalians, Moravians, Lutherans, and others combined for 1 percent of the total. By 1890 these bodies reported a membership of 240,305, then 43 percent of all Tar Heel Negroes and 1 percent above the rate of church membership for the state's whites. Much of this growth occurred within the Baptist denomination, whose state convention (founded in 1867) sent evangelists, Sunday school organizers, and charity workers to a plenteous harvest in the state's eastern counties. With its General, Central, and Western conferences in place by 1891, in North Carolina the A.M.E. Zion church built its largest following in thirty states. But it still ranked second in the contest of evangelistic outreach. The Baptists' 41 local associations, 1,270 edifices, 908 ministers, and 140,205 communicants in 1900 outdistanced the A.M.E. Zion church's 65 station circuits, 600 edifices, 395 ministers, and 130,000 communicants. By 1900, Baptist, Congregational, Episcopalian, Methodist, and Presbyterian memberships totaled 305,709, or 49 percent of the North Carolina Negro population.[28] With the number of followers doubling within twenty years, the church seemed more nearly ubiquitous than any other institution.

Its omnipresent ethos of faith and piety linked social concerns and spiritual values. To most ordinary churchgoers, in Du Bois' judgment, "God was real. They knew him. They had met Him personally." Intense spirituality, especially at revival services, could be an emotional outlet to relieve and renew communicants for life's demands. Worship was also an occasion to express joy or grief and reaffirm "kin obliga-

28. Thomas W. Yonker, "The Negro Church in North Carolina, 1700–1900" (M.A. thesis, Duke University, 1955), 68–69, 73–74, 76, 78, 82, 98–99, 158–59; U.S. Bureau of the Census, *Negroes in the United States, 1920–32* (1935), 9–10; *Eleventh Census, 1890: Abstract*, 259; U.S. Bureau of the Census, *Religious Bodies, 1906* (2 vols.; 1910), I, 58, II, 100–101; Logan, *The Negro in North Carolina*, 165, 166; J. A. Whitted, *A History of the Negro Baptists of North Carolina* (Raleigh: Edwards and Broughton, 1908), 34; J. W. Hood, *One Hundred Years of the A.M.E. Zion Church* (New York: A.M.E. Zion Book Concern, 1895), 624–25.

tion," marital sanctity, and bonds of mutuality in families and communities. That 51 and 55 percent, respectively, of North Carolina black females and males aged fifteen and over were married in 1900 (compared with 54 and 57 percent of this age category in the entire population) probably owed something to the moral authority of churches. Church networks fostered the ideal of monogamous marriage. Another ideal was mutuality. Thomas O. Fuller served several rural congregations, one of which worshipped "in a log hut used for public school purposes." Members of this congregation not only kept "together by holding prayer-meetings," but they also donated time to build "our lovely house of worship." Such "abiding faith and loyalty," to Baptist historian J. A. Whitted, heightened "the general uplift of the colored people of North Carolina." Educated blacks who went to church rarely displayed spiritual emotionalism, but they still did much for the cause of the gospel and the race. A.M.E. Zion layman J. C. Dancy, the widely known editor of the *Star of Zion*, was, according to his son, "very religious and practiced his religion in day-to-day fashion. None of us ever sat at the breakfast table without reciting a verse from the Bible prior to having our meal." By faith the young would be disciplined and the group saved. For it was the church, declared Bishop James W. Hood, that "opened the way for the development of the race in a material and intellectual sense." It aimed to fulfill the needs of body and soul together.[29]

Critical to the church's work were ministers and missionaries. Bishop Hood, "in his day one of the most influential men of color in the United States," and Joseph C. Price, "idol of the Zion Church," outshone the rest of the clergy. Spellbound by Price's eloquence, the New York *Times* deemed him "a noble specimen of the Negro. He is six feet tall and of massive frame, and his face . . . suggests a man of marked intelligence." But a "who's who" of the ministry must also include Nicholas F. Roberts and S. Augustus Shepard, each a former slave and

---

29. Du Bois, *Black Reconstruction*, 124; Whitted, *The Negro Baptists of North Carolina*, 23, 25, 33; Herbert G. Gutman, *The Black Family in Slavery and Freedom, 1750–1925* (New York: Pantheon, 1976), 204–11; Rawick (ed.), *The American Slave*, XV, 306; *Negroes in the United States*, 151–52; *Thirteenth Census, 1910: Abstract with Supplement for North Carolina*, 593; Fuller, *Twenty Years in Public Life*, 29–30; John C. Dancy, *Sand Against the Wind* (Detroit: Wayne State University Press, 1966), 60; Hood, *One Hundred Years of the A.M.E. Zion Church*, 22–23.

a Baptist. A son of Shaw University, Roberts studied theology at the University of Chicago, joined Shaw's faculty, and in 1893 became acting president. Editor of the school's *African Expositor* and president of the Baptist State Convention and the Baptist State Sunday School Convention, he remained "a conspicuous, indispensable factor in everything which meant the uplift of the denomination." Shepard distinguished himself in the parish rather than in the academy. After finishing Shaw, he served as state missionary for the American Baptist Publication Society while founding the Sunday School Convention and the Colored Orphan Asylum at Oxford. By 1901 he had become pastor of White Rock Church in Durham, where his son would later launch North Carolina College. Despite "the tide of the more intelligent ministry which swept most of the pioneers from the stage," Shepard stood "among the ablest ministers of the State." Of outstanding churchwomen, the wives of Shepard and Hood were the best known and probably the most visible. Pattie G. Shepard, head of the Baptist Women's Home Mission Convention, demonstrated "unmistakable evidence of her ability to lead women," J. A. Whitted noted. By virtue of "her command of a choice flow of language and her great executive mind, she swayed great audiences wherever she appeared." Katie P. Hood, secretary and eventually president of the A.M.E. Zion Woman's Home and Foreign Missionary Society, attended St. Francis Academy in Baltimore, where she developed a fierce "determination to go through with what she undertakes." Embodying "strong force of character," she became "a perspicacious leader" in "the mission cause" of benevolent work and Christian education. At home and abroad, she won the respect of intelligent men and women and the love of little children.[30]

The church directed much of its moral discourse at youth, and lessons abounded. Christian parents must give "their children a rich legacy of industry and character" and impress upon them "the merits of good, plain common sense." At the proverbial "Children's Day

30. Carter G. Woodson, *The History of the Negro Church* (Washington, D.C.: Associated Publishers, 1921), 196, 213; clipping from Raleigh *Banner*, April 28, 1881, Scrapbook, 1880–86, in Hunter Papers; New York *Times*, quoted in *A.M.E. Zion Church Quarterly*, III (1893), 437; *Paths Toward Freedom*, 182; Whitted, *The Negro Baptists of North Carolina*, 112, 204, 207–208; Hood, *One Hundred Years of the A.M.E. Zion Church*, 282–85; William J. Walls, *The African Methodist Episcopal Zion Church: Reality of the Black Church* (Charlotte: A.M.E. Zion Publishing House, 1974), 404.

exercises," the young heard about "the carpenter, the son of Mary," from whose toils came "that which we prize most dear." Black heroes were described as models of righteousness. Frederick Douglass was a "gentle man without spot or blemish," who lived "an entire life beyond reproach." Joseph Price could be "at home among the humblest of his race, as he was the most fortunate." In 1898 several thousand prints, which could "be had for almost nothing," were made for those who had "long wanted large and good pictures of the late and brilliant J. C. Price to frame and hang in their homes." There were also other didactic forms, particularly parades, poems, prayers, and sermons on Emancipation Day—January 1. Following the annual Emancipation Day "line of march," the crowd might hear a poem addressed to "the colored school boy," such as: "Boys, please be true!/The girls will gladly lend a helping hand,/Provided you/Will for your rights and country bravely stand." No prayer failed to render "thanks for the emancipation of our country, and humanity itself, from the terrible sin of Negro slavery." Young persons would also often read history lessons on black heroes such as freeborn "John Chavis, colored, who . . . was sent to Princeton University . . . and was prepared for the ministry of the Presbyterian Church." The young also heard speakers such as the Zionite who declared that "energy of character . . . and integrity" were required "to win a great prize."[31]

For the laity and the public, sermons and theological opinion invoked similar maxims and spoke to the social context in which black people lived. To see the average congregation only as "plain Negroes" with an unlearned preacher is to miss the diversity of congregations and ministers. Whether educated or uneducated, ministers were expected to be moral leaders. Their members also wanted them to preach in what theologian Henry H. Mitchell has called "the hermeneutic style." According to Mitchell, the term *hermeneutic* is "a code word for putting the gospel on a tell-it-like-it-is, nitty-gritty basis." This creates intimate dialogue between speaker and audience because it addresses circumstances in their world. It blends folk and formal aspects of black

31. Fuller, *Twenty Years in Public Life*, 13; Dancy, *Sand Against the Wind*, 61; Whitted, *The Negro Baptists of North Carolina*, 32; unascribed clipping, 1877, Scrapbook, 1833–79, clippings from New York *Observer*, 1881, Weldon *North Carolina Republican*, May 22, 1884, Scrapbook, 1880–86, unascribed clipping, January 8, 1898, Scrapbook, 1887–99, in Hunter Papers; Salisbury *Star of Zion*, August 27, 1891, June 16, 1898; *A.M.E. Zion Church Quarterly*, III (1893), 512, IV (1894), 178–79.

preaching to achieve emotional expression as well as informed ex-
egesis of the text.[32]

Bishop Hood, whom A.M.E. Zion layman Simon Atkins esteemed
"above any other Afro-American, living or dead," emerged as the
quintessential practical preacher. Hood's *The Negro in the Christian
Pulpit* (1884), an anthology of sermons and one of the first by a black
North Carolinian, demonstrated "a rich variety of doctrine, style and
thought" in the Negro's proclamation of the Word. Most of the twenty-
six sermons deal with themes of personal consecration, good stew-
ardship, self-denial, and brotherly love—foundations of Christ's
church and the true community. Throughout his texts, though artic-
ulating a need for individual spirituality, Hood never countenanced
unrestrained emotionalism. "Christianity bears the marks of intelligence," he preached. The most important virtue in the consecrated
life was service to God by serving one's fellow man and woman. The
faithful steward, therefore, fulfilled the daily mission of sharing his
material and spiritual resources and talents with others. Were not
these exhortations to serve and share essential to Negroes' freedom
and independence? They must "work out their own salvation," Hood
believed, by inculcating such values in churches, schools, and other
Negro institutions. To deny oneself, the meaning of Jesus' call to discipleship, was another essential value. Hood particularly condemned
selfishness and intemperance. Selfishness could lead to ultimate tor-
ment for the soul, as in the case of the rich man who "belonged to the
favored race" and gave the beggar Lazarus only crumbs from his table.
"How many here today are copying his example?" Hood asked. And
intemperance seemed to bind people in a way worse than slavery.
"Death released the victims of our late system of slavery. . . . We have
no such hope respecting the victims of intemperance. Death sinks
them deeper." The bishop summed up his Christology in the maxim
"Love to God, and love to man." He expounded on another theme—
deliverance or liberation—in *The Plan of the Apocalypse* (1900). Ministers
were told "to teach the people prudence," for "their cry unto God for
deliverance" had been heard. The wrath of God's imminent judgment

32. Logan, *The Negro in North Carolina*, 165, 169; Henry H. Mitchell, *Black Preaching*
(Philadelphia: J. B. Lippincott Co., 1970), 30–31.

would "put down every opposing power" of oppression and persecution. Appropriate to this triumph of good over evil was the verse "To patient faith the prize is sure, / And all that to the end endure / The cross, shall wear the crown." Using images of Armageddon, Hood spoke symbolically to blacks' hope for complete freedom.[33]

Enlarging that vision were other blacks who spoke out on racism and religion. Representative of their statements was an article in the Raleigh *Gazette* in 1891 by Charles N. Hunter. He asked: "Are the American people willing to appeal the so-called 'Negro problem' to the Bible and abide the judgment of God as it issues out of the sacred pages of the Holy Writ? Are they—the white people of the American Republic ready to trust the whole matter to an Alwise God?" Hunter doubted it, but he added, "We should understand at once that applied Christianity is the only means by which we may ever hope for the removal of this great obstruction to the development of the South." In 1899 a sermon by A.M.E. Zion minister J. J. Adams appeared in the *Star of Zion*. Raising a biblical question, "Sirs, what must I do to be saved?" (Acts 16:30), he feared that blacks were in danger of social death. He cited racist pronouncements by white clergymen and public officials, plus "cruel injustice and bloody outrages perpetrated upon the Negroes," to prove that "our political life in many parts of the country is but a death through politics." Yet he still hoped for racial justice. "It was right that all men should be free, and the question of American slavery could not be settled till the nation recognized the freedom of her sable sons," he declared. Concerning just what must be done to assure Negro salvation, Adams explained: "I am not able to offer a solution now. But I believe our policy should be Christianity first, peace next, and anything after that, which assures protection to home life and liberty." Not only did he "appeal to the white ministry of the land to aid the colored race in this effort," but Adams also implored "the young people of the race to cling closer to the Church and its institutions. If we turn away from God, our cause is lost." His homily is a reminder that black churchmen did face day-to-day reality. Their religion may have

33. J. W. Hood, *The Negro in the Christian Pulpit* (Raleigh: Edwards and Broughton, 1884), 6, 8, 30–31, 68–70, 118–19, 157, 285; J. W. Hood, *The Plan of the Apocalypse* (York, Pa.: P. Anstadt and Sons, 1900), xii–xiii, 40–42, 44.

been less otherworldly in its outlook than socialist E. Franklin Frazier postulated.[34]

Even as the faithful sang, "I am bound for the promised land," ministers' orientation to the real world continued. Study "the great questions of the day," recommended A.M.E. Zion pastor E. George Biddle, who believed a good shepherd should keep abreast of "politics and all economic subjects that relate to the health and wealth of his flock." Clearly, the relevance of church and pastor depended upon education and enlightenment. "The pulpit is demanding prepared men for its occupancy. The pew demands talent that can lead and instruct it in the truths of the Gospel," declared the *A.M.E. Zion Church Quarterly.* "Thought, well presented, must take the place of sound and noise, and senseless harangue and twaddle. These will not do in this enlightened time." But the letter without the spirit profited nothing, for the task warranted "weight in character." It demanded empathy, integrity, sobriety, and uprightness. "If he [the pastor] lets a rumor get out on him, it will dig a grave deep enough to bury his salary, the general fund and all together," added Zion bishop I. C. Clinton, giving a charge on responsibility. "We must teach the sacredness of the marriage relation. We must protect our females. . . . Teach our people that we cannot be respected until we respect ourselves." Preaching on the benevolence of Dorcas in Acts 9:30, a fellow Zionite acknowledged the church's historic debt to Christian womanhood (meaning black women) for proven charity and discipleship. The look toward heaven was not denied, but earth-oriented matters were hardly overlooked.[35]

Black Carolina enjoyed in its churches what Frazier termed "an opportunity for self-expression and status." Pride, for instance, was frequently evident church news, which might speak of a parson as "one of the most intelligent, boldest, and bravest members of the race," of denominational growth as "astonishing," or of a parish as "the leading colored church." Pulpits could host a bishop who thanked the Almighty that "the sun of liberty has been shining upon us," a white judge who warned that God "can lift up the weak and pull down the

34. Clippings from Raleigh *Gazette*, May 30, 1891, Salisbury *Star of Zion*, January 26, 1899, Scrapbook, 1887–99, in Hunter Papers; E. Franklin Frazier, *The Negro Church in America* (New York: Schocken, 1964), 46.

35. *Songs of Zion*, 54; *A.M.E. Zion Church Quarterly*, II (1892), 311, 418, III (1893), 497; Salisbury *Star of Zion*, January 19, 1899; clipping from Littleton *Reformer*, July 25, 1900, Scrapbook, 1900–1902, in Hunter Papers.

strong," or a layman who scoffed that "the white pulpit of the South is wholly independent of the Negro . . . and hence can ignore his claims." The conservative Raleigh *Biblical Recorder* saw in such jeremiads the Negro's ambition "to rule a superior race. He can never rise to power."[36]

In the meantime, black churchgoers proved themselves to be fallible, as complaint, dissension, and heresy sometimes threatened their fellowship. Critics of disharmony said that it arose from evils such as "the tongue of slander," hypocrisy, intemperance, sponsoring "anything to draw a crowd," and other "degrading practices." The latter included excursions, according to one critic, because "we need every penny of our money to buy ourselves homes and to educate our children." High churchmen similarly scorned the cakewalk, whose undignified dance routines meant "playing the monkey . . . for the white man," and they also condemned "disgusting and injurious face and hair" products. "The Negro who is not contented with his color and hair is a fool," a joint pastoral letter proclaimed. Hence church people assumed moral authority and attempted to regulate behavior. Another controversy involved segregation. Opponents of "separated ecclesiastical relations" (segregated churches) argued that these made impossible "the recognition of the equality of our manhood in church and state." Proponents deemed all-black connections legitimate and demanded whites' tolerance of them, arguing that "intolerance is the golden wedge in the camp, and until it is removed it is folly to talk about the settlement of this question." Tolerance was also needed within the black church. A.M.E. and A.M.E. Zion bishops' dialogue on merger, for example, led the emigrationist Henry M. Turner to reject Hood's effort to eliminate "the term African from our church title" and to denounce "lies, slander, misrepresentations, low cunning, wicked juggling, abuse and vilification . . . on both sides." So in spite of the argument that "there ought to be a union," parochialism stood in the way. Hood's insistence upon Zion's ascendancy in a united body had been "unreasonable" to Turner, leading to a rejection of the A.M.E.

36. Frazier, *The Negro Church*, 46; clipping from Salisbury *Star of Zion*, September 11, 1885, Scrapbook, 1880–86, clippings from Enfield *Progress*, June 3, 1887, Salisbury *Star of Zion*, June 13, 1889, Charlotte *Africo-American Presbyterian*, August 20, 1891, Raleigh *Gazette*, April 25, 1891, July 2, 1892, Scrapbook, 1887–99, clipping from Raleigh *Biblical Recorder*, November 5, 1902, Scrapbook, 1900–1902, in Hunter Papers.

proposal for equitable jurisdiction between two boards of bishops. Hood also rebuked Booker T. Washington for "his wild, random, thoughtless, and as I fully believe, slanderous statement" that many preachers lacked character: "One man proves immoral and a big noise is made about it. Ten others in the same body are pure and upright and no mention is made of them." Thus, the conflicts arising from blacks' freedom to discuss, to debate, and to "be somebody" in God's house sometimes undermined the "broad charity that will at least enable us to feel our brother's care."[37]

Churches, nevertheless, nurtured the ethos of cooperation that bonded sacred and secular institutions of uplift. Benevolent groups (the Royal Knights of King David, the United Order of True Reformers, and the Household of Ruth) and fraternal organizations (the Masons, the Odd Fellows, the Good Templars, and the Sons of Ham) evolved in the faith and existed in such abundance that the Atlanta *Christian Index* commented: "No race has as many societies among them as the colored. . . . Let us unite and work for our own common good." Some ordinary folk accused these orders of hindering religion. One devout man, asked by a reporter how his church was getting on, replied: "Mighty poor, mighty poor, brudder. De 'cieties . . . is just drawin' all de fatness an' marrow outen de body an' bones" of the church. Business, educational, political, and religious leaders, by contrast, eyed the orders as agencies of character building and self-help. With a statewide Grand Lodge, the Masons promoted solidarity, thrift, mutual aid, and Christian morality right beside the Baptist State Convention. Annual meetings usually were held in large city churches, whereas the locals gathered at church-owned lodge halls. In 1895, the A.M.E. Zion church owned eleven lodge halls whose seating capacity totaled 1,200. Sharing space, church and lodge might recruit and retain the critical mass of consumers necessary to support Negro insurance, retail, and service establishments. To wit, without twenty churches and fourteen lodges to promote patronage between 1891 and 1901, Raleigh's black businessmen and professionals would have been hard-pressed to sur-

37. Clippings from New York *Christian Herald*, July 19, 1884, Washington *Republic*, January 11, 18, 1885, Scrapbook, 1880–86, in Hunter Papers; Salisbury *Star of Zion*, October 10, November 28, 1884, February 6, July 17, September 10, 1886, January 5, 1888, May 30, 1889, January 15, 1891, March 11, 1897, December 21, 1899, November 1, December 20, 1900.

vive. Such interdependence received more and more emphasis as this era went on. "The influence of the pulpit in this regard can hardly be over estimated. It is a great . . . stimulant, affecting many, many lives that other influences fall short of," stated J. Milton Steel of Zion connection. Religion strengthened institutional ties even as it gave meaning to black freedom.[38]

Freedom of the ballot—the untrammeled right to vote—complemented the economic, educational, and religious freedoms blacks aspired to during the period. Politics is probably the most widely discussed subject in the historiography of the nadir. Historians have agreed that a significant number of Negro men voted and held office in North Carolina and the South until their disfranchisement around 1900. The record also shows that blacks generally remained loyal to the Grand Old Party, though racism was rampant in and outside the party and culminated in the Democratic party's success. Less is known about how much Negroes viewed voting and office holding as priorities or weighed the blessings and risks of those liberties. But political participation at least provided them a means to legitimate their citizenship and to protect racial interests. Many thought that the race's ultimate survival, which Douglass questioned at the exposition in 1880, would swing on the pendulum of politics.

Black Carolinians, ever testing the limits of white tolerance, made themselves conspicuous in the electorate and in public office. Between 1880 and 1896 they furnished between 90,000 and 109,000 voters, mostly easterners who allied with western, formerly unionist whites in a strong state Republican party. In gubernatorial contests from 1880 to 1896, Democrats never received more than 54 percent of the vote, and an average of 78 percent of eligible black males cast ballots, three out of four of them for Republican candidates. This trend helped to make North Carolina elections the most competitive and perhaps the most democratic among the southern states. The leverage possessed by Negroes and Republicans did not come from Democrats' goodwill (ballot box stuffing, intimidation, and lynchings occurred) but resulted

38. Logan, *The Negro in North Carolina*, 203; *Christian Index*, quoted in Salisbury *Star of Zion*, November 26, 1886; Salisbury *Star of Zion*, November 13, 1885, January 5, 1888, January 11, 1894; Dorothy A. Gay, "Crisis of Identity: The Negro Community in Raleigh, 1890–1900," *North Carolina Historical Review*, L (1973), 132. On the central institutional role of the church, see Hood, *One Hundred Years of the A.M.E. Zion Church*, 13–26, and especially the documents on 525–30.

mainly from their power in the Second Congressional District, known as "the Black Second," where eight of ten counties boasted Negro majorities. Democratic resistance to sharing power with a minority party and race, however, soon led to racist suffrage restrictions, namely a poll tax, literacy and property tests, and a grandfather clause. Eighty-seven percent of eligible blacks voted for governor in 1896, and in 1900 the rate was 67 percent (of an estimated 120,000 who were eligible). Four years later, virtually no blacks voted. Prior to this purge hundreds of Negroes were elected or appointed to local, state, and federal offices. In the cities and towns, Negroes held the positions of alderman, attorney, constable, and policeman; in the counties, blacks served on boards of education and in the offices of school commiteeman, county commissioner, coroner, jailer, magistrate, register of deeds, deputy sheriff, and surveyor. At the state level, blacks served primarily in the General Assembly. From 1877 through 1890, Negro members numbered 43 in the House and 11 in the Senate; they served 65 House and 16 Senate terms. Only 22 black legislators served during the sessions of 1891–1897, and the session of 1899 seated but 5, only 1 a senator. Occasionally a black would be a state asylum director, inspector, or solicitor. The most prestigious officeholders, of course, served in Washington: United States congressmen James E. O'Hara (1883–1887), Henry P. Cheatham (1889–1893), and George H. White (1897–1901). Blacks from the Tar Heel State also, at various times, held positions as customs collector at the port of Wilmington, commander of a Negro regiment in the Spanish-American War, and minister to Liberia. In addition, there were scores of black postmasters. Black Carolinians thus held office at all three levels of government, "though never in proportion to their population strength."[39]

The decline and elimination of Negro office holding mirrored the broader context of political and social inequality. In analyzing postbellum North Carolina politics, historian Eric Anderson sees the

39. Logan, *The Negro in North Carolina,* 18, 43, 45–47; Jeffrey J. Crow, "Cracking the Solid South: Populism and the Fusionist Interlude," in Lindley S. Butler and Alan D. Watson (eds.), *The North Carolina Experience: An Interpretive and Documentary History* (Chapel Hill: University of North Carolina Press, 1984), 335, 338; J. Morgan Kousser, *The Shaping of Southern Politics: Suffrage Restriction and the Establishment of the One-Party South, 1880–1910* (New Haven: Yale University Press, 1974), 183, 194; Escott, *Many Excellent People,* 181; Anderson, *Race and Politics in North Carolina,* 246–51; Edmonds, *The Negro and Fusion Politics,* 111–12; Salisbury *Star of Zion,* August 9, 1900.

period 1878–1901 as one that witnessed a progression from equilibrium to realignment to extremism. Black office-holding and patronage gains were lost in the Democrats' counterattack against fusion (the Republican-Populist alliance) and in their implementation of statutory white supremacy. Oppression and slavery remained grim realities. Women were being bought for "$20 to $120 a head" in Tunisia, and Brazil's recent abolition of slavery barely allowed it to be classed as a "civilized nation," but North Carolina claimed to be a democracy. It was at least possible for a former governor, who had been impeached and removed from office, to defend his efforts to implement the Republican Reconstruction policies. A black Republican editor could eulogize a former president as "a strong abolitionist," and another black editor could extol his race's "gallantry in the war with Spain." But the state's white officials were thoroughly Negrophobic, politically and socially. The ugly manifestations of such Negrophobia—in segregated public travel, in the cruelty and neglect of the convict lease system, and in the way children learned prejudice from their elders—convinced the Raleigh *Gazette* that racial hatred "reaches deep down beneath the foundations of our free institutions. . . . In its settlement is involved the final triumph or the final ignominious failure of free democratic government."[40]

Democracy was central to Negro political rhetoric, which vacillated between ideologies of conflict and consensus. To practice the principle of equality, too long deferred, the state would have to implement "the organic law under which we live," as one black leader put it. Yet civil rights (particularly those defined in the Thirteenth, Fourteenth, and Fifteenth amendments) were addressed differently by the main factions. Whether appealing to "the white people of the state" or meeting with presidents, Congressman Cheatham, legislator George L. Mabson of New Hanover County, and other moderates relied upon moral suasion and petition. They believed conscience, enlightenment, good-

---

40. Clippings from Raleigh *News and Observer*, December 6, 1881, Weldon *North Carolina Republican*, May 22, 1884, Scrapbook, 1880–86, clippings from Raleigh *State Chronicle*, May 10, 1889, Raleigh *Gazette*, April 9, May 5, 1892, unascribed clipping, December, 1898, Scrapbook, 1887–99, clipping from Raleigh *News and Observer*, April 13, 1901, Scrapbook, 1900–1902, in Hunter Papers; Salisbury *Star of Zion*, November 26, 1886, May 24, 1888, October 15, November 12, 1891, January 19, 1893; editorial in *A.M.E. Zion Church Quarterly*, II (1892), 319; Anderson, *Race and Politics in North Carolina*, 61–62, 145–46, 240–41.

will, and gradualism, not rhetorical threats, offered the best means to reform "public sentiment." But agitation was the forte of Congressman White and a few militants, who labeled lynching "a systematic thinning out of the colored voters" and white supremacy a euphemism for "fraud, intimidation, carnage and death." They believed equity, independence, and respect for life and limb necessitated protest. The two ideologies frequently clashed. Acrimony filled the air when the moderate Charles N. Hunter argued that to forge interracial peace, blacks must forgo office holding, which he thought was a bad lesson from Reconstruction and a basis of the existing corrupt leadership. That allegation did some fearless officeholders great injustice, the militant Bishop Turner replied. "Had they been as cowardly as the present generation, the Negro would have had no rights to-day, civil or political." Outspoken A.M.E. Zion bishop Alexander Walters, furthermore, said he harbored "no sympathy with that class of leaders who are advising the Negroes to voluntarily eschew politics in deference to color prejudice." Booker T. Washington, who preached that message of retreat while enjoying wide popularity, made the militants' fight even more difficult. Perhaps the most heated exchanges came in patronage squabbles between the camps. Fired for opposing Congressman O'Hara, deputy internal revenue collector E. R. Dudley, complaining to his pliant superior, reacted, "Mr. O'Hara is not my master, but I am truly sorry to learn that you are his slave." Yet, though tactics differed, the factions did agree on democratic goals for American blacks: a racially inclusive government, equal protection under the law, continued enfranchisement, educational opportunity, and "a fair chance to compete in the labor world," affording "the black boy the chance to make the best of himself."[41]

It was according to these shared goals, then, that the political parties would be judged. Negroes were allied to Republicanism, though dis-

41. Clippings from Goldsboro *Enterprise*, February 19, Raleigh *Banner*, May 19, 1881, Winston *Western Sentinel*, November 8, 1883, Scrapbook, 1880–86, clippings from Raleigh *Outlook*, February 25, 1887, Nashville *Southern Recorder*, March 2, 1888, Raleigh *Gazette*, April 23, July 23, 1892, Raleigh *Visitor*, September 21, 1898, Raleigh *News and Observer*, January 3, 1899, Scrapbook, 1887–99, clipping from Raleigh *News and Observer*, April 21, 1901, Scrapbook, 1900–1902, in Hunter Papers; Salisbury *Star of Zion*, May 15, September 1, 27, 1887, February 9, 1888, July 25, 1889, September 11, December 4, 1890, December 8, 1898, January 5, February 9, September 28, October 26, 1899, May 31, July 12, August 2, 23, 30, December 6, 1900.

agreements over civil rights and patronage forced many to question this relationship. Intraparty tension is therefore evident—from the time of O'Hara's convention resolutions of 1881, which called for the appointment and election of "competent and deserving colored men," through New Hanover County blacks' complaint of 1898 that they cast "about 95 per cent of the total Republican vote" but received "less than 20 per cent of the offices directly in the hands of the County Commissioners." The complainants indeed had limited options. Most tried to stand on the middle ground between dissatisfaction and loyalty, "condemning our enemies in the party" without leaving it. Others made it obvious that they much preferred an admittedly flawed GOP to a southern Democracy "of brutality savagery and inhumanity." After all, blacks did dissent and plead their case in the Republican party, which heralded as members Frederick Douglass and Judge Albion W. Tourgée, a former North Carolina carpetbagger and "staunch friend of the race." Those unwilling to trust in image alone favored alliances with "the liberal and progressive element among Southern whites" along bipartisan lines. Few dissenters joined the state "Colored man's Republican party" of 1889 or the National Negro party of 1900, but many of them endorsed the Farmers' Alliance third-party movement because it was "giving the regular Democracy a lot of worry, not to say trouble." In the years 1894–1898, many black regulars voted the fusion ticket while seeking more offices. Negro officeholders and voters, however, were compelled to compromise with powerful county Democratic bosses and were vulnerable to racial terrorism. Commentators contended that black men had "as much right to divide their votes as white men. They should be slaves of no one party." But the Democratic party's extreme antiblack campaigns and "cry to repeal the fifteenth amendment" eclipsed that argument. "How any self-respecting Negro can be an honest Democrat is a mystery beyond my comprehension," confessed Bishop Hood.[42]

42. Clippings from Raleigh *Banner*, June 25, 1881, Charlotte *Messenger*, June 30, Fayetteville *Sun*, October 3, 1883, Weldon *North Carolina Republican*, May 22, Statesville *American*, June 30, 1884, clipping of article entitled "North Carolina Election Returns by Congressional Districts for the Year 1884, Compared with Elections of 1880 and 1882," from Washington, D.C., *Press*, March 7, 1885, Scrapbook, 1880–86, clippings from Raleigh *Gazette*, May 21, 1892, Wilmington *Daily Record*, March 26, 1898, Scrapbook, 1887–99, in Hunter Papers; Salisbury *Star of Zion*, March 19, 1886, July 12, September 13, 1888, August 29, 1889, August 14, 1890, March 24, 1892, November 9, 1899, June 14, July

As blacks groped to respond in a principled manner to an unprincipled situation, they clung to their heritage as free men and women. To several of the Federal Writers' Project informants, politics was "'bout . . . de Ku Klux," and their words evoked a folk image of armed terror during Reconstruction that events of the 1880s and 1890s confirmed. Although lynchings and pogroms carried out by Klansmen, Red Shirts, and Whitecaps in Georgia and the Carolinas were deplorable, these activities did not surprise the state's Negro spokesmen. For example, they discerned the relationship between Tar Heel suffrage restriction ("How many Negroes are there in North Carolina who can give date and place of birth?") and the triumph in South Carolina of governor-elect Benjamin R. Tillman, who promised "to see that white supremacy is maintained in her borders." Constitutional disfranchisement there, of course, hastened it in the Old North State. Even those whom the black man considered political friends opposed him or warned him of "the inevitable." The Afro-American plea for justice went unheeded and was followed by a bloody riot at Wilmington and the "unfair, unjust, and inhuman proposition to disfranchise," as the Littleton *Reformer* called it. The *Star of Zion*, for its part, predicted that "thousands of the best Negroes will emigrate." That statement proved prophetic, for many of the educated, fearful of losing all constitutional freedoms, left the state, as the Exodusters had done two decades earlier. An omen of the times, Emancipation Day in 1900 was cold—too cold for a parade. Rather, those who assembled adopted their "Address to the White People of North Carolina." Declaring "there can be no middle ground between freedom and slavery," the address urged a rejection of the Democrats' proposals to repeal the Thirteenth, Fourteenth, and Fifteenth amendments by amending the state's constitution: "Repeal them and slavery again becomes lawful," the address stated. The campaign "not only to restrict our right to vote,

---

5, October 18, 1900; North Carolina Democratic party broadsides, *ca.* 1898, 1900, and statement of North Carolina Republican Executive Committee (Colored), 1916, in North Carolina Collection, University of North Carolina, Chapel Hill. See also Jeffrey J. Crow, "'Fusion, Confusion, and Negroism': Schisms Among Negro Republicans in the North Carolina Election of 1896," *North Carolina Historical Review,* LIII (1976), 364–84; and John Hamilton Haley, "The Carolina Chameleon: Charles N. Hunter and Race Relations in North Carolina, 1865–1931" (Ph.D. dissertation, University of North Carolina at Chapel Hill, 1981), 145–48.

but to deny that right altogether," was un-Christian, undemocratic, and unpatriotic.[43]

The nadir, as Rayford W. Logan labeled the period of postbellum Negro life and thought from 1877 to 1901, was a time of transition in Afro-American and southern history. Situated between the end of Reconstruction and the emergent Age of Segregation, it occasioned a downswing to "the lowest point in the American Negro's struggle for equal rights." Whether one agrees or disagrees with Logan's nomenclature and chronology, historians generally accept the view that the status of blacks deteriorated as white racism triumphed during the last two decades of the nineteenth century. W. E. B. Du Bois pronounced the extreme oppression of those years "the long step backward toward slavery." John Hope Franklin similarly suggested that "'The Long Dark Night' continued until 1923."[44] In any case, blacks endured the worst of times and then made a long climb toward equal civil rights that lasted more than half a century and culminated in the 1960s. They were able to accomplish these things largely because of their resilient heritage of freedom and hope for equality.

The post-Reconstruction generation saw itself, in Frederick Douglass' words, "as a free people . . . on trial." Freedom's future mandated the enforcement and preservation of the Thirteenth, Fourteenth, and Fifteenth amendments. Survival depended critically upon a collective vigilance. "Having achieved by a bloody war and through the great Emancipator, Abraham Lincoln, our freedom, and later by enactments of Congress our citizenship and enfranchisement in theory," Bishop Alexander Walters told the 1900 National Afro-American Council, "we are now face to face with the question of our complete civil and

---

43. Clipping from Fayetteville *Sun*, September 26, 1883, Scrapbook, 1880–86, clippings from New York *Independent*, November 14, 1889, Wilmington *Messenger*, November 14, 1898, Atlanta *Constitution*, March 17, 1899, Scrapbook, 1887–99, clipping from Raleigh *Morning Post*, January 2, Raleigh *News and Observer*, March 11, May 11, Littleton *Reformer*, July 25, 1900, Raleigh *Biblical Recorder*, November 5, 1902, Scrapbook, 1900–1902, in Hunter Papers; Salisbury *Star of Zion*, January 2, 1889, May 16, 1895, December 1, 1898, March 2, June 22, 1899, February 1, March 8, June 28, August 9, September 3, November 29, 1900; editorial in *A.M.E. Zion Quarterly Review*, X (July–September, 1900), 54. Cf. the Democratic party broadside *The Negro Smith Scores Populist Johnson* (1899), and the speech by John T. Morgan, *Negro Suffrage in the South, January 8, 1900*, in North Carolina Collection, University of North Carolina, Chapel Hill.

44. Logan, *The Betrayal of the Negro*, 3, 11; Du Bois, *Black Reconstruction*, 708. Franklin is quoted in Logan, *The Betrayal of the Negro*, 11.

political rights, from the struggle for which we dare not retreat." Black Carolinians, too, appreciated the general emancipation, demanded constitutional protection, and moved determinedly forward. During the 1880s and 1890s, according to historian Frenise A. Logan, "the Negroes who remained in the state were optimistic; yet at the same time they were acutely conscious of the obstacles in the path of their advancement." That double consciousness significantly influenced blacks' perceptions of the white world and substantially shaped their core values.[45]

It was shared concepts of freedom that formed the crucible of black North Carolina's institutional and intellectual life in the nadir. The state's blacks consciously and constantly identified themselves as a recently freed people with entitlement to full citizenship under federal and state constitutions. A common memory of slavery as inhumane permeated oral and written testimony on the past. A catechism on being free, God fearing, educated, independent, self-reliant, and unified as a race was followed by all black institutions.

However, efforts to enlarge opportunity through economic, educational, religious, and political means mirrored patterns of intraracial conflict as well as consensus. In an increasingly complex statewide community, both elite and folk responses were apparent. Racial thought and action brought together the intelligentsia with the rank and file. The black experience in this era included the lives of Exodusters, nonmigrating farm tenants, propertyless and unskilled laborers, businessmen and -women, clergymen, editors, educators, students, the rural and urban uneducated, church members, politicians, officeholders, and voters, and expressions of feelings and opinions survive from all these groups. A cross-section of a dynamic if oppressed society, North Carolina blacks began to pluralize Negro ideology and strategy. For instance, there were differences in outlook that were based on social class. The numerically larger peasantry displayed a bread-and-butter, no-nonsense orientation and showed a greater impulse to migrate. The small, influential middle class opposed migration and viewed freedom more explicitly in petit bourgeois terms of individual liberty, moral development, and material progress.

45. Clipping from Raleigh *Journal of Industry,* October 9, 1880, Scrapbook, 1880–86, clipping from Raleigh *Morning Post,* January 2, 1900, Scrapbook, 1900–1902, in Hunter Papers; Salisbury *Star of Zion,* August 30, 1900; Logan, *The Negro in North Carolina,* 219.

Meanwhile, public competition and debate among middle-class leaders themselves often revealed conflicting perspectives. Divergent priorities and tactics were expressed by black moderates, militants, and emigrationists; advocates of self-help and civil rights; proponents of industrial and classical education; otherworldly and politically active church members; Democrats, Republicans, independents, and fusionists. Their pronouncements—on appropriate responses to racism and white officialdom, on the role of traditional values in strengthening group pride and solidarity, or on prescriptions for poverty, illiteracy, lynching, Jim Crow, and disfranchisement—mixed strategies of accommodation and protest.[46]

Overall, however, the framework of racial consensus seemed to reduce class strain. To a generation with fresh memories of slavery, always dominated by white North Carolina, race was much stronger than class per se. Therefore, the Negro community could effectively contain many schisms via its broad agreement on goals, including the efficacy of basic freedoms (to earn and learn, of religion and the ballot) that it must preserve and pursue. Core values—good character, industry, thrift, mutuality, and race unity—represented another wide area of accord. Such agreements, which merged ordinary people's aspirations with those of institutional leaders, provided an ideological buffer against external realities. Finally, black North Carolina, as America's and the South's sixth-largest minority population in 1880 and seventh-largest in 1900, typified a number of major trends in southern black history. These trends included, among others, the building of autonomous institutions, the emergence of clergymen as perhaps the most important leadership element, mass outmigration, and significant political participation from the 1870s to the early 1900s. Portraying black southerners' relentless determination to be truly free even in the nadir of Afro-America, black North Carolina remained a major participant in "the contest over the meaning of freedom" into the twentieth century. Thus, it was only appropriate that in 1960, when the sit-ins swept North Carolina and the South, young blacks who sat in at "white only" lunch counters carried signs that read "FREEDOM NOW."

46. Cf. Meier, *Negro Thought in America*, 69–82.

7 / JEFFREY J. CROW

An Apartheid for the South: Clarence Poe's Crusade for Rural Segregation

By almost any measure, Clarence Hamilton Poe, editor of the *Progressive Farmer* from 1899 to 1953, was an archetypal southern Progressive. He rose from the grinding poverty of the postbellum southern farm to edit, own, and publish the most influential farm journal in the region (circulation 1.5 million). Poe had a keen intellect and a prodigious appetite for knowledge. His books, articles, speeches, and editorials—written in a clear, forceful, expository style—revealed the deep convictions of a middle-class moralist whose Baptist upbringing allowed him to quote effortlessly from the Bible and the classical literature in which he immersed himself. Largely a self-taught man, Poe learned from observing. During two trips to Europe (1908 and 1912) and a journey around the world (1910–1911), he studied foreign agricultural problems and systems and applied the insights he gathered from those experiences to southern agriculture. All of Poe's energies were directed toward improving the southern farmer's community life, education, agricultural methods, and status in a rapidly modernizing society. Poe had a penchant for statistics and pored over census data with a social scientist's eye for detail, comparison, and analysis. In the words of a contemporary educator, Poe was a "rural sociologist."[1]

---

1. Bion H. Butler, biographical sketch of Clarence Poe (Typescript in Clarence H. Poe Papers, North Carolina State Archives, Division of Archives and History, Raleigh). Ar-

Poe's progressive views on building a New South could have defined a political agenda for the region. He favored better care for the mentally ill, reformatories for young criminals, and child-labor laws. In North Carolina he led the fight for prohibition, adopted in 1908, and for six-month compulsory school attendance laws. Presidential primaries, the initiative and referendum, federal regulation of trusts and railroads, and lower tariffs for a free market also won his endorsement.[2] If he had any political heroes, they undoubtedly were fellow Democrats Woodrow Wilson and Charles B. Aycock, governor of North Carolina (1901–1905), whose daughter Alice the young editor married in 1912. In one other important respect Poe shared the southern Progressive ethos of the age: he propounded a conservative, racist ideology.

Although not a conscious race-baiter in the mold of Benjamin R. Tillman, James K. Vardaman, and Hoke Smith—the type of people Poe classed as "bitter or destructive . . . 'negro agitators' "—he espoused a paternalistic view of white supremacy and black inferiority that castigated lynch law on one hand and defended disfranchisement and segregation on the other. In Poe's analysis of the South's social, political, and economic ills, however, blacks represented only part of the problem. Above all, Poe championed the independent white yeoman farmer, an endangered species as the economic and demographic trends of the twentieth-century South gained momentum. Poe clung to a Jeffersonian, agrarian vision of the South, one inhabited by prosperous white farmers safely removed from what he perceived as the baleful effects of a poor, licentious, and ignorant black population. In the words of one admirer, when Poe assumed the editorship of the *Progressive Farmer*, "he determined . . . [to] take up for the white man a

---

chibald Henderson, mathematics professor and historian at the University of North Carolina at Chapel Hill, was the educator mentioned in the text. A full-scale biography of Poe (1881–1964) is long overdue. Poe's voluminous papers in the North Carolina State Archives invite an in-depth study of his long career. His published autobiography, *My First Eighty Years* (Chapel Hill: University of North Carolina Press, 1963), is rambling, superficial, and conspicuously silent about the issues central to this essay. More helpful are two studies by Joseph A. Coté: "Clarence Hamilton Poe: The Formative Years, 1899–1917" (M.A. thesis, East Carolina University, 1969), and "Clarence Hamilton Poe: Crusading Editor, 1881–1964" (Ph.D. dissertation, University of Georgia, 1976).

2. Coté, "Clarence Poe: Crusading Editor," 88. For an authoritative account of the reform movement in the South, see Dewey W. Grantham, *Southern Progressivism: The Reconciliation of Progress and Tradition* (Knoxville: University of Tennessee Press, 1983).

task that a great humanitarian had begun not long before for the black man—emancipation."[3]

Although he promoted a variety of Populist panaceas for white farmers—from cooperatives to rural credit associations—Poe in time also came to advocate rural segregation.[4] His crusade to divide black and white farm populations into separate enclaves on the basis of land-ownership stirred considerable debate in the columns of the *Progressive Farmer* and throughout the South. Indeed, his ideas resonated with echoes of policies then being enacted in South Africa. The debate reached all the way to the North Carolina Senate, which in 1915 voted on a constitutional amendment to effect such a plan. Poe, therefore, was no ordinary southern Progressive. His racial views placed him in the vanguard of Anglo-American theorists who were designing and justifying a rigid system of apartheid in South Africa and the American South.

Clarence Poe was born in 1881 in Chatham County, North Carolina. Located in the rolling piedmont of the state on the fringes of the antebellum plantation economy and the postbellum industrial boom, Chatham County was deeply hurt by the agrarian depression of the 1890s. Poe's family nearly lost its farm, and he learned firsthand what it was like for a farm family to move to the city (in his case, Greensboro) and live and work in an industrialized urban environment. The experience profoundly impressed young Poe, who developed an idyllic vision of what life on the farm should be and could be with fundamental reforms to alleviate the farmers' economic distress.

In 1897 Poe attracted the attention of James W. Denmark, editor of the *Progressive Farmer*, who invited the sixteen-year-old youngster to come to Raleigh to serve as assistant editor. Two years later, before his nineteenth birthday, Poe assumed full editorial responsibilities. In 1903 he bought the weekly journal, which then had 5,504 subscribers. Four years later, the *Progressive Farmer* changed from a state to a regional

---

3. Butler, biographical sketch of Poe, in Poe Papers.
4. For an excellent introduction to Poe's land-segregation plan, see Jack Temple Kirby, "Clarence Poe's Vision of a Segregated 'Great Rural Civilization,'" *South Atlantic Quarterly*, LXVIII (1969), 27–38; Jack Temple Kirby, *Darkness at the Dawning: Race and Reform in the Progressive South* (Philadelphia: J. B. Lippincott Co., 1972), 119–30.

publication and expanded into Virginia, South Carolina, Georgia, and Tennessee. By buying out small agricultural newspapers, Poe raised the number of his journal's subscriptions to 150,000 in 1911. Six years later, Poe operated four regional offices and claimed a circulation of 200,000.[5]

When Poe joined the staff of the *Progressive Farmer*, the journal was an organ of the North Carolina Populist party. Founded in 1886 by the legendary Leonidas LaFayette Polk, the *Progressive Farmer* was present at the birth of the Farmers' Alliance. During the 1890s the journal followed embattled farmers into the People's party. For a brief period Populist and Republican fusionists wrested control of the state from the Democracy, which had held power since the end of Reconstruction. The Populist-Republican coalition controlled two legislatures, those of 1895 and 1897, and elected a Republican governor in 1896. The Democrats responded with furious appeals to the racial prejudices and fears of white voters. Regaining control of the General Assembly in 1899, the Democrats drafted a suffrage amendment to disfranchise blacks, who were overwhelmingly Republican, and poor whites, many of whom had supported the Populists. In the bitter, violent white-supremacy campaigns of 1898 and 1900, Poe secretly supported the Democrats and gubernatorial candidate Charles B. Aycock at the very time the Populist party was fighting for its survival. In 1900 the young editor privately solicited letters in support of the disfranchisement amendment to publish in the *Progressive Farmer*. "I have had a confidential request from the editor of the *Progressive Farmer*, for something in favor of the Amendment for his paper," one Democrat informed a colleague. "*He must not be known as soliciting these contributions, as he might loose his job if it were known.* Get your friends in different sections to write along the same lines. . . . Persons can use a *non de plume* [*sic*] or their names as they prefer." Writing years later, Poe recalled that in 1900 the Democratic party circulated thousands of copies of the *Progressive Farmer* containing his articles in favor of the suffrage amendment. "I still remember one of the closing incidents of the campaign," Poe related to Josephus Daniels, publisher of the Raleigh *News and Observer*, in 1941, "[when] from one small county postoffice in a single day seven sub-

5. Coté, "Clarence Poe: Crusading Editor," 23, 34–35, 37.

scribers stopped their paper because I had praised Candidate Aycock as 'a high-toned Christian gentleman.'"[6] The suffrage amendment passed and Aycock was elected governor.

Poe established his credentials as a nationally respected southern Progressive early in the twentieth century. Reaching beyond his agrarian constituency, Poe published articles in such prestigious periodicals as the *North American Review, Atlantic Monthly,* and *Outlook.* In 1902 he defended suffrage restriction in the South as a progressive measure to cleanse politics, foster better race relations, and return principle rather than party to the ballot box. In the same article he termed blacks a "child race" that needed to be educated before it could vote.[7]

Two years later, Poe decried lynching as an evil. The mob, he admitted, "is not always actuated by fear of a guilty man's escape. Sometimes the ruling passion is only a savage, diabolical bloodthirstiness. Sometimes it is sheer and fiendish bullyism tormenting the weak and defenseless." Poe called for a "stringent, but flexible" antilynching law with a wide range of penalties. To Poe, women's fear of rape and black men's fear of lynching were "twin perils that menace Southern peace." He urged more safeguards for rural women, such as telephones and stiff vagrancy laws, "against the reckless, roving elements of blacks" from which "the criminal class is chiefly recruited." The agrarian editor recommended a "rural police force" to function in the same manner as the antebellum slave patrol. Black leaders, he counseled, could reduce Negro crime through industrial education, religious training, and opposition to "unwholesome notions of social equality and intermarriage." White men, too, must assume some responsibility for encouraging "immorality among negro women," he said. The thought of supposed concupiscence offended Poe's sensibilities: "The bestiality of negro men is fostered by the unchastity of negro women. No form of racial amalgamation must find toleration among the whites."[8]

6. T. B. Parker to J. Bryan Grimes, May 7, 1900, Clarence Poe to Josephus Daniels, March 13, 1941, quoted in *ibid.,* 70–73.

7. Clarence H. Poe, "Suffrage Restriction in the South: Its Causes and Consequences," *North American Review,* CLXXV (1902), 534–43.

8. Clarence H. Poe, "Lynching: A Southern View," *Atlantic Monthly,* XCIII (1904), 155–65. In 1906 North Carolina governor Robert B. Glenn thanked Poe for his support on the antilynching issue. R. B. Glenn to Clarence Poe, June 15, 1906, in Poe Papers. See also Raleigh *Progressive Farmer,* January 4, 1913.

Poe's paternalism toward blacks was especially evident in his attitudes about black education. He opposed efforts throughout the South to divide school funds between the races in proportion to the amount of taxes paid by each. In Poe's opinion, such a policy would only aggravate the "Southern race problem." Education, he contended, was always preferable to ignorance and illiteracy. A division of the tax moneys, he believed, would undermine the public school system. Because whites now controlled government and education, they had the "power to adapt the negro's education to his needs, and select the worthiest and safest black men to direct the education and influence the principles of the young negroes." Many southern Progressives did not follow Poe in his support for equal, if separate, education for blacks. In practice blacks were taxed proportionally more than whites, and black children received less per capita expenditure on education.[9]

At the national level Poe shared many of the Progressive movement's ideas about economic democracy and the Progressives' faith in science and the scientific method to promote economic efficiency, one of Poe's favorite themes when discussing the needs of southern agriculture. He railed against "unfair accumulations of great wealth" and trusts that burdened the common man. Poe opposed "distributing wealth in any Socialistic manner," but he wished to ensure "every man the enjoyment of the wealth that he creates." Wary of the class appeals of unnamed "demagogues and agitators," Poe argued for the removal of special privilege and the recognition of the "rights of capital as well as the rights of labor." He stood for "justice and a square deal"; only "weaklings" sought "special rights or class privileges."[10]

Writing in 1915, Poe commented privately that "there is no reason for us to feel that we [southerners] are chained down by the inheritance of the ignorance and stagnation of the ante-bellum period." The South's "unprogressiveness," he declared, grew out of "ignorance rather than . . . innate conservatism."[11] Yet, Poe never entirely escaped

9. Clarence H. Poe, "Should Southern Whites Aid Negro Schools? A Southerner's View," *Outlook*, August 23, 1910, pp. 1010–1013; J. Morgan Kousser, "Progressivism—For Middle-Class Whites Only: North Carolina Education, 1880–1910," *Journal of Southern History*, XLVI (1980), 169–94.

10. Clarence Poe to Charles B. Aycock, March 9, 1912, in Poe Papers.

11. Clarence Poe to J. G. de Roulhac Hamilton, April 1, 1915, *ibid.*

the shadow of the past. Reconciling the South's agrarian heritage with its industrial and urban future challenged the editor's fertile mind and facile pen.

In a speech at Trinity College in Durham in May, 1906, Poe defined the three major problems facing the South as illiteracy, lower per capita wealth than that of other sections, and unexploited natural resources. Journalists, he asserted, had a part to play in curing the South's economic ills. "The crying need of the South today," he declared, "is for the newspaper dedicated not to politics but to community development."[12] This statement succinctly expressed Poe's credo. In speeches and editorials he sought to articulate the white South's problems and his proposals for solving them. Education, political economy, and, increasingly, the settlement of the "race problem" ranked high on his list of priorities.

Poe recognized that the South remained overwhelmingly rural. Thus, he reasoned, "the whole problem of re-building the South hangs on the improvement of farming and farm life." There "is great room for the development of manufacturing," he admitted, but the "supreme task and opportunity of our day" must be "to train the man behind the plow to the highest degree of efficiency." Poe wished to redeem southern farming "from the inherited curse of slavery," which fostered the idea that farm work was undignified for white men. Farming skill in the North and West, Poe pointed out, was held in higher esteem. Southern farming, on the other hand, had been left to the "shiftless negro slave, and then the shiftless tenant." Poe called for diversified crops, more livestock, machinery, fertilizers, good roads, and schools. He was especially critical of black farmers, "ignorant and illiterate, little more than a generation removed from slavery, and with ten times as much confidence in the changes of the moon as in experiment stations, and a hundred times as much faith in Old Master's ways of farming as in the views of modern leaders of agriculture."[13]

Speaking before the Southern Commercial Congress in Washington, D.C., in 1907, Poe echoed the sentiments of fellow editor and North Carolinian Walter Hines Page. Prosperity, Poe asserted, depended

12. Clarence Poe, "The Young Men of Journalism," *ibid.*
13. Clarence Poe, speech at Clinton, N.C., July 4, 1906, *ibid.*

upon the well-being of the common, average man. Merchants, lawyers, bankers, railroads, and manufacturers must see that the farmer prospered. The doctrine applied equally to blacks and whites. He cited the "ignorant negro" as the South's greatest economic burden. Having traveled in ten southern states, Poe postulated "as a principle of political economy" that communities prospered "in proportion to their white population." The editor mused: "I do not know what we are going to do with the negro. I do know that we must either frame a scheme of education and training that will keep him from dragging down the whole level of life in the South . . . or else he will get out of the South and give way to the white immigrant."[14]

In the same speech Poe condemned the South's refusal to educate and train its poorer classes. For too long the South had feared that education "would spoil the working man." He labeled "cheap, untrained labor . . . a curse" and argued that the New South must be predicated on an agricultural revolution. He demanded an educational crusade to modernize the farm and train "country children" in the ways of scientific farming.[15]

Year after year, before numerous forums Poe reiterated these themes linking education, prosperity, and race. At Littleton, North Carolina, in 1908 he noted that the average Tar Heel farmer produced only about half as many salable crops as the average American farmer; Ohio farmers, Poe observed, had accumulated six times as much property as North Carolina farmers.[16] The main explanation for this discrepancy, he contended, lay in "political economy." This meant that "where skill and intelligence begins . . . profit begins." Throughout the United States in "every class," he declared, "all are prospering just in proportion as they add mental labor—thought, skill, science, knowledge, education, training—to muscular labor." Poe deplored the southern

14. Clarence Poe, "The Agricultural Revolution," *ibid.*
15. *Ibid.*
16. Clarence Poe, speech at Central Academy, Littleton, N.C., May 12, 1908, *ibid.* Poe's comparison of northern and southern farm productivity was correct. In 1900 the average number of acres of cropland harvested per farm in North Carolina was 25; the figure declined to 22.6 in 1910. Along with Mississippi, which had similar figures, these statistics ranked lowest in the South. The respective figures for Kansas were 104.4 and 111.9. In 1899 the approximate value of farm products in North Carolina was the lowest in the South—$398 per farm; the figure rose to $694 in 1909. Comparable figures for Iowa were $1,598 and $2,759. Gilbert C. Fite, *Cotton Fields No More: Southern Agriculture, 1865–1980* (Lexington: University Press of Kentucky, 1984), 235, 237.

plantation owner's opposition to education, but he also warned: "If the negro will not become efficient, he will be crowded out." To make North Carolina the leading state in the New South, Poe posited, Tar Heels must combine "the courage, culture and chivalry of ante-bellum days with the progress and cosmopolitan outlook of the twentieth century."[17]

Poe repeatedly emphasized the putative relationship between prosperity and the proportion of whites in a state's or community's population. "And this is true," he argued, "not because the negro is a negro, not because he is black, or kinky-headed, or flat-nosed, but because he is less efficient, because in intelligence and character he is inferior to the white man." Poe blamed southerners for following "prating demagogues decrying taxation for universal education." He also scored an educational system "made by city people for city people." Textbooks failed to impart to farm children "the possibilities of science and training in agricultural work." Poe demanded longer school terms, compulsory attendance, and practical education in "agricultural science" for rural schools.[18]

Poe, however, continued to return to the Negro as the source of the region's poverty. In a commencement address to the North Carolina Agricultural and Mechanical College for the Colored Race at Greensboro in May, 1910, Poe identified himself as a descendant of slaveholders and the "blood . . . of Confederate soldiers and of the Ku Klux." Even so, he associated himself with Governor Aycock, who had offered pledges of goodwill and assistance to elevate blacks in the wake of the 1900 white-supremacy campaign. Educating field hands, the editor declared, must take precedence over politics, but progress must come "without social intermingling." Terming the "ignorant negro field hand" an economic curse, Poe asserted that "the presence of the negro in the South has made the whole section and my entire race poorer—and chiefly by reason of this same time-worn half-sacred Southern fetish of an ignorant, illiterate field hand as the ideal agricultural laborer." The fault, Poe confessed, lay with whites for allowing blacks to remain untutored and unschooled. Untrained labor, he be-

17. Poe, speech at Central Academy, 1908, in Poe Papers.
18. Clarence Poe, "Prosperity of Every Man Depends upon Prosperity of Average Man," *ibid.*; Poe, "Making Education Fit the Farmer's Needs," *ibid.*; Poe, "What North Carolina Needs," *ibid.*

lieved, "has not only failed to make immediate profits but has laid waste the capital of the landholder as well." Poe said the South had long ago repudiated "the fallacy that slavery was an economic good." It must now "repudiate once and for all time the no less monstrous heresy that ignorant labor is better than intelligent labor." Farm laborers and field hands, Poe insisted, must be "able to read intelligently about the principles of fertilizing, crop rotation, plant breeding, seed selection, soil management, and a thousand other things."[19]

The farm editor reminded his black audience that ten years of suffrage restriction under "Democratic rule" had not produced the dire effects predicted. The school term had been extended, and efforts "to curtail the negro's school fund" had been thwarted. The grandfather clause had expired in 1908. "In a word then," he solemnly intoned, "the South is going to give you [blacks] a square deal." Poe said the destinies of whites and blacks in the South "in the industrial sense . . . are surely linked together." He concluded, however, with a warning for the black college graduates. Racial "purity" must be respected; "pride of race" among whites and blacks must be nurtured. If educated blacks allied with "low and immoral" whites or took "their ambitions" north "or elsewhere 'over the line,'" Poe thundered, they would provoke "titanic fury" from whites. This, then, was Poe's "message of hope" to blacks, a message not of hatred, he maintained, but "of most generous sympathy."[20]

Poe also carried his homily of racial purity and homogeneity to white audiences. In a speech to the South Carolina Press Association in June, 1910, Poe declared, "Both Carolinas need and must have a larger proportion of white people." The eleven southern states of the old Confederacy were too sparsely settled: they supported a population of sixteen million, ten million of whom were white. "Of course," he observed, "we do not want the lower-class European immigration" that was then inundating the North. He preferred the western and northern European "blood" that composed "our vigorous American stock." Poe welcomed immigration from England, Scotland, Ireland, Germany, Sweden, and Holland. "From some countries of Southern and Eastern Europe, on the other hand," he noted, "immigration is [of] a decidedly

19. Clarence Poe, "The Message of the White South to the Negro Race," *ibid*.
20. *Ibid*.

lower order and objectionable because of a low standard of intelligence and efficiency." Poe urged southern states to attract farmers from the North and West who were migrating to Canada. "I should favor it [white immigration] as our surest deliverance from our race problem," he said. "The proportion of negroes to whites is too large in every Southern State." In Poe's opinion, blacks should constitute no more than 20 percent of the population of any state.[21]

To prove his point to the South Carolina newspapermen, Poe estimated that the economic worth and efficiency of the Negro was only one-half that of the white man. Therefore, in a county with a population equally divided between whites and blacks, its overall efficiency would be only 75 percent that of an all-white county. The Tar Heel editor restated his commitment to "practical education . . . suited to the needs of a great, awakening agricultural citizenship such as ours." He left his fellow journalists with this admonitory watchword for the South: "Education and Immigration—Both of the Right Sort."[22]

Although Poe strongly opposed "indiscriminate European immigration," an infusion of sturdy white Anglo-Saxon stock seemed to offer the South the best short-run solution to its large black population. What he hoped to engender was a "great democracy of thrifty, prosperous home-owning small farmers" who would eliminate rural isolation with a patchwork of eighty-acre farms. To effect this agrarian democracy, Poe encouraged white tenants to buy land. He also proposed levying graduated taxes on large landholders and the "unearned increment in urban or rural land values." Such taxes would discourage large accumulations of property and promote land sales to white tenants and small farmers. But Poe had ambivalent feelings about black landownership. Black tenants who bought land deprived white tenants of that benefit. It would be unfortunate, Poe decided, if blacks became "the dominant land-owners in any section because they need and must have the leadership of the progressive white farmer in order to make large success themselves."[23]

At the same time Poe pleaded with northern and western farmers to come south, he cautioned them about blacks. Blacks, Poe advised,

21. Clarence Poe, "How to Build Up the Carolinas," *ibid.*
22. *Ibid.*
23. Clarence Poe, "Dr. Seaman A. Knapp: What He Did for Southern Farmers . . . ," *ibid.*; Raleigh *Progressive Farmer*, December 23, 1911.

were good workers, but they had two faults: "slovenly work when not watched" and a proclivity to attend the "baptizin'" or "big meeting" rather than keep strict hours. Nor did Poe believe white immigrants would find blacks desirable neighbors. "You will not like too many black neighbors," he counseled, but having two or three "colored families within easy reach when you want some odd jobs done" was an asset. As a class, blacks lacked "the energy, prudence, foresight and mental ability necessary to make a country thrifty and progressive." The black man, he said, should not be treated as a white man, but "given a square deal and kept in his place," a black "will do you no harm and cause you no trouble."[24]

Poe's artfully homey advice and paternalistic interpretation of southern race relations, by his own admission, began to falter as he came to view the South's large black population, even after disfranchisement, as a major impediment to the southern reform movement. Upon returning from a visit to his old family farm in Chatham County, Poe sadly observed, "There has been . . . a tie of affection between the negroes and the families of their former owners that made strongly for peace between the races—a tie now rapidly weakening." Economic dislocations had forced white families to move to the city; the vacuum they created was being filled with blacks, which in turn impelled other whites to leave "for social reasons." He disagreed with the old dictum that blacks were a source of wealth. Black tenants were poor farmers. The Negro, he argued, was "one of the greatest breeders of poverty—a fact, of course, for which he is not to blame, and which is to be remedied not by repressing him but by making him efficient."[25]

The "presence of negro farmers in the South is a great drawback to successful co-operation," Poe told a convention of state farmers' unions in 1912. For cooperative enterprises to flourish, there must be an adequate white population, which was why Poe so fervently advocated white immigration. A cooperative association, he declared, "must be composed of men on the same level, men who meet on a perfect equality of 'give and take' and who are kept divided by no bar, social or otherwise." How was the South to achieve this "homogeneous population"?[26]

24. Raleigh *Progressive Farmer*, October 26, 1912.
25. Clarence Poe, "A Snapshot of Southern Rural Life," in Poe Papers.
26. Clarence Poe, "Business Co-Operation—What Can We Do About It?" *ibid.*

In 1911, white farmers in Okfuskee County, Oklahoma, forced black farmers to sell their property at a sacrifice and leave the community. The coerced exodus occurred after the death of a white farmer, evidently at the hands of blacks. In an editorial, Poe criticized efforts to deprive blacks of human or property rights and defended blacks' equal protection before the law. But, clearly intrigued by the episode, Poe insisted that whites had "every right to use legitimate means to encourage white settlers and discourage the coming of more negroes." Oklahoma farmers had formed a "White Farmers' Congress and Immigration Bureau" to establish all-white neighborhoods. The farmers' organizations required that "no member . . . sell or lease land adjoining that of a white farmer to a negro." Poe applauded the concept. Segregation, he declared, helped each race build up "a better society of its own."[27] To what lengths Poe would extend segregation soon became apparent.

During the summer of 1912, Poe toured the British Isles and Low Countries to study European agricultural methods and organizations. What he saw impressed him. Unlike on the vast North American continent, with its open spaces and isolated farms, in Europe farms stood in close proximity and farmers lived in village clusters. Moreover, cooperative credit societies permitted European farmers to avoid the snare of crop liens and one-crop agriculture. To a Jeffersonian such as Poe, the agricultural systems he observed in Europe held great appeal. They also reinforced his own views about the reforms needed in the agrarian South.[28]

Of even greater consequence, however, was Poe's meeting with Maurice Smethurst Evans (1854–1920), S.M.G., whom he described as a distinguished citizen of the newly formed Union of South Africa. Evans, a merchant and politician from Durban, Natal, had been born in Manchester, England, and had migrated to Natal in 1875. In 1910 he helped frame the constitution uniting the four provinces of the Trans-

27. Raleigh *Progressive Farmer*, September 15, 1911. Such violence directed at black landowners was not unusual. In early 1911 night riders around Hominy, Oklahoma, dynamited Negro homes and forced blacks to flee the community on the midnight train. Several months earlier, land speculators had sold land to blacks for cotton farms. New York *Times*, January 24, 1911; Norman L. Crockett, *The Black Towns* (Lawrence: Regents Press of Kansas, 1979).

28. Kirby, *Darkness at the Dawning*, 121–22.

vaal, Natal, the Orange Free State, and Cape Colony. He also helped draft the Native Lands Act of 1913, which ordained strict racial segregation in the rural areas of South Africa.[29] The act decreed "possessory segregation"; that is, it prohibited Africans from purchasing land outside designated native reserves and from entering sharecropping arrangements in "white" agricultural areas. Later the law came to define the physical place of Africans, permitting them to reside outside the reserves only when the interests or conveniences of whites required them elsewhere.[30]

Poe clearly found Evans' ideas on segregation provocative and instructive. In a lengthy article in the *Progressive Farmer* titled "The Negro Problem in Two Continents," Poe reported his interview with Evans and pointed out the differences and similarities between South Africa and the American South. In South Africa there was as yet "no common race policy for the entire nation." Blacks were not treated as citizens, and they faced very discriminatory laws. Poe noted that legislation in the United States must "apply to whites and blacks alike." In the Transvaal, for instance, blacks could not walk on the sidewalks and instead had to walk the streets with horses and cattle. In Natal blacks could not purchase or carry firearms, and the only schools for blacks in South Africa were operated by missionaries. Poe decided, "Our Southern Negro, so far from being the oppressed, abused and mistreated child of destiny he is so often represented as being, is, in fact, the best-off colored man on the face of the earth."[31]

29. Raleigh *Progressive Farmer*, July 6, 1912. Evans became a recognized authority on race relations because of the publication of two books: *Black and White in South East Africa: A Study in Sociology* (London: Longmans, Green and Co., 1911) and *Black and White in the Southern States: A Study of the Race Problem in the United States from a South African Point of View* (London: Longmans, Green and Co., 1915). For a perceptive analysis of Evans' thinking on segregation, see John W. Cell, *The Highest Stage of White Supremacy: The Origins of Segregation in South Africa and the American South* (New York: Cambridge University Press, 1982), 28–33. See also *Who Was Who, 1929–1940* (London: Adam and Charles Black, 1941), 423.

30. George M. Fredrickson, *White Supremacy: A Comparative Study in American and South African History* (New York: Oxford University Press, 1981), 236–53. Fredrickson correctly pointed out the vast demographic differences between South Africa and the American South. In 1911 whites constituted 21.37 percent of the South African population, whereas whites composed 68 percent of the South's population in 1900. As the Poe-Evans link suggests, white supremacists on both continents were well aware of each other's practices and ideologies. Cell, *The Highest Stage of White Supremacy;* Kenneth P. Vickery, "'Herrenvolk' Democracy and Egalitarianism in South Africa and the U.S. South," *Comparative Studies in Society and History*, XVI (1974), 309–28.

31. Raleigh *Progressive Farmer*, July 6, 1912.

Evans warned Poe that the South must separate whites and blacks to prevent "infinite trouble." He argued for a plan that "silently, gradually and steadily" made black sections "blacker" and white sections "whiter through the voluntary migration and segregation of each class." Like Poe, Evans disagreed with the "considerable class of white men who erroneously believe that ignorant, Negro labor is an asset." The South needed "homes rather than plantations" to create "a vastly more prosperous white democracy of thrifty, home-owning small farmers."[32]

Evans also believed blacks should own land, "but I would have them acquire land in districts of their own instead of having the Negro farms mixed in with the white farms—thereby further scattering or diluting your already too small white population and retarding the growth of that richer social life possible only in the thickly settled homogeneous white communities." Blacks, Evans contended, should form their own communities, provided their leaders received training from such schools as Hampton and Tuskegee and conducted their affairs under white supervision.[33]

The South African politician also complained about a class of whites on both continents "who are not progressing, landless people who formerly subsisted by hunting and fishing or by freighting (hauling) and who in the present condition of things have grown idle and shiftless." Such people must, he said, be taught industrial efficiency and the dignity of labor.[34]

Finally, Evans and Poe agreed that the "supreme duty" of both South Africa and the American South was to preserve "racial purity." If social lines broke down, chaos would result. White men who imperiled the "purity of our blood," asserted Evans, "should be treated as traitors to their color and to their country."[35]

Poe's meeting with Evans marked an important watershed in the development of the editor's reform plans for the South. For more than a decade Poe had searched for some method to advance the cause of a rural, white democracy made up of small, landowning farmers. Sharecropping, tenancy, forced migration to the cities, and rural isolation

32. *Ibid.*
33. *Ibid.*
34. *Ibid.*
35. *Ibid.*

inhibited strong community ties of church, school, and farm organization and seemed to presage the South's future in the twentieth century.
Moreover, the presence of a large, unskilled, unpropertied black population tied to the land in virtual peonage obstructed economic and
social reform. During the early years of the twentieth century, South
Africa monitored closely the American South's treatment of blacks and
adopted some of the same practices. But South African politicians such
as Maurice Evans had devised their own system of apartheid to subju-
gate a much larger black population. In at least one respect, concluded
Poe, the South African model was worthy of emulation.

In the summer of 1913, Poe launched a crusade for land segregation
that lasted for nearly two years. In so doing, he sparked a vigorous,
often bitter, debate over fundamental issues: the destiny of blacks in
the South; the meaning, intent, and constitutionality of segregation;
the question of miscegenation; and the economic future of the southern white farmer. The debate exposed the very core of the South's class
and caste structure. Poe's plan for land segregation provoked predict-
able opposition from black leaders and farmers and from lawyers, politicians, and constitutional experts. But perhaps surprisingly
to Poe, it also alienated the South's propertied upper class, in
whose hands southern farmlands were becoming more and more
concentrated.

Poe's proposal for land segregation evolved during the year following his interview with Evans. He prepared his readers for the idea in
the spring of 1913 with editorials entitled "More White Farmers the
Hope of the South" and "We Must Save the Rural South to the White
Race." Poe expressed alarm about the increase in tenancy and absentee
landlordism. The editor urged "some remedy" to preserve white communities and to halt "the menacingly rapid encroachment of the Negro
farmer on white territory." Poe wanted to make the South "a permanently great and forceful section" of democratic, home-owning,
thrifty, small white farmers. "We should like to see the Negroes own
the land they till, as we should like to see all other classes," Poe conceded, "but we want to see them buy in colonies of their own." The
agrarian editor saw a "striking parallel" between the South's race problem and California's situation with respect to Japanese farmers who
were buying land from whites. The California legislature resolved the
problem in 1913 by barring the Japanese from owning land. Said Poe,

"Substitute Negroes for Japanese and does this not describe the situation in the South today?" He continued, "Let the Negroes build up their own communities and co-operate in their communities as the whites in theirs."[36]

In a flurry of speeches and editorials in July and August, 1913, Poe unveiled his plan for "a great rural civilization in North Carolina." At Mooresville, North Carolina, the farm editor explained his rationale for concentrating the white population "in both country and city." The "wisdom of such a policy" had long been recognized in southern towns, he asserted; it was now paramount for "our whole Southern country" to group races in "rural sections," as he termed them. "If a negro should attempt to buy a home on one of the main white residence streets in Raleigh or Columbia or Charleston or Atlanta, the power of an unwritten law would make itself felt against him instantaneously and most imperiously." But white farmers had no such "protection." Without "a satisfying white society for the family or a sense of safety and protection for the wives and the young women," whites fled their farms. Poe's own father had given up his Chatham County farm, which had been in the family for four generations, "simply because the place became surrounded by negroes." Poe's cousin still lived on part of the land—"a hero of the rear-guard of our ancient Anglo-Saxon civilization."[37]

Poe hypothesized that if two adjoining school districts each included fifty white families and fifty black families, an "impetus to progress" would result from regrouping the population so that a hundred white families and a hundred black families lived in separate communities. This "white nucleus" would attract other white families, and white schools, churches, rural telephone systems, roads, libraries, and lyceums would flourish. Poe demanded a law to "make it illegal for a negro to buy land in a white community if a majority of the resident voters or land-owners petition against sales to negroes."[38]

The *Progressive Farmer* headlined "A SOUTH-WIDE CAMPAIGN FOR RACE SEGREGATION" on August 2, 1913. "The white people will not be content to have present conditions continue indefinitely," Poe editorialized, "will not consent forever to see their white communities

36. *Ibid.*, March 15, June 7, 14, 1913.
37. Clarence Poe, "A Great Rural Civilization in North Carolina?" in Poe Papers.
38. *Ibid.*

broken up by the wholesale and promiscuous butting-in of Negro tenants and land-owners, depriving their families of an adequate social life and imperilling the safety of white farm women." He argued, "The proposition of segregation is not a measure of injustice to the Negro, but a measure of justice to the white man." Segregation was now the rule everywhere except farms, Poe declared. It applied to Orientals in California; to blacks in cities, churches, and schools; to Indians on reservations; and to Africans in South Africa. Atlanta had passed an ordinance allowing a majority of property owners on a city block to prevent the sale of land to a different race. Georgia, Poe insisted, must pass a similar law for its rural sections.[39]

The same week that the *Progressive Farmer* inaugurated its campaign for rural segregation Poe traveled to Columbia, South Carolina, to spread his message. There he introduced another disturbing reason, in his view, for promoting land segregation. Poe had rejoiced at preliminary estimates from the 1910 census suggesting that the rural South was growing "whiter." But the complete census figures, which became available in 1913, revealed that between 1900 and 1910 the land cultivated by white farmers in North Carolina had actually decreased by 500,000 acres and in South Carolina by 600,000 acres. In the same period, North Carolina blacks had increased their holdings by over 200,000 acres, and South Carolina blacks by about 150,000 acres. For all the South Atlantic states, white farm acreage had decreased 3 percent, whereas black farm acreage had increased 13 percent. Poe interpreted these figures as further evidence that blacks were "driving white people off the farms and taking the rural South" for themselves. Southern states, he said, must pass laws allowing white landowners to delineate a district in which blacks could not purchase land. Such legislation would also create areas where whites could not purchase land, at least in theory. But it was the white farmer who was uppermost in Poe's mind. Anticipating some of the objections to such a legal scheme, Poe promised that the legislation would apply only to future sales. "White owners in black districts," he said, "could continue to rent land or could sell it to negroes."[40]

39. Raleigh *Progressive Farmer*, August 2, 1913.

40. Clarence Poe, "What Must We Do to Develop a Great Rural Civilization in the Carolinas?" in Poe Papers; Raleigh *Progressive Farmer*, July 15, 1911. The rising number of black farmers delighted Booker T. Washington. Kirby, *Darkness at the Dawning*, 160–61.

Poe's analysis of black demographic trends in the South was correct, if only temporarily. Between 1900 and 1910 every southern state experienced an increase in the number of black farmers, both as tenants and landowners. In 1900, North Carolina counted 53,996 black farmers; in 1910, it counted 64,456. The trend continued until 1920, but the number of black farmers has declined ever since.[41]

Poe's audacious plan for land segregation potentially challenged both the South's economic structure and its legal-constitutional system. In particular the reform editor wished to foster economic cooperation among farmers, but he found that the "wholesale sandwiching of whites and Negroes in our rural districts" proved the main obstacle to such cooperation. "Everybody knows that the Negroes stand together," Poe asserted. "They are notoriously clannish in everything. They help one another even to the extent of shielding Negro criminals from the law."[42]

But blacks were not the perpetrators of the overall problem. City landowners, merchants, and large planters, declared Poe, had "practically taken sides against the struggling white tenant and small farmer in favor of the Negro." Poe recounted his conversation with an absentee plantation owner from Mississippi who lived in Memphis. The planter admitted he did not want white tenant farmers on his land. "They won't spend money and run accounts at our stores like the Negroes will," the planter conceded, "and besides they soon want to buy land themselves. The Negroes make more money for us." A South Carolina farmer told Poe that the strongest opposition to rural segregation came from merchants, horse dealers, and landowners. "Large farms are a curse to the South," said the farmer. A Chatham County reader reported that merchants in towns sold small plots of twenty, thirty, or forty acres to blacks and furnished supplies to make a crop. Consequently, blacks seldom escaped debt unless they went "to public works [nonfarm jobs]." Poe decried absentee landlordism. Because such planters were not resident land owners, they did not care whether the rural South was "a fit place for a white man to live."[43]

Similarly, Poe argued that his land-segregation scheme would not violate the Fourteenth Amendment. The South, he predicted confi-

41. Fite, *Cotton Fields No More*, 238.
42. Raleigh *Progressive Farmer*, August 9, 1913.
43. *Ibid.*

dently, would find a way to make his plan legal, as "in the case of Negro disfranchisement despite an iron-bound Amendment specifically designed to prevent it." Poe did not favor prohibiting black ownership of land. That was "specifically unconstitutional" because blacks were citizens. In California the situation differed; the Japanese were not citizens. Neither did Poe sanction for the South the "extreme" Native Lands Act of South Africa, which restricted Africans to only 13 percent of the land areas. However, he noted, segregation ordinances were being adopted in Atlanta, Richmond, Norfolk, and Greenville, South Carolina, and the Maryland Court of Appeals had recently upheld Baltimore's segregation ordinance by virtue of the city's police powers. Poe, therefore, felt certain that his plan could avoid entanglements with state or federal constitutions. He proposed "that wherever the greater part of the land acreage in any given district that may be laid off is owned by one race, a majority of the voters in such a district may say (if they wish) that in future no land shall be sold to a person of a different race." According to Poe's plan, such action must be approved by a reviewing judge or board of county commissioners.[44]

Although Poe continued to insist that the law would apply equally to both races, he never acknowledged one simple truth: after the adoption of suffrage restriction across the South, blacks could not vote and thus were precluded from making or opposing such a decision. Disfranchisement also effectively eliminated black office holding. For example, the collapse of Populist-Republican fusion and the Democratic ascendancy in the North Carolina General Assembly after 1899 essentially barred from elective or appointive office blacks who might have viewed sympathetically the plight of Afro-American farmers and tenants. Despite Poe's disingenuous defense of "equal" treatment for both races, however, he did identify a harsh and disturbing aspect of southern agricultural life—tenantry.

Tenantry in the South rose from 36 to 49 percent of all farms between 1880 and 1910. In North Carolina, tenants operated 42.3 percent of the state's farms in 1910. Among white farmers, 33.6 percent were tenants; among black farmers, 67.2 percent. Moreover, the size of Tar Heel farms was shrinking. The average size of a farm in North Carolina in 1910 was 88.4 acres, down from 101.3 acres in 1900. White farmers

44. *Ibid.*, August 9, 30, 1913.

owned and operated an average of 116 acres in 1910, whereas black farmers owned and operated an average of 55.8 acres. Among tenants the figures declined even more sharply. White tenants worked 10 fewer acres, 67, in 1910 than they had in 1900. Black tenants worked 8 fewer acres, 44.[45]

In short, southern tenancy, one-crop agriculture (usually cotton or tobacco), crop liens, sharecropping, absentee landlords, and furnishing merchants who advanced credit at high rates of interest all stood in Poe's path toward reordering the southern economic and social landscape. Poe was sensitive to the "tenant problem" and continually urged farmers to own the land they cultivated. He propounded "a plan for State loans," rural credit societies, and long amortization periods. Farmers, the Progressive editor declared, were true creators of wealth. Denying that he wished to stir up class prejudice, he nonetheless criticized merchants, bankers, lawyers, and insurance men as nonproductive components of the economy. Poe honored "the man who works . . . an actual creator of values . . . the young men in jeans and overalls who make the Commonwealth richer by doing productive labor."[46]

Poe's attack on southern tenantry through his land-segregation scheme brought a flood of comments from readers of the *Progressive Farmer*. Small producers blamed large planters and nonresident landowners for tenantry and the decay in southern rural life. One North Carolina farmer asserted that a certain class of white landowners treated black tenants as peons. "They furnish their tenants everything in the spring at high rates and in the fall take everything at low rates," he explained. The farmer knew a black tenant who bought on credit a mule worth $90 for $150, "and after fifteen years of hard work the mule died without being paid for. In the meantime, the white man got all the Negro made. Such land-owners don't want intelligent white tenants. They want those they can use to their advantage." A Tennessee farmer

45. *Thirteenth Census, 1910: Abstract with Supplement for North Carolina*, 596–613, 624, 625; Fite, *Cotton Fields No More*, 34–35, 235, 237. See also Dwight B. Billings, Jr., *Planters and the Making of a "New South": Class, Politics, and Development in North Carolina, 1865–1900* (Chapel Hill: University of North Carolina Press, 1979), and Dolores E. Janiewski, "From Field to Factory: Race, Class, Sex, and the Woman Worker in Durham, 1880–1940" (Ph.D. dissertation, Duke University, 1979).
46. Poe, "A Great Rural Civilization in North Carolina?" in Poe Papers.

echoed the same complaint. Opposition to land segregation originated with "white people who own large farms in the South. . . . They believe there is more money to be made from the Negro than from the poor whites." Wealthy whites, he opined, favored black labor, "the same . . . as before 1865." Another North Carolina farmer reported a large landowner in his county who held four thousand acres and would not "let a white man live on it."[47]

Even Francis D. Winston, former lieutenant governor of North Carolina (1905–1909), superior court judge, legislator, and major architect of disfranchisement, acknowledged the evils of easy credit, the time merchant, the tenant system, and absentee landlordism. From "personal knowledge of merchants" in his home county of Bertie, he described an economic system in which merchants rented thousands of acres of land "and then sub-let to hundreds of small tenants." The merchants' only purpose was to generate trade for the store. "The statistics for land rented and sub-rented in this way," Winston said, "would startle you." These merchants, he contended, had no interest in improving lands or raising livestock. What they sought was the largest cotton crop that tenants could raise and at the same time a "store account larger than the biggest crop the land is capable of and at a prospective price the market would not warrant." Winston recommended raising taxes on rented lands to discourage such practices.[48]

While Poe's segregation scheme evoked class-conscious protests from small farmers, it also generated fears about a loss of labor from larger planters. Poe argued that segregated white communities would attract more white renters. Consequently, land values would rise, allowing owners to sell land at a fair price to white farmers, a process that Poe characterized as better than "renting . . . to shiftless, soil-destroying tenants." The farm editor admitted that blacks might resist going into all-white communities to work, but he curiously labeled such hesitancy "industrial suicide." Poe predicted that labor shortages

47. Raleigh *Progressive Farmer*, September 20, December 6, 1913. The perils of black land tenure are discussed in Manning Marable, "Politics of Black Land Tenure, 1877–1915," *Agricultural History*, LIII (1979), 142–52; and Sydney Nathans, "'Gotta Mind to Move, A Mind to Settle Down': Afro-Americans and the Plantation Frontier," in William J. Cooper, Michael F. Holt, and John McCardell (eds.), *A Master's Due: Essays in Honor of David Herbert Donald* (Baton Rouge: Louisiana State University Press, 1985), 204–22.
48. Raleigh *Progressive Farmer*, February 6, 1915.

would be made up by "young Southern white men," by "good white labor" from other sections of the nation, and by European immigrants, who once shunned the South because of competition from blacks.[49]

Others were not so sure. A correspondent from Memphis who signed himself "Interested Cotton Farmer" claimed "the Negro is absolutely indispensable to the cotton planters around here." White families, he said, were "not physically able to cope [compete] with the Negroes in the cultivation of cotton. The Negro is constitutionally fitted for the long, hot cotton season." The Tennessee planter portrayed white sharecroppers as "thriftless, unscrupulous and careless." A landowner could compel blacks to work, he stated knowledgeably, whereas white tenants resented "anything like being dictated to." He declared, "As long as you pay up your Negroes you never lack help." The cotton farmer's success, he confessed, rested on "black shoulders," and until mechanized farming could be perfected, "the Negro will have to be used as a substitute." The South, concluded the philosophical planter, was "pre-eminently a white man's country," and "so long as you let a Negro know that the white man is master you need not fear them [blacks]."[50]

A Mississippi farmer expressed the same sentiments. He had tried farming with white labor and had failed. "The white man does not take to the hoe and plow like the colored man," he commented, "and is more expensive as a general thing. He wants his coffee three times daily and everything else in proportion. You can tell the colored man what to do and what you want done." The Mississippi farmer did not believe the South could get along without blacks. He concluded, "The day comes when they are segregated, I want to go with the Negro."[51]

A farmer from Alabama who owned four hundred acres and worked it with black labor decided that the movement for land segregation emanated from "'one-horse farmers' who can do their work in one day." If blacks left his community, he speculated, 90 percent of the crops on each farm could not be grown, and land values would plummet "not less than one-half."[52]

Many readers zealously applauded Poe's land-segregation proposal.

49. *Ibid.*, October 4, 1913.
50. *Ibid.*, December 5, 1913.
51. *Ibid.*, November 8, 1913.
52. *Ibid.*, December 5, 1913.

An Arkansas correspondent stated that his township long ago had informally barred blacks from renting or settling there. An adjoining township, however, had permitted blacks to move in, and they now dominated as owners and renters. "Give us segregation for those who are willing to work for a living," said the farmer, "and let those who want to have the Negro always with them be segregated with the Negro." A Virginia farmer charged that blacks worked with "the white man's capital—his land, team, etc."—until they could buy their own land and hire "the Negro that is worth hiring for wages." White farmers, he groused, were left with the "shifting and shiftless Negroes." Racist northerners also supported the concept of rural segregation. "A man does not need to live in the South," asserted a resident of New Jersey, "to see that it is either Segregation, Annihilation, Deportation or Degradation. What is the Southerner waiting for—to be treated like the French in Haiti or San Domingo?"[53]

Poe's campaign for land segregation also exposed a dark side of race relations that increasingly had come to preoccupy the southern white mind at the turn of the twentieth century. Fears of miscegenation, the rape of white women by black "beasts," and the apparent growth of the nation's mulatto population all fed white racial and sexual fantasies. Mulattoes were blamed for the alleged rise of crimes against white womanhood in the 1890s, which in turn spawned periodic orgies of lynching. Mulattoes' "white blood" was said "to replace native humility and cowardice with Caucasian audacity." Because whites viewed blacks as a class possessing criminal tendencies, southern spokesmen easily justified and legitimized racial repression, disfranchisement, and segregation.[54]

An Alabama physician favored Poe's plan for rural segregation because it would "improve the morals and uplift both races." Having practiced medicine for nineteen years, the country doctor claimed he had witnessed the spread of the "disease and immorality now prevalent." The increasing proportion of mulattoes in the South especially disquieted him. "Our youths," he averred, "should be taught that 90

53. *Ibid.*, December 5, 1913, April 11, 1914.
54. George M. Fredrickson, *The Black Image in the White Mind: The Debate on Afro-American Character and Destiny, 1817–1914* (New York: Harper & Row, 1971), 277–78, 282; Joel Williamson, *The Crucible of Race: Black-White Relations in the American South Since Emancipation* (New York: Oxford University Press, 1984), 306–10.

per cent of the Negro race is diseased. Segregation will teach both races self-reliance; it will lessen disease and amalgamation." A subscriber from Warren County, North Carolina, similarly deplored the health risks to white women "from their own husbands, who in their youth contract nameless diseases from dissolute colored women."[55]

Poe plainly championed such views. He published excerpts from an article by Pitchfork Ben Tillman, which appeared in *Trotwood's Magazine*. The South Carolina senator declaimed: "Amalgamation is the hope and ultimate purpose of the Negroes, the obliteration of the colored line; and many whites, too many, oblivious to their duty to their race and caste, are voluntary criminals in this regard, while, thank God, our white women prefer death to such a fate." In addition, Poe printed analyses of recent census figures showing a tremendous growth in the nation's mulatto population between 1870 and 1910. Although critics of these figures pointed out that census takers' definitions of mixed-bloods had changed since 1870, Poe maintained that there was "no warrant for optimism so long as the races continue to occupy the same territory." With demagogic fury, Poe inveighed: "When the Negro was a wild, black, jabbering, dirty savage, fresh from the jungles of Africa, we might the easier have prevented the mixing of the races, but now the tragic penalty of the white man's sin is that as the Negro takes on more and more the Caucasian's features and the Caucasian's intelligence and the Caucasian's nature, his physical repulsiveness grows less and less, and the peril grows greater rather than less."[56]

Census officials agreed with Poe's critics. In 1870 a total of 584,049 mulattoes were counted in the census; in 1910 the number was 2,050,686. Whereas mulattoes constituted 12 percent of the Negro population in 1870, they made up 20.9 percent forty years later. But the same definition had not been used in every enumeration. Moreover, the statistics compiled depended on each individual enumerator's ability to perceive traces of Negro or Caucasian blood in the persons counted. As a percentage of the Negro population, the mulatto population grew from 15.2 percent to 20.9 percent in the two decades between 1890 and 1910. As census officials explained, such an increase

55. Raleigh *Progressive Farmer*, November 8, 1913, March 28, 1914.
56. *Ibid.*, February 21, June 13, 1914.

"might naturally result—even without any continuous infusion of white blood—from the intermarriage of mulattoes with blacks." Children of such unions would be mulattoes under the definition of the term adopted in 1910—"the admixture of white blood in the Negro population"—despite "some uncertain degree of accuracy."[57]

Black leaders responded fiercely to Poe's segregation plan. In particular, Plummer B. Young, editor of Norfolk's black newspaper, the *Journal and Guide*, ridiculed Poe's scheme. "If Editor Poe doesn't mind," Young teased, "when he gets his racial segregation law through, some of his white constituents who are too lazy to do their own work will starve to death." Young traveled through North Carolina and found "very little sentiment . . . among the better class of whites in favor of the Poe proposition." Booker T. Washington and W. E. B. Du Bois, both of whom Poe had praised in earlier times, and James B. Dudley, president of the state college for blacks at Greensboro whose graduating class Poe addressed in 1910, also denounced the idea.[58]

Poe bridled at the opposition from black farmers as well as black leaders. In an editorial titled "The 'Revolution and Bloodshed' Talk and Its Significance," Poe declared: "The full-blooded Negro is submissive and easily managed, but when our imperious, commanding, domineering white blood, the blood that knows no master, mixes with Negro blood in the mulatto, it begins to work like a smoldering volcano." Poe termed mulattoes the "greatest menace to white supremacy." He quoted I. N. Ross, a black minister in Washington, D.C., who instructed his race "to quit buying pianos and go to buying guns, and to quit going to dancing schools and begin going to military schools."[59] Without segregation, it appeared to Poe, racial conflict was ineluctable.

In the spring of 1914, Poe traveled to Memphis to address the National Conference of Charities and Corrections and to attend the Southern Sociological Congress. His speech, titled "The Rural Problem and the Rural Community," reiterated the plea for separate "white and colored communities." But at the congress Poe came face to face phys-

57. For estimates of the mulatto population and a discussion of difficulties in defining mulattoes, see *Negro Population, 1790–1915* (Washington, D.C.: Government Printing Office, 1918), 208–209.

58. Raleigh *Progressive Farmer*, November 8, December 27, 1913, January 24, 1914, January 30, 1915.

59. *Ibid.*, January 24, 1914.

ically with the reality of actual social equality. He was horrified. In an open letter to Governor William Hodges Mann of Virginia, president of the congress, Poe tendered his resignation from the organization. He bitterly condemned the integrated meeting in Memphis: "White men and white women, Negro men and Negro women, [were] all admitted on equal terms of equality as members and as participants in the Congress." In his view, it was offensive to have blacks seated on the first floor instead of separately in the balcony. He opposed "mixed-race organizations" and concluded the time had come "to say that each race should have its own sociological organization."[60]

Ironically, Booker T. Washington addressed the integrated assemblage and stated that blacks did not seek "social mixing." Poe thought the congress "soothed and lulled" by such promises. However, he had heard another speech in Memphis that chilled his segregationist sensitivities. W. E. B. Du Bois, speaking in a church "packed to suffocation with Negroes and mulattoes fired by an entirely different gospel," espoused a radical message. Du Bois proclaimed "the doctrine that the Negro must break down every barrier and that every discrimination must be swept away until nothing stands in the way of intermarriage, Negro office-holding, or anything else." Poe warned whites not to "let soft-heartedness run into soft-headedness."[61]

Poe's angry editorial fueled a debate already raging among black and white reformers about how to respond to the land-segregation scheme. Booker T. Washington confessed privately that Poe's incendiary comments on the Memphis meeting could have an injurious effect on the work of the Southern Sociological Congress. But the Tuskegee leader refused to take Poe's land segregation plan seriously. Not only was Poe's scheme "utterly impracticable," according to Washington, but there also was "no . . . sentiment among the substantial landowners in this section of the South in favor of such a proposition." Washington thought the farm editor merely wished "to advertise his paper." Washington had never heard a "single white man" propound "segregation in the farming districts." If it became known that a black farmer had a few hundred dollars to invest in land, said Washington, the farmer was "constantly beset by white people who want to sell him

60. Clarence Poe, "The Rural Problem and the Rural Community," in Poe Papers; Raleigh *Progressive Farmer*, May 30, 1914.

61. Raleigh *Progressive Farmer*, May 30, 1914.

land." The real problem, in Washington's mind, was that blacks did not have sufficient money to buy all the land whites offered them for sale.[62]

Other observers of American race relations remained less sanguine than Washington. Oswald Garrison Villard, a founder of the National Association for the Advancement of Colored People and editor of the New York *Evening Post*, accused the Tuskegee leader of "fiddling" while blacks were subjected to one injustice after another. "There has developed in North Carolina," Villard declared, "the greatest menace yet, a movement under the leadership of Clarence Poe, which will undoubtedly result in legislation, segregating the Negro on the farm lands, thus giving the lie to Washington's advice to his people that if they will only be good and buy land they will be let alone and will flourish."[63]

Villard's ideological ally, Du Bois, agreed with that analysis. In the pages of the *Crisis*, the journal he founded and edited, Du Bois counterattacked. Poe's comments about the Memphis meeting and the integrated Southern Sociological Congress particularly offended him. He characterized Poe's statements as "reactionary suppression" and grouped the North Carolinian with Governors Cole Blease of South Carolina and James K. Vardaman of Mississippi, "demagogues . . . radical on everything except the Negro problem." Du Bois continued, "On that they are reactionary, vindictive, and positively indecent to a degree which is almost inconceivable." Du Bois acidly described the Memphis meeting of the Southern Sociological Congress as a "mischief-making combination" composed of "the struggling, emerging Negro, the cowardly white North, the advanced white southern reformers, the Negro hating southern radicals and the reactionary Poes." The black editor also denigrated whites' contradictory attempts to justify urban segregation on one hand while deploring rural segregation on the other. He saw no "inherent difference between separating the races in cities and rural districts" and on railroads and in public places. "All are equally wrong."[64]

Poe remained oblivious to such arguments by blacks. To his way of

62. Louis R. Harlan and Raymond W. Smock (eds.), *The Booker T. Washington Papers* (13 vols.; Urbana: University of Illinois Press, 1972–84), XII, 296, 308–310, 488–89, XIII, 5–6, 40–41.

63. *Ibid.*, XII, 472–73.

64. *Crisis*, VIII (1914), 125–26, 197.

thinking, he spoke for "humbler white brethren out on the farms and in the shops and factories." He denied charges such as "'You hate the negro' or 'You would treat him unjustly.'" More galling to Poe were southern leaders and the "dominant white classes . . . [who] set at perfect ease in segregated portions of our towns and cities, and never have occasion to think of the negro other than as a servant—never as a competitor." Such "vast uncomprehension" obscured the economic struggle between white farmers and blacks, "but recently barbarian with an inferior civilization and with correspondingly low living standards."[65]

Implicitly, Poe's system of apartheid, if less draconian than the South African model, was designed to assure the South a permanent under-class of cheap black labor, but one that could not compete directly against small, landowning white farmers, who would be safely shel-tered in exclusive communities to work out their economic and social destinies in cooperative enterprises. In brief, Poe sought what George Fredrickson has termed a *Herrenvolk* democracy. Demographic and economic trends in the New South—from increasing urbanization and industrialization to growing tenancy and improverishment on the farms—had intensified the competition between white and black la-bor. Poe meant to end that competition and to make vast areas of the rural South a white man's country. After a year of crusading, however, his dream was no closer to realization. A new strategy was needed.

During the spring of 1914, Poe's proposal suffered two major reversals. First, a North Carolina convention of Progressive Democrats, held in April, refused to entertain Poe's controversial segregation plan as part of its platform. Major reforms such as a statewide primary, revision of the tax system, child-labor legislation, and a minimum school term of six months took precedence. In view of the fact that Poe was one of the convention's principal organizers, the deletion of the rural segregation plank, to which he belatedly agreed, still amounted to repudiation.[66]

Second, the North Carolina Supreme Court overturned a segrega-tion ordinance adopted by the city of Winston. The case of *State* v.

65. Clarence Poe, "The Editor Must Be a Crusader," in Poe Papers.
66. Joseph F. Steelman, "The Progressive Democratic Convention of 1914 in North Carolina," *North Carolina Historical Review*, XLVI (1969), 95–97.

William Darnell clearly had implications for Poe's plan. Attorney General Thomas Walter Bickett, later to become governor (1917–1921), and Gilbert T. Stephenson of Winston-Salem represented the state before the high court. Stephenson's role in the case is of interest because he was a noted authority on the subject of race and the law. A graduate of Wake Forest College and Harvard Law School, Stephenson published *Race Distinctions in American Law* in 1910. Moreover, writing in the *South Atlantic Quarterly*, the Winston-Salem attorney had criticized Poe's proposal on moral grounds, though he admitted that a constitutional justification of it probably could be found. Stephenson oddly defended urban segregation, based on a philosophy of noblesse oblige, at the same time he denounced rural segregation as "immoral."[67] In the case of the Winston ordinance, however, the state supreme court struck down such inherent contradictions.

In 1912 the Winston board of aldermen adopted an ordinance making it unlawful for any "colored person" to occupy any residence on a block where a greater number of residences were occupied by whites. The board modeled the ordinance after a similar one in Richmond, Virginia. When William Darnell, "colored," moved into a house on a predominantly white street and block in 1913, he was tried in municipal court, found guilty, and fined. He appealed to the Forsyth County Superior Court, which upheld the decision. The state of North Carolina admitted that Winston had no express power to pass a segregation ordinance, but under its charter, Bickett and Stephenson contended, the municipality could exercise police powers "for the good order, good government, or general welfare of the city."[68]

Chief Justice Walter Clark, a renowned Progressive and jurist in his own right, demurred. The city's charter could not be construed to allow an ordinance to establish "a public policy which has hitherto been unknown in the legislation of our State," Clark wrote in his opinion. Similar restrictions, he argued, could be extended to Re-

67. Gilbert T. Stephenson, "The Segregation of the White and Negro Races in Cities," *South Atlantic Quarterly*, XIII (1914), 1–18; Stephenson, "The Segregation of White and Negro Races in Rural Communities in North Carolina," *ibid.*, 107–17; Clarence Poe, "Rural Land Segregation Between Whites and Negroes: A Reply to Mr. Stephenson," *ibid.*, 207–12; Kirby, *Darkness at the Dawning*, 128–29; Steelman, "The Progressive Democratic Convention of 1914," 95–96.
68. *State* v. *William Darnell*, 166 N.C. 300 (1914).

publicans and Democrats, Protestants and Catholics, Germans and Irish. The ordinance also usurped the right to own, sell, lease, buy, rent, or dispose of property as one chose. Conceivably, Clark pointed out, a white or black property holder could be denied use of his or her own house.[69]

But the chief justice did not stop there. Clark stated further that county commissioners could not pass similar restrictions "for country districts." Otherwise, "a white manager" or "white tenant" could not "reside on a farm where a majority of the tenants or hands are colored." The chief justice therefore ruled that the Winston ordinance had been "adopted without authority of law," and he dismissed the action.[70]

Poe apparently never commented publicly on this state supreme court decision, but it must have come as a blow. For a year he had been urging southern legislatures to enact rural segregation laws. Now his own state supreme court had annulled a city ordinance based on the same principle as his land-segregation plan. Rather than concede defeat, however, Poe simply shifted goals. Instead of a statute for land segregation, he began agitating for a state constitutional amendment. An amendment had two advantages, he reasoned. First, it would remove the possibility of a measure being in conflict with the state constitution; second, it would allow the people (that is, white voters) to decide on the matter. Poe compared a land-segregation amendment with disfranchisement. Those who had said no constitutional plan for disfranchising blacks could succeed, he reminded critics, had been proved wrong. Rural segregation, as much as disfranchisement, was a necessity.[71]

The test for Poe's segregation amendment came in the North Carolina General Assembly of 1915. As the legislature prepared to convene in January, Poe confessed that farmers were "up against powerful interests," some of the most "influential and politically powerful men in the South," but the crusading editor remained undeterred. He ex-

69. Ibid.

70. Ibid. See also North Carolina Supreme Court, Original Cases, 1909–1929, February term, 1914, Case No. 337, North Carolina State Archives, Division of Archives and History, Raleigh.

71. Raleigh Progressive Farmer, October 31, 1914, January 2, 16, 30, February 20, 27, March 6, 1915.

coriated "the Shylocks and vultures" among whites who profited from blacks' "ignorance and weakness." Poe had no desire to be "unjust to the Negro," but he believed deeply the "disadvantaged man" in the South was "not the Negro, but the laboring white man." The remedy, Poe contended, was already being utilized by "our brother white men of our same race and tongue" in South Africa. There blacks were forbidden, under a law that became effective in June, 1914, to buy or lease "land in the districts set apart for white ownership."[72] North Carolina, in his opinion, must be the next sovereign government to enact such a plan.

To lobby the legislature for a constitutional amendment providing for land segregation, Poe called on the North Carolina Farmers' Educational and Cooperative Union. First organized in 1908 with 928 members, the Farmers' Union reached its peak in 1912–1913 with 33,000 members and 1,783 local chapters. The *Progressive Farmer* was the union's official organ, and together the Farmers' Union and editor Poe promoted numerous progressive farm measures to break up trusts, to repeal the crop-lien law, and to lower interest rates.[73]

When Poe asked the local chapters to clip the text of the segregation amendment from the *Progressive Farmer*, sign it, and send it to their legislators, the farmers responded immediately. Petitions poured into the General Assembly. Some petitions included letters from officers of the local farmers' unions. "We the signers do think this is the greatest thing for the farmers that could be passed," wrote a Vance County farmer. "And may God help you all to pass it." Several petitioners complained that they did not have sufficient time to collect signatures. "I'm satisfied if I had the timne I could get ever body in this communities, to sign it for ever body I saw sign[ed] it," declared a Nash County farmer. Not every farmers' union, however, endorsed the measure. A Bertie County farmer admitted "that some . . . I waited upon refused to sign." And the secretary-treasurer of a Person County chapter announced tersely, "We . . . do not favor a Constitutional amend-

72. *Ibid.*, January 2, 16, 1915; Clarence Poe, "The Greater North Carolina—How May It Be Developed?" in Poe Papers.

73. Charles P. Loomis, "The Rise and Decline of the North Carolina Farmers' Union," *North Carolina Historical Review*, VII (1930), 305–25; Loomis, "Activities of the North Carolina Farmers' Union," *ibid.*, 443–62.

ment." At least one petition was sent by women. A women's club in Asheboro (Randolph County) "heartily urge[d] the passing of some practical land ownership segregation law."[74]

A total of 234 petitions bearing 5,867 signatures were submitted to the General Assembly (see Table 1). Sixty of North Carolina's one hundred counties were represented by these petitions; the counties generally fell within the state's cotton and tobacco belts. In the state's old antebellum plantation counties of the east, such as Edgecombe, Halifax, and Warren, large black populations were matched by high rates of farm tenancy. But even in western counties with relatively small black populations, such as Iredell and Lincoln, farm tenancy was clearly a deep concern. In Rockingham County, the state's largest producer of tobacco, blacks composed 28.7 percent of the population. However, 54.5 percent of the farms were operated by tenants.[75]

A comparison of the number of members in the Farmers' Union, which coordinated the petition drive, with the number of petitioners from each county also shows that support for the land-segregation scheme was particularly evident in the old plantation belt (see Table 2). Pasquotank, Vance, Halifax, Edgecombe, and Person counties—among others—contributed a substantial number of signatures from members of the Farmers' Union. Members from counties farther west with high rates of tenancy but relatively small black populations—such as Rockingham, Iredell, Catawba, and Wilkes—also demonstrated their support for the land-segregation scheme.

But despite the backing of nearly six thousand petitioners, the movement for land segregation remained as shallow as it was broad. Counties with significant numbers of members in the Farmers' Union as well as sizable populations of tenant farmers and blacks returned relatively few signatures in favor of land segregation. Bertie, Chatham, Granville, Pitt, and Northampton—among other counties—failed to mobilize the massive support that might have made Poe's plan a rallying point for struggling white farmers.

On February 16, 1915, Senator Mark Majette of Tyrrell County introduced Senate Bill 827, "An Act to Amend the Constitution of North

74. Raleigh *Progressive Farmer*, February 20, 27, 1915; petitions regarding land segregation, in Box 57, General Assembly Papers, Session of 1915, North Carolina State Archives, Division of Archives and History, Raleigh.
75. See Table 1. *Thirteenth Census, 1910: Agriculture*, VIII, 230–31.

Table 1 Petitions for Land Segregation Submitted to the North Carolina General Assembly, 1915

COUNTY (N = 60)[a]	Number of Petitions	Number of Signatures	Percentage (%) of Black Population, 1910	Percentage (%) of Farm Tenancy, 1910
Alamance	1	31	25	28.3
Alexander	1	16	7.9	21.6
Beaufort	4	57	41.9	28.4
Bertie	2	60	58.6	45.9
Buncombe	2	35	16	26.9
Burke	1	16	12	28.1
Cabarrus	3	66	23.2	56
Caldwell	1	22	11.7	24.1
Caswell	4	83	51.5	56.2
Catawba	4	138	12.4	27.4
Chatham	4	56	33.9	39.3
Cleveland	1	25	19.6	50.6
Currituck	2	91	33.8	36.2
Davie	1	10	17.5	43
Durham	1	12	35.1	56.5
Edgecombe	1	42	60.8	72.8
Forsyth	2	29	29.6	25.9
Franklin	4	127	46.8	64.6
Gaston	3	47	22.9	49.8
Gates	3	105	44.9	28.2
Granville	1	21	48.8	57.6
Greene	1	21	46.6	72
Guilford	3	59	25.4	27.3

(continued)

Table 1 (Continued)

COUNTY (N = 60)[a]	Number of Petitions	Number of Signatures	Percentage (%) of Black Population, 1910	Percentage (%) of Farm Tenancy, 1910
Halifax	5	228	64.6	64.2
Harnett	2	32	29.1	34.8
Henderson	1	42	11.2	21.3
Hoke[b]	4	105	—	—
Hyde	5	73	41.9	51.8
Iredell	6	252	21.7	39.5
Johnston	4	126	24.6	47.4
Lincoln	1	59	16.3	41.5
Macon	1	28	4.7	27.3
Mecklenburg	3	30	38	64.2
Montgomery	6	108	24.5	36.6
Nash	7	141	41.8	62.1
Northampton	2	30	58.5	56.8
Onslow	1	20	30	34.1
Orange	6	160	32.7	37
Pasquotank	7	156	50.1	48.1
Person	10	143	43.1	59.9
Pitt	1	26	49.8	64.9
Randolph	4	70	11.6	20.9
Richmond	1	12	46.9	57
Robeson	1	22	43.3	54.2
Rockingham	6	176	28.7	54.5
Rowan	3	108	24.2	37.8
Rutherford	1	25	15.1	46.1

	Petitions	Signatures	%	%
Sampson	3	74	33.5	33.2
Stokes	6	108	12.7	47.8
Swain	1	41	1.8	30.4
Transylvania	1	16	8.9	23.3
Union	2	67	28.1	56.8
Vance	4	143	51.5	59.2
Wake	1	141	40.9	54.3
Warren	5	87	65.2	54.8
Watauga	1	19	1.8	17.7
Wilkes	6	261	8.6	25.1
Wilson	2	111	43.7	69.1
Yadkin	2	31	7.6	27.3
Other				
Ash/Watauga	1	13		
Union/Montgomery	1	34		
Chinquapin	1	56		
Unidentified	59	1,324		
Totals	234	5,867		

SOURCES: The number of petitions and the number of signatures on them were culled from Box 57, General Assembly Papers, Session of 1915, North Carolina State Archives, Division of Archives and History, Raleigh. The percentages for the black population in each county and for the farms operated by tenants in each county were gleaned from the *Thirteenth Census, 1910: Abstract with Supplement for North Carolina,* 596ff.

[a]In 1915 there were a total of 100 counties in North Carolina.

[b]Hoke County was formed in 1911 from Cumberland and Robeson counties. Therefore, no statistics are available for 1910.

Table 2 Number of Members of Farmers' Union, 1912, Compared with
Number of Signatures on Petitions for Land Segregation, 1915

COUNTY	Number of Members[a]	Number of Signatures	Percentage (%)[b]
Alamance	417	31	7.4
Alexander	365	16	4.3
Beaufort	477	57	11.9
Bertie	476	60	12.6
Buncombe	590	35	5.9
Burke	360	16	4.4
Cabarrus	333	66	19.8
Caldwell	219	22	10.0
Caswell	393	83	21.1
Catawba	338	138	40.8
Chatham	601	56	9.3
Cleveland	371	25	6.7
Currituck	0	91	—
Davie	180	10	5.5
Durham	239	12	5.0
Edgecombe	93	42	45.1
Forsyth	618	29	4.6
Franklin	524	127	24.2
Gaston	495	47	9.4
Gates	86	105	122.0
Granville	370	21	5.6
Greene	317	21	6.6
Guilford	731	59	8.0
Halifax	218	228	104.5
Harnett	306	32	10.4
Henderson	382	42	10.9
Hoke	132	105	79.5
Hyde	182	73	40.1
Iredell	1,007	252	25.0
Johnston	667	126	18.8
Lincoln	433	59	13.6
Macon	74	28	37.8
Mecklenburg	417	30	7.1
Montgomery	351	108	30.7
Nash	492	141	28.6
Northampton	604	30	4.9
Onslow	492	20	4.0

(*continued*)

Table 2 (Continued)

COUNTY	Number of Members[a]	Number of Signatures	Percentage (%)[b]
Orange	442	160	36.1
Pasquotank	67	156	232.8
Person	385	143	37.1
Pitt	697	26	3.7
Randolph	852	70	8.2
Richmond	257	12	4.6
Robeson	277	22	7.9
Rockingham	907	176	19.4
Rowan	795	108	13.5
Rutherford	203	25	12.3
Sampson	106	74	6.9
Stokes	1,287	108	8.3
Swain	36	41	113.8
Transylvania	56	16	28.5
Union	450	67	14.8
Vance	362	143	39.5
Wake	844	141	16.7
Warren	306	87	28.4
Watauga	411	19	4.6
Wilkes	954	261	27.3
Wilson	455	111	24.3
Yadkin	642	31	4.8

[a]See Charles P. Loomis, "The Rise and Decline of the North Carolina Farmers' Union," *North Carolina Historical Review*, VII (1930), 312–14.

[b]These are projected percentages, assuming everyone who signed a petition was a member of the Farmers' Union. As figures for Currituck, Gates, Halifax, Pasquotank, and Swain counties suggest, not every petitioner was a member of the union. It is also important to note that no blacks were members of the union. Moreover, at least 21 of the 1,783 local chapters in North Carolina included an unspecified number of women members. Loomis, "The Rise and Decline of the Farmers' Union," 312, 314–15.

Carolina . . . Relating to Ownership of Lands." The bill faithfully articulated Poe's plan.

The General Assembly by regulations applicable to all races, may provide that by vote of the qualified voters or of the freeholders of any prescribed district within a county, the lands in such district may be segregated to the ownership, use or occupancy of a particular race. But the percentage of the lands of the State segregated to any particular race by districts shall not be greater than the percentage which the population of that race bears to the total population of the State; nor shall such segregation impair the vested rights of persons who have previously bought or leased land in such districts, nor prevent a person of the race to which such district is segregated from employing persons of a different race as his servants, laborers, or agricultural croppers or tenants and providing homes for them on his land. Provided, also, that no election shall be held under the provisions of this section except upon petition of a designated proportion of the freeholders within the proposed district presented to a reviewing judge or board of county commissioners and a finding by said reviewing authority that the establishment of the proposed district will promote the general welfare of the people of the district, after allowing time for the presentation of counter petitions or petitions for changes in the boundary lines of the proposed district, and that no school district or township in which the land is wholly owned by persons of one race shall be included in any district segregated to any other race.[76]

Poe's land-segregation amendment apparently made one concession to disfranchised blacks. Presumably, black freeholders—that is, property owners—could have voted either to create segregated rural districts for themselves or to oppose white efforts to establish all-white communities. Only a handful of black freeholders, however, would have been able to vote in the election to ratify a constitutional amendment.

As Poe pointed out in the *Progressive Farmer*, the bill had several built-in safeguards. First, like the suffrage amendment, he argued, it would not conflict with the federal Constitution. Second, no race could segregate a greater proportion of the state's lands than its proportion of population. In other words, since whites composed approximately 68 percent of the state's population, no more than 68 percent of North Carolina's acreage could be segregated to them. However, Poe shrewdly observed that if blacks owned all the land in one small district, then whites could thwart black segregation by petitioning for a larger district in which whites held a majority. Third, the bill did not prevent a farmer from hiring laborers and tenants of a different race or interfere with those farmers who already owned land. Finally, no school district or township in which land was owned wholly by one race could be segregated to the other. Poe considered the proposed

76. S.B. 827, in Box 35, General Assembly Papers, Session of 1915; *North Carolina Senate Journal*, 1915, pp. 275, 340.

amendment propitious as well as historical. Coming fifty years after Appomattox and emancipation, he declared, it must be adopted to save "a half-dying rural civilization in the South." In sum, the amendment was needed to halt "the rapid Africanization of the rural South."[77]

On February 27 the Committee on Constitutional Amendments reported S.B. 827 unfavorably, but the committee offered a substitute and recommended its passage. The substitute bill, actually much simpler and more direct in its language, removed Poe's complicated provisos, which he had devised in anticipation of various objections. The substitute bill read:

The General Assembly by general laws equally applicable to all races resident in the State, may provide that by vote of the qualified voters or of the freeholders of any prescribed district within a county, the lands in such district may be segregated or set apart to the ownership of a particular race. In such districts where the ownership of land shall be segregated or set apart to any particular race, no transfer of land in such district, whether by deed, descent, or will, or lease longer than one year, shall be made to any person other than a member of the race to which said land has been segregated or set apart; but no such general laws nor acts done thereunder shall impair the vested rights of a person of a different race then owning land in such district.[78]

As its special order for March 5, 1915, the North Carolina Senate considered the land-segregation amendment. Senator Majette, who introduced the original bill, spoke in favor of the scheme. Opposition to the amendment, however, quickly showed a bipartisan dimension. Charles A. Jonas of Lincoln County, one of only seven Republicans in the fifty-member state senate and a future congressman (1929–1931), denied that he had "ulterior motives" as a Republican and declared that North Carolina should not "deprive a lower race of its rights." Frank Nash, a prominent Orange County Democrat, lawyer, and historian, made the most compelling arguments against passage. "I do not

77. Raleigh *Progressive Farmer*, February 20, 27, March 6, 1915.
78. *North Carolina Senate Journal*, 1915, p. 477; S.B. 827, in Box 35, General Assembly Papers, Session of 1915. Senators on the Committee on Constitutional Amendments were R. L. Stedman, chairman (Halifax County); Mark Majette (Tyrrell County); H. W. Stubbs (Bertie County); Arthur M. Dixon (Gaston County); W. L. Cohoon (Bladen County); B. F. Davis (Burke County); E. B. Cloud (Polk County); D. F. Giles (McDowell County); and Ezra Parker (Johnston County). Only Parker was a Republican; all others were Democrats.

recall since the Legislature of 1868, perhaps," he asserted, "that there has ever been a measure proposed on the floor of this body so antagonistic to democracy, property rights, and the constitution." As a "superior race," he said, whites had a duty of enforcing "absolute justice." Nash disparaged the idea that the amendment provided voluntary land segregation. Should the amendment be submitted to the people for a vote, he noted, blacks would not be able to cast ballots for or against it. Nash proved persuasive. In a narrow vote the North Carolina Senate rejected the measure, 15 to 17.[79] Actually, the magnitude of Poe's defeat was a bit greater than he ever admitted publicly. To amend the state constitution required an affirmative vote by three-fifths of the members present in each house of the General Assembly. Thus, Poe's proposal needed twenty yeas from the thirty-two lawmakers present to pass its first reading in the state senate.

Although chagrined, Poe feigned optimism. Most of the negative votes, he observed, came from west of Greensboro, traditionally an area suspicious of eastern interests and race-related legislation. Only four eastern senators had opposed the measure. Moreover, Poe maintained that a majority in the North Carolina House of Representatives supported the amendment. The "plan is coming and coming fast," asserted the farm editor, and the fight must continue in 1917.[80]

In truth Poe's plan was dead. Although he never entirely abandoned the scheme, the idea of rural segregation never won widespread acceptance. When South Carolina considered a similar proposal in 1916, Poe addressed the South Carolina House of Representatives. He blamed his defeat in North Carolina on the "mountain sections where the race problem is not an issue." If the South had adopted such a policy after the Civil War, Poe argued, any attempt to overthrow it would inspire a "revolution." If it was good policy fifty years ago, queried the editor, "why is it not good policy now?"[81]

79. *North Carolina Senate Journal*, 1915, pp. 556, 682; Raleigh *News and Observer*, March 6, 1915.

80. Raleigh *Progressive Farmer*, March 20, 1915.

81. Clarence Poe, "Legislation Needed by Our Farming Interests," in Poe Papers; Raleigh *Progressive Farmer*, February 12, December 16, 1916, May 26, 1917; Clarence Poe, "The Crusade for a Richer Country Life," in Poe Papers. See also Poe's 1915 commencement address at the University of Virginia, which was titled "What Is Justice Between White and Black? A Study of Conditions in the Rural South," in Poe Papers; and Clarence

In the years after World War I the parallel race problem affecting South Africa and the American South continued to fascinate Poe. He attributed postwar unrest among blacks on both continents to the African race's extremely "bitter mood," but he failed to comprehend the reasons for that mood. In the South, at least, "so-called 'protective' organizations" among blacks had sprung up in response to a resurgence of the Ku Klux Klan. Poe censured the modern Klan as an attempt to exploit "the history of another day and the prejudice of our own." With the adoption of women's suffrage in 1920, the Progressive editor stated that the South should be run on the same basis as South Africa, which he characterized as "equality for the whites and justice for the blacks."[82]

Poe never wavered in identifying the ultimate beneficiaries of his reform proposals: "Caucasian . . . men and women . . . , inheritors of the same racial history, traits and tendencies." Such people, Poe averred, were "indeed 'created equal.'" Poe's plea for a southern *Herrenvolk* democracy appealed to small, struggling white farmers who, like Progressive spokesmen nationwide, wished to elevate the common man. Southern Bourbons, however, remained adamantine. Poe's entreaties and notions of justice for either race impinged little on the collective conscience of merchants, bankers, and planters. Poe's land-segregation scheme emphatically censured the South's economic arrangements and threatened to democratize property holding at a time when all trends—demographic, social, and economic—were in the opposite direction. Poe's plan could not dilute the concentration of land and wealth in fewer hands, end tenantry, or interdict urbanization and industrialization in southern society. However, Poe's greatest fear—the "Africanization" of the southern countryside—never occurred. The Great Migration of the First World War and after sent black migrants streaming north and west in search of better economic opportunities and less political repression. In fact, out-migration from the South was not limited to blacks. In the half century after 1910, an estimated nine million black and white southerners—equal to 34 per-

---

Poe, "The South: Backward and Sectional or Progressive and National?" *Outlook*, October 11, 1916, pp. 328–31.
    82. Raleigh *Progressive Farmer*, July 12, 1919, September 11, 1920.

cent of the entire 1910 population of the South—migrated to other parts of the country.[83]

In the end Poe's plan for rural segregation collapsed from the weight of its own complexities. Poe's scheme, purposely vague, invited too many legal and constitutional questions about how it could be implemented without violating property rights. Opponents of the idea, at least partially imbued with humanitarian impulses, couched their objections in paternalistic utterances about protecting an "inferior race." Inevitably, Poe collided head on with large agricultural and commercial interests, which had no desire to reform economic patterns that rewarded them so handsomely or to jeopardize the availability of cheap black labor.

At every turn Poe's friends and foes thwarted him. The Progressive Democratic convention refused to include the land-segregation scheme in its platform. A quasi alliance of planters, merchants, and blacks voiced strident disapproval of the proposal. The North Carolina Supreme Court nullified a Winston segregation ordinance, with grave implications for Poe's plan. Finally, a constitutional amendment to effect land segregation failed by five votes to pass the North Carolina Senate.

Still, Poe's crusade is instructive. It reveals a conservative, even reactionary, side to the Progressive movement in the South. Poe was never able to break out of the rigid confines created by the banishment of blacks and poor whites from the political process. He alternately patronized blacks, accused planters and merchants of intentionally propagating tenancy and absentee landlordism, and blamed Afro-Americans for the South's poor economic conditions. These contradictions reflected the narrowed political universe of southern politics, in which blacks became a scapegoat for the region's problems. Poe's solution—land segregation—did not necessarily attack tenancy. Rather than build a political movement based on class or economic interests, he attempted to manipulate the races into separate spheres and preserve a system of vertical racial stratification. His vision of cooperation, racial homogeneity, and social harmony idealized a Jeffersonian past that was disintegrating under the relentless forces of modernization.

83. Clarence Poe, "Have Faith in North Carolina," in Poe Papers; Jack Temple Kirby, "The Southern Exodus, 1910–1960: A Primer for Historians," *Journal of Southern History*, XLIX (1983), 585–600.

Those same forces, so profoundly alarming to Poe, were eroding class and caste distinctions and impoverishing blacks and whites alike.

Even within the virulently racist atmosphere of the early twentieth century, Poe's views represented a radical strain. The Progressives who ushered the South into the reform movement have been characterized as racial moderates. They instituted disfranchisement and Jim Crow laws, to be sure, but they also defended educational opportunities for blacks and righteously fought lynching. As Poe's crusade demonstrates, the description is inadequate. Race was the Progressives' moral blind spot. Pledges of friendship and paternalistic solicitude for blacks as a "child race" notwithstanding, southern Progressivism also carried within it an immoderate and potentially dangerous element. W. E. B. Du Bois recognized the threat when he termed Poe and other Progressives of that ilk reactionary.

For a brief period on the eve of the First World War, the South stood at a crossroads, with Clarence Poe pointing in the direction of South Africa. Despite his best efforts, an American apartheid failed to materialize, and the South was spared the trauma in the 1960s of undoing two generations of rural segregation.

The Proto-Dorian Convention: W. J. Cash and the Race Question

Only the eccentric, idiosyncratic W. J. Cash would have made up (and dared to use) the expression "the Proto-Dorian Convention" to characterize his argument that the white South had been, throughout its history, unalterably committed to white supremacy. A newspaperman by trade when he published *The Mind of the South* in 1941, Cash was an audacious, brilliant—if obscure—writer who had lived all but a handful of his days in the Carolina piedmont. There racism was constant and palpable: in lynchings, in bloody race riots, in racist novels and newspaper headlines, and in the blatant demagoguery of southern politicians. Cash saw the best and the worst men and women of his time welded together—in a subtle but profound agreement that obscured the real issues of life—to enforce racial segregation and to deny the vote to the recently emancipated former slaves. That bonding of the highest and lowest white classes was "the Proto-Dorian Convention."[1]

1. W. J. Cash, *The Mind of the South* (New York: Vintage, 1969), 40, 69, 86–88. For an appreciative, sprightly, but uncritical look at Cash's life see Joseph L. Morrison, *W. J. Cash, Southern Prophet: A Biography and Reader* (New York: Knopf, 1967). The first to spy (and decry) Cash's contention was Donald Davidson, "Mr. Cash and the Proto-Dorian South," *Southern Review,* VII (1941), 4–5, 20. Davidson's review is reprinted in his *Still Rebels, Still Yankees and Other Essays* (Baton Rouge: Louisiana State University Press, 1972), 191–212. See also C. Vann Woodward's review of *The Mind of the South* in the *Journal of Southern History,* VII (1941), 400.

An omnivorous reader, Cash knew that others before him, many of them distinguished historians, had said much the same thing—admittedly in a more restrained manner. He also knew that his predecessors were imbued with the very racism they chronicled. This was true of no less an authority than Ulrich B. Phillips, whose books on slavery dominated scholarly thought from the moment they appeared after the First World War. Phillips had concluded that white dominance was "the central theme of Southern history." Twenty-five years earlier, the widely read journalist and historian William Garrott Brown had made much the same argument, as Cash doubtless knew. He agreed with the argument, and said so sweepingly—and extravagantly, as his critics have maintained. But these same critics, almost all of whom have been liberal academics troubled by the lurking determinism in *The Mind of the South*, have failed to give Cash proper credit for exposing and slashing the racist underpinnings of his predecessors and contemporaries. Nor have his critics, friendly or otherwise, explored the context of Cash's life as a means of seeing how deeply mired in racism his region was and how and why he was able, finally, to escape and expose the lockstep that racism had fastened on the "master" race, the Dorians of high and low estate.[2]

Wilbur Joseph Cash was born on May 2, 1900, in Gaffney, South Carolina, into a hardworking, respectable family that prized the Cherokee Avenue Baptist Church and the Limestone Mill, where his father ran the company store. Gaffney numbered four thousand in 1900 and was, for all its pride in its churches and New South boosterism, a rough, hard-drinking, fist-fighting, grimy piedmont textile mill town

2. Ulrich B. Phillips, "The Central Theme of Southern History," *American Historical Review*, XXXIV (1928), 30–43; Bruce Clayton, *The Savage Ideal: Intolerance and Intellectual Leadership in the South, 1890–1914* (Baltimore: Johns Hopkins University Press, 1972), 179–204. For commentaries on Cash's thought see C. Vann Woodward, "The Elusive Mind of the South," in Woodward, *American Counterpoint: Slavery and Racism in the North-South Dialogue* (Boston: Little, Brown, 1971), 261–84; Michael O'Brien, "W. J. Cash, Hegel, and the South," *Journal of Southern History*, XLIV (1978), 379–98; Michael P. Dean, "W. J. Cash's *The Mind of the South*: Southern History, Southern Style," *Southern Studies*, XX (1981), 297–302; Edwin M. Yoder, Jr., "W. J. Cash After a Quarter Century," in Willie Morris (ed.), *The South Today: 100 Years After Appomattox* (New York: Harper & Row, 1965), 89–99; Bertram Wyatt-Brown, *Yankee Saints and Southern Sinners* (Baton Rouge: Louisiana State University Press, 1985), 131–54; Fred Hobson, *Tell About the South: The Southern Rage to Explain* (Baton Rouge: Louisiana State University Press, 1983), 244–73; Richard King, *A Southern Renaissance: The Cultural Awakening of the American South, 1930–1955* (New York: Oxford University Press, 1980), 146–72.

just below the North Carolina border. Blacks knew their place in Gaffney. Rigid racial segregation prevailed throughout the piedmont and the South by 1900, and violence, much of it racial, was commonplace news on the front page of the Gaffney *Ledger*. Blacks were the objects of humor or ridicule in the press, in sermons, and in literature. Warnings abounded about the dangers of abandoning white supremacy even for a moment.[3]

Following Mississippi's lead, South Carolina had constitutionally disfranchised its blacks in 1895. Louisiana followed in 1898, and North Carolina, with racist Red Shirts intimidating and harassing blacks and recalcitrant whites, disfranchised and segregated blacks in 1900. And so it went across the South. For sensitive Carolinians, the traumatizing and symbolic event of white supremacy was the Wilmington, North Carolina, race riot of 1898, which left at least eleven blacks dead and many more wounded. The city completed the job by electing as mayor the leader of the mob, a former Confederate officer and congressman. South Carolinians who approved of the region's racism gloried in the words and deeds of Pitchfork Ben Tillman, who in 1900 was at the height of his national fame as a racist politician. Tillman and his successor, Coleman Blease, who was even more of a red-neck than Tillman on race, loudly defended lynchings.[4]

Blease, hero of the wool-hat boys and mill workers, was a frequent visitor to Gaffney and the region. He triumphantly toured the town in 1911 after capturing the governorship from the more moderate forces behind former governor Clinton Heyward. Coley Blease came as a special guest of the local order of the Red Men, a nativist group open only to "men of pure white blood and under the tongue of good repute." Other fraternal organizations admitted blacks to segregated groups, but not the Red Men, Blease reminded the throng that trailed after him as the Gaffney Cornet Band filled the air with "Dixie." The *Ledger*, a New South paper devoted to pumping for prohibition, economic growth, and moral reform (and given to worrying that harping

3. See, for example, Gaffney (S.C.) *Ledger*, February 27, May 5, 1903, April 1, 1904, August 28, 1906, March 23, 1909.
4. C. Vann Woodward, *Origins of the New South, 1877–1913* (Baton Rouge: Louisiana State University Press, 1951), 321–49, 350; Paul D. Escott, *Many Excellent People: Power and Privilege in North Carolina, 1850–1900* (Chapel Hill: University of North Carolina Press, 1985), 254; Francis Butler Simkins, *Pitchfork Ben Tillman, South Carolinian* (Baton Rouge: Louisiana State University Press, 1944), 393–407.

on racial violence, however deplorable, would distort and hurt Gaffney's image), noted with approval that the normally coarse governor
had refused to comment on a recent lynching, because "there were
ladies in the crowd." But Blease had shouted that "when a nigger laid
his hand upon a white woman the quicker he was placed under six feet
of dirt, the better."[5]

Like other southern newspapers, the *Ledger* reported black crime, at
home and throughout the South, with a thoroughness bordering on
the compulsive. When a jury in 1911 acquitted a white man charged
with recruiting some Negroes to kill another white, editor Ed DeCamp
noted approvingly that the disgruntled judge had severely criticized
"whites who attend negro meetings, saying that such whites are a
disgrace to their race." DeCamp insisted that Gaffney's respectable
folks abhorred the more barbarous lynchings. Stories of blacks being
burned alive or their bodies mutilated by savage crowds, sometimes in
the presence of schoolchildren, were routinely reported, but DeCamp
was usually at pains to show that the better sort of whites were not
involved. The *Ledger* refused to believe the news from Statesboro,
Georgia, in 1904 that the "best citizens of the community" had led a
savage burning of "black brutes." The mob was obviously "composed
of illiterate white trash."[6]

Two years later, and just a month before news of the Atlanta race riot
shocked the nation, a mob of over a thousand whites in nearby Greenwood County took an accused Negro rapist from jail, tied him to a tree,
and riddled his body with bullets for ten minutes. "The negro's head
was literally shot into pulp," the *Ledger* reported, "his brains covering
his hat and face." The crowd would have been even more savage and
burned the man alive if Governor Heyward had not been there. As a
result of Heyward's plea for decency, "a humane man pulled the
doomed negro's hat over his face before the crowd started shooting."[7]

What Cash the young boy thought of all this is unknown, but as an
adult he would have none of this New South liberalism that constantly
blamed the white masses for the racial ills of the South. Educated,
respectable people were "above" racism, went the litany; the problem
was "out there" in the unwashed, the ignorant who would be weaned

5. Gaffney (S.C.) *Ledger*, November 21, 1911.
6. *Ibid.*, March 7, 1911, August 26, 1904.
7. *Ibid.*, August 21, 1906.

from their thirst for blood by education. Until then, the masses should listen to their betters. In *The Mind of the South* Cash rejected this view as so much self-congratulatory delusion, saying: "The common whites have usually done the actual execution. . . . But they have kept on doing it only because their betters either consented quietly or, more often, definitely approved." Always intensely personal, Cash re-counted, "I have myself known university-bred men who confessed proudly to having helped roast a Negro."[8]

Long before Cash knew any university-bred men, he was confronted with the imposing popularity of the Reverend Thomas Dixon, from nearby Shelby, North Carolina, who had shed his clerical garb to become the South's premier author of racist novels. First had come *The Leopard's Spots* (1902), a racist saga of Reconstruction, and it was followed in 1905 by the runaway best seller *The Clansman*, which Dixon reworked into a play before seeing it become a hugely successful racist film, *The Birth of a Nation*.[9] Staged, *The Clansman* was spectacular, requiring a large theater to accommodate a troop of horses. Its appearance in Gaffney in 1907 was greeted with a packed house and thunderous applause. No one in town, not even a youngster, could have missed the hoopla and deep emotional meaning of Dixon's extravaganza, which was performed repeatedly in the piedmont during these years. Young Cash probably did not see the play—his parents were, as he would later say, "foot-washing Baptists" who did not hold with theatergoing—but he saw the film in 1916. What impact it made on the sixteen-year-old is hard to say. Later, speaking as an adult after having taken on a certain tough-guy persona, he said that he remembered "watching the Rev. Tom Dixon's Ku Kluxers do execution on uppity coons and low-down carpetbaggers, and alternately bawling hysterically and shouting my fool head off."[10]

The movie deeply touched white southerners. In Chattanooga, Ralph McGill's boyhood hometown, the film caused a sensation and played "night after night to a packed house." Visiting New Orleans

---

8. Cash, *The Mind of the South*, 310–11.
9. John C. Inscoe, "*The Clansman* on Stage and Screen: North Carolina Reacts," *North Carolina Historical Review*, LXIV (1987), 139–61. For more on Dixon see Joel Williamson, *The Crucible of Race: Black-White Relations in the American South Since Emancipation* (New York: Oxford University Press, 1984), 140–79.
10. Gaffney (S.C.) *Ledger*, April 5, 12, 1907; W. J. Cash, "Southland Turns to Books with Full Vigor," Charlotte *News*, February 9, 1936.

with his parents in 1916, nine-year-old Hodding Carter sat trembling as he watched the movie in a theater jam-packed with Confederate veterans who screamed the rebel yell from the opening scene on. His father, caught up in the crowd's emotions, hollered and flung his hat into the air, "never to see it again." The play's appearance in Shelby in the 1920s—when Cash may well have seen it—made such an impression on one of Cash's young friends that she could not sleep that night, so fearful was she of an attack by a black. Even in her seventies, after a lifetime of reading and yearning to shake free of racial prejudices, she still felt a moment of terror whenever an unknown black man walked behind her.[11]

It is impossible to gauge the emotional impact of Dixon's now forgotten writings. However melodramatic and limited his literary skills, he embodied something profoundly important in the white psyche. In *The Leopard's Spots* some Negroes, brandishing pistols, invade a white wedding party and carry off the bride. The rescuers are told to shoot to kill, even if it means killing the young virgin. "There are things worse than death," the father screams. Following the accidental shooting of the young girl, the father consoles the aggrieved rescuers: "It's all right boys. . . . You've saved my little gal." Even a horrible death was preferable to rape by a black.[12]

This maudlin intertwining of sexual purity and racism was far more than the outpouring of a popular novelist's tortured psyche. Dixon touched and expressed something profoundly sensitive in the nation's racism—his work was enormously popular everywhere in America. For white southerners, Dixon expressed (or merely repeated) what the majority truly believed. There was an uncanny, but understandable, similarity between Dixon's words and one of Tillman's characteristic outbursts: "I have three daughters, but, so help me God, I had rather find either one of them killed by a tiger or a bear and gather up her bones and bury them, conscious that she had died in the purity of her maidenhood, than to have her crawl to me and tell me the horrid story

11. Ralph McGill, *The South and the Southerner* (Boston: Little, Brown, 1963), 129; Hodding Carter, "Furl That Banner?" *New York Times Magazine*, June 25, 1965, pp. 8–9; John T. Kneebone, *Southern Liberal Journalists and the Issue of Race, 1920–1944* (Chapel Hill: University of North Carolina Press, 1985), 9; interview with Bea Morris, September 15, 1984.

12. Thomas Dixon, *The Leopard's Spots: A Romance of the White Man's Burden, 1865–1900* (New York: Doubleday, Page, 1902), 125–26.

that she had been robbed of the jewel of her womanhood by a black fiend."[13]

Just when and what young Cash read of Dixon's writings is unknown. The chances are at least good that Cash would have thrilled to Dixon's stirring romances. Later in life, he recalled himself as a typical starry-eyed southern boy, imagining himself a dashing young Confederate charging with Pickett and dying gallantly for the Lost Cause. That may be an accurate portrait of the young boy's psyche; it may also be a product of Cash's dramatic turn of mind and phrase and part of his strategy to prove how all-inclusive "the mind of the South" was. It is clear, though, that by his late teens, when he started college, he had little but contempt for the literary tradition Dixon embodied. By the time Cash was a man struggling to become a writer and break free of the southern sentimental novel, he was embarrassed by Dixon and appalled by the adoration his neighbors in Shelby—Cash and his family had moved to Boiling Springs, North Carolina, in 1913—lavished on the writer. When Cash wrote *The Mind of the South*, he gave Dixon little but the back of his hand. Aside from Ellen Glasgow and James Branch Cabell, Cash wrote, describing southern literature in 1914, "the literary state of the region was to be accurately measured by Thomas Dixon, Jr., whose many rabid novels, and especially *The Clansman* . . . probably contributed no little to stirring up racial feeling and the creation of the Ku Klux Klan."[14]

The specters of Dixon, Tillman, and Blease seared Cash's conscience. They had the same effect on fellow North Carolinian Gerald W. Johnson and other members of a rising generation of liberal southern writers and journalists, including Tennessee's George Fort Milton, Virginia's Virginius Dabney, and Georgia's Ralph McGill. In Mississippi, young William Alexander Percy watched in disgust the racist, rabble-rousing antics of James K. Vardaman. In Alabama, Clarence Cason recoiled in horror at J. Thomas Heflin's racist demagoguery. As adults, Cash and his contemporaries never for a moment accepted the fiction that Tillman, Blease, and their kind championed the poor, however much they might rant, as Tillman did, about sticking a "pitchfork" in the rich. To Cash, Tillman was a "nigger-baiting" demagogue,

13. Simkins, *Pitchfork Ben Tillman*, 397.
14. Cash, *The Mind of the South*, 385.

the first in a line extending through Tom Watson and Hoke Smith of Georgia, Jeff Davis of Arkansas, and the notorious Vardaman, whose race-baiting spelled the end of the aristocratic Percys' dominance. And Blease, said Cash, was "the capstone of it all." All were vulgar but shrewd captains, as Cash would say, of the Proto-Dorian Convention.[15]

Cash's emancipation from the assumptions of his region probably began early. He was no ordinary youngster. Exceedingly bookish and awkward, he was not very good at games and shy to the point of reclusiveness. On warm days, his idea of fun was to crawl under the front porch with a book and shut out the world. Hidden away from others, clutching Shakespeare or Thomas Carlyle, he allowed his active imagination to run free, whether about the Civil War or about defending a beautiful woman. Although he had to be prodded to be enthusiastic about his family's narrow brand of religion, he was emotionally quite close to his mother and would remain so all his life. Apparently, as man and boy, Cash felt distanced from his father, who, in the years when Cash was growing up, was away at the mill most of the day. Named Joseph Wilbur Cash—and thus having the same initials as his father, John William—Cash reversed his given names while he was still a teenager. He did this quietly, without fanfare, perhaps in defiance of his father, perhaps out of what might be thought of as innocent adolescent passion for his own identity. Whatever the reason, it appears certain that even as a youngster Cash was, except perhaps in the secret recesses of his imagination, different. And part of that differentness was his lack of assertiveness, particularly outward physical assertiveness. He was a retiring, reclusive sort. Appropriately, his boyhood friends dubbed him Sleepy, a nickname of psychological disguise and one he liked.[16]

Sleepy complained some when his family insisted that he attend Wofford College, a Methodist school in nearby Spartanburg, South Carolina. Cash spent a year (1917–1918) there before dropping out to work in naval shipyards and cantonments, most of the time with his

15. Ibid., 253–56; William Alexander Percy, Lanterns on the Levee: Recollections of a Planter's Son (New York: Knopf, 1941), 140–55; Clarence Cason, 90° in the Shade (Chapel Hill: University of North Carolina Press, 1935), 72–89; Kneebone, Southern Liberal Journalists, 112.

16. Interviews with Allan Cash, August 7, 1984, Henry Cash, August 9, 1984, and Elizabeth Cash Elkins, August 20, 1984.

father at Spartanburg's Camp Wadsworth. Before settling in at Wake Forest College, a Baptist institution, in 1920, Cash endured an unhappy semester in Indiana at Valparaiso University, then known as the People's University. While there, states Cash's biographer Joseph L. Morrison, a Negro sat down beside him, only to be turned away rudely when Cash declared he was not "about to sit with a nigger." Nor would he as long as he lived, according to Morrison. Cash's friends, including some who knew him well in 1919, have said that they find Morrison's account impossible to square with the young man they remember. The imputation to Cash of such aggressive behavior is simply not in keeping with his personality or character. Cash may not have been entirely liberated from the assumptions of white supremacy—he would have been quite extraordinary had he escaped all the lurid images of blacks that saturated his culture—but Morrison's portrayal seems unsupportable.[17]

Cash experienced an immersion in modern, liberating ideas when he went to Wake Forest in 1920. He encountered teachers who did not blink at the mention of Darwin or evolution or blanch when someone mentioned naughty Virginia novelist James Branch Cabell or H. L. Mencken, who had a few years earlier blasted the South as "the Sahara of the Bozart." Wake Forest was an intellectual oasis for a thirsty young man such as Sleepy Cash, who immediately took on advanced ideas and started whooping it up for Mencken. Cash latched on to Darwin, Nietzsche, and Wagner and may have begun reading Freud. Before long, as editor of the sprightly campus newspaper, the *Old Gold and Black*, he was poking fun at religious fundamentalists, puncturing myths, and luxuriating in the open-minded atmosphere of Wake Forest. "Light streamed from its windows over a darkling land," said Gerald W. Johnson, another Tar Heel writer who prized his student days at Wake Forest.[18]

The guiding force at the school was President William Louis Poteat, a German-trained Ph.D. in biology who championed freedom of inquiry and expression. His son Hubert M. Poteat, the indulgent faculty ad-

17. Morrison, *W. J. Cash*, 21; interviews with Harriet Doar, September 17, 1984, Irma Dunn, August 30, 1984, and Charles A. McKnight, September 15, 1984.
18. Morrison, *W. J. Cash*, 25–34; H. L. Mencken, "Sahara of the Bozart," in Mencken, *Prejudices: Second Series, 1920* (New York: Knopf, 1920), 136–54; Fred Hobson (ed.), *South-Watching: Selected Essays by Gerald W. Johnson* (Chapel Hill: University of North Carolina Press, 1983), x.

viser to the *Old Gold and Black*, preferred reading aloud to the students from the writings of iconoclastic Texan W. C. Brann to telling them how to edit the paper. Young Poteat also organized discussion groups to foster a more humane attitude toward the Negro. In these discussions and in history and political science courses Cash came into contact with New South liberalism, that positive creed that fervently espoused industrialization and benevolent treatment of the Negro, treatment organized by well-meaning academics and professional people who willingly accepted segregation and disfranchisement as necessary "reforms" to bring racial harmony.[19]

Wake Forest, like many similar colleges at the time, was a bastion of what Cash would later dismiss as shallow New South liberalism. In addition to being an embattled leader in the cause of science—though he could always assure his bitterest critics that he had never questioned the biblical account of creation—President Poteat helped found the Commission on Interracial Cooperation (CIC). Early in 1919, Poteat, YMCA leader Will Alexander, M. Ashby Jones, and others, received a grant from the YMCA to start the organization. Together the leaders persuaded various college presidents, professors, and liberal newspaper editors to meet for calm consideration of the race situation. They hoped to improve race relations and undermine the leaders of what they considered the extremists of the right and the left. Basically, the CIC was a conservative group, but racists feared and hated it. Poteat was chairman of the North Carolina branch, which brought members of both races together to discuss conditions, seek better educational facilities for blacks, and call for harmony and cooperation between the races.[20]

Still, Wake Forest was an all-white school in rural Wake County, some fifteen miles north of Raleigh. The more humane students probably considered themselves quite emancipated from the racism of the era—and they doubtless were, to an extent. Editorials in the *Old Gold and Black*, such as the one entitled "The Negro Question" when Cash

19. Morrison, *W. J. Cash*, 26–28; Clayton, *The Savage Ideal*, 185–217.

20. Suzanne Cameron Linder, *William Louis Poteat: Prophet of Progress* (Chapel Hill: University of North Carolina Press, 1966), 100–101. See also Wilma Dykeman and James Stokeley, *Seeds of Southern Change: The Life of Will Alexander* (Chicago: University of Chicago Press, 1962), 59–68, 102–109, 131–37. For an expression of liberal opinion by one of Cash's Wake Forest professors, see C. Chilton Pearson, "Race Relations in North Carolina: A Field Study of Moderate Opinion," *South Atlantic Quarterly*, XXIII (1924), 109.

was managing editor, lauded Poteat's view "as a true solution of a vital question" and warned blacks not to heed the bad advice of those such as W. E. B. Du Bois, "whose policy is to wage bitter and aggressive war against the White race and their principles." The editorial repeated the familiar "We know the Negro best" litany. The Negro should be given the vote, the paper declared, but first he must prove that he is capable of exercising the ballot and "does not intend for political equality to pave the way for social equality." That, in essence, was the variety of New South racism that went hand in glove with paternalism.[21]

The campus was an island of paternalistic decency in a sea of racism. The college loved its "old-timey" Negro, Tom Jeffries, who had been a janitor at the school for over forty years. At any college function "Dr. Tom" showed up in cutaway coat and was listed on the program, much to the delight of the old grads. Installments of Dr. Tom's "philosophy," sounding gratifyingly similar to Uncle Remus' manner of speaking, were legendary around campus. Once, at a watermelon cutting, Dr. Tom expounded on the fine qualities of the Wake Forest men to a group of young ladies: "I jus wan to admin' de young ladies here dat any of you dat gets a Wake Fores' boy sho' will get a prolific enterprise."[22]

Cash graduated in 1922, did a meaningless year at Wake Forest Law School, taught school for two years, and then worked off and on for the Charlotte newspapers—the liberal *News* and the conservative *Observer*. In between he suffered through the agonies of an unrequited love affair, did a stint on a Chicago newspaper, and fought off bouts of depression brought on by his fear of being sexually impotent. He continued devouring Mencken, Cabell, Shakespeare, and more recent loves: Voltaire, Montaigne, Dreiser, Gibbon, Dostoevski, and Willa Cather. He was particularly taken with William Hazlitt, whose essay "On the Disadvantages of Intellectual Superiority" helped Cash's own emerging sense of irony develop, and Joseph Conrad, whose subtle but all-encompassing dissection and denunciation of racism left a permanent mark on Cash's sensibility. A loner and, by his own admission, an "odd duck" who did not seem to fit anywhere and who worried about everything, Cash burrowed into Freud, looking for answers.

21. "The Negro Question," *Old Gold and Black*, February 3, 1922.
22. Linder, *William Louis Poteat*, 86; "'Dr.' Tom," *Old Gold and Black*, April 21, 1921.

Freud may not have helped him to understand himself, but the Freudian concepts of ego and defense mechanisms were invaluable for understanding his fellow whites, their attachment to white supremacy, and their willingness to sacrifice real political and economic gains for the psychological gratification that racism provided.[23]

In short, Cash had, by the mid-1920s, become an intellectual, the real kind, a cosmopolitan, someone who knew a world that was different from and better than the flawed ones of Boiling Springs and Shelby, the towns where he had spent his youth, and Charlotte, where he lived and worked intermittently in the 1920s and early 1930s. North Carolina and the South in the 1920s were far from any idealized world an intellectual might have chosen. Intolerance and religious bigotry reigned. Racism was woven into the very texture of life. True, the number of lynchings had declined from the shockingly high figures of the prewar years. But the Ku Klux Klan had reemerged in 1915 and was flourishing everywhere in the South and in the Midwest by the mid-1920s. The Invisible Empire now identified itself with Americanism and denounced Catholics and Jews, as well as blacks. By late 1924 the Klan claimed a national membership in the millions, and it was a highly disruptive force at that year's Democratic national convention.[24]

By the fall of 1924 the Invisible Empire was visible everywhere in the piedmont, staging well-attended rallies and parades in Shelby, Gastonia, and Charlotte, North Carolina, and Spartanburg and Greenville, South Carolina. The Shelby Klan vehemently denounced interracial activities—never mind that there were none—and intimidated the town's few Catholics and non-Protestants. In June, 1925, two hundred robed Klansmen paraded through Shelby carrying fiery crosses on their way to the courthouse steps in the town square, where a Klan exhorter held forth. Nobody in town had ever seen anything like it, the *Cleveland Star* reported with a touch of pride. The newspaper estimated

23. For a fuller discussion of this point see Bruce Clayton, "A Southern Modernist: The Mind of W. J. Cash," in Bruce Clayton and John A. Salmond (eds.), *The South Is Another Land: Essays on the Twentieth-Century South* (Westport, Conn.: Greenwood Press, 1987), 171–85.

24. George B. Tindall, *The Emergence of the New South, 1913–1945* (Baton Rouge: Louisiana State University Press, 1967), 173–75, 187–94, 242, 243; David M. Chalmers, *Hooded Americanism: The History of the Ku Klux Klan* (2nd ed.; New York: Franklin Watts, 1981), 28–39, 202–15.

the crowd of onlookers to be close to five thousand. A year later, Klan delegations from some fifteen neighboring towns converged on Shelby to parade, exhort, and recruit. Perhaps Shelby was chosen because the local Klan was headed, according to the *Star*, by "one of the best known men in town, who is a mixer and has the reputation of being a good fellow." The local theater obliged by showing a Klan film, and the town took on a carnival atmosphere as the Klan brought back "colorful memories of the Old South."[25]

Nationally, North Carolina was considered to be one of the Klan's showcase states. Klan leaders beamed with approval when the highly respected and popular Judge Harry A. Grady, recently elected to the North Carolina Superior Court, agreed to be the state's grand dragon in 1922. Klaverns sprang up across the state; respected editors, clergymen, and businessmen joined. But in 1927, when Imperial Wizard Hiram Wesley Evans and the Klan's national leaders called upon state legislatures to forbid interracial marriage, marriage between Protestants and Catholics, and attendance at Catholic schools, Judge Grady resigned. Others did the same. The news created a sensation, and some papers, including the *Star*, initially exaggerated the extent of the disillusionment. Most chapters reaffirmed their allegiance to Evans, denounced Grady, and swore allegiance to the new grand dragon, Amos C. Duncan, who moved the state's headquarters from Raleigh to Charlotte. Still, the Klan had suffered a major blow in North Carolina and throughout the South.[26]

Cash had a front-row seat. Following a summer in Europe in 1927, where on doctor's orders he had gone to regain his health by walking and bicycling, he was living with his parents in Boiling Springs and making regular trips over to Shelby to talk and see friends. In the fall he filled in as state editor of the Charlotte *News* and in early 1928 convinced the paper to run a weekly column. (Cash was unwelcome at the *Star*, where he was thought, quite rightly, to be unreliable on politics and race.) He launched his column, which he called "The Moving Row," by denouncing Americanism and its demand for intellectual uniformity. He preferred Voltaire's "I do not agree with a word you say,

25. *Cleveland Star* (Shelby, N.C.), June 23, 1925, June 14, 1926, February 23, 1927; Chalmers, *Hooded Americanism*, 92–97.

26. Chalmers, *Hooded Americanism*, 94–95, 291–99; *Cleveland Star* (Shelby, N.C.), February 23, 1927.

but I will defend to the death your right to say it." In his best Mencken imitation Cash said: "The Kluckers are granted full right to believe and proclaim that the Pope is a cannibal with dark designs on Baptist babies. They are merely asked to remember that the Constitution, which they invoke, does not proscribe Catholics or Jews or Niggers." In another installment Cash poked at the narrowness of "the Neolithic [Cole] Blease."[27]

Cash's career as the Mencken of the piedmont ended after just four installments of "The Moving Row." He fell again to the neurasthenia that had plagued him off and on since his college days. "I landed in a hospital, and eventually had to give up work and retire to the ancestral village," he reported later. By fall, after a summer of long walks and wood chopping, he was sufficiently recovered to be able to accept the editorship of a new semiweekly, the *Cleveland Press*. Published in Shelby and meant to be a competitor to the *Star*, the first issue of the *Press* appeared on September 20, 1928, just in time to be in the thick of the heated presidential race between Herbert Hoover and Al Smith.[28]

When the Democrats nominated Smith, a Catholic and a wet, the veteran Senator Furnifold M. Simmons resigned from the Democratic national committee and announced his anti-Smith feelings and his break with the state's party chieftains, who were remaining loyal to Smith and his running mate, Senator Joseph T. Robinson of Arkansas. Shelby's O. Max Gardner, the party's gubernatorial nominee, and his brother-in-law Clyde R. Hoey—the other half of the Shelby Dynasty— reviled Simmons, and the battle lines were marked off. By the time the *Cleveland Press* appeared, the anti-Smith Democrats were well orga- nized and headed by Frank R. McNinch, a former mayor of Charlotte. The Klan, now securely headquartered in Charlotte, was actively op- posed to Smith, saying it based its stand solely on Smith's wetness, not his religion.[29]

But Cash thought differently. During his brief editorship of the paper

27. W. J. Cash, "The Moving Row," Charlotte *News*, March 4, April 12, October 30, 1928.

28. Application for a John Simon Guggenheim Memorial Fellowship, October 20, 1932, in Joseph L. Morrison Papers, Southern Historical Collection, University of North Carolina, Chapel Hill; Joseph L. Morrison, "Found: The Missing Editorship of W. J. Cash," *North Carolina Historical Review*, XLVII (1970), 40–50.

29. Joseph L. Morrison, *Governor O. Max Gardner: A Power in North Carolina and New Deal Washington* (Chapel Hill: University of North Carolina Press, 1971), 48–51; Morrison, "Found," 44–45; Chalmers, *Hooded Americanism*, 96–97.

(it expired after six weeks), Cash hammered at the Klan, both for its religious intolerance and its racism. His first signed column, his revived "The Moving Row," singled out the Klan's anti-Catholicism and denounced its hate sheet, the *Fellowship Forum*. The *Forum* was widely distributed in Shelby and throughout the state. The Carolina piedmont, as Cash knew, was Klan country. Still, he had to admit that the Klan-backed anti-Smith forces did not have a monopoly on racism. Smith's people, including Gardner, Hoey, and the rival *Star*, welcomed Cole Blease's racist demagoguery when he campaigned in North Carolina and warned that a Hoover victory meant a return to "Negro rule." A newspaperman, Cash reported on Blease's visit to Cleveland County as objectively as possible, hoping that fair-minded people would be offended by Blease's racism. "His picture of black men crowding white women from the street and wantonly insulting them stirred the crowd's fire," Cash reported, "and the Senator's promise that such activities in his own state would be greeted by men 'who know how to tie a rope to a tree and to the other end, too' brought laughter and whoops."[30]

On the whole the *Press* was forthright and, considering Cash's strong feelings and Menckenesque style, temperate in its reporting and editorials. He rebuked the clergy for its attacks on Smith and encouragement of the Klan. He was particularly incensed when leading churchmen like Virginia's Methodist Bishop James A. Cannon, Jr., vehemently attacked Smith on the ground that the New Yorker had injected the religious issue into the campaign. The argument was preposterous on the face of it and in no way justified Cannon's distributing some 380,000 copies of his anti-Catholic pamphlet that denounced Catholicism's alleged intolerance.[31]

Hoover defeated Smith handily and in the process broke the Solid South. Not since 1888 had a Republican carried one southern state. Hoover won five, including North Carolina. For years historians have debated the significance of the Klan and the religious issue in the election. To Cash it was clear that the Klan's religious bigotry, working

30. W. J. Cash, "The Moving Row," *Cleveland Press* (Shelby, N.C.), September 20, October 30, 1928.
31. Editorials, *ibid.*, October 2, 26, November 6, 1928; Cash, "The Moving Row," *ibid.*, October 30, 1928; Morrison, "Found," 47–48.

in league with the main-line Protestant churches, had been instrumen-
tal in swinging North Carolina into Hoover's column, but Cleveland
County followed Gardner and Hoey rather than the Klan and went for
Smith. As David Chalmers has pointed out, some of North Carolina's
counties where the Klan was strongest went for Smith while others
went for Hoover.[32]

Nevertheless, Cash gained some important experience from his brief
sojourn with the *Press* as he watched the moving row of southern
politics. Just before the paper folded on November 26, 1928, Cash had
launched an attack on Furnifold M. Simmons. He did not call Simmons
a bigot, but he did accuse him of tolerating and fostering bigotry. Cash
immediately converted his anti-Simmons editorials into a slashing
piece that he submitted to Mencken's *American Mercury.* Published as
"Jehovah of the Tar Heels," it aped Mencken's extravagant, vi-
tuperative style and breezy use of *nigger, coon,* and *Ethiop* to castigate
Simmons' opportunistic racism.[33]

Cash's immersion in political reporting left him with a lifelong contempt for the Klan and a conviction that the Klan, far from being the
work of red-necks and poor whites, did the bidding of "the best people" and was honeycombed with the clergy. By the time he wrote *The
Mind of the South,* Cash's ideas about the Proto-Dorian Convention had
been germinating for more than a decade.

Thus, when he wrote his great work, Cash had been thinking and
brooding about himself and the South for a long time. He went on from
the obscure, soon-to-be-forgotten *Cleveland Press* to write a half dozen
or so scorching essays for Mencken's *American Mercury.* In a Menckenesque style he would never completely abandon, Cash outlined
what would become, when fully developed in his book, his overarching ideas. After lacing into Simmons, Cash explored the bitter strike at
Gastonia in 1929 for Mencken's readers, slapped at Charlotte's Calvinist bourgeois leaders, heaped abuse on Duke University for being
J. B. Duke's conservative academy—a slander he would later recant—
and sarcastically chided Dixie's clergy for failing to exploit the hard
times that had come with the Great Depression. By the early 1930s,

32. Chalmers, *Hooded Americanism,* 97.
33. Cash, "The Moving Row," *Cleveland Press* (Shelby, N.C.), October 30, 1928; W. J.
Cash, "Jehovah of the Tar Heels," *American Mercury,* XVII (1929), 185–92.

Cash had coined the expression "Proto-Dorian Convention," but he had not developed the idea.[34] It would take time for all the notions rolling around in Cash's head to find expression, just as it would take time for Cash to finish the great book he had promised Alfred A. Knopf he would write.

Following the lead of Cash's stylish biographer Joseph L. Morrison, it has become fashionable to assume that Cash should have produced his book much sooner than he did. He signed a contract with Knopf in 1931 and, like most authors, told Knopf (and himself) that he could complete the task quickly. He did not. For the rest of the decade he would promise Knopf to have the manuscript ready by a certain date. Knopf finally became so disgusted with what he considered Cash's procrastination that he threatened in 1939 to publish what he had. Cash did procrastinate and do other things, such as plan to write other books and apply for grants that would allow him freedom from his dependence on his family, when he should have been writing. But the psychological question aside—whether a writer of Cash's admittedly neurotic nature can, in fact, write before he feels himself ready—it is arguable that Cash's experiences with the Charlotte *News*, which he joined in 1935, enabled him to refine and rethink, perhaps unconsciously, what he knew about the mind of the South. And it is also arguable that during the time he worked for the *News*, Cash acquired even greater insight, which would be invaluable to the book.[35]

When Cash joined the *News*, first as a book reviewer and occasional editorialist and then, in 1937, as a full-time editor, the paper had a deserved reputation as a liberal voice in a conservative town. The morning paper, the *Observer*, was higher toned and decidedly conservative, whereas the *News* prided itself on being brash and attracting bright, creative young writers. At thirty-five, Cash was not quite youthful in 1935, but he was bright and creative. And he joined an editorial room where his iconoclastic turn of mind was not only tolerated and encouraged but expanded.[36]

---

34. W. J. Cash, "The War in the South," *American Mercury*, XIX (1930), 163–69; Cash, "Close View of a Calvinist Lhasa," *ibid.*, XXVIII (1933), 443–51; Cash, "Buck Duke's University," *ibid.*, XXX (1933), 102–110; Cash, "Holy Men Muff a Chance," *ibid.*, XXXI (1934), 112–18; Cash, "Paladin of the Drys," *ibid.*, XXIV (1931), 146.

35. Morrison, *W. J. Cash*, 48–75.

36. The following are a few southern writers who got their start with the Charlotte *News*: Harry Ashmore, Burke Davis, Marion Hargrove, Tom Pridgen, Reed Sarratt, and

Cameron Shipp, an old Shelby friend, was responsible for bringing Cash to the paper, and through the years he helped Cash immensely. A bona fide liberal, Shipp had chafed at the restrictions placed on him at the *Star*—one of which was not to use Cash. When Shipp jumped to the *News* in 1935, he immediately persuaded J. E. Dowd, the liberal-leaning editor and publisher, to hire Cash. In addition to doing a little bit of everything at the paper, Shipp got out a highly literate book page each Sunday. He liked to give Thomas Dixon and Thomas Nelson Page a good bashing now and then and to encourage newer, younger writers who were emancipated from the magnolia and mint-julep school of fiction. Shipp also saw to it that serious works by and about blacks got reviewed.[37]

Shipp's coming to the *News* reinforced the paper's liberal point of view on social issues. He was one of the driving forces behind the *News*'s commitment to publicizing lynchings and other forms of racial violence. The number of lynchings continued to decline in the 1930s, but some incidents reached new levels of bestiality, such as the slow burning of two Negroes by blowtorch in Mississippi in April, 1937. The paper reported such grisly news, editorialized against it, and said, over and over again, that the police could stop lynchings whenever they wanted to—a point Cash would underscore in *The Mind of the South*. During the first thirty years of the century only twelve lynchers were brought to justice.[38]

Throughout the decade the *News* hammered away at violence in the South and in Charlotte. It was a matter of shame and urgency to Shipp, Dowd, and young liberal journalists such as Reed Sarratt and Charles ("Pete") McKnight that Charlotte's murder rate made the city "the murder capital of the United States," as the paper annually announced at the beginning of a new year. For example, in 1936, with 55 homicides and a population of nearly 90,000, Charlotte was, relatively speaking, the nation's most violent city. To have the same murder rate as New

Walter Spearman. See also Jack Claiborne, *The Charlotte "Observer": Its Time and Place, 1869–1986* (Chapel Hill: University of North Carolina Press, 1986), 168–95.

37. See, for example, Cameron Shipp, "Marginalia," Charlotte *News*, March 1, October 25, 1936, and Walter Spearman's sensitive review of Zora Neale Hurston's novel *Their Eyes Were Watching God*, *ibid.*, October 3, 1937.

38. Editorial, Charlotte *News*, April 14, 1937; Cash, *The Mind of the South*, 310; Pete Daniel, *Standing at the Crossroads: Southern Life Since 1900* (New York: Hill and Wang, 1986), 58.

York City, which had 329 homicides that year, Charlotte's population would have had to be 1,250,000. Grand Rapids had had two murders in a city of 168,592; to match its rate, Charlotte would have had to be a city of two million, the *News* pointed out. Month by month the paper totaled Charlotte's murders and computed its murder rate, noting whenever possible that the city had either maintained its supremacy or slipped behind some other southern city. The *News* observed with mock pride that Charlotte's 35 murders in 1939 allowed the city to nose out Montgomery, Alabama—30 murders, population 66,000—and keep its ignominious title as the nation's murder capital. Two-thirds of the way through 1940 the *News* noted that with 36 murders the city had already surpassed the previous year's total and had a chance to outdistance all its competitors.[39]

To those who complained that the paper was airing the city's dirty linen, the reply was that the truth had to be faced. To those who argued that the paper should put the blame where it belonged—on the presence of a large number of Negroes—the editors replied that other southern cities had equally large if not larger black populations. The paper acknowledged that most of the murders were committed by blacks but argued that the dominant white society could bring that to an end by changing the social and economic position of blacks and by insisting that blacks who murdered other blacks be punished to the full extent of the law. For too long, the paper editorialized, whites had exhibited a subtle racism by blinking at black crime when the victim was black. It was an irony of southern history that the the city's liberal journalists would find themselves having to argue for harsh punishment for blacks.[40] Even so, Cash discovered around the offices of the *News* a group of men and women who refused to duck the issue of southern violence and who were prepared to state and face up to tough moral decisions. His experiences in Charlotte deepened his awareness of violence, toughened his attitude toward facing it openly, and provided him with further justification for his contention, made starkly and without equivocation in *The Mind of the South*, that violence was an integral part of the southerner's identity.

Early in 1937 the *News* startled the community and much of the

39. Editorials, Charlotte *News*, November 25, 1937. November 28, 1939.
40. Editorials, *ibid.*, March 30, May 9, 1936, June 11, July 30, 1937, March 7, 1938.

region by publishing Shipp's muckraking exposé of Charlotte's slums. For four unrelenting days the front page screamed in eight-column headlines and biting journalism that Charlotte had some of the worst living conditions known to man. Shipp, accompanied by a photographer, had gone into the most wretched black sections of the city— Blue Heaven, Black Bottom, and Sugaw Creek—looking for the truth. What they found was filthy, fetid, unsanitary conditions and widespread disease. Often two or three families were cramped into a shotgun house that was pitch dark even in the middle of the day. "Strike a match in this hut," Shipp's first slashing exposé began, "to see a black child dying of tuberculosis." Everywhere Shipp turned, he found poor people huddled in the slums, many suffering from tuberculosis, gonorrhea, syphilis, and colitis. There were perhaps as many as seven thousand of them all together—human beings living like animals.[41]

"MURDER LIVES IN THE SLUMS," the News thundered at its shocked readers. Murder, like disease, was a product of social conditions. Change the way people live, the News pleaded. If living conditions for the oppressed could be changed, everyone would gain.[42]

On the fourth and final day, Shipp and the News headlined another part of the awful truth: "WHITE PEOPLE EXIST IN AREAS OF MISERY." Shipp and the others doubtless knew that many of their readers, however shocked they might be, would put the whole business out of their minds by saying that the black slums existed because blacks were slovenly, shiftless, and ignorant. Such a "defense mechanism," as Cash said in the News and in The Mind of the South, allowed both respectable whites and red-necks to agree that though such deplorable social conditions might exist, blacks had only themselves to blame. But Shipp's concluding piece of muckraking made it clear that poverty and slums did not stop at the edge of Blue Heaven.[43]

Shipp's exposé brought results. Citizens' leagues, both black and white, sprang up to work for slum clearance. Churches and social organizations sponsored discussions of Shipp's revelations and urged their representatives in Congress to make sure that Charlotte received its share of funds allocated under the New Deal's Wagner-Steagall Act, which provided millions of dollars for slum clearance. Civic groups in

41. Ibid., February 7, 8, 1937.
42. Ibid., February 9, 1937.
43. Ibid., February 10, 1937.

nearby Gastonia demanded that its tenement sections be condemned as slums. By late 1938 Charlotte's city council was pressing the city's housing authority for action. A year later, the city was actively winning federal funds and building low-cost housing. But the task was staggering. In early 1940 the *News* reported that after all that had been done, there were still more than five thousand dwellings in the city without proper toilets and more than ten thousand without bathtubs.[44]

Cash was learning valuable things about the South, things he could not learn in any of the standard books. He loved the camaraderie of the newsroom, where the air was usually blue with cigarette smoke and some old editor's cursing. The editors and writers were serious, but they laughed and drank and cherished a good story, particularly those about crooked cops, Sabbath breakers in Presbyterian Charlotte, or the popularity of bootleggers in dry Mecklenburg County. Cash even allowed himself a sheepish grin when Shipp loudly announced to newcomers to the *News*, particularly some college boy or girl down from the school of journalism at the University of North Carolina, that they were to remember that Jack Cash was somebody, that he was writing a book for Mr. Knopf and had written for old Mencken. (Actually, as Shipp knew full well, most of the newcomers had already heard of Cash and regarded him with awe.) It was Shipp who would take an irate J. E. Dowd by the arm and assure him that Cash would cut down on his drinking and get to work on Mondays. Each time, Dowd softened and said Cash could stay on, but he reminded Shipp that Cash was a radical at heart and had better be restricted to reviewing literary works and editorializing only on foreign affairs, which few people in town paid any attention to. Cash wrote well, Dowd admitted, and Shipp convinced him that Cash was writing a great book that would bring renown to the *News*.[45]

The enforcement of Dowd's wishes, Shipp's eagerness for Cash to finish his book, Cash's wide-ranging reading, and his obsession with denouncing Hitler and fascism meant that Cash rarely touched on the Proto-Dorian Convention in the *News*. But his editorials excoriating

44. *Ibid.*, March 11, August 29, 1937, January 26, 1938, January 23, 1939, March 6, 1940.
45. Burke Davis to author, November 1, December 18, 1984; interview with Reed Sarratt, November 30, 1984; Reed Sarratt to author, December 12, 19, 1984; interview with Charles McKnight, September 15, 1984.

Hitler were slashing attacks on racism.[46] And his columns and book reviews celebrated Conrad's subtle scoring of white racism, applauded Erskine Caldwell for telling the truth about southern whites, and championed Julia Peterkin, DuBose Heyward, Paul Green, and Howard Odum for trying to deal sympathetically with blacks in their novels, plays, and other works. Cash's appreciation of Thomas Wolfe and William Faulkner continued to deepen and mature.[47] No reader of the *News* could miss the point when Cash dismissed Thomas Dixon and praised Langston Hughes and other black writers. The book page was Cash's soapbox for spreading Franz Boas' anthropological arguments that all races come from mixed evolutionary backgrounds and that any talk of pure races and distinctive, immutable racial characteristics was scientifically unsound. Cash felt compelled to say such things—when Shipp and others were urging him to concentrate on writing his book—because he feared that many Americans, and not just southerners, might succumb to fascism because of its blatant racism.[48]

Cash was even allowed to do a bit of local muckraking. In mid-1939 he did an exposé of the wretched conditions in the local tuberculosis sanatorium. It was overcrowded, dark, poorly ventilated, and understaffed; ceilings and floors were rickety and barely safe. In the sections for blacks, conditions were even worse. What passed for an isolation ward was a tiny corner big enough for just three beds. "They put the far-gone cases there either to take a change for the better or to die— usually to die," Cash wrote. "If they die audibly . . . the other patients hear their rattling gasps, their moans and their mutterings. Most of them can see their contorted faces and bodies as they struggle for the last precious breath. The bodies of the dead must be carried out under the eyes of the whole ward."[49]

---

46. See for example, W. J. Cash, "Europe's Ku Kluxers," Charlotte *News*, September 5, 1937.

47. For his rejection of the Fugitives and Agrarians see W. J. Cash, "That for Tate: Classics and the Soil," *ibid.*, March 29, 1936. For Cash's view of Faulkner, Caldwell, and other southern writers, white and black, see Cash, "An Epithet: Oh, So Sad," *ibid.*, April 5, 1936; Cash, "Literature of the Negro," *ibid.*, July 26, 1936; Cash, "This Sentimental Cult," *ibid.*, March 28, 1937; Cash, "William Faulkner," *ibid.*, November 8, 1936. For Cash's admiration for Conrad see Cash, "The Strange Story of Conrad," *ibid.*, October 3, 1937, and Cash, "Death with Honor," *ibid.*, April 3, 1938.

48. W. J. Cash, "Papa Franz Boas," *ibid.*, July 12, 1936; Cash, "Literature of the Negro," *ibid.*, July 26, 1936; Cash, "The Negro and His Poetry," *ibid.*, April 11, 1937.

49. W. J. Cash, "A Visit to Mecklenburg Sanatorium," *ibid.*, June 11, 1939.

Unlike most of the white patients, few of the blacks survived. Treatment of blacks was inadequate, and most arrived at an advanced stage of illness. "Every year, an appalling number of blacks is literally condemned to death by the fact that the hospital has no way to take care of them," Cash noted. Speaking directly to his white readers, he said that if this news failed to move them, they should "remember that over half of the incoming black patients work as domestics in white homes."[50]

Perhaps if Cash had had a free hand at the *News*, he might have become quite a crusading liberal. The *News* was progressive, but it conformed to the liberal racial assumptions and practices of the day. At no time during the 1930s did the liberals at the *News* attack either racial segregation or disfranchisement of blacks, nor did Virginius Dabney at the Richmond *Times-Dispatch* or Ralph McGill at the Atlanta *Constitution*. The front page exploited black crime in sensationalistic headlines and news articles that would sound racist to modern ears. Darky cartoons sometimes appeared, and editorials and articles lapsed into darky dialect occasionally. When mentioned in the paper, blacks were always identified as such, usually by the label "colored." They were always referred to by their given names, never as Mr., Mrs., or Miss, as whites were. If the *News* erred and identified a white as a Negro, the policy of the paper was to get in touch with the offended person immediately and offer compensation for the insult. Blacks were seldom mentioned in a positive light before the late 1930s, and news about blacks was ignored for the most part. The paper ran few photographs of blacks other than black criminals. "No pictures of niggers or snakes," one editor liked to bark.[51]

What sort of newsman Cash would have become is moot. By late 1940 his book was finally done. When it appeared in early 1941 to a chorus of praise, Cash married, won a Guggenheim Fellowship, and packed his bags and left for Mexico City to write a novel to be set in the late nineteenth-century South of the piedmont mill country.[52]

At the beginning of *The Mind of the South*, in the section on the Great South of plantations and slavery that had emerged by 1820, Cash

---

50. *Ibid.*

51. Kneebone, *Southern Liberal Journalists*, 74–96, 196–214; interview with Reed Sarratt, November 30, 1984.

52. When Donald Davidson learned of Cash's death, he tried to withdraw his review (which was unfavorable), but he was unsuccessful.

explained that the presence of Negro slaves and the arrogance of the planters had threatened to degrade the common whites, rob them of their self-esteem, and thus develop in them a sullen, angry mood, perhaps even a genuine class consciousness. But ironically, little or none of that had happened. Slavery, however much it might degrade the common man, was built on racial consciousness, the assumption and the assurance that, come what may, to be white was to be superior to all blacks. Thus, slavery elevated the common white "to a position comparable to that of, say, the Doric knight of ancient Sparta." And thus was the common white intricately and mysteriously connected once and for all with his betters. A great potential rift, what Marx would call the class struggle, was permanently averted.[53]

Although poor whites were dominated by the region's "ruling class," Cash argued over and over again that southerners were not ruled by class but by their egoistic need to identify themselves, no matter what their station in life, with a grand, romantic, heroic, gallant idea of "the South." The ruling class, whether planters or twentieth-century capitalists, was quite small numerically, mainly because it was made up of aggressive, self-made men who believed their rule to be a natural consequence of their struggle to survive on a crude frontier. But mainly they ruled because they were able to implant in the common southerners' mind the belief that they were "the South." The ruling class, aiming to convince and disarm the Yankee, may even have come to believe it themselves, Cash wrote, but the true believers were the common whites. They looked up to the planters, admired them, and saw in them examples of what they themselves might become. This belief was pure fantasy, of course, said Cash, but it was a fantasy that coddled the ego of the common white and was thus integral to maintaining the Proto-Dorian Convention.

Having lived his entire life in the South and having dipped generously into Freud and a host of modernist intellectuals, Cash had an angle of vision that prompted him to probe what he considered irrational behavior. Why would common people, many of them poor and downtrodden, identify with their rulers? Why did such folks—exploited by their masters and frequently made the object of ridicule, often scorned as "red-necks," "lint-heads," and "white trash"—fight

53. Cash, *The Mind of the South*, 40.

to defend slavery? Indeed, they volunteered, fought courageously, and died. Many commentators on the Old South have wondered why the slaves did not rebel. Cash, who would have been the first to spy the uninformed racism in that question, wondered rather why the common white did not rebel. He did not, because "like every other good Southerner, he so absolutely identified his ego with the thing called the South as to become, so to say, a perambulating South in little."[54]

Thus, the Proto-Dorian Convention subtly and profoundly served the self-interest of the ruling class and the psychological needs of the common whites. Later, after the Civil War had been lost and Reconstruction overthrown, when the South fell in love with the machine and industrialization, fell in love with moneymaking, fell in love, that is, with Progress, said Cash, the Proto-Dorian Convention was still safely intact. White solidarity was the rallying cry of the Redeemers, who threw off the Yankee yoke in 1877. White supremacy was the cry of the disfranchisers, who saved the South from another Reconstruction in the 1890s. The men who built the mills, the politicians who pumped for schools, the clergy who prayed over the whole enterprise promised Progress—if whites would only stick together. Racial solidarity once again assuaged the ego of the (white) man furthest down. And this ploy the ruling class continued to understand. It raised the flag of white supremacy whenever the white masses threatened to rebel—to join the Populists or form a union and call a strike. No matter what happened, "the planter and, for that matter, the better sort of farmer had other effective bolsters for their essential ego than this one superiority. The cracker didn't. Let him be stripped of his proto-Dorian rank and he would be left naked, a man without status."[55]

But to Cash's mind, the deceivers, the ruling class that manipulated the psyche of the common whites, was itself deeply involved in self-deception. The planter's bragging and boasting about his contented slaves, the beauty and virtue of his women, the purity of the races, the never-say-die courage of Johnny Reb was meant to conceal guilt—and fear that none of it was true. Much of it was propaganda to rebut the Yankee slur. And much of it was believed. Take the troublesome slander that the slave was physically and sexually exploited in the cabins at night. It was all true, said Cash. Slave owners had their way

54. *Ibid.*, 115.
55. *Ibid.*, 112.

with black women, the most defenseless creatures in the land, finding in the slave cabins passionate pleasures that were denied them by their wives' Puritan prohibitions. Southern moralists railed against miscegenation, but in vain. Everybody knew the truth. But nothing could be admitted. What followed was more and more dollops of the mythology: that the South was the soul of virtue and that the purity of southern womanhood was living proof of the region's virtue.

The result was that the southerner as Dorian was a man entangled in a labyrinth of self-deceptions and illusions of innocence and purity, all of them intertwined with race and sex. Thus southerners came to believe, down in the recesses of their souls, that since woman was the very "perpetuator of white supremacy," they were defending purity itself whenever they shouted for Dixie or helped preserve the ancient pattern of relationships. "I verily believe," Cash wrote, "the ranks of the Confederacy went rolling into battle in the misty conviction that it was wholly for her [woman] that they fought."[56]

No wonder Cash had trouble writing his book. He was, and he knew it, treading on forbidden ground. Sex was not talked about, certainly not in foot-washing Baptist circles; sex was "dirty." And here was Cash, a southern white man, not only admitting that miscegenation was widespread, but also saying far more. Cash went on to argue that the southern mind was in the grip of the "rape complex": a half-understood, but passionate feeling that everything was, at bottom, sexual, since the South had identified itself with Purity, which, of course, was woman. "It is obvious that the assault on the South would be felt as, in some true sense, an assault on her also, and that the South would inevitably translate its whole battle into terms of her defense."[57]

It is tempting to brush all of this aside as nothing more than the pseudo-Freudian musings of a writer whose imagination had run amok. But Cash was one of the few soaringly original minds the South has produced. He and his book must be confronted particularly in light of one of the central paradoxes of the South's history: the South's touchy reticence to talk about sex and its obsession with rape, violence, and sexual purity—taboos Tillman and Dixon exploited so ruthlessly and so destructively. Cash reiterated what every authority before him had stated clearly—that rape was seldom the reason for lynchings. A

56. *Ibid.*, 89.
57. *Ibid.*, 118.

white woman's chances of being raped by a black male, said Cash, was much less "than the chance that she would be struck by lightning." And yet lynch mobs, many of which engaged in obscene sexual torture, screamed about rape.[58]

Cash's observations on what lynchings really meant and on what they revealed deserve attention. As already noted, Cash dismissed the standard view that lynchings were the work of the irrational masses, who could be cured by education. Such a view, while commendable as an argument for enlightenment, did not square with the facts, Cash argued. Moreover, from Cash's perspective, that view perpetrated the easy rationalization that education would end lynchings. Having known some educated lynchers and been around educated men and women who held racist views, Cash looked for other meanings in lynchings.

The frequency of lynchings, to say nothing of the falseness of the customary defense, prompted Cash to contend that given the massive fears whites felt toward blacks and given the white South's obsession with the black rapist, lynchings were really public acts of racial solidarity and patriotic expression that the community, in fact, honored. In truth, lynchings were acts of chivalry with definite "ritualistic value in respect to the entire Southern sentiment." It is striking to note that in seeing lynchings in this way—in looking beneath the surface of what was obviously a public event with well-defined and widely understood rules—Cash predated by almost forty years those anthropologists and historians who study seemingly obvious public events and places for their inner meaning, both for individuals and for the community.[59]

For all of his insights and despite his emancipation from the Proto-Dorian Convention, however, Cash's journalistic generalizations, particularly when taken out of context, sound racist. The Negro is "notoriously" a romantic, a hedonist infatuated with lovely words, heaping

58. *Ibid.*, 117.
59. *Ibid.*, 121. See, for example, the sophisticated way a modern southern historian examines the Ku Klux Klan in Charles L. Flynn, Jr., *White Land, Black Labor: Caste and Class in Late Nineteenth-Century Georgia* (Baton Rouge: Louisiana State University Press, 1983), 44–46. Flynn builds on the creative work of Natalie Zemon Davis, *Society and Culture in Early Modern France: Eight Essays by Natalie Zemon Davis* (Stanford: Stanford University Press, 1975), and E. P. Thompson, "'Rough Music': Le Charivari Anglais," *Annals*, XXVII (1972), 286–87.

"them in redundant profusion one upon another until meaning vanishes and there is nothing left . . . but the play of primitive rhythm upon the secret springs of emotion." The Negro "is a creature of grandiloquent imagination, of facile emotion, and above everything else under heaven, of enjoyment."[60]

But as the insightful literary historian Richard King has observed, "whatever critical comments Cash made about blacks he attributed the same or worse to whites." Nor should it be overlooked that Cash's book was a searing indictment of white racism. Drawing on his experience with the Charlotte News, Cash wrote caustically about black slums and the wretched, soul-crushing living conditions most blacks had to endure. And Cash chronicled the success of those few blacks who were able to overcome the enormous obstacles of racism. King errs when he criticizes Cash for failing to show that the Negro had to live in two worlds and was far more complex that Cash realized. Cash may not have said much about the black mind, but he convincingly shows that blacks were forced to live in their own segregated world. And as Fred Hobson has cogently argued, Cash would have thought it presumptuous of someone like himself to "explain" the black mind. Cash's modesty alone, to say nothing of his profound appreciation for the modernist awareness of the relativity of knowledge, would have kept him from saying much about blacks.[61]

After forty years of reading, thinking, brooding, worrying, talking, and writing, Cash had shaken free of his region's racial prejudices and illusions. He understood, as few southern whites of his era did, what W. E. B. Du Bois meant in The Souls of Black Folk when he said that blacks always hide their true feelings from whites. Blacks hide behind a veil, a mask, said Du Bois, and are forever inscrutable to whites. Understanding that and much more about his countrymen, Cash was forever free from embracing the white southerners' cherished notion, expressed by racist and well-meaning liberal alike, that they "understood" the Negro and knew what was best for both races. Cash, too, looked at the Negro face but he saw the mask of mystery and a rebuke to centuries of southern boasts and illusions. "What was back there, hidden?" asked

60. Cash, The Mind of the South, 51–53.
61. King, A Southern Renaissance, 163; Hobson, Tell About the South, 264.

Cash about those black, grinning faces. "What whispering, stealthy, fateful thing might they be framing out there in the palpitant darkness?"[62]

Cash did not know. He thought he knew all about the cries and whispers, hopes and fears, good and evil of his own race, whose mind he had tried so desperately to understand, help, and, yes, in the language of his people, "save." Unfortunately he would never know that his book would become a classic—a controversial one, but a classic all the same. He ended his life by his own hand in a lonely hotel room in Mexico City in July, 1941, as far away as he could get from the Proto-Dorian Convention.

62. Cash, *The Mind of the South*, 326–27.

Contributors

Eric D. Anderson received his Ph.D. from the University of Chicago. He is the author of *Race and Politics in North Carolina, 1872–1901: The Black Second* (1981). Currently, he is professor of history and chair of the Department of History at Pacific Union College.

Bruce Clayton is the Harry A. Logan, Sr., Professor of History at Allegheny College, Meadville, Pennsylvania. He has published *The Savage Ideal: Intolerance and Intellectual Leadership in the South, 1890–1914* and *Forgotten Prophet: The Life of Randolph Bourne.* He is the coeditor, with John A. Salmond, of *The South Is Another Land: Essays on the Twentieth-Century South.* He is at work on a biography of W. J. Cash.

Jeffrey J. Crow received his Ph.D. in 1974 from Duke University, where he was elected to Phi Beta Kappa. With Robert F. Durden, he coauthored *Maverick Republican in the Old North State: A Political Biography of Daniel L. Russell.* His articles, essays, and books have spanned both the American Revolution and the New South. His article "Slave Rebelliousness and Social Conflict in North Carolina, 1775 to 1802" won the award as the best article in the *William and Mary Quarterly* in 1980. Currently, he is administrator of the Historical Publications Section of the North Carolina Division of Archives and History and editor in chief of the *North Carolina Historical Review.*

Ruth Currie-McDaniel received her Ph.D. degree from Duke University in 1974. Since then, she has taught in several colleges and universities, including Marymount College, Palos Verdes, California; UNC-Charlotte; and Winthrop College, Rock Hill, South Carolina. Currently, she teaches at Whitworth College in Spokane, Washington. From 1984 to 1988 she held the position of Command Historian for the U.S. Army Strategic Defense Command in Washington, D.C., and Huntsville, Alabama. She is the author of several articles on society and politics in the nineteenth century. Her book *Carpetbagger of Conscience* was published in 1987.

PAUL D. ESCOTT earned his B.A. degree from Harvard College and his Ph.D. from Duke University, where he studied with Robert F. Durden from 1971 to 1974. He is the author of *After Secession: Jefferson Davis and the Failure of Confederate Nationalism, Slavery Remembered: A Record of Twentieth-Century Slave Narratives*, and *Many Excellent People: Power and Privilege in North Carolina, 1850–1900*. He is professor of history at Wake Forest University in Winston-Salem, North Carolina.

CHARLES L. FLYNN, JR., was born in New Haven, Connecticut, and received his undergraduate training at Hamilton College (B.A., 1974) and his graduate training at Duke University (M.A., 1975; Ph.D., 1980). He is currently an associate professor of history at Washington and Jefferson College. His published works include *White Land, Black Labor: Caste and Class in Late Nineteenth-Century Georgia*.

RAYMOND GAVINS (Ph.D., Virginia) is associate professor, specializing in Afro-American and southern history, at Duke University. In addition to articles, chapters, and essays on black life and thought in the South, he is author of *The Perils and Prospects of Southern Black Leadership: Gordon Blaine Hancock, 1884–1970*. Currently working on a general history of blacks in North Carolina, he is especially interested in the intellectual and social history of black southerners during the half-century before the Brown decision of 1954.

RICHARD L. WATSON, JR., is professor emeritus of history at Duke University. He served on the Board of Editors of the *Journal of Southern History* from 1969 to 1972 and was president of the Southern Historical Association in 1976–1977. The author or editor of various books and articles on twentieth-century United States history, he contributed the chapter "From Populism through the New Deal" to *Interpreting Southern History* (1987), edited by John B. Boles and Evelyn Thomas Nolen.

Index